# BEYOND THE RESOURCES OF POVERTY

# Cities and Society Series

Series Editor:
Chris Pickvance, Professor of Urban Studies, University of Kent, UK

Cities and Society is a series disseminating high quality new research and scholarship which contribute to a sociological understanding of the city. The series promotes scholarly engagement with contemporary issues such as urban access to public and private services; urban governance; urban conflict and protest; residential segregation and its effects; urban infrastructure; privacy, sociability and lifestyles; the city and space; and the sustainable city.

# Beyond the Resources of Poverty

*Gecekondu* Living in the Turkish Capital

ŞEBNEM EROĞLU
*University of Essex, UK and University of Kent, UK*

Routledge
Taylor & Francis Group

LONDON AND NEW YORK

First published 2011 by Ashgate Publishing

2 Park Square, Milton Park, Abingdon, Oxon OX14 4RN
711 Third Avenue, New York, NY 10017, USA

*Routledge is an imprint of the Taylor & Francis Group, an informa business*

First issued in paperback 2016

**British Library Cataloguing in Publication Data**
Eroğlu, Şebnem.
  Beyond the resources of poverty : gecekondu living in the Turkish capital. —
  (Cities and society)
  1. Squatter settlements—Turkey—Ankara. 2. Poor—Turkey—Ankara—Attitudes.
  3. Income—Turkey—Ankara. 4. Households—Economic aspects—Turkey—Ankara.
  5. Ankara (Turkey)—Economic conditions—21st century.
  6. Ankara (Turkey)—Social conditions—21st century.
  I. Title II. Series
  339.4'6'09563–dc22

**Library of Congress Cataloging-in-Publication Data**
Eroğlu, Şebnem.
  Beyond the resources of poverty : gecekondu living in the Turkish capital / by Şebnem Eroğlu.
    p. cm. — (Cities and society)
  Includes index.
  ISBN 978-1-4094-0746-1 (hbk. : alk. paper)
  1. Poverty—Turkey—Istanbul. 2. Poor—Turkey—Istanbul. 3. Squatters—Turkey—Istanbul—
Istanbul—Case studies. 4. Squatter settlements—Turkey—Istanbul—Case studies. I. Title.
  HC495.P6E76 2011
  339.4'60949618–dc22

                                                                          2011000112

ISBN 978-1-4094-0746-1 (hbk)
ISBN 978-1-138-26084-9 (pbk)

# Contents

# List of Figures

# List of Tables

# Acknowledgements

This book is drawn from research funded by the School of Social Policy, Sociology and Social Research at the University of Kent, Foundation for Urban and Regional Studies and Universities UK. I am grateful for the financial support they provided for my research.

A number of contributors helped me speak about those whose lives and struggles often pass without note. Most of all, I am thankful for the guidance and invaluable feedback generously given by Professor Chris Pickvance who also improved my work through his meticulous editing. His ever-present support saw this book safely through to completion.

I also owe thanks to my family members; to my husband Jeremy Hawksworth for his extensive proof-reading and above all, for his patience and moral support; to my father İsmail Eroğlu for giving his time and expertise during lengthy discussions on the broader economic climate in Turkey, to my mother Deniz Eroğlu for helping to gather material in Turkish and to my sister Çiğdem Eroğlu who assisted with photography.

There are many others to whom I am greatly indebted but who cannot be named for reasons of anonymity. These are the people of the *gecekondu* who allowed my entry into their lives with great hospitality, humour and openness. Without them, this research would not have been possible. Special thanks go to my generous host 'İnci' whose hospitality provided the foundation from which trust could be built with other dwellers in the settlement.

With the permission of the publisher, this book reuses material from the following articles already published by myself: 'Informal finance and the urban poor: an investigation of rotating savings and credit associations in Turkey', *Journal of Social Policy*, 2010, 39(3), 461-81. 'The irrelevance of social capital in explaining deprivation: a case study of Turkish *gecekondu* households', *Tijdschrift voor Economische en Sociale* Geografie, 2010, 101(1), 37-54. 'Patterns of income allocation among poor *gecekondu* households in Turkey: overt mechanisms and women's secret kitties', *The Sociological Review,* 2009, 57(1), 58–80. 'Developing an index of deprivation which integrates objective and subjective dimensions: extending the work of Townsend, Mack and Lansley and Halleröd', *Social Indicators Research*, 2007, 80(3), 493–510.

This book is dedicated to the memory of my grandfather, Hayrettin Baransel, who recently passed away.

# Chapter 1

# Introduction

The aim of this book is to understand how households respond to poverty and why some are more successful in reducing their deprivation than others. The book draws on longitudinal research carried out between April and October 2002 in a *gecekondu*[1] settlement in the Turkish capital city of Ankara (Eroğlu 2004).

How households cope with their impoverished circumstances is a crucial question for Turkey given its character as a middle income country with high incidence of poverty and income inequality. The most dramatic changes in income distribution have taken place since the early 1980s, which marks a passage from an era of planned economy to one of trade and financial liberalisation (Boratav 1988, 1994, Boratav et al. 2000, Yeldan 2001, 2004, Şenses 2008). Throughout the last decade, the income gap between the richer and poorer segments of the population has remained remarkably wide, as is evident from the respective Gini coefficients of 0.43 and 0.41 for the years 2003 and 2008 (TURKSTAT 2006, 2010a).

Concerning trends in poverty, it remains difficult to map out the course of change since the pre-research period due to the unavailability of complete time series data. The nearest poverty statistics available to the time of field research were produced for the year 1994. An estimate by World Bank (2000) shows that, in that year, 35 per cent of the overall population was unable to meet their basic food and non-food needs and the figure was 55 per cent for the urban population (World Bank 2000). The first official statistics were generated for the year 2002, using the measurement methods prescribed by the World Bank. The earliest series were based on expenditure, but since 2006 income-based ones have also become available. Taken at face value, both indicate a downward trend but the observed levels of poverty vary between the two series. According to an expenditure-based estimate, the proportion of the overall population unable to meet basic food and non-food needs appears to have fallen from 27 per cent in 2002 to 17 per cent in 2008. The respective rates for the urban population were 22 and 9.4 per cent (TURKSTAT 2009a). However, a less optimistic picture emerges from income-based estimates[2], which demonstrate that 30.9 and 29.4 per cent of the overall population had an income below 70 per cent of the median

---

1  *Gecekondu* in Turkish means 'built overnight' and is used initially to refer to squatter housing a large part of which has been authorised in the early 1980s.

2  These are based on equivalised disposable per capita household annual income, and calculated for thresholds set at 40, 50, 60 and 70 per cent of the median income. The 70 per cent threshold corresponded to 4430 YTL – i.e. 21 per cent below the net minimum wage in 2008 (TURKSTAT 2010a).

in 2006 and 2008 respectively. These figures indicate a slower pace of decline from a much higher base than their expenditure-based counterparts. This also seems true for the urban population given the respective rates of 16.7 to 15.2 per cent (TURKSTAT 2009b, 2010a).

Whether the official statistics present an accurate picture of poverty and inequality in the country remains a contested issue (see e.g. Sönmez 2009). In my view, substantial reductions in poverty are unlikely given a) the persistence of high unemployment at 10.3 and 11 per cent in 2002 and 2008 respectively (TURKSTAT 2003a, 2010b), b) the depreciation in real wages, which for instance reached 18.2 per cent within manufacturing sector between 2000 and 2006 (BSB 2007), c) the high level of informalisation within the labour market, evidenced by the fact that in 2008, 43.5 per cent of the working population had no social insurance (TURKSTAT 2010b), d) the limited share of public social expenditure within the GDP, which only increased by 1.54 per cent between 2002 and 2008, from a very low base at 13.54 per cent (SPO 2010), and e) the lack of substantial state provisions for poverty and unemployment that extend beyond a fragmented social assistance mechanism (including a number of means-tested in-kind and cash benefits), training-centred activation programmes and insurance-based unemployment benefits. The overall proportion of these provisions within the public spending remained highly restricted indeed – e.g. in 2005, means-tested benefits outside health and education constituted only 0.38 per cent of the GDP (SPO 2010) whereas others had a share of 0.1 per cent each (OECD 2010). In further support of this is the evidence that, in 2008, 95 per cent of all social transfers were composed of pensions that are contribution-based, and only 3.5 per cent of the total transfers were allocated to the bottom 20th percentile while the top received 45 per cent (TURKSTAT 2010a). Given these considerations, it can be suggested that the high incidence of poverty has continued to be a persistent feature within the Turkish society. Thus, the question of coping remains of significant concern to a considerable portion of the population.

The subject of this book is given further significance due to the recurrent circumstances of economic crisis which hit the country in 2000, 2001 and 2008. This book captures a critical period when the crisis conditions created by the first two waves, e.g. further wage squeeze, informalisation of labour force and unemployment, continued to set particular challenges for the poorer parts of the population, making it imperative to seek alternative ways to cope with poverty.

The space allocated to the question of coping within the Turkish literature is disproportionately small as compared to the scale of poverty and income inequality in the country. There in fact exists an extensive *gecekondu* literature, exploring the socio-economic characteristics, labour and housing market behaviour of the low-income rural-to-urban migrants living in these settlements and/or their interactions with bureaucratic organisations, but the bulk of this literature revolves around the question of urban integration rather than the poverty struggle of the *gecekondu* dwellers *per se* (see e.g. Eke 1982, Erder 1994, 1996, 1997, Gökçe et al. 1993, Güneş-Ayata 1991, Heper 1982, 1983, Karpat 1976, Kartal 1982, Kongar 1972,

Öğretmen 1957, Şenyapılı 1978, 1981, Tatlıdil 1989, Türkdoğan 1974, Yasa 1966, 1973, Yörükhan 1968). There is also a growing research interest in poverty which coincides with the production of this book (see e.g. Buğra and Keyder 2003, Erdoğan ed. 2002, Işık and Pınarcıoğlu 2001, Oktik ed. 2008, Özdek ed. 2002, SPO 2001, UPL 2001, World Bank 2003, 2005). However, the number of studies with a specific focus on survival/coping remains restricted to a few (Boratav 1994, Demir 1991, Kalaycıoğlu and Rittersberger-Tılıç 2002, UPL 2000). These studies approach to so-called survival strategies from a perspective of labour market processes, social network relations and/or consumption, but do not account for some core areas of behaviour such as intra-household income allocation. More fundamentally, however, they do not offer a comprehensive framework whereby to explain factors that lead to success or failure by these strategies – a generic limitation that is also evident within research from other parts of the world.

The wider literature also tends to explore the socio-economic behaviour of poor households from a strategy-based perspective but the terminology used for depicting behavioural responses to poverty varies considerably. 'Survival strategies', 'family strategies', 'household strategies', 'household work strategies', 'livelihood strategies', 'coping strategies', 'getting by' and 'making ends meet' illustrate some of the most frequently used conceptions. The use of terminology is nevertheless not the only point of diversity. The number of disciplines which took an interest in the subject also varies. The relevant research comes from various academic disciplines ranging from anthropology, economics, sociology and social history, and dates back at least to the first anthropological studies on ghetto poverty (Liebow 1967, Peattie 1968, Stack 1974). Since then, a vast amount of research has been conducted within different parts of the world, extending from economically less advanced (see e.g. Bartolome 1984, Beall et al. 2000, Beneria and Feldman eds. 1992, Chant 1991, Eames and Goode 1973, Edin and Lein 1997, Frayne 2994, Gonzales de la Rocha 1994, Hoodfar 1988a, 1996, Logan 1981, Lopez-Gonzaga 1996, Meer ed. 1994, Moser 1996a, 1996b, 1996c, Norris 1988, Pryer 2003, Sharma 1986, Wolf 1990) to more developed (see e.g. Andreotti 2006, Kempson et al. 1995, Kempson 1996, Leonard 1992, McCrone 1994, Meert et al. 1997, Mingione 1983, 1985, 1987, Morris 1990, Pahl 1984, Pahl and Wallace 1985, Smith and Macnicol 2001, Vinay 1985) and former socialist countries (see e.g. Clarke 1999, Lokshin and Harris 2000, Rose 1994, 1998, Tchernina and Tchernin 2002, Walker 1998). The question of how households manage to live on a tight budget has also attracted attention in the field of journalism (see e.g. Abrams 2002a, 200b, Toynbee 2003). Most of these studies have an urban focus. Further research on developing countries explores the socio-economic behaviour of households living in rural areas or at the urban-rural interface (e.g. Agarwal 1992, Baker 1995, Beck 1989, Ellis 1998, Hart 1986, Heyer 1989, Meert 2000, Muica et al. 2000, Pak 1996, Swift 1989, Taal 1989). Part of the literature concentrates upon the survival of particular social groups e.g. women, lone parents and older people. For instance, much research places women's poverty struggle at the centre of analysis, and examines the distribution of tasks and resources as well as the cost of survival at the intra-household level (e.g. Beneria and Roldan 1987, Beneria and Feldman eds. 1992, Chant 1985, 1991, 1994, 1996, Dwyer and Bruce eds. 1988, Meer ed. 1994, Pak 1996, Patterson 1994, Tacoli 1995).

Although the chosen topic has been studied extensively, this book is distinct from previous research both theoretically and empirically. Above all, it critically examines existing approaches to understanding the socio-economic behaviour of poor households, e.g. household survival, livelihood and coping strategy, and then proposes an alternative model based on a division of 'household responses to poverty' into four key types: income generation, income allocation, consumption and investment. In explaining household responses and their outcomes for poverty, the roles of different resources are explored, along with wider structural processes and household characteristics that affect the availability and or benefit delivery capacity of these resources.

The model advanced here diverges from the variants of the resource-based approach used previously in that it a) incorporates a comprehensive behavioural dimension into the model, b) establishes a theoretically well-founded, clear-cut and exhaustive list of resources that are critical to poverty, and c) identifies household characteristics as a set of factors with potential effects on household resources and choices of action that are separate from wider structural processes.

A further point of divergence relates to the empirical application of the resource-based perspective. The majority of the existing research, in theory, subscribes to the idea of agency vs. structure, but in practice reduces poverty to a resource management problem. These studies, by under-emphasising the structural effects on poverty, overstate the resilience of the poor. However, a minority of recent studies stresses the importance of examining the role of structural forces in shaping livelihood (coping or survival) resources and strategies (Bebbington et al. 2007, Dercon 2002, Gonzales de la Rocha 2001a, 2007, Haan and Zoomers 2005, Zoomers 2006). For example, Bebbington et al. (2007) demonstrate the restrictive effects of broader political economic and trade policy. Gonzales de la Rocha (2007) shows how 'the myth of survival' is created in the face of neo-liberal economic adjustment policies that foster unemployment and poverty. Dercon (2002) draws attention to the poverty impact of limited social security coverage. From this work, there emerges the idea that without appropriate policy intervention to address macro constraints on poverty and to enable poor people to benefit from the economic rewards of the society, survival or livelihood strategies alone are unlikely to bring relief to the lives of the impoverished (Gonzales de la Rocha 2007, Zoomers 2006). By examining empirically the labour market conditions and state housing and social security policies, the research presented here confirms the relevance of this newly emerging viewpoint.

More specifically, this book challenges the argument that (relative) household success is due to better management of available resources and/or having more or more varied resources. Studies from this perspective, for instance, suggest that having a higher number of earners, a wider range of income sources, or a larger stock of (social) capital leads to reduced deprivation (see e.g. Ellis 2000,

Gonzales de la Rocha 1994, Grootaert 1998, Narayan and Prichett 1999, Piachaud 2002, Selby et al. 1990). Instead it is demonstrated here that household success depends more on the capacity of resources to deliver benefits and that this depends on structural constraints, such as the general conditions of economic decline, informal, seasonal and casual conditions of work and state housing and social security policies. This explains why key differences in deprivation are found between households with and without labour-based entitlements to social security and who do or do not benefit from the redevelopment of *gecekondu* housing.

Methodologically, the distinctive features of this book are two-fold. First, it advances an innovative method for measuring the poverty outcomes of household resources and behavioural responses from a deprivation perspective. The method involves a unique way of addressing two central questions: a) what are those standards of living whose absence indicates deprivation and b) how can one determine the value of each standard of living? It incorporates three 'objective' dimensions of deprivation (i.e. monetary, consumption and work-related) and weights them according to the subjective perceptions of respondents regarding which items are more critical to deprivation. The weights are obtained through the application of factor analysis. The result is thus a more sophisticated instrument than deprivation indices used previously.

Secondly, the book adopts a robust research design. A random sample of 17 households was chosen from a typical *gecekondu* settlement in Ankara with controls placed on household size, structure and life cycle stage. Separate interviews were conducted with both spouses in each of the two visits to the field – a short term longitudinal design. The book uses both qualitative and quantitative approaches to data analysis and includes analyses of the entire sample and case studies of three households displaying different levels of deprivation.

The structure of the book is organised as follows. Chapter 2 presents a critical overview of the relevant theoretical literature in order to provide a sound basis for understanding poverty and socio-economic behaviour of the poor households. The chapter reviews the existing debates about the conceptualisation and measurement of poverty and clarifies the position taken within these debates. The methodological underpinnings of the poverty instrument devised for this study are summarised in Appendix A. It then calls into question the appropriateness of the popular notions of household survival, livelihood, and coping strategy in conceptualising behavioural responses households devise to counter poverty. This is followed by a description of the four types of behaviour distinguished in this study: income generation, income allocation, consumption and investment. Chapter 3 critically examines two current frameworks used to explain household survival or livelihood strategies, one of which is based on Polanyi's three modes of economic integration and the other represents the resource-based approach to livelihoods. The chapter then introduces the explanatory model advanced here to expand upon the earlier variants of the latter approach. Finally, it presents a review of previous research findings and the main hypotheses set out for the field research. Chapter 4 sketches the research base for this book. It outlines the research design, sampling technique and methods of data collection and analysis, and describes the key features of the research setting, placing it within the wider context of *gecekondu* settlements and dwellers in the capital.

The subsequent five chapters present the results obtained from the field research. Chapters 5 to 7 draw upon the analysis of the entire sample. The aim here is to uncover the causal processes behind household success with a specific focus on the link between household deprivation and the availability and benefit delivery capacity of resources mobilised within different types of behaviour. In exploring this relationship, Chapter 5 focuses on the area of income generation and Chapter 6 looks at the three remaining areas: income allocation, investment and consumption. Chapter 7 re-examines these types of behaviour in relation to changes in household deprivation between April and October 2002, and explores whether households have experienced short or long spells of poverty. Chapters 8 to 10 are, on the other hand, dedicated to case studies of three households with varying levels of deprivation to provide further insight into the lives of *gecekondu* households and how they cope with their impoverished circumstances. The concluding chapter evaluates the contributions of the book to theory, research and policy-making, and provides a presentation of research limitations and an agenda for future research.

# Chapter 2
# Conceptualising Household Responses to Poverty: A Critical Perspective

This chapter critically examines the relevant theoretical literature in order to enhance our understanding of household responses to poverty. The chapter is organised into three parts. The first part briefly reviews the debates surrounding the definition and measurement of poverty and clarifies the position taken in this study. This is followed by a critique of the popular concepts of household survival, livelihood and coping strategy. The chapter concludes with a presentation of my own classification of household socio-economic behaviour.

## Defining and Measuring Poverty

The definition of poverty has given rise to an extensive academic debate which has long centred on the question of whether poverty is an absolute or a relative concept. From an absolute perspective, poverty is understood as 'having less than an objectively defined minimum' (Hagenaars and De Vos 1987:212), or as a condition emerging when a core of human needs are partly or fully unsatisfied. Earlier absolutist approaches to poverty are two-fold. The *subsistence approach* focuses on the minimum income required for basic survival and is often associated with the works of Charles Booth (1891) and Joseph Rowntree (1910). Rowntree (1910:x), for instance, defines 'primary poverty' as having insufficient earnings to obtain the necessities for the maintenance of physical efficiency. The *basic needs approach* extends the scope of this subsistence concept to include two main elements: a) minimum requirements for private consumption (e.g. food, shelter and clothing), and b) essential services provided by and for the community at large (e.g. safe drinking water, sanitation, public transport and health and education) (ILO 1976, Streeton et al. 1981). Both are however found to be limited for two fundamental reasons. First, they are considered to lack conceptual depth. For instance, the subsistence approach is criticised for restricting the scope and depth of human needs, whereas the basic needs concept for confining them primarily to physical needs (Mack and Lansley 1985, Townsend 1993). Second, they are condemned for their lack of recognition of the fact that the requirements of life vary across time and space (Townsend 1979, 1985).

This represents the view of human needs underlying the notion of relative poverty. Two approaches can be identified from this perspective. The *relative deprivation approach* views poverty as being deprived of a minimum standard of living generally approved or shared by a given society. Townsend appears as the main representative of this approach. In his studies of poverty in the United Kingdom, Townsend (1993:36) considers people to be 'relatively deprived if they cannot obtain at all, or sufficiently, the conditions of life – that is the diets, amenities, standards and services – which allow them to play the roles, participate in the relationships, and follow the customary behaviour which is expected of them by virtue of their membership of society'. For him, the conception of relative deprivation involves a shift in the poverty paradigm, not simply towards a broader set of indicators of objective material and social deprivation and their links to income, but to an understanding of poverty which takes into account the time and context dependent nature of deprivation. The *inequality approach* defines poverty as a condition of having less than others in the society. From this viewpoint, people who for instance earn less than half of median income in a given country are considered poor. This approach is considered significant in terms of the challenges it sets against the ideology underpinning the income and welfare distribution prevalent within the society (George 1988).

Until recently, there has been a consensus over the relative view of poverty. The relativists demonstrate that scholars such as Rowntree, whose works are often associated with the absolutist viewpoint, in fact, employed context specific indicators in their measurements. They argue that ultimately, all conceptions of poverty are relative in that it is impossible to detach the definition of even physical needs from the customs and conventions of the society in which these needs arise (George 1988, Spicker 1990, Veit-Wilson 1986, Walker and Walker 1994). Thus, according to relativists, central to the conception of poverty is not the absolute vs. relative distinction but 'the degree of generosity and parsimony built into the definition' (Walker and Walker 1994:45).

This consensus has however been subject to significant challenges. The relativists are criticised for ignoring the conceptual distinction between poverty and inequality.[1] Sen (1983) for instance argues persuasively against the view that in a very affluent society people would still count as poor if they could not afford to buy a car every year. Equally, he suggests that 'there is ... an irreducible absolutist core in the idea of poverty ... If there is starvation and hunger, then – no matter what the relative picture looked like – there is clearly poverty' (Sen 1983:159). Thus he concludes that the idea of 'absolute need' should be maintained in order to distinguish poverty from wider inequalities. A more explicit critique of the relative understanding of human needs is developed by Doyal and Gough (1991), based on the distinction between 'needs' and 'need satisfiers'. Although the latter is believed to be context-specific, basic needs are considered universalisable on the grounds that if they are not satisfied then this will lead to serious actual harm (see also Gough et al. 2007). Hence, these challenges lend support to the basic needs

---

1   In Berthoud's (1976:18) words, 'inequality is concerned with some people having less than others, the others being either the average or the comparatively rich' whereas poverty is with 'not having *enough* to live on' (emphasis in original).

thinking that has reappeared within recent perspectives on poverty and well-being, two of which are worthy of particular attention.

The first refers to Sen's *capability approach*, according to which neither opulence (e.g. income and commodity command) nor utility (e.g. happiness and satisfaction) but human functioning(s) and capability to achieve valuable functioning(s) constitute the right focus. Sen (1999:7) defines the term functioning as 'an achievement of a person: what he or she manages to do or to be', whereas he uses the notion of capabilities more broadly to refer to 'the alternative combinations of functionings the person can achieve, and from which he or she can choose one collection' (Sen 1993:31). Although Sen speaks of certain intrinsically valuable functionings (e.g. being able to live long, read and be well nourished) and operationalises them in terms of longevity, literacy and schooling within his famous Human Development Index (HDI) (UNDP 1990, 1996), he refuses to prescribe a definitive list of core capabilities.

For some scholars, the lack of a prescribed list is seen as an advantage in that it makes the capability approach applicable to the evaluation of individual advantage within a broad range of areas from poverty, well-being and human development to agency, inequality and social justice (Alkire 2002, Clark 2006). However, significant questions have been raised regarding the operationalisability of this approach. First of all, scholars emphasise the complexities arising from the fact that the capability set includes actual as well as counterfactual opportunities (i.e. those available but not chosen by the individual and hence unobserved). Even the restriction of focus to the actual capabilities is seen to be of little help because, as Gough et al. (2007) points out, the scope of valuable functionings remains potentially too wide. This requires excessive data as well as an explicit method for inter-personal and group comparisons, which Sen's capability approach is unable provide (Alkire 2007). Moreover, some scholars view the absence of a theory-driven list of capabilities as a potential weakness because this makes it hard to pin down human needs beyond the basic functionings that Sen incorporated into the HDI (Gough et al. 2007, Nussbaum 2000).

Several attempts have been made to develop such a list. The most influential is proposed by Nussbaum (2000). Her cross-cultural list of core capabilities is drawn largely from an Aristotelian framework, and includes the following categories: life, bodily health, bodily integrity, sense-imagination-and-thought, emotions, practical reason, affiliation, concern for other species, play and control over the environment. Nussbaums's approach is praised for portraying a richer picture of human flourishing than Sen (Gough et al. 2007). However, it is argued that there is little empirical evidence to confirm its claims to universal applicability (Clark 2006).

The second approach represents the *theory of human needs*, formulated by Doyal and Gough (1991) independently of Nussbaum, to establish universal categories of basic needs. Here basic needs are seen as a requirement for successful social participation, including two main elements: physical health and (critical) autonomy. Acknowledging that there is a variety of ways in which common human needs can be satisfied, universal features of need satisfiers, i.e. intermediate needs, are then identified. These include adequate nutritional food and water, adequate protective housing, non-hazardous work and physical environments, appropriate health care, security in childhood, significant primary relationships, physical and economic security, safe birth control and childbearing, and appropriate and basic and cross-cultural education. The focus of this theory on emancipation and societal conditions to be met for need satisfaction, according to Dean (2003), makes it a less individualistic perspective than Sen's capability approach. However, he finds the theory rather limited in terms of capturing 'the sense in which human needs or capabilities must themselves incorporate the capacity for voice, deliberation and the negotiation of need itself' (Dean 2003:7).

Overall, despite differences in their understanding of human needs, the above approaches make a significant contribution to the development of an objective view of poverty. However, three major concerns have been raised against this particular perspective. The first refers to the attainability of an entirely objective definition/measurement given that neither the determination nor the interpretation of poverty indicators is free from the arbitrary decisions and value judgements of the experts (Gordon 2000, Piachaud 1981, 1987). The second relates to the failure of objective approaches to take account of the voices of the poor, who are likely to have a better understanding of their own circumstances than the experts whose encounters with them tend to be short-lived (Chambers 1997). Finally, the notion of objective poverty is completely rejected by scholars who favour the idea that 'poverty lies only in the eyes of the beholder' as a feeling or perception of having less than others (Orchansky 1969 cited in Mack and Lansley 1985:30). From this viewpoint, those who have a tendency to compare themselves against the worse off may not count as poor even though they lack access to certain basic necessities. This comprises one among many examples to demonstrate why poverty cannot be reduced to a subjective feeling or perception. I am of the opinion that there is actual poverty whether or not the subjects are aware of it. The possibility for people to have a limited awareness of their needs and circumstances makes expert judgement still relevant even if it contains some normative elements. However, this is neither to suggest that subjective perceptions or feelings of poverty should be ignored nor that the poor should not be given a voice. Hence, in my view, the best option would be to combine the expert knowledge with the experiences of the bearers of poverty.

Previous applications and extensions of the deprivation, capability and human needs approaches has sought to develop innovative ways to build subjective perceptions or feelings of respondents into their measurement of poverty or well-being. A thorough review of these literatures is beyond the scope of this book. However, since the book seeks to take the deprivation perspective in a new direction, previous studies from this viewpoint are reviewed here in brief (for an extended review see Eroğlu 2007). These studies conceive of poverty as 'the enforced lack of socially perceived necessities' (Gordon et al. 2000, Halleröd 1994, 1995, Halleröd et al. 1997, Mack and Lansley 1985). The methods they developed and used to measure poverty are built upon Sen's critique of Townsend's relative deprivation approach. In his own words,

> The choice of 'conditions of deprivation' cannot be independent of 'feelings of deprivation'. Material objects cannot be evaluated in this context without reference to how people view them, and even if the 'feelings' are not brought in explicitly, they must have an implicit role in the selection of 'attributes'. Townsend has rightly emphasised the importance of the 'endeavour to define the style of living which is generally shared or approved in society' ... one must, however, look also at the feelings of deprivation in deciding on the style and the level of living the failure to share which is regarded as important (Sen 1982:16).

Two rather distinct methods appear to have evolved from this critique; one is formulated by Mack and Lansley (1985) and the other by HallERöd (1994). The former draws upon social perception in selecting necessities from an initial list of consumer items, and includes only those items perceived by more than 50 per cent of respondents as necessities of life. The latter is a refined version of this method, seeking to determine the weights for each initially listed item according to the proportion of the population which regarded the item as a necessity. Fundamentally, these methods are significant in terms of the central role they give to social perception in measuring poverty. However, they suffer from three generic limitations. First, the choice of necessities is, to a great extent, confined to consumer items, indicating their exclusive preference for the direct measurement of poverty. Second, majoritarian thinking dominates the way subjective perceptions of necessities were evaluated (see also Veit-Wilson 1987). Thus, these methods fail to provide solutions in cases where the practices of poor people do not match the priorities of the majority. Finally, in contrast to those scholars who view the separate exploration of wants and affordability as an advantage in terms of capturing the poor that are truly constrained (Piachaud 1987), I believe this type of enquiry has the potential weakness to produce invalid results, given the possibility for people's desires to be already constrained by their life circumstances (Sen 1987).

In light of the above considerations, this study takes a deprivation-based approach to the definition and measurement of poverty, but diverges from the works of Townsend (1979), Mack and Lansley (1985) and HallERöd (1994) both conceptually and methodologically. It defines poverty from a multiple deprivation perspective, based on the absence of living standards that are deemed necessary to maintain a decent life. Unlike Townsend's relative deprivation concept, the view of poverty favoured here recognises the universality of human needs, and occupies a middle ground between the two poles of the objectivity-subjectivity continuum.

Furthermore, the study proposes a unique way of addressing two questions that are central to deprivation index development: a) what are those standards of living whose absence indicates deprivation, and b) how should the value of each living standard be determined? (Sen 1987). The new method incorporates three 'objective' dimensions of deprivation (i.e. monetary, consumption and work-related) and weights them according to subjective perceptions of respondents regarding which items are more critical to deprivation. An original application of factor analysis is performed here both to finalise the list of measures and determine their weights. The end product is referred to as the Factor Weighted Index of Deprivation (FWID) and the stages of its development are outlined in Appendix A.

The proposed method makes significant advances on those used by Townsend (1979), Mack and Lansley (1985) and Halleröd (1994) to produce an index of deprivation. A detailed discussion of these can be found in Eroğlu (2007). First of all, it captures a broader range of actual deprivations on key dimensions. Second, it reconciles direct and indirect (i.e. income-based) methods of measurement which tend to be used independently of each other. Such reconciliation makes it possible to demonstrate a) the differences in (household) capacity to convert income into consumption items and assets, and to obtain them without deploying income, b) the forces likely to affect this capacity (e.g. the level and type of skills, information, social support, and institutional entitlements available and patterns of income allocation), and c) the labour market-related sources of poverty beyond the level of earnings. Third, it helps identify a set of core measures in a way that is less susceptible to arbitrary selection, and hence retains a capacity to differentiate between choice and constraints more reliably than earlier methods based on separate analysis of wants and affordability. Last but not least, it leads to a more inclusive measurement that represents every respondent's perception of deprivation. The outcome of the proposed method is thus a more robust and theoretically sophisticated instrument.

## Conceptualising Socio-Economic Behaviour of Poor Households

A variety of concepts have been used to describe the socio-economic behaviour of households in poverty, the most popular of which is 'household survival strategy'. This section questions the appropriateness of this notion by examining its three elements in turn. Two alternatives to the idea of survival, coping and livelihood are also considered.

### The Household: Can We Speak of Household Behaviour?

This section discusses whether the household constitutes an appropriate unit for analysing behavioural responses to poverty given the feminist critique of the notion of the household as an undifferentiated entity. Feminist scholars have questioned the treatment of the household as a 'black box' (Whitehead 1981) or as an individual by another name' (Folbre 1986a) as though it had a logic and interests of its own. They have directed our attention to the inequalities and conflicts of interest in the sharing of responsibilities and benefits along the lines of gender and generation within the household. There now exists a substantial body of literature which confirms the presence of divergences in interests along age and gender lines in many life course decisions made, and also imbalances in the distribution of tasks and in access to resources within the household (see e.g. Beneria 1992, Beneria and Roldan 1987, Chant 1991, Fapohunda 1988, Gonzales de la Rocha 1994, Harris 1981, Hoodfar 1988b, Kanji 1994, Mencher 1988, Moser 1996a, 1996c, Perez-Aleman 1992, Rodriguez 1994, Roldan 1988, Safilios-Rothschild 1984, Sharma 1986, Wolf 1990).

One key question raised within this literature concerns whether the idea of 'household (survival) strategy' truly reflects the ways in which decisions are made within the household (Bruce 1989, Folbre 1986b, 1988, Morris 1990, Rakodi 1991, Schmink 1984, Wolf 1990). It is argued here that what appears to be a household strategy can typically be a decision of the male head of the household or individual members (Bruce 1989, Wolf 1990). Since the absence of collectively produced decisions makes it difficult to speak of a household strategy in the full sense of the term, some scholars urge caution against the use of the term (Crow 1989) whereas others abandon the concept entirely. Wolf (1990:44) for instance rejects the term household strategy on the ground that it 'misinterprets intra-household behaviour, obscures intra-household stratification by gender and generation and stifles the voices of the unempowered and usually females and the young'.

The above considerations challenge the idea of the household as an entity with real joint interests. This view is questioned by scholars who argue that the household cannot be reduced to an agglomeration of individuals since the very basic objective and mutual obligations of survival make the household something more than the sum of the trajectories of its members (Crow 1989, Pahl and Wallace 1985, Rakodi 1991, B. Roberts 1991, Sharma 1986). One should therefore expect to see some co-operative outcomes in relation to who decides what, who does what and who obtains what goods and services. Indeed, there exists some evidence that household members do work out solutions which contribute towards the enhancement of collective welfare (Fernandez-Kelly 1982, Gonzales de la Rocha 1988).

Consequently, the household remains an appropriate unit for analysing behavioural responses to poverty given its character as 'a mix of cooperation and conflict' (Sen 1990). This feature of the household, as Folbre (1988) points out, reveals an important question for our research: Does poverty make it more likely that households will act collectively? This question will be pursued when examining the patterns of income allocation within the household.

Turning to define the scope of the term household, the literature offers several alternatives. Some studies depict it as a unit of reproduction (Chant 1991, Gonzales de la Rocha 1994, Lomnitz 1977, Roberts 1991, Schmink 1984); others as a unit of resource (e.g. income and labour) pooling and sharing (Friedman 1984, Sharma 1986, Stauth 1984) or an organisational unit sharing mutual obligations of 'survival' (Fontaine and Schlumbohm 2000, Mingione 1991). Each of these definitions emphasises an important function of the household, but tells us very little about its boundaries.

Three key criteria are jointly applied in this study to define the household. The first criterion is co-residence, which is often omitted from anthropological definitions (P. Roberts 1991, see e.g. Friedman 1984, Lomnitz 1977, Martin and Beittel 1987, Mingione 1991, Wong 1984). In contrast, this study retains the criterion because its omission would blur the analytical distinction between the household and wider social relationships and hence leave questions like 'what integrates a household, what makes the household a separate unit and to what extent we can stop dealing with the household in order to start dealing with social networks' unresolved (Gonzales de la Rocha 1994:20). However, in order to prevent the reduction of the household to a residential group, a second criterion is introduced; i.e. members living under the same roof must feel obligated to other residents in terms of making ends meet. This criterion is significant in that it emphasises the fact that there is more to the household than its economic functions. As Schmink (1984) points out, definitions using this criterion take into account the economic as well as social, ideological and subjective determinants of household behaviour. However, one issue emerging from the use of this criterion concerns how to treat groups of individuals who live apart but continue to share mutual obligations of making a living (seasonal workers, those with a pied-à-terre, etc.). Here, in my view, the temporal dimension of living arrangements becomes important in terms of maintaining the distinction between the household and wider social networks. From this perspective, only those who temporarily or periodically live apart can be treated as a household unit. The first two criteria are also attributable to the family. In order to distinguish the household from a family, a third criterion is employed; i.e. household members do not have to be linked to each other through kinship or biological ties.

Consequently, the household is understood here as a unit where members who are not necessarily tied to each other through kinship, permanently or intermittently co-reside and enter into explicit or implicit 'negotiations' as to how resources should be mobilised and allocated to make ends meet, albeit not on an egalitarian basis.

*Strategy: Do Poor Households Plan their Actions?*

The existing literature tends to take a strategy-based approach to understanding household livelihood, coping or survival behaviour. The concept of strategy has been favoured for two main reasons. The first is to challenge the notion of the poor as 'passive victims' whose actions are determined by structural forces. The second is to counter the idea of the poor as living in a 'culture of poverty'; a set of self-perpetuating deprivations and learned behaviour patterns continuing across generations (Gonzales de la Rocha 1994, Pahl and Wallace 1985, Roberts 1991, Schmink 1984). The term is thus of particular relevance to poverty research. However, it is often applied indiscriminately, i.e. without paying attention to theoretical boundaries and/or providing empirical evidence (Schmink 1984, Wolf 1990). This section focuses on the key meanings attached to the concept in the sociological literature in order to identify its boundaries, and then discusses whether we can ascribe strategic value to socio-economic behaviour of poor households.

The concept of strategy was, as Fontaine and Schlumbohm (2000) point out, first used in military terms and then transferred to economics through game theory. The game theory perspective on strategy found its reflections within the sociological literature. Most notably, Crow (1989) uses the term to refer to rational, long-term and conscious actions that require choosing between alternatives. The strength of Crow's definition derives from his clear identification of the scope of the actions that can be called 'strategy'. This helps prevent the erosion of its analytical value through indiscriminate application. However, scholars dispute the idea that the strategy is meaningful only when actors are aware of the choices and the rationale behind their actions, and argue that unconscious elements, such as culturally transmitted practices, can be part of strategic action (Anderson 1971, Bourdieu 1977a, 1977b, Certeau 1984, Fontaine and Schlumbohm 2000, Morgan 1989, Pickvance and Pickvance 1994).

For instance, drawing on a theory of practice which recognises the limits of awareness in lived experience, Bourdieu (1977b) argues that agents engage in strategic action by means of *habitus*, i.e. an 'inter-subjective environment' incorporating past experiences (Calhoun 1993). From this perspective, the term strategy is understood as complex combinations of the aims of actors and the principles guiding their choices of means, which neither requires complete awareness of all possible options nor an unrestricted choice of action (Fontaine and Schlumbohm 2000). This means that strategic actions no longer involve choosing among several objective possibilities or making predictions (Calhoun 1993, Certeau 1984, Fontaine and Schlumbohm 2000).

The strength of Bourdieu's approach stems from his emphasis on habit rather than strict rational calculation. By introducing the concept of *habitus*, he draws our attention to the fact that agents' decisions and actions are deeply influenced by tradition (culture) and past experiences, and hence they are prone to involve elements either in the form of misrecognition or non-recognition. However, the scope of his definition remains potentially too wide: it involves unconscious as well as pragmatic actions, and hence risks losing the cutting edge of the term strategy.

Hence, it seems more appropriate to follow scholars who take a middle ground between Crow and Bourdieu's approaches to strategy by defining it as actions that involve a choice regardless of whether they are a product of conscious thought processes or not. From this point of view, can we attribute strategic value to the socio-economic behaviour of poor households? Some scholars argue that we cannot due to the limited nature of choices available to them (Clarke 1999, Crow 1989). As B. Roberts (1991:138–9) quotes from Haguette (1982), the idea of the poor as pursuing strategic action may be a 'myth' which is 'little but an euphemism for crushing poverty in which survival depends on selling one's own and one's family labour cheaply and whatever conditions offered'. This is a plausible argument;

however, there remain areas where strategic actions are likely for those in poverty. For instance, my research on rotating savings and credit associations demonstrate that however small their savings, poor households can make plans as to how to use them (Eroğlu 2010a).

Thus, the concept of strategy remains relevant to understanding the socio-economic behaviour of poor households, despite the problem of its indiscriminate application which we have sought to overcome here by reinstating the boundaries of the concept.

*Survival: A Useful Concept?*

Interestingly, despite its widespread use, the term survival is often employed as a catch-all phrase lacking definite boundaries (see also Davies 1993). This section outlines two distinct meanings attached to the concept, and discusses how useful they are in understanding the socio-economic behaviour of poor households.

The dominant approach associates survival behaviour with short to medium-term actions leading households to stay in a given socio-economic position in contrast to social advancement. This usage is evident within family (life) studies which distinguish between survival and social mobility strategies (see e.g. Cornell 1987, Folbre 1987, Hareven 1982, Roberts 1994, Tilly 1987). To illustrate, Roberts (1991:139) defines survival strategies as 'a set of decisions-actions performed to organise the household to get by in the short or medium term' whereas he uses social mobility strategies to refer to 'allocative decisions such as those over children's education, the purchase of a house, or improvement in job qualifications that will bear fruit in the longer term.' Hareven (1982:360) also differentiates between two types of life plan. One is defensive plans 'designed to cope with the recurring crises and insecurities' and the other is long range-plan, 'often spanning two or three generations designed to assure basic security and achieve advancement.'

Some studies from this perspective use the term to embrace households' economic practices directed towards subsistence, as well as collective actions (e.g. protests) they carry out with the wider community to further their economic interest and secure shelter and other aspects of urban welfare (Daines and Seddon 1991, Roberts 1991). The inclusion of the latter was justified on the grounds of their direct or indirect contribution to human survival or to the active struggle of the households engaging in survival strategies. Daines and Seddon (1991:9) support this viewpoint by arguing that 'all struggle involves an active engagement with the immediate environment and always has the potential for the development of more effective, more sustained and more collaborative forms of struggle, even when taking place at the most 'basic' individual level, with the most 'limited' and 'immediate' of objectives'. Conversely, other scholars separate survival practices from collective actions (Elson 1992, Harari and Garcia-Bouza 1982). Elson (1992), for instance, draws a distinction between survival and transformation strategies, and associates the latter with activities that can enable a sustained growth and development both at a personal and a national level.

The second approach defines survival in terms of reproduction, and uses the term beyond its strict sense of 'getting by' to include practices which might bring about the promotion of welfare and possibly social mobility across generations (Mingione 1991).

Comparing the usefulness of the two approaches to survival, despite issues surrounding the inclusion of collective actions, the first approach makes a clear attempt to give the concept a distinctive meaning. However, the distinction between survival and social mobility still remains rather blurred because, as Hareven (1982) herself points out, long-term plans e.g. about home buying and migration are likely to permeate aspects of everyday life. By contrast, despite its attempts to separate 'basic' from 'inessential behaviour', the second approach serves no purpose beyond calling reproduction by another name. Moreover, there are issues concerning the temporal dimension of these approaches. The problem with the first one is that it does not clarify how short term an action should be in order to be regarded as survival, and with the other, the problem stems from its neglect of the fact that what is reproductive in the short term can be a disaster in the long term.

More fundamentally, however, these approaches are flawed due to their failure to recognise that, even where it is equated with aim, outcome or bare existence[2], the term survival remains unworkable for the following reasons. First of all, equating survival with aim runs the risk of assuming that the outcomes will be as intended. Yet, linking it with outcome is not a viable option either, as this leads to the risk of attributing effects to behaviour without further evidence. Finally, if the term is related to bare existence, then 'non-survival' becomes unobservable. Thus, the term is inherently susceptible to indiscriminate application, and is not used here.

## Coping and Livelihood: Viable Alternatives?

The literature approaches the socio-economic behaviour of poor households also from the viewpoints of coping and livelihoods. This section briefly discusses whether these concepts constitute viable alternatives to survival.

Two distinct meanings are attributed to the term coping. Some studies describe it as getting by on a daily or weekly basis and solving problems as they arise (Anderson et al. 1994, McCrone 1994), whereas others use it to indicate activities devised to combat crisis conditions (e.g. famine) (Corbet 1988, Davies 1993). The former offers clear boundaries for the concept but excludes planned actions. The latter, due to its reference to transient conditions, seems inapplicable to household behaviour against chronic (or long-term) poverty. Hence the term coping provides only a partial coverage of possible responses to poverty.

Turning to the notion of livelihood that has found widespread support from both academic circles (see e.g. Beall et al., Chambers and Conway 1991,

---

2    I thank Professor Chris Pickvance for bringing these aspects of survival to my attention.

Chambers 1995, Ellis 2000a, Grown and Sebstad 1989, Pryer 2003, Rakodi 1999, 2002, Scoones 1998) and development agencies such as CARE, DFID, Oxfam and the UNDP (Carney et al. 1999), the literature offers a series of definitions for the concept. According to Chambers and Conway (1991:6), 'a livelihood comprises the capabilities, assets (stores, resources, claims and access) and activities required for a means of living'. Similarly, Grown and Sebstad (1989:941) define the 'livelihood system' as 'a mix of individual and household survival strategies, developed over a given period of time that seeks to mobilise available resources and opportunities'. The concept of livelihood embraces various ways of making a living, only one of which is employment. In Grown and Sebstad's (1989:942) own words, '[t]he livelihood systems concept does not connote the sense of a fixed time and place of work and of employer-employee relationship. It conveys more readily the dimensions of seasonality and of multiple overlapping or sequential tasks, and captures more completely the ways that individual members of a household are deployed.' Thus, the term has a close connection with the concept of 'work'; used in its broader sense to include both formal and informal spheres of economic activity (see Gershuny 1983, Leonard 1992, Pahl 1984, 1985, Pahl and Wallace 1985, Papanek 1979, Sharma 1986, Vinay 1985).

The strength of the livelihood concept stems from its combining two elements: ways of making a living and the resource base required for it. However, in my view, its connotations of earning an income limit the behavioural coverage of the concept. For example, practices such as intra-household income allocation, considered to have significant repercussions for 'secondary poverty' remain outside its remit (Chant 1985, Eroğlu 2009, Rowntree 1910, Vogler and Pahl 1994, Wilson 1987). Thus, the notion of livelihood also remains only partly relevant to understanding the socio-economic behaviour of poor households.

Overall, the above considerations indicate that an alternative conceptualisation of household behaviour is required a) to embrace a broader range of actions than the notions of livelihood, coping and strategy will allow, and b) to avoid the problem of indiscriminate application inherent to the term survival. Thus, this study rather employs the term 'household responses to poverty' to incorporate both strategic and non-strategic actions that are devised against transient or persistent poverty, along with practices of income allocation (For its previous applications within an urban context see e.g. Moser 1996a, 1996b, 1996c).

**Classifying Household Responses to Poverty: Towards a Comprehensive Division**

This section aims to identify core areas of behaviour in which household responses can be developed. Four areas are distinguished: income generation, income allocation, consumption and investment. Studies from diverse literatures address one or more aspects of this division, based on a range of ideas; for example, income diversification, income-consumption smoothing, money management, asset strategies etc. The proposed division is however distinctive in that it offers a more comprehensive framework which unifies core elements of behaviour.

In arriving at this division, I have also considered the decisions and activities involving changes to the household size and structure, such as nesting (i.e. integrating members of other households), fission (i.e. disintegration of the family members) and fertility control, as well as those related to the household relocation, such as migration (Moser 1996a, 1996b, 1996c). However, in what follows, only the above mentioned types of behaviour are explained in detail, firstly because I controlled for the household size, structure and life-cycle, and secondly because neither the location nor characteristics of respondent households had changed between the two visits to the field. The types of behaviour outlined below do not represent any sequential order.[3]

*Income generation* involves formal and informal[4] activities whereby households mobilise their labour and non-labour resources to obtain an income. This behaviour category thus allows a focus on gender divisions within the labour market and the specific ways in which adult and child labour of both sexes contribute to household income. Unlike survival studies that define income as 'everything that comes into the household in cash or kind' (Gonzales de la Rocha 1994, Hoodfar 1996), income is understood here to have monetary elements only. These include: a) wages from public or private sector employment, b) earnings from formal or informal petty commodity production or petty commerce, c) money obtained from social contacts in the form of gifts, inheritances, remittances, etc., c) rent from housing, land, equipment, animals, etc., d) interest from financial assets such as savings, and e) transfer payments from state and other institutions and associations (e.g. pension, subsidies, donations, insurance and tax repayments). This view of income is influenced by the work of the Household Research Working Group at the Fernand Braudel Centre (see e.g. Friedman 1984), but rejects extending the term to home-made consumable goods since, in my opinion, these act more as a compensation for income than income *per se*.

*Income allocation* refers to decisions and practices concerning the distribution of income between different areas of savings and expenditure for both the overall household and its individual members. The outcome of these decisions and practices is referred to as the actual income distribution. Income is conceived

---

3    For studies researching 'household response sequencing' during famine see Agarwal (1992), Corbet (1988) and Devereux (1993).

4    There exists some controversy over the status of the concept of informal. Some consider it to be a distinct sphere of the economy, which lies outside state regulation (Ferman and Brendt 1981, Portes and Castells 1989). Others argue that it should neither be seen as a separate economy nor be restricted to market activities (Mingione 1987, Pahl 1985, 1988, 1989). Nonetheless, both positions allow a focus on the labour market processes and the varying implications of the formal-informal divide for exploitation, which I think is most critical to poverty.

as being allocated through overt and covert mechanisms operating within the household.

Overt mechanisms comprise those that are known to and seemingly approved by both spouses, and are based on the distinction drawn, as in the work of Pahl (1983) and Vogler (1994), between the concepts of 'financial control' and 'financial management' to emphasise 'the hierarchy of financial responsibility' within the household (Morris, 1990:106). 'Financial control' involves making important decisions concerning how income will be distributed, and how responsibilities for different expenditure areas will be shared. Financial control is often operationalised by looking at which spouse has the final say in the financial matters. On the other hand, 'financial management' refers to the process whereby these decisions are implemented in practice (Pahl 1983). This study is largely based on the financial management typologies developed by Pahl (1980, 1983, 1989) and later refined by Vogler (1994). Pahl identifies four main types. The first is the 'whole-wage system' where one partner is responsible for managing the entire household income remaining after the main earner has taken out his or her share for personal spending. The second is the 'housekeeping allowance system' where the main earner makes only part of his or her earnings available to the household and keeps the rest for household and/or personal spending. The third is the 'independent system' where neither partner has access to the other's income. The last one is 'shared management' where both partners have access to the household income, and are responsible for managing this common pot. Vogler (1994) breaks down this category into 'female-managed pool', 'male-managed pool' and 'joint-pool', based on the evidence that in some cases of shared management, one partner was held more responsible for managing household finances.

The distinction drawn between financial management and control is of significant value in understanding poverty in that it draws our attention to 'the hierarchy of financial responsibility' and its implications for power relationships within the household. However, the existing typologies of financial management are of limited help in understanding poverty due to a) their lack of focus on the actual distribution of income, and b) the limitations of the contrast drawn in these typologies between 'household' and 'personal' spending. According to Pahl (1990:121), household spending represents a 'legitimate claim' on members' pooled or non-pooled income, whereas personal spending is taken from one's own earnings. Pahl uses the source of funding to distinguish between the two forms of spending without discussing whether personal spending can also be deemed legitimate or not. However, in my view, the question of legitimacy becomes crucial to poverty especially when the purpose of personal spending is concerned. This is critical because some personal spending could ultimately serve the 'collective good' by helping the overall household and/or its individual members to achieve or maintain living standards that they deem critical to pursuing a decent life.

This leads me to propose a distinction between 'fair' personal spending that contributes to the achievement of such standards and 'controversial' spending which does not. I acknowledge that, in theory, each spouse could have a different conception of what counts as 'fair' or what is a 'collective good'. But, in practice, based on the examples of personal spending in my study, such differences are unlikely. Typical examples of 'fair' personal spending include work-related food and travel expenditures (e.g. money spent by men in specialist coffeehouses where casual labourers gather to search for jobs), whereas spending on alcohol, gambling and smoking constitute the usual 'controversial' forms.

On the other hand, covert mechanisms are understood to operate when either spouse withdraws a portion of the total income without the explicit agreement of the other spouse, and exerts exclusive discretionary power over how to allocate this money. The money obtained in this way can be kept as savings and/or used as a budget for various expenditures. One study of low-income Turkish households reports that this type of savings is called *vallah billah kesesi* (i.e. oath pouch) by women who created them (Şenol-Cantek 2001). I rather refer to them as 'secret kitties'.

*Consumption* refers to those activities situated on a continuum from commodified (paid for) to non-commodified (i.e. unpaid for), which indicates the level of monetisation within consumption practices, and hence the extent to which they a) enable access to goods and services (monetised or otherwise), and b) counteract income shortfalls.

The underlying idea here is that once income has been generated, poor households, by definition, would experience an income deficit, i.e. an imbalance between their income and consumption needs, which they are obliged to redress by gaining additional money (e.g. through borrowing or realising financial or non-financial assets) and/or reducing the cost of consumption through engagement in commodified to non-commodified spheres.

The commodified end of the spectrum includes activities performed to reduce the cost of monetised goods and services. Substituting certain consumption items by their cheaper market equivalents, reducing their quantity and going without illustrate such practices. The semi-commodified sphere involves activities which allow access to goods and services that are subsidised or partially non-monetised. Self-provisioning[5] epitomises semi-commodified consumption, but not exclusively so. Finally, the non-commodified sphere embraces activities which enable access to goods and services that are unpaid for, at least at the point of entry. Use of free national health services, electricity theft and receipt of donations in kind constitute a few examples. In an attempt to counteract inadequate income, households are likely to try combinations of activities from each sphere, as a result of which 'balance' can be achieved at such levels that a 'surplus' may be obtained for investment.

---

5   As Leonard (1998:94) points out, self-provisioning generally refers to 'the production of specific goods and services from within the household for consumption of household members and includes activities that are seen as useful indicators of the degree to which households substitute for formally produced goods and services' (e.g. home baking, knitting, dress-making, hairdressing, household maintenance and car repairs).

*Investment* includes those practices whereby households create financial and non-financial assets such as generating a 'surplus income', borrowing an investment loan from formal and informal credit sources, and converting assets previously acquired.[6] Furthermore, in principle, investment is considered here as an area that is distinct from insurance as the latter is aimed specifically at protection against potential future risks. However, in practice, the distinction between the two areas can be rather blurred; for example, a flat bought today for shelter may help compensate for the loss of earnings in old age.

## Conclusion

Based on a critical review of the relevant theoretical literature, this chapter set out the approach taken in this study a) to define and measure poverty and b) to conceptualise behavioural responses devised to counter it. Poverty was defined from a deprivation perspective and measured based on a new methodology which combines its 'objective' and subjective dimensions. Furthermore, the notions of coping, livelihood and survival strategy were rejected in favour of the term 'household responses to poverty' on the grounds that the latter allows a focus on a broader range of actions and avoids the risk of indiscriminate application associated in particular with the concept of survival. Finally, a four-fold division was proposed to distinguish core areas of behaviour: income generation, income allocation, consumption and investment. It was argued that although these behavioural elements can be found elsewhere, the proposed division is distinctive in unifying key areas in which household responses to poverty can be devised.

---

6   The practices of borrowing and asset sale are viewed here as integral to both consumption and investment as households can engage in these activities for either purpose.

# Chapter 3

# Explaining Household Responses to Poverty: Towards an Improved Framework

The aim of this chapter is to put forward a coherent framework for explaining household responses and their outcomes for poverty. The chapter starts with a critical examination of two major frameworks previously used to explain household survival or livelihoods, and then introduces the explanatory model designed for this study. Finally, it presents a review of previous research findings and sets out hypotheses.

**Current Explanatory Frameworks: An Overview**

This section reviews two main approaches, referred to here as the economic integration and resource-based models. The first model explains 'survival' behaviour in terms of the three forms of integration Polanyi (1977) used originally to classify economies, i.e. reciprocity, redistribution and exchange (see e.g. Meert et al. 1997, Meert 2000). For Polanyi, each form specifies an institutionalised movement of goods and persons whereby the elements of economic process (e.g. material resources and labour) are linked together, and effective integration of these movements depends upon the pre-existence of supporting structures, i.e. institutions. The mode of reciprocity involves the flow of resources between at least two symmetrical groups whose members display similar economic behaviour towards each other. Redistribution concerns the distribution of resources accumulated in 'a recognised centre' by virtue of custom, law or ad hoc central decision making. Polanyi mentions that redistribution not only applies to society as a whole, but also to smaller groups, such as tribes and households. Finally, exchange signifies a bi-directional movement of goods between persons dispersed or randomly placed in the system, and hinges on the existence of a market.

The economic integration model allows us to explore the role of key institutions such as the market, the state and household/community networks in household choices of action. Institutions are deemed to play a 'mediating role' in constraining the free play of interactions as well as providing resources for actions to take place (Kazepov 2005). This particular role of the institutions gives the model its ability to bridge macro and micro levels. However, although the focus on three modes of integration enables a broad coverage of behaviour, the model excludes certain actions that are significant to poverty. For example, the redistribution mode can only be partially applied to income allocation since not all income systems require the use of a recognised centre (e.g. systems where spouses manage their earnings separately).

Turning to what I refer to as the resource-based framework, this model has been applied within both urban and rural contexts and been given a variety of names in the literature, such as the 'livelihood framework', 'capital assets framework', 'asset vulnerability framework' and 'resource profiles approach'. Here, resources (assets or capital) are viewed as an essential element of making a living, and hence a key determinant of poverty. Individuals and households are treated here as agents in control of a resource portfolio, but structural limits to their agency are also recognised.

Studies from this perspective conceptualise the content of the resource portfolio in different ways (for variations of the model see e.g. Bebbington 1999, Bebbington et al. 2007, Carney et al. 1999, Chambers and Conway 1991, Chambers 1995, Grown and Sebsdat 1989, Ellis 2000a, McGregor and Kebede 2002, Moser 1996a, 1996b, 1996c, 1998, Meikle 2002, Piachaud 2002, Pryer 2003, Rakodi 1999, 2002, Saltmarshe 2002, Scoones 1998, Swift 1989, White and Ellison 2007). For reasons of space, I shall illustrate a few of these variations only. Swift (1989:11) uses the term 'livelihood assets' to refer to 'a wide range of tangible and intangible stores of value or claims to assistance which can be mobilised in times of crisis.' These 'livelihood assets' are categorised into investments (human investments, individual productive assets, collective assets), stores (food stores, stores of real value such as jewellery, bank accounts) and claims (on the community, patrons, the government and international community). Moser (1996a) also distinguishes between tangible and intangible 'vulnerability assets' but classifies them rather differently into labour, productive assets (e.g. land and housing) human capital, household relations and social capital. Extending the work of Moser, Carney et al. (1999) group livelihood assets into human capital (time, number of household members, health and skills), social capital, physical capital, financial capital and natural capital.

Given its emphasis on resources available for action, the above model offers a more micro approach to poverty than the economic integration perspective. Nevertheless, there still remains room for linking micro and macro levels since the model takes account of structural forces and their role in enabling and constraining access to resources. Hence, I consider it to be an important step in the direction of explaining household responses and their outcomes for poverty. However, three common limitations with the variants of the model restrict its value.

First of all, the conceptualisation of the resource portfolio is often problematic for two reasons; one being the indiscriminate application of the term resource. The scope of the concept is indeed rather wide, embracing both material and non-material objects that imply a capacity (Pickvance and Pickvance 1994). However, some variants of the model use the term too broadly, for instance, to include health, household size and/or religion within the resource portfolio (see e.g. the works of Carney et al. 1999, Rakodi 2002, White and Ellison 2007). I believe this problem results from the failure to separate the means that are directly deployable (e.g. labour power) from the factors that determine the availability or capacity of these means (e.g. health and religion). In my view, only the former forms a sound basis for identifying resource types.

The other reason concerns the failure to produce jointly exhaustive and mutually exclusive resource categories. Key resources have mostly been brought to light by different variants of the model but no single variant contains all key resources. For instance, the classification by Carney et al. (1999) overlooks the categories of bodily resources (e.g. human organs) and institutional entitlements (e.g. rights to social security). Moreover, some variants of the model make joint use of resource types that imply a similar capacity. For example, Bebbington (1999), who treats cultural and human capital as distinct resource types, disregards the theoretical foundations of the concepts laid out respectively by Bourdieu (1986) and Coleman (1990), and hence overlooks the fact that they both cover educational skills and qualifications. Unlike some writers (e.g. White and Ellison 2007), I find the overlapping use of resource categories problematic in that it jeopardises the empirical applicability of the model.

Secondly, the resource-based framework completely ignores the behavioural dimension of poverty. The absence of such a dimension makes the current framework less workable in that it prevents the systematic examination of resource mobilisation within specific areas of behaviour.

Finally, the prevailing framework provides only a partial picture of the possible effects on household resources and responses to poverty. There is an emerging consensus that its disproportionate emphasis upon resources obscures our understanding of the structural effects on poverty (Beall and Kanji 1999, Gonzales de la Rocha 2001a, 2001b, Haan and Zoomers 2005, McGregor and Kebede 2002). Despite attempts to provide a detailed account of the potential structural forces (see e.g. Carney et al. 1999), this remains a significant problem with most variants and empirical applications of the model. Yet, as is widely known, the model, at least in principle, subscribes to the idea of structure vs. agency. Thus, in my view, a more fundamental problem with this model lies in its failure to separate household characteristics (i.e. size, structure and life-cycle stage) from resources and to recognise their potential effects on resources that are distinct from wider structural processes.

Consequently, it appears from the shortcomings of the resource-based model that there is a need for an improved framework which a) allows a more systematic analysis of the relationship between household resources and choices of action, b) draws on a theoretically well-founded classification that contains mutually exclusive and jointly exhaustive resource types, and c) clearly separates out key effects on resources. The model presented below seeks to address this need.

**The Household Response Model: Beyond the Resource-Based Framework**

This section outlines the key features of the model developed and used in this study to answer two main research questions: a) how do households respond to poverty, and b) why some households are more successful than others in their responses to poverty. The proposed framework is referred to here as the household response model, which draws on the four types of behaviour distinguished earlier: income generation, income allocation, consumption and investment, and explores them in terms of the relationships summarised in Figure 3.1.

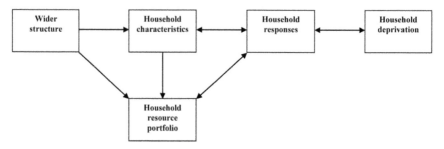

**Figure 3.1    Main components of the household response model**

The three sets of factors hypothesised to have an effect on household responses and their outcomes for poverty include: a) the wider structure, b) the composition of household resource portfolio and c) household characteristics (i.e. size, structure and life-cycle stage). Before describing each element in detail, two points needs to be clarified. First, as can partly be seen from Figure 3.1, the nature of interactions between the main components of the model is neither static nor uni-directional. I shall only illustrate here the possible relationships between household behaviour and poverty and their implications for other aspects of the model. The ways households respond to poverty can have an effect on its extent and/or intensity, but the reverse is also true. Poverty can lead households to respond in ways that would reshape their size, structure and resources as well as the structural conditions to which they are exposed; for instance, household practices of restructuring (e.g. merging with members of other households) and relocation (e.g. international migration) are likely to produce such effects (Moser 1996a).[1] Second, although not shown in Figure 3.1, the model recognises the role of norms, values and beliefs (including religion) in shaping household members' attitudes and behaviour, but for reasons explained in the previous section, they are considered to be distinct from household resources.

The remainder of this section focuses on three major influences hypothesised to affect household behaviour. The *wider structure*[2] embraces economic, social,

---

1    Social movements can also contribute to removing structural constraints on households' choices of action, but are not explored here in detail because the model is focussed more on the individual practices of households than collective actions.

2    In developing the structural aspects of this model, I was inspired by the livelihood framework devised by Carney et al. (1999:7, 9, 11) and adopted by Lloyd-Jones (cited in Rakodi 2002:9).

cultural, political and environmental forces operating at the global, national and local levels. Hence it represents a wide range of factors that are beyond the household's immediate control. For instance, they extend from broader policies driven by supra-national bodies (e.g. structural adjustment programs and trade policy) and government policies designed centrally or locally (e.g. housing and social security policy) to external influences relating to the cultural, urban or neighbourhood context (e.g. patriarchal structures and conditions prevalent within the urban labour and property markets). The wider structure is understood to have a bearing upon household characteristics, resources and behaviour. To illustrate, the conditions of unemployment can affect household decisions about child bearing and hence numbers available for work, which might lead small households to make intensive use of their labour resources by having one or more members engaged in more than one job. Furthermore, neighbourhood characteristics can play a role in the production and maintenance of social capital or solidarity networks (see e.g. Forrest and Kearns 2001, Sönmez 2007) while the wider urban context can shape the way low-income families manage their work and time demands (Roy et al. 2004).

*Household characteristics*, which consist of size, structure and life-cycle stage, are construed to have potential effects on household resources, behaviour and poverty. Previous studies have shown that these characteristics equip the households differently in their struggle against poverty (Gonzales de la Rocha 2001b). Research attention has been drawn to the role of household size, structure or life-cycle in shaping poverty, the extent of household involvement in informal work and/or women's labour market participation (Chant 1991, Gonzales de la Rocha 1994, Grootaert et al. 1995, Krishna 2004, Lokshin and Yemstov 2001, Vinay 1985, World Bank 2005). Household structure was also seen as an object of decisions/actions households take to combat poverty, or more specifically to change their dependency ratios (see e.g. Cornia et al. 1987, Hackenberg et al. 1984, Moser 1996a, Selby et al. 1990). Merging with members of other households illustrates such actions. Consequently, household characteristics have a dynamic quality which partly emanates from the control households have over their size and structure.

Finally, *household resources* are viewed as capacities that can be mobilised in their own right or in combination with others to generate material and/or immaterial benefits (e.g. information, money, goods, services and moral support) from a variety of sources such as the market, the state and the household. These capacities are hypothesised a) to determine the nature of household responses and hence the outcomes for poverty and b) to be bound by household characteristics and the wider structure. A new distinction is drawn between the *availability* and *benefit delivery capacity* of resources to demonstrate the specific effects of these two forces. To illustrate, while the stage in the life cycle would determine the availability of labour resources, the competition between informal and formal sectors of the economy would rather affect their capacity to generate an income. A similar distinction is drawn by Leach et al. (1999:233) who applies the concepts of endowments and entitlements to separate 'rights and resources that social actors have' from utilities they derive from legitimate effective command over goods and services. This distinction differs subtly from my own in that it places emphasis on benefits obtained, whereas I stress the ability of resources to provide benefits.

Households are construed to have a portfolio that potentially includes the resource types listed below. The portfolio is broadly seen as a possession of the household (members) but the resources contained within it can either be internal or external to the household.

Internal resources
1. Time
2. Bodily resources
3. Labour resources
4. Cultural capital
5. Economic capital

External resources
6. Social capital
7. Public resources
8. Institutional entitlements.

I shall next elaborate upon each component of the household resource portfolio.

*Time, Bodily and Labour Resources*

Time is a significant resource used in combination with others, but on its own it implies little capacity (Pickvance and Pickvance 1994). Concerning *bodily resources*, except for the work of White and Ellison (2007) which I came across after developing my own model, these are not treated as a distinct category within the existing variants of the resource-based framework. Some variants of this framework place them under human capital, but this de-emphasises the distinct ways in which bodily resources can be mobilised to obtain benefits without mobilising labour power. Examples of this include the sale of organs in return for a passport as in the film 'Dirty Pretty Things' directed by Stephen Frears (2002). *Labour resources* can be employed both for paid and unpaid work. Hence, the focus on labour allows an exploration of age and gender divisions likely to occur within the domestic as well as the labour market sphere.

*Three Forms of Capital*

The three forms of capital incorporated into the household portfolio were originally formulated by Bourdieu (1986). While the categories of cultural and economic capital are adopted from his work, this study departs considerably from his conception of social capital, although the idea of them being mutually convertible is retained. Before moving to elaborate on each form of capital, the controversy surrounding the status of the term 'capital' needs to be addressed. Some scholars contend that the definition of household resources in terms of capital leads to reification of the concept and hence should be avoided (McGregor and Kebede 2002, see also Schuller et al. 2000 for a review). However, others draw attention to the metaphorical value of the term, resulting from its emphasis on the potential for investment and appropriation of surplus value by the individuals or masses (Lin 2001). Besides, Bourdieu's three forms of capital are considered to have real foundations given the references they make to tangible and intangible objects such as language, qualifications, assets, etc. (Schuller et al. 2000). Thus, it seems to me that even where capital is no longer equated with objects, there still remains room to use the term in a metaphorical sense.

*Cultural Capital*

According to Bourdieu (1986), there are three forms in which cultural capital can exist. First is the embodied state where cultural capital is inherent to the dispositions of the mind and body. This process of embodiment implies a labour of inculcation and assimilation and costs time which must be a personal investment of the investor. I will refer to this form of cultural capital as informal. In my view, hustling comprises one particular type of informal cultural capital, although Wacquant (1999) regards it as a 'mastery of a particular type of symbolic capital'. In his study of coping in the American ghetto, Wacquant (1999:142) defines hustling as 'the ability to manipulate others, to inveigle and deceive them, if need be by joining violence to chicanery and charm in the pursuit of immediate pecuniary gain'. The second is the objectified state where cultural capital is materialised in cultural goods such as pictures, books, dictionaries, instruments, machines. The last is the institutionalised state where cultural capital is objectified in the form of educational qualifications. I will call this formal cultural capital. Overall, in this study, cultural capital will be used in the sense of information, skills and qualifications individuals acquire through formal education as well as their personal life experience.

*Economic Capital*

Following Bourdieu (1986), economic capital is defined here as resources which are immediately and directly convertible into monetary terms and may be institutionalised in the form of property rights. Economic capital thus includes monetary income, financial (e.g. jewellery, foreign exchange and bank accounts) and non-financial assets (e.g. land, car and house). The last two aspects of economic capital are self evident. As for the content of monetary income see Chapter 2.

## Social Capital

Among the three forms of capital, social capital is the most fashionable and controversial. Thus, the ways in which the term is defined and used require very careful consideration. In the last two decades, the concept of social capital has been applied to micro, meso and macro-level research from a variety of disciplines and fields of study in order to understand a wide range of phenomena, including families and youth behavioural problems, schooling and education, collective action, community life, democracy and governance, economic development, health and well-being, household welfare, poverty, work and organisational behaviour. One generic problem with this body of research concerns the indiscriminate use of the term. The aim here is not to construct a conceptual framework applicable across various disciplines or different levels of empirical research. It is rather to establish a clear and workable definition in order to guide micro-level research in which social capital is understood as a feature of individual actors rather than that of nations. There are in fact debates as to whether social capital is a collective or an individual good (Portes 1998). I agree with scholars who consider it to be a feature of both due to its potential benefits for the collectivity as well as for particular individuals (Lin 2001). However, for our research purposes, we will seek a definition where social capital is construed as a characteristic of individual agents. In pursuit of this, I will leave aside many of the meanings attached to social capital in empirical research and concentrate on the seminal work concerned with its theoretical foundations.

I shall start by clarifying the position taken here in relation to earlier debates about the status of social capital. First, unlike scholars who find the term decontextualised and hence unworkable (Fine 2001, Fine and Green 2000, see also review by Schuller et al. 2000), I favour the view that the term can be used as a metaphor to connote an individual's investment in social relations for expected returns (Lin 2001). I find this view plausible because, although economic motivations may not govern why people establish social relationships, people generally take an interest in receiving material and/or immaterial rewards from social interaction (Blau 1968). Second, in contrast to the large part of the literature which takes for granted social capital as an 'absolute good' or a 'metaphor for advantage' (e.g. Burt 2001), I agree with scholars who consider it as being neither a positive or negative phenomenon (e.g. Woolcock 1998). This is because, as shown by earlier studies, besides providing benefits, social interaction can also have a 'downside' e.g. it can be exclusive, impose restrictions on individual freedom or put 'downward levelling pressures' on the parties involved (Cleaver 2005, Portes and Landolt 1996, Staveren 2003). Consequently, social capital is understood here as a neutral phenomenon, and will be used in its metaphorical sense, which I believe is not problematic as long as the concept is a) based on existing theoretical frameworks; b) 'analytically productive'; and c) empirically operationalisable (Schuller et al. 2000). I will thus now turn to discuss how social capital is defined within the existing literature.

One of the earliest uses of the term, in a sense that is close to that of today, can be found in Jacobs's (1961) work on social networks in American cities (Woolcock 1998). Jacobs (1961:138) refers to social capital as the network connections of urban dwellers: 'networks are a city's irreplaceable social capital. Whenever the capital is lost, from whatever cause, the income from it disappears, never to return until and unless new capital is slowly and chancily accumulated'. The French sociologist Bourdieu, recognised as one of the founders of social capital, slightly diverges from Jacob in his definition of the concept. He conceives of social capital as an 'aggregate of the actual and potential resources which are linked to the possession of a durable network of more or less institutionalised relationships of mutual acquaintance and recognition – or in other words, to membership in a group – which provides each of its members with the backing of the collectivity-owned capital, a 'credential' which entitles them to credit, in various senses of the word' (Bourdieu 1986:248–9). It thus seems that for Bourdieu social capital embraces the social relationship itself that allows agents to claim access to resources embedded in these networks, as well as the amount and the quality of the network resources (see also Portes 1998). In my view, this duality poses an empirical problem for poverty studies by preventing us from drawing a clear contrast between social contacts and the outcomes of likely interactions between these contacts.

Independently from Bourdieu's instrumental line of thinking, a similar conception of social capital has been established and used in other contemporary sources. In the work of the economist Glen Loury, the term social capital is used to capture the differential access to opportunities through social connections for minority and non-minority youths (Portes 1998, Woolcock 1998). Portes (1998) criticises Loury's use of the concept as being devoid of any detailed or systematic analysis to reveal its relation to other forms of capital. Loury's work nevertheless leads Coleman (1988, 1990) to develop a more refined analysis of the role of social capital in the formation of human capital. In Coleman's analysis, the term social capital is defined with a specific emphasis on its function as 'varieties of entities with two elements in common: They all consist of some aspects of social structures, and they facilitate certain action of actors –whether persons or corporate actors – within the structure' (Coleman 1990:302). Portes and Sensenbrenner (1993), in my view correctly, criticise Coleman's approach for a) failing to answer the question of what those entities enabling individuals to attain their goals are, and b) conceptualising social capital only as a positive socio-structural force. Portes and Sensenbrenner (1993:1323) redefine the concept as 'expectations for action within a collectivity that affect the economic goals and goal-seeking behaviour of its members, even if these expectations are not oriented towards the economic sphere'. Although these writers acknowledge the idea that economic motives are not the sole determinant of social action, their definition becomes less useful since the operationalisability of these expectations remains a problem. A few years later Portes (1995:12) defined social capital rather differently as a 'capacity of individuals to command scarce resources by virtue of their membership in networks and or broader social structures'. This definition is in fact conceptually well suited to my research purposes as it clearly conveys the instrumental role of social relationships in providing access to resources. However, how to operationalise individuals' capacity to command scarce resources remains an empirical problem.

More recently, scholars have begun to use the concept in order to depict an individual's stock of social networks (Wellman and Frank 2001), or 'resources embedded in a social structure which are accessed and/or mobilized in purposive actions' (Lin 2001:12). These definitions fail to offer clear-cut boundaries for the concept. The latter understanding of social capital is, for instance, too broad to avoid indiscriminate use of the term as there is a high risk of interpreting 'resource' as any means that serves an end within a given interaction. Neither does the former set of definitions fully address the boundary issue as it remains unclear in what ways social capital is distinct from social networks.[3]

Another widely held perspective views social capital as a generalised disposition to trust (Fukuyama 1995, Inglehart 1997, Putnam 1993). For Putnam (1993:167), social capital signifies the 'features of social life – networks, norms and trust – that facilitate co-operation and co-ordination for mutual benefit'. Similarly, Inglehart (1997:118) refers to it as 'a culture of trust and tolerance in which extensive networks of voluntary associations emerge'. The empirical shortcomings of this usage are also evident in trust-based definitions, due to the difficulty of measuring how trusting people or nations are.

Overall, there appear two generic limitations with the above definitions of social capital; these concern problems with boundary setting and empirical applicability. In my view, a sound response to the conceptual and empirical limitations of these definitions comes from Pizzorno who construes social capital as 'the relations in which more or less durable identity of participants are recognized' (2001:5). Pizzorno's definition offers well-defined boundaries for the term, which can be operationalised e.g. by asking whether the respondent intends to maintain links with a given social contact in the foreseeable future. However, Pizzorno excludes the market from the domain of social capital, which I believe is rather problematic given the evidence that informal transactions can take place between employers and employees (see e.g. Kalaycıoğlu and Rittersberger-Tılıç 2001, White 1994). For instance, in her research on small scale enterprises in Turkey, White (1994) describes the interactions between employers and employees as a kind of fictive kinship relationship with an implicitly exploitative character.

Thus, in contrast to Pizzorno (2001) who restricts social capital to non-market based contacts, I shall use the concept in a broader sense to refer to relatively durable social contacts established inside or outside markets. I consider these contacts to have a potential downside as well as a capacity to deliver material and non-material benefits. This is to suggest that social capital can act as a resource in

---

3    There is in fact little agreement upon the precise meaning of the term social network. However, by referring to it as a specified set of links among social actors, Mitchell (1969), in my view, provides a useful and generally acceptable definition for the concept.

which individual agents invest and which they use to gain access to information, jobs, money, goods, services, etc.

The body of relationships described above as social capital is by no means uniform in character. Of the various types of social capital identified previously, the distinction drawn between 'bridging' and 'bonding' capital has attracted the most attention (Field 2003, Narayan 1999, Putnam 2000, Woolcock 1998). Scholars now speak of a third dimension called 'linking social capital' (Halpern 2005). However, the literature offers no clearly defined criteria to determine which aspects of social capital provide a distinctively bridging or bonding character, and this renders such classifications less workable.

Hence, I propose to develop an alternative classification based on exchange theories, given that the flow of benefits in a social environment is mediated by the rules of social exchange (Bourdieu 1986). The classification advanced here draws on market-based approaches[4] to social exchange as they are more sympathetic to the idea of social interaction being influenced by economic motives. More specifically, it represents a synthesis of two approaches developed by Blau (1964, 1968) and Sahlins (1974). Blau (1964:91) refers to social exchange as 'voluntary actions of individuals which are motivated by returns they are expected to bring and typically do in fact bring from others'. While Blau limits social exchange to actions which are rational, voluntary and rewarding, Sahlins (1974) extends it to include unrewarding transactions as well. This study favours the extended definition as it is better suited to the idea that social capital can have a downside.

My own classification of social capital rests partly on Blau's (1964) contention that social exchange transactions can either be 'unilateral' or 'reciprocal' in nature. For Blau, these transactions share two basic characteristics; i.e. trust and pretence of disinterested generosity. The point of distinction between them lies in the reciprocity element. A social transaction is considered to be 'unilateral' when the parties fail to reciprocate on an 'equal' footing, which in turn creates power differentials between them. This type of transaction implies a direct cost of subordination for the subjects of power. On the other hand, a social transaction is regarded as 'reciprocal' when the parties meet the obligation to reciprocate on an 'equal' footing. In developing this concept further, Sahlins (1974) identifies three distinct forms of reciprocal transaction, drawing on the idea that social exchange is situated between the unsociability and solidarity extremes. Accordingly, 'negative reciprocity', where each party is seeking to obtain an advantage at the expense of others, is located at the 'unsociable extreme'. In between is the 'balanced reciprocity', which is based on the simultaneous exchange of exactly the same types and quantities of goods within a finite and limited period. Finally, at the

---

4   Non-market approaches suggest a sharp distinction between the market and social exchanges, denying the utilitarian concerns in social interaction and the economic value of the items transacted (e.g. Levi-Strauss 1966, Malinowski 1922) The adoption of a market-based approach within this study does not mean that the mentality of *homo economicus* is assumed to govern social interactions.

solidarity end, exchange transactions take the form of 'generalized reciprocity', by which Sahlins (1974:193–94) refer to 'putatively altruistic transactions' where assistance is provided and returned if possible and when necessary.

The above hybrid of social exchange theories leads me to identify two major forms of social capital. One refers to *reciprocal contacts* with which one enters into social transactions on a balanced or generalised basis, sometimes with the intention to accumulate advantage at the expense of others. The other involves *power-based contacts* with which one complies in exchange for the benefits such compliance produces. The latter is in my view embodied within patron-client relationships, whose significance for the lives of low-income urban groups is well-documented (Lomnitz 1977, Nelson 1979, Norris 1988, Roberts 1991 – see below for an extended review). In what follows, I shall therefore outline the key features of these relationships which can either be established in urban areas or be a continuation of traditional, ethnic or rural relationships reproduced in urban areas (see e.g. Cornelius 1975, Erder 1994, Güneş-Ayata 1991, Hannerz 1974, Karpat 1976, Nelson 1979, Oakley 1979, Sandbrook 1982, Wolf 1966).

Two broad clusters of meanings are attributed to the term clientelism. The anthropological literature refers to it as a specific type of dyadic relationship, which ties people with unequal status or power and which depends on exchange of favours between these actors (Boissevain 1974, Burgwal 1995, Eisenstadt and Roniger 1984, Foster 1963, Lande 1977, Scott 1977, Wolf 1966). This is illustrated by interrelations of patronage and brokerage which are respectively defined according to whether the powerful party is in direct or indirect control of resources. In the political science literature, clientelism is understood as a 'political machine' by which mass-based parties mobilise political support (Banck 1986, Chubb 1982, Nelson 1979, Weingrod 1977). This machine operates on the principle of distributing or promising to distribute public resources as favours by political power holders/seekers and their respective parties in exchange for votes and other forms of political support (Banck 1986). Nelson (1979), in my view accurately, portrays the political machine as an 'outgrowth' of interpersonal patron-client ties, as the two forms have many aspects in common. The main difference between the two forms of clientelism seems to lie in the actors involved. In political clientelism, the role of the patron is undertaken by the party organisation, which derives its power from state resources of all kinds (e.g. political, bureaucratic or strictly economic) and uses this power to elicit electoral support (Chubb 1982).

Following Eisenstadt and Roniger (1984), common characteristics of the two forms of clientelism can be outlined as follows: First, they are based on direct exchange of favours. The benefits exchanged in these transactions include 'instrumental and economic as well as political ones on the one hand, and promises of reciprocity[5], solidarity and loyalty on the other' (Eisenstadt and Roniger 1984:48). Second, in spite of their seemingly enduring and binding nature,

---

5   Some scholars from this literature regard reciprocity as an attribute of clientelist relationships without making explicit in what sense they use the term (see e.g. Scott

both relationships are entered into voluntarily. Thirdly, they are neither legal nor contractual in character. This is why the patron-client bond requires a strong basis of trust and loyalty. Last but not least, the exchange transactions contain a strong element of inequality and power differential between patrons and their clients. Scott (1977) indicates that patrons, occupying positions critical for clients, such as factory owners, are in an ideal position to demand compliance from clients who are desperate for these scarce resources. Consequently, in my view, both interpersonal and political clientelism can be captured by Blau's (1964) conception of 'unilateral exchange' in that within both forms of clientelism the transaction of favours depend on the compliance of the less powerful party (Eroğlu 2000).[6]

So far, I have sought to define the boundaries of social capital and proposed an alternative way to distinguish between its different forms. As a result, social capital is confined to individuals' stock of relatively durable contacts with varying capacities for ensuring flows of information, money, goods and services. Depending on the type of exchange relationship parties enter into, these contacts are understood to assume either a reciprocal or power-based character. The advantages of this framework are as follows. First of all, it avoids the indiscriminate use of the term, as well as offering a sound basis for its operationalisation. Second, it allows an emphasis on the instrumentality of social relationships as a potential resource with varying capacities to deliver benefits. Finally, it provides further insight into the 'downside of social capital' through a focus on negative forms of reciprocity, relationships of subordination and various other constraints on the flow of benefits.

*Public Resources*

This category encapsulates all man-made and natural resources owned collectively by public bodies (e.g. state-owned land, forests, rivers, water and electricity), and hence has a broader coverage than the widely used notion of 'natural capital' (see e.g. Carney et al. 1999 and Rakodi 2002). One peculiar example of this resource type comprises the public waste that can be recovered through scavenging.

*Institutional Entitlements*

The idea of entitlement comes from Sen's (1982) work on famines, and is applied broadly to the study of urban and rural livelihoods in the form of 'claims' and 'access' (Chambers and Conway 1991, Swift 1989), or 'endowments' and 'exchange' (Pryer 2003). By entitlements, Sen (1982) refers to the totality of rights and

---

1977). As far as Blau's (1964) social exchange theory is concerned, reciprocity cannot be considered as a feature of clientelism as it implies a lack of clear power differentials.

6   For an alternative exchange-based conception of patron-client relationships refer to Lomnitz (1971, 1988) who draws on Polanyi's mode of redistribution. Here, Blau's (1964) perspective on social exchange is preferred primarily due to its concern with power differentials between the parties involved in an exchange transaction.

opportunities available to an individual. However, the term is used here in a more restricted sense to indicate entitlements created by governmental or non-governmental institutions. They, for instance, concern rights of access to state welfare benefits and services (e.g. social security, health services and public housing), squatter regularisation and redevelopment schemes and charitable aid. The focus on entitlements forms a bridge between macro and micro levels as they are often shaped by state policies.

## An Overview of Research Findings: What Brings Success?

This chapter has so far sought to clarify the theoretical foundations on which this study is based. The remainder of the chapter presents a review of conclusions reached within diverse literatures in order to set out hypotheses. The review discusses the key influences likely to affect household success in reducing deprivation with reference to the four types of behaviour outlined earlier: income generation, income allocation, consumption and investment.

### Income Generation and Diversification

One central idea here is that livelihood diversification is key to understanding poor households' socio-economic situation. Debates about livelihood diversification mostly concern the rural parts of the developing world, but nevertheless remain relevant to understanding the determinants of urban households' success in income generation. Ellis (2000b:290) broadly defines livelihood diversification as 'the maintenance and continuous adaptation of a highly diverse portfolio of activities in order to secure survival'. Although the concept is claimed not to be equivalent to 'income diversification', most economic and quantitative studies use the term in its rather narrow sense to denote the range of cash earning activities from various sources (cf. Ellis 1998, Hussein and Nelson 1998). I will employ the term in the same sense as these economic studies, not only because it makes the concept analytically easier to work with but also because it captures the distinct characteristic of livelihood diversification; which is, as Ellis (1998:15) points out, its emphasis on 'variety of dissimilar income sources'. These sources are often understood in terms of farm and non-farm activities. A number of studies which apply the term to the urban context conceive of income diversity in terms of formal and informal sector activities (Gonzales de la Rocha 2001a). The focus of this study will be on the resources directly used in dissimilar income generating activities.

Concerning the poverty implications of diversification, Ellis (1998, 2000b) argues that having diverse alternatives for income generation makes people's livelihood systems less vulnerable. Research performed in urban and rural areas is supportive of this argument (e.g. Bird and Shepherd 2003, Grootaert et al. 1995, Krishna et al. 2006, Moser 1996a, Reardon et al. 1992 and for detailed reviews see

Ellis 1998 and Hussein and Nelson 1998). The idea that households with a diverse income portfolio are likely to be more successful makes sense particularly in the context of risk and uncertainty, since diversification may enable low co-variation of risk between the components of income portfolio. However, as indicated by Dercon (2000), the observed patterns of diversification might not necessarily help reduce risk or manage it effectively. There is research evidence to support this argument (e.g. Dercon and Krishnan 1996). Dercon (2000) argues that livelihood diversification may prove ineffective due to 'entry constraints' which force poor households to participate in low return activities. These constraints range from the need for skills and assets to more structural factors such as the functioning of product, labour, and asset markets. In light of these considerations, *I do not expect households with more diverse income options to be necessarily associated with lower levels of deprivation* (Hypothesis A). Let us now discuss some of the likely constraints with reference to resources that may be of potential use in generating income. I will begin with labour.

Most studies report labour to be one of the most frequently used resource types by the poor households (Gonzales de la Rocha 2001b, Moser 1996a, 1996b, 1996c). Thus, *I also expect labour to be the most significant resource that households use to generate income* (Hypothesis B). Research evidence from developing countries suggest that mobilising additional labour – principally women's labour but in the poorest households even children's labour – constitutes a frequent household response to a declining income (Chant 1991, Cornia et al. 1987, Latapi and Gonzales de la Rocha 1995, Logan 1981, Moser 1996a, 1996b, 1996c, Norris 1988). A few Turkish studies also point to the fact that especially since the 1980s rural-to-urban migrant women have increasingly become part of the labour force due to economic hardship (Ecevit 1998). According to the official figures, women's participation rates in the Turkish urban labour force rose by 39 per cent between October 1988 and 2001 (TURKSTAT 2003a). These figures may prove even higher if their informal sector employment and home-based income earning activities, which often go unreported due to women's perception of these tasks as non-work, are also taken into account (Özbay 1995). According to one survey, women constitute 11 per cent of the informal sector participants in Turkey (TURKSTAT 2003b). Further studies also demonstrate the significance of informal sector employment and home-working in women's income generating practices in urban Turkey (Çınar 1994, Kalaycıoğlu and Rittersberger-Tılıç 2001, White 1994). Nevertheless, the size of the urban female labour force in Turkey remains rather small, comprising only 20 per cent of the total urban labour force in 2001 (TURKSTAT 2003a). A full account of the factors restricting female labour participation is beyond the scope of this study, but I concur with the idea that given the decline in the potential of the urban labour market to provide employment particularly since the 1980s, low female labour participation rates cannot be explained simply in terms of religious and patriarchal influences but the structural problems of the urban economy should also be taken into account (Ecevit 1995). Increasing unemployment or unfavourable working conditions are likely to be responsible for low level of female labour participation.

As a matter of fact, a World Bank study (1999) shows that the low status, low paid, low security job options available to the rural-to-urban migrant women in Turkey, as well as potential sexual harassment in the work place, make staying at home a more desirable and prestigious alternative.

The acknowledgement of such structural pressures however does not mean that traditional norms, values or beliefs no longer have any relevance. *Alevi*s and *Sünni*s constitute the two main Islamic sects in Turkey. Scholars argue that in comparison to *Sünni* families, women in *Alevi* families enjoy more power and autonomy, and take a more active role in the public sphere as gender segregation is not part of their religious practices (Ayata 1997, Erman 2001, Shankland 1996). Studies in *gecekondu* areas of Turkey confirm that employment participation rates of *Alevi* women tend to be higher than those of their *Sünni* counterparts (Erman 1998, Erman et al. 2002, Gökçe et al. 1993).

However, before reaching a firm conclusion on this, one also needs to consider the impact of patriarchal ideology in which female employment is strongly opposed due to the perceived threats to male authority, masculine pride and family honour (Erman et al. 2002). Within the urban context, there are indeed forces which work against patriarchy. For instance, urban migration, by enabling a rupture from the migrant family's circle of kin and villagers, may present women with an opportunity to challenge 'classic patriarchy' (Kandiyoti 1988). However, as Erman (2001) points out, cultural institutions and values as well as the capitalist system which integrates women into the urban economy as a cheap and flexible labour force help patriarchal ideology to reproduce itself in the urban context. A study by Başaran (1982) in an Aegean city of Turkey, for example, indicates that 42 per cent of villagers and 52 per cent of workers find it inappropriate for women to have paid employment. Negative attitudes against female employment are also reported to be prevalent within rural-to-urban migrant families (Çınar 1994, Erman et al. 2002, Erman and Türkyılmaz 2008, Kalaycıoğlu and Rittersberger-Tılıç 2000). This leads me to argue that the fact that both Islamic sects are embedded in an overarching patriarchal society could well override the differences between the labour market behaviour of *Alevi* and *Sünni* women. Moreover, in my view, the possibility of doing home-based work, which is more compatible with the dominant patriarchal ideology and which is becoming popular among the urban female labour force in Turkey[7], may also blur the differences between the two groups. Nevertheless, *as far as their employment outside home is concerned, I expect Alevi women to be more active than their Sünni counterparts. However, given the prominence of patriarchal influences, female employment is likely to be seen as a 'last resort'* (Hypothesis C).

Even if 'non-primary' labour resources are increasingly mobilised for income generation, does this mean that households with greater labour market participation are better off? Scholars consider the number of dependants as being

---

7    Strikingly, the number of home-based female workers rose by 52 per cent between October 1995 and 2001 (TURKSTAT 2003a).

crucial to economic and social success (Hackenberg et al. 1984, Kalaycıoğlu and Rittersberger-Tılıç 2002, Selby et al. 1990). Research from Mexico and the Philippines indicates a strong tendency for better off households to have lower dependency ratios (i.e. the ratio of dependants to workers) (Hackenberg et al. 1984, Selby et al. 1990). The rationale here is rather straightforward: the greater the number of working household members, the higher the household income. Longitudinally speaking, an increase in the number of labour market participants might be seen as a successful response to a decline in real income (Latapi and Gonzales de la Rocha 1995). However, in contrast to the proponents of the dependency argument, I believe the key to success does not simply depend on numbers contributing to household income, but more broadly on how many are able to have decent working conditions. This extends the matter beyond the level of pay to include access to social insurance, occupational health and safety, etc. As is reported in many studies from the developing world, economic restructuring programs have led to the deteriorating labour market conditions (Beneria and Feldman eds. 1992, Gonzales de la Rocha 2001b, Kanji 1994, Meer 1994, Roberts 1995). The Turkish economy is no exception to this rule. Macro-economic studies on Turkey draw attention to the link between structural adjustment programs and declining real urban wages – especially from 1994 onwards –, and increasing marginal sector participation in return for low wages and no social insurance (Boratav et al. 2000, Yeldan 2001). Such conditions prevalent within the Turkish labour market are unlikely to have improved in the face of the 2001 economic crisis.[8] *These considerations lead me to hypothesise that differences in household dependency ratios are unlikely to be reflected in overall deprivation levels since adverse conditions in the labour market are likely to restrict the benefit delivery capacity of the labour resources deployed* (Hypothesis D).

The factors that determine the benefit delivery capacity of labour resources may stem from the demand and supply side of the labour market. The sector of employment may be regarded as one of those demand side influences. Some studies view the informal sector as an important source of livelihood for poor households (Cornia et al. 1987, Jiggins 1989, Massiah 1989, Moser 1996a, 1996c, UPL 2000). Others also regard it as an opportunity to earn a reasonable income, and yet acknowledge the lack of access to welfare services as a drawback of the informal sector (Eke 1982, Roberts 1989, 1991, 1994). A further group of scholars, however, more radically challenge the idea that the informal sector can offer the poor or unemployed people a life-line (Amis 1995, Pahl 1988). This critique makes great sense given the evidence that the informal sector provides casual

---

8  The Turkish economy witnessed a severe financial crisis in February 2001, which led to a dramatic decline in growth rates and an increase in inflation and unemployment rates. The growth rates declined from 6.1 per cent in 2000 to −9.4 per cent in 2001. The annual rate of inflation increased from 39 per cent in 2000 to 68.5 per cent in 2001 (Akyüz and Boratav 2003). Finally, the unemployment rate based a narrow definition, rose from 6.4 per cent in 2000 to 8.4 per cent in 2001 (TURKSTAT 2003c).

and legally unprotected forms of employment and lower hourly income rates (Beall et al. 2000, Beneria 1992, Mingione 1983, Perez-Aleman 1992, Safa and Antrobus, 1992). The argument of this study will be in line with the critical view of the informal sector, primarily because access to state pensions and healthcare in Turkey are heavily dependent on work-based contributions, which require the employee and his/her employer(s) to formally register with the system (see also Eke 1982). Considering the poverty inducing effects of limited social insurance coverage, *I expect those households with lower levels of formal sector participation to suffer from increased deprivation* (Hypothesis E).[9] However, my reservation concerning this hypothesis is that the differences in the deprivation levels of formal and informal sector participants may be blurred due to the fact that elements of irregularity (e.g. illegal employment arrangements) can also be observed in the tax-paying segments of the private sector.

Supply-side influences may also have direct or indirect effects on the benefit delivery capacity of labour resources. We have already discussed some of these influences, i.e. religion and patriarchal attitudes against female employment. Further supply-side influences relate to the components of the household resource portfolio, among which economic, cultural and social capital are of particular relevance. Starting with economic capital, this resource may be influential in cases where financial or non-financial assets are deployed for entrepreneurial purposes alongside labour. However, as Dercon (2000) correctly points out, the portfolio of assets available to poor households is, in general, limited and highly susceptible to economic shocks. The same may be true for the work-related assets of *gecekondu* households who are reported to have frequent engagement in small scale entrepreneurship (Şenyapılı 1981, UPL 2000, 2001). This type of employment may also be evident in my research. However, *I expect the level of economic capital deployed by the poor households in small scale 'enterprises' to be almost invariably low , or even non-existent , and to fail to offer protection against conditions of economic crisis* (Hypothesis F).

Cultural capital (i.e. formal or informal skills), which is often deployed in combination with labour, constitutes another resource likely to affect the benefit delivery capacity of labour resources and hence levels of household deprivation. The impact of formal education on deprivation is often discussed within the context of human capital (see e.g. Rakodi 2002). Previous research on poor social groups reveals that higher levels of human capital are significantly associated with higher levels of household welfare in general (Grootaert et al. 1995, Grootaert 1998, Grootaert et al. 2002, Grootaert and Narayan 2001, Lokshin and Yemtsov

---

9   With the enactment of the Social Security and General Health Insurance Law in 2008, it became possible to make voluntary contributions to the state health and pension schemes but the system continues to exclude those who are unable to contribute on a regular basis (see also Appendix B). The poverty implications of limited social insurance coverage are also addressed by a number of studies published subsequent to my field research (Buğra and Keyder 2006, Saaw and Akpınar 2007).

2001, Maluccio et al. 2000, Narayan and Pritchett 1999). Likewise, rural livelihood research demonstrates low returns to uneducated labour (Carter and May 1999). A Turkish study of rural-to-urban migrant households shows that higher levels of education can improve the likelihood of finding a better job and ensure 'higher levels of absorption' (Eke 1982). However, Eke is careful to note that education does not necessarily guarantee a better job since low-income migrants, usually having no schooling beyond primary education, are unable to pass the level which is crucial for enhancing household income. Bearing this in mind, *I anticipate that the greater the level of formal cultural capital possessed by the households, the more likely they are to experience reduced deprivation* (Hypothesis G).

Social capital may also impact upon the benefit delivery capacity of labour by virtue of its role in the job search process. Based on theories of social resource (Lin 1982), social network and social capital, an extensive body of research examines the relationship between social capital and status attainment (see Lin 1999 for a detailed review). These studies formulated and tested a number of propositions either by focusing on 'accessed social capital' (i.e. resources accessed in an individual's general social networks) or 'mobilised social capital' (i.e. the use of social contact and the resources provided by the contact in job finding). Two of these propositions are of particular relevance here. The first is 'the social resource proposition': the higher the accessed or mobilised resources embedded in social networks (i.e. social capital) the better the outcome of an instrumental action (e.g. attained status). The second is 'the strength of ties proposition': the higher the use of weaker ties the better the access to social resources. Previous research consistently provides confirmatory evidence for the social resource proposition, using various social capital measures (Lin 1999). Those testing the effects of 'mobilised social capital' often focus on the status of the contact person (e.g. Marsden and Hurlbert 1988), whereas those dealing with 'accessed social capital' measure social capital with reference to a) network diversity, i.e. contacts' occupational and educational status (e.g. Erickson 2001), b) structural positions salient in a society such as occupations and class (e.g. Lin et al. 2001), or c) extent of contacts (e.g. Boxman et al. 1991).

These studies tell us little about the role of social capital in the status achievements of disadvantaged groups, who, as Lin (1999) points out, tend to use informal channels. Previous research on Turkey confirms the frequent use of informal channels by low income groups (*gecekondu* dwellers, migrants, factory or piece workers, house cleaners etc.) in job search and recruitment processes. Kin and *hemşehri* (i.e. people from the same village or town) groups are reported to play a particular role (Dubetsky 1976, Erder 1994, 1996, Gökçe et al. 1993, Güneş-Ayata 1991, 1996, Karpat 1976, Şenyapılı 1978, Tatlıdil 1989, UPL 2000, 2001, White 1994, Yasa 1966). Earlier studies claim that these informal channels are residues of rural life-style, and therefore will gradually lose their significance in the urban environment and give way to formal channels (Kartal 1982, Kongar 1972, Karpat 1976, Şenyapılı 1978, Tatlıdil 1989, Yasa 1966). However, in keeping with Duben's (1982) argument, recent research confirms that in urban Turkey, informal channels retain their significance for finding jobs or seeking other forms of support. However, in my view, these studies fail to convincingly establish the impact of these informal channels on the overall well-being of disadvantaged groups. A few studies on the developed world explore this relationship empirically. A Dutch study for instance indicates that those using informal job processes do not necessarily attain better jobs (Flap and Boxman 2001). How far this evidence is valid for the Turkish case remains to be seen. *In the Turkish labour market, where recruitment procedures are not entirely rationalised and informal employment is quite a common occurrence, poor households are expected to use their informal channels (i.e. social capital) extensively* (Hypothesis H). However, unlike studies which use number of contacts to measure social capital, *I am not expecting households with larger volumes of social capital to attain better positions in the labour market and thereby experience less deprivation* (Hypothesis I). This is because 'volume' implies little about the benefit delivery capacity of social contacts mobilised in the job process. In my view, a more appropriate way to assess the benefit delivery capacity of social contacts is to focus on the contact status. This research will explore the impact of contact status in relation to clientelist ties where poor households come into contact with people of higher status.

Turning to patron-client relationships, the bulk of research demonstrates that they are an important source or strategy of survival and social mobility for the urban poor (Banck 1986, Gonzales de la Rocha 1994, Lomnitz 1977, Nelson 1979, Norris 1984, 1988, Roberts 1970, 1973, 1991, 1995). Turkish studies report these relationships to be of significant use in job finding or gaining access to money, goods and services including *gecekondu* housing and public services (Dubetsky 1976, Erder 1996, Heper 1982, Işık and Pınarcıoğlu 2001, Kıray 1982, Magnarella 1970, Kalaycıoğlu and Rittersberger-Tılıç 2001). Some scholars however question the capacity of urban patrons to provide for their clients. Nelson (1979) for instance argues that patron-client relationships operating at the interpersonal and political level can provide few tangible benefits for many of the urban poor. However, these ties, particularly those of a political nature, are likely to bring economic and social advancement only for the aggressive and favoured minority. Additionally, many scholars suggest that forces such as increasing specialisation, variety of government activities, growing market contacts and widened needs and desires on the part of ordinary people, which operate more strongly in the urban context are likely to cause limited, partial, contingent and sporadic patterns of clientelist ties to emerge. This is claimed to reduce the quality of benefits delivered (Nelson 1979, Norris 1984, Roberts 1973).

In the Turkish literature, even where a decline in the capacity of clientelist relationships is claimed or implied (Işık and Pınarcıoğlu 2001, Kalaycıoğlu and Rittersberger-Tılıç 2002), I have found no convincing explanation as to why, and in what ways, their capacity is declining and how the urban poor will be affected.[10] Işık and Pınarcıoğlu (2001) seem to make this claim on the basis of the fact that since 1985 no amnesty law has been passed to authorise *gecekondus* built after 1985; allowing some *gecekondu* owners to enjoy speculative profits in the urban land market. This presumption is, in my view, unjustified in that it ignores the possibility of another amnesty in the future. Exploration of the influences affecting the capacity of clientelist relationships in Turkey is beyond the scope of this book. Nevertheless, one tendency is worth mentioning. It appears that some governmental positions in Turkey are gradually losing their potential as a source of patronage power. Güneş-Ayata (1996) claims that access to governmental positions via *hemşehri* relationships is becoming difficult due to the rationalisation of recruitment process through exams etc. I suspect any rationalisation is only superficial. I also believe that mass privatisation of State Enterprises plays a part in restricting access to such positions. Whatever the reason; this tendency indicates a reduction in the capacity of clientelist relationships to provide access to relatively secure jobs in the public sector. The exploitative nature of these relationships can also have adverse implications for the benefits delivered by urban patrons. Obviously, patrons do not deliver favours for altruistic reasons; they engage in these transactions with the intention of profit maximisation or political advancement (Chubb 1982, Kıray 1982, Spicer 1970). The patrons provide benefits in return for loyalty, which may impose certain costs on the clients. *These considerations lead me to hypothesise that those engaging in clientelist transactions when finding work may not necessarily be more successful* (Hypothesis J). It may well follow from this that higher status contacts do not always provide better job opportunities. Let us now examine whether the tie characteristics are effective in job attainment.

Despite the consistent confirmation of the 'social resource proposition' in the status attainment literature, there remains much debate about the 'strength of weak ties' thesis originally posed by Granovetter (1973, 1982). Granovetter contends that weaker ties are more likely to ensure better job information, as they tend to form bridges between dissimilar information sources. By this contention, Granovetter establishes a positive association between weak ties and information transfer rather than occupational achievement. The strength of weak ties proposition upon which the status attainment research is based constitutes a version of Granovetter's original contention modified to test whether weak ties provide better access to resources. However, there exists no consistent empirical evidence to support even this modified proposition (see Lin 1999). The wider social network literature also provides conflicting evidence. In his study of poor households in urban Chile, Espinoza (1999) finds that weak ties which constitute specialised labour market contacts of the urban poor lead to better employment conditions. On the other hand, Grieco (1987) shows that strong ties can be of significant use in recruitment. Yakubovich (1999) generalises this finding to all forms of support. Two points

_____

10   The Turkish studies on the subject mainly focus on the characteristics and historical development of clientelist party politics (see e.g. Güneş-Ayata 1994, Özbudun 1981, Sayarı 1977).

can be made as to why weak ties may not work in the labour market. First of all, weak ties offer little incentive for exchange (Lin 1999). Secondly, the type of ties favoured in the job search process depends on the conditions of the labour market; in situations of recession, for instance, strong ties are claimed to be of more importance (Grieco 1987). Thus, *given the conditions of economic crisis in Turkey, I anticipate that poor households may predominantly use strong ties to find jobs with better pay and working conditions and hence experience deprivation to a lesser extent where such contacts are formed* (Hypothesis K).

In addition to labour, other types of resources can be used directly in generating an income. Economic capital comprises one such type. Households may deploy some of their financial and non-financial assets to derive income in the form of rent or interest. However, *I do not expect the asset portfolios of the poor households to have a significant capacity to promote income* (Hypothesis L). The reasons for this will be explained when discussing investment and insurance behaviour. Within the Turkish context, gecekondu appears as one specific means whereby poor households can obtain rent. Those who legally or illegally occupy a gecekondu with an extension(s) or additional storey(s), or more than one gecekondu, can generate some rental income. However, those whose rights to gecekondu ownership were secured by the Redevelopment Law (no 2981) can enjoy higher levels of rent, following the transformation of their gecekondus into apartment blocks.[11] This however primarily depends on two factors. The obvious one is the location of the neighbourhood, and the other is the land share which determines the number of flats to be allocated to them in the new blocks, if any. Consequently, *I do not expect the households in my sample to get involved in gecekondu speculation beyond meeting their immediate shelter needs, and hence to generate rent from their gecekondus* (Hypothesis M).

Turning to social capital, this resource type can also directly facilitate income generation. In the literature, the link between social capital and household welfare is well established. Mostly World Bank led studies associate greater social capital with increased levels of household welfare although its degree of significance in relation to other resources (e.g. human capital) varies from one case to another (Grootaert 1998, Grootaert and Narayan 2001, Grootaert et al. 2002, Maluccio et al. 2000, Narayan and Pritchett 1999, Narayan 1997, Rose 1999). In measuring household welfare, these studies often use proxies of income or expenditure. As for social capital, they either treat number of group memberships, group characteristics (i.e. degree of heterogeneity) and group values and norms as separate measures of social capital, or combine these dimensions within an index. In discussing the relationship between social capital and position attained in the labour market, we have already established that volume of social capital is less likely to be effective as it has few implications for the benefit delivery capacity of social contacts. In my view, this is also true as far as their role in direct income generation is concerned,

---

11   For different models of *gecekondu* transformation see Dündar (2001), Türker-Devecigil (2005) and Uzun (2005).

since under conditions of economic hardship, the capacity of social contacts to provide support for each other may become eroded and the spirit of solidarity may begin to be replaced with more individualistic concerns. As a matter of fact, the findings from economically less developed parts of the world, including Turkey, point to the declining capacity of solidarity networks in circumstances of economic hardship and recession (Bora 2002, Buğra and Keyder 2003, 2006, Gonzales de la Rocha 2001b, Moser 1996a, Şen 2002, World Bank 2003).

One counter-argument is that the probability of coming into contact with people of higher benefit delivery capacity is higher for those possessing larger volumes of social capital. This sounds plausible but, as is the case with most World Bank research, what is not considered here is the fact that at least two parties are involved in social exchange, and that the flow of resources in such transactions is maintained on the basis of the reciprocity principle. It is well acknowledged that failure to reciprocate poses threats to the independence of the receiver (Blau 1964, Finch and Mason 1992). Often due to their limited reciprocal capacity, the poor households may avoid asking for help to keep their independence, or reciprocate at a balanced level as long as their own resources allow them to. Of equal importance, they may be denied support due to concerns over their creditworthiness (Moser 1996a). Thus, what the poor households can get out of their social contacts is likely to be bound by what they can offer. Transactions with close relatives which tend to be based on generalised reciprocity might be an exception. However, as discussed earlier, their capacity to provide support could be fragile as well. Given these considerations, *I expect social capital to make a rather limited contribution to household income, and hence to play a limited role in reducing deprivation* (Hypothesis N).

Finally, institutional entitlements can be mobilised for income generation. It was suggested that those with access to more entitlements are less likely to suffer from poverty (Kirkby and Moyo 2001). This proposition should be approached with care since it overlooks the likely constraints upon the benefit delivery capacity of this type of resources. At the time of research, a number of contributory and non-contributory cash benefit entitlements were granted by the central as well as local governments. The former include entitlements to old-age pension and unemployment insurance whereas the latter involve pensions for specific groups such as the elderly and the disabled and emergency cash relief awarded for educational and medical purposes.[12]

However, the capacity of these entitlements to solve poor households' income problems can be constrained by various structural factors. One set of constraints relates to the strict conditions set out for access to benefit entitlements (e.g. means-test, premium requirements). To illustrate, in 2001, in order to become eligible for unemployment insurance, the employee had to accumulate 600 days' worth premium within the three years prior to redundancy and 120 days of this had to

---

12    For details on social assistance mechanisms in Turkey see e.g. Buğra and Keyder (2006).

be uninterrupted. This means that casual and informal workers are likely to be faced with exclusion from such benefits.[13] A second set of constraints concern gate-keeping. Access to some of the cash benefit entitlements, especially those granted locally, tends be controlled by gatekeepers, often for clientelist purposes. A third set of constraints limit the size, duration and regularity of cash benefits provided. Thus, most entitlements available to the poorer groups in Turkey are far from acting as an adequate and consistent source of income. This is also confirmed by more recent research, which emphasises the inadequacies of existing social assistance mechanisms in tackling poverty in Turkey (Buğra and Keyder 2003, Güneş-Ayata and Ayata 2003, METU 2003, World Bank 2003). In light of these considerations, *I expect institutional entitlements to make a rather limited and inconsistent contribution to household income, and hence to have little effect on reducing household deprivation.* (Hypothesis O).

*Income Allocation*

One central idea here is that how income (and also goods) is allocated within the household determines the degree to which its members experience or avoid 'hidden' or 'secondary poverty' (Chant 1985, Pahl 1980, Rowntree 1910). The term 'secondary poverty' was formulated by Rowntree (1910) and used by survival studies to refer to situations where household members experience greater poverty than would be the case if all of the wage earners' income was made available for general household use (Chant 1994). In what follows, the likely effects of income allocation will be discussed in terms of the distinction drawn between overt and covert mechanisms. These mechanisms are understood to have an effect on deprivation occurring both at the *overall* household and intra-household levels. The former concerns standards of living whose absence directly affects all members (e.g. access to housing) or produces a shared sense of deprivation, and takes into account access to resources whose benefits are shared collectively (e.g. a flat used as a family home). The latter refer to differences between members' standards of living, for example in personal areas of consumption.[14]

Without referring to the overt vs. covert distinction, a substantial body of research explores the broader implications of the former for gender inequalities within the household. The evidence reveals three quite distinct patterns of inequality. One well-established pattern is that women are as likely as men to manage the household income while men reserve the right to have the final say in financial matters (Burgoyne and Lewis 1994, Land 1969, Pahl 1983, 1989). Women from low-income households, especially, are shown to shoulder the responsibility for financial management single-handedly (Ayers and Lambertz

---

13   As a matter of interest, in 2000, 11 per cent of the urban labour force comprised casual workers (TURKSTAT 2003a) and 12 per cent informal workers (TURKSTAT 2003b). There may be an overlap between casual and informal employment figures.

14   The FWID measures the former type of deprivation.

1986, Goode et al. 1998, Graham 1984, Kempson et al. 1995, Rubin 1976, Vogler and Pahl 1993, 1994, Vogler 1994, Wilson 1987). Alternatively, Rake and Jayatilaka (2002) demonstrate the prevalence of joint control among low-income households. However, the study raises doubts about the validity of this finding by drawing attention to a few cases where women who claim to control finances jointly also say they have difficulties in challenging men's spending behaviour.

There exists further research focusing on financial arrangements made within the household, but these studies neglect the useful distinction drawn between the concepts of financial management and control. Only a few of these studies confirm that women are more likely to manage the finances in low-income households (Moser 1996a). The rest reveal divergent results. A survey by the Turkish Ministry of Health on married and working women (cited in UNDP 1999) and a qualitative study of money-earning activities among migrant women (Erman et al. 2002) conclude that men tend to be the main managers of the family budget. Further research from other parts of the world suggests that women in poor and middle class households are more likely to retain control over household finances (Mencher 1988, Papanek and Schewede 1988). The mixed results may be due to cultural differences but can also attributed to differences in the conceptual approaches used.

Consequently, the above depicted pattern of inequality is likely to apply to the Turkish households studied here, given that they are mostly composed of first generation rural-to-urban migrant couples from a gecekondu settlement, among whom patriarchal values and norms tend to be prevalent (see e.g. Erman 2001). Therefore, *I propose that male spouses from these households are likely to retain control over household finances while their wives manage the household income as an extension of their domestic duties* (Hypothesis P). More recent research substantiates this hypothesis by demonstrating that women are more likely to manage household finances where 'traditional breadwinning ideologies' are expressed (Vogler 2005, Vogler et al. 2006).

A second pattern of inequality concerns the differences in spouses' experience of 'financial deprivation'. Most studies conclude that men generally enjoy better living standards than their wives, and hence experience less 'financial deprivation' when income is tight (Chant 1985, Vogler 1994, Vogler and Pahl 1993, 1994, Wilson 1987). Although this pattern is shown to persist across all management systems, scholars insist that these systems make a significant difference to the living standards of the individual household members. However, the literature contains no consistent evidence to confirm that any particular management system is more or less conducive to producing poverty. Some studies demonstrate that the largest differences in 'financial deprivation' occur within households using female-managed and housekeeping allowance systems (Vogler 1994, Vogler and Pahl 1994), whereas others reveal that in households where the husband manages or controls the finances, inequality between the partners and the experience of deprivation by the wife and children are likely to reach extreme levels (Wilson 1987). By contrast, further evidence suggests that in times of hardship all or most household members can sacrifice their individual welfare and spending in favour of the collective welfare (Fernandez-Kelly 1982, Gonzales de la Rocha 1988). Thus, *I hypothesise that the actual income distribution within the sample households is likely to serve the 'collective good', and to make a greater difference to overall household deprivation than the systems of management and control adopted* (Hypothesis Q).

A third pattern of gender inequality is shown to exist in access to personal spending money (PSM). The research consensus here is that women tend to withhold less money for personal use, and that men have greater access to PSM (Ayers and Lambertz 1986, Björnberg and Kollind 2005, Blumberg 1991, Burgoyne 1990, Burgoyne and Lewis 1994, Hoodfar 1988b, Jiggins 1989, Mencher 1988, Pahl 1989, Rake and Jayatilaka 2002, Treas 1993, Vogler and Pahl 1994, Wilson 1987).

In contrast to overt mechanisms of income allocation, covert mechanisms are little explored. Only a few studies in sociology and social history demonstrate the use of such mechanisms in different parts of the world. Research from Turkey (Erman et al. 2002, Şenol-Cantek 2001) and the USA (Zelizer 1997) draws attention to the concealed savings created by women through the use of various manipulative techniques, such as keeping quiet about a portion of their own income, taking money from their husbands' pockets, or inflating the claimed expenditure. On the other hand, Tichenor's (1999) study of married couples with female breadwinners in the USA reports two cases where men kept separate accounts without the knowledge of their wives, by using techniques similar to those outlined above.

Thus, little is known about the logic of financial secrecy. Nevertheless, existing debates about financial autonomy and separate accounts are of some relevance to understanding why women keep secret kitties. It is argued that one key requirement for each spouse to obtain a sense of financial autonomy is to preserve exclusive ownership rights over a portion of their income (Burgoyne and Lewis 1994, Fleming 1997 cited in Elizabeth 2001). According to Hertz (1992), separate accounts used by couples with relatively equal incomes allow the development of substantial autonomy for each spouse, thereby redressing the traditional balance of power within marriage. On the other hand, scholars who studied couples with female breadwinners suggest that men's separate accounts may have a role in counterbalancing any 'money power' associated with the female breadwinning position (Stamp 1985, Tichenor 1999).

With few exceptions, the separate accounts studied earlier differ from secret kitties in that they were set up with the knowledge of the other spouse. However, both mechanisms seem to play a similar role in affecting the balance of power between spouses, which I consider to be critical to understanding women's motives for using secret kitties. In my view, by enabling women to avoid direct confrontation with men about financial matters, secret kitties might on the surface help preserve the traditional imbalance of power. However, they allow women to counteract men's authority indirectly by giving them exclusive discretion over a hidden sum of money. Therefore I believe secret kitty use by women epitomises a particular way of 'bargaining with patriarchy' to use Kandiyoti's (1988) phrase, which fits in well both with her description of 'female conservatism' as a response to the breakdown of classic patriarchy, and with Bolak's (1997) conception of 'traditional defiance'. The defining characteristic of 'traditional defiance' is 'neither accommodation of power nor overt contestation for power, but a curious combination of ritualistic adherence to traditional norms in public on the one hand and private mockery and manipulation of husbands on the other' (Bolak 1997:227). This type of domestic bargaining is likely to be quite a common occurrence in Turkish society given the reported tendency for low-income and/or rural-to-urban migrant women to avoid direct confrontation with their husbands in situations of conflict and to retain their low power status despite participation in paid work (Bolak 1997, Erman 1997, 1998, 2001, Erman et al. 2002, İsvan 1991, Kandiyoti 1982, Kuyaş 1982).

In short, I conceive of secret kitty keeping as a covert mechanism whereby women challenge the established patriarchal authority silently to increase their levels of financial agency. Although Hertz (1992) suggests that financial autonomy is more likely for women with income than for those without, it is clear from the manipulative techniques used in accumulating kitty money that women with no income can also enjoy an enhanced sense of financial autonomy to a degree. In light of these considerations, I hypothesise *that women in low-income households where finances are predominantly controlled by men are more likely to keep secret kitties regardless of whether they earn an income or not* (Hypothesis R).

Given the prevalence of patriarchal norms and values among *gecekondu* households, secret kitty keeping by women is likely to be a common occurrence, but what does this mean in terms of poverty? When a sum of money is withdrawn from the total household income, the logical expectation would be to see increased deprivation for other members of the household and/or the overall household. However, there is a wealth of evidence from different parts of the world to suggest that this is not true of women's secret kitties. The bulk of this evidence demonstrates that women are more likely than men to spend a greater portion of their income on areas relating to the household and children, or that their personal spending tends to be (more) family-oriented. (Blumberg 1991, Chant 1985, Gonzales de la Rocha 1994, Hoodfar 1988b, Jiggins 1989, Morris 1990, Mencher 1988, Nyman 1999, Pahl 1989). Further supportive evidence suggests that women in countries such as Egypt and Turkey tend to associate their personal needs with those of their households (Bolak 1997, Hoodfar 1988b). For these reasons, *I hypothesise that women's secret kitty keeping is unlikely to inflict further deprivation on the overall household or its individual members, especially children* (Hypothesis S).

*Consumption*

Having introduced my expectations as to which households are more likely to avoid 'secondary poverty', I shall now discuss the influences likely to affect the success of household consumption practices in counteracting income shortfalls. The literature draws attention to self-provisioning (or subsistence production) as one way to counterbalance the effects of insufficient income. However, as also indicated by Leonard (1998), households differ in their ability to engage in self-provisioning activities. Some studies consider it to be a more viable option for relatively well-off households due to the monetary costs involved (Clarke 1999, Pahl 1984, Pahl and Wallace 1985), whereas others demonstrate poor households' involvement in self-provisioning activities such as growing and preserving food (Demir 2002, Mingione 1985, UPL 2000). However, most of these studies also acknowledge their limitations in terms of meeting households' 'survival' needs, and counteracting income deficit in monetised economies (Demir 2002, Mingione 1985).

I will follow the same line of argument, placing it within the broader context of consumption extending from commodified to non-commodified spheres. In my view, practices that take place within the former sphere are less likely to offer an effective solution to income deficit in that they often involve going without or compromising on the quality and/or quantity of goods and services. Semi-and-non-commodified practices are likely to combat income shortfalls more successfully since, however limited, they allow access to goods and services without putting as much pressure on household income. Nonetheless, the success of these practices depends on the type of resources mobilised. In my view, most beneficial resources include entitlements to social insurance and *gecekondu* type assets, and hence those who possess such resources are likely to fare better. In contrast to more recent research which draws attention to the significance of social capital in 'consumption smoothing', i.e. the maintenance of consumption levels prior to economic crisis (Carter and Maluccio 2003), I consider this particular resource to be of little value in terms of enabling access to critical goods and services such as healthcare, housing etc. without putting pressure on the household income (see also Eroğlu 2010b). Overall, it is likely that most resources mobilised for consumption purposes will have a limited benefit delivery capacity. Therefore, I anticipate that *neither households with increased participation in semi-and-non-commodified consumption, nor those who mobilise a greater range of resources within these spheres of activity are likely to display reduced deprivation.* (Hypothesis T).

*Investment, Insurance and Credit Use*

This final section explores which influences are likely to affect household success by investment and insurance practices. Given income-related constraints, one obvious expectation for poor households might be to have no engagement in asset building activities. There is however evidence from both economically advanced and less developed parts of the world to confirm that households can build an asset portfolio at times of economic hardship (see e.g. Carter and May 1999, Hogan et al. 2004). Assets poor households accumulate can be few in number, but investment-related poverty is not simply a question of having a few assets but assets of low benefit delivery capacity. This view is also supported by research from development economics which demonstrate a tendency for poor households to have a 'low-yielding' portfolio due to constraints on the household's ability to make effective use of the assets possessed (Carter and May 1999, Zimmerman and Carter 2003). Subsequently, *I hypothesise that poor households are unlikely to generate an income surplus sufficient to accumulate assets of high benefit delivery capacity; that is, assets with a significant potential to a) generate an income, b) promote further capital accumulation and/or c) provide future financial security. These households are, for instance, unlikely to make sizeable savings to benefit from the Turkish financial market which at the time of research offered highly favourable options to investors* (Hypothesis U).

Potentially, some external resources can be mobilised for asset acquisition. Social capital comprises one such resource which can be put to various uses. First of all, social capital may act as a source of direct financial support. Remittances from family members working abroad are one particular form in which such aid can be delivered. For poor households, remittances are claimed to comprise a fundamental source of income (Frayne 2004, Hoodfar 1996, Kalaycıoğlu and Rittersberger-Tılıç 2002, Safa and Antrobus 1992). In addition to their contribution to income generation, remittances may also play a role in the making of asset portfolios. However, as Itzigson (1995) shows in his study of four different countries within the Caribbean basin, remittances are least accessible to low income families. For the reasons discussed earlier, it seems to me that the likelihood of poor households' social contacts providing gift money is rather limited.

Second, social capital can operate as a means to asset inheritance whose impact on poverty is understudied. Given their migrant backgrounds, *gecekondu* households may have rural land passed on through inheritance, but the benefit delivery capacity of this asset type is likely to be restricted by factors such as decline in agricultural subsidies, increasing cost of agricultural production, youth migration to cities and land fragmentation which often leads to conflict between siblings.

Third, social capital can be of potential help as a source of informal credit. Research on Turkey and other parts of the world confirms the extensive use of social contacts by poor households for borrowing purposes (Colin et al. 2000, Frayne 2004, UPL 2000). It is widely known that poor households tend to rely more on informal credit sources due to restricted access to formal financial institutions – a problem encountered even in micro-credit programmes targeted specifically at the poor (see e.g. Cuong 2008, Tipple and Coulson 2007). However, the same problem appears to apply also when informal borrowing is concerned. Research evidence documents exclusion of poor households from informal credit opportunities due to their lack of creditworthiness (Moser 1996a, see also a review by Gonzales de la Rocha 2001b). For those who retain their creditworthiness in the eyes of their contacts, or those who are linked to relatively well-off people with whom they interact on the basis of generalised reciprocity, informal borrowing may remain an option. Dercon (2000) argues that informal credit and insurance opportunities enable households to cope with unpredictable incomes. Borrowing from social contacts may help delay the pressure to generate an income surplus or spread it over time; yet does not remove it. Moreover, in an economic environment where returns on financial means of investment such as deposit accounts, gold, or foreign exchange exceed the annual rate of inflation, borrowing may prove a disadvantage, inducing further deprivation. Recent research evidence indeed demonstrates the high transaction costs involved in informal credit and how it prevents women from moving out of poverty (Schindler 2010).

Finally, social capital may also form a base for organising rotating savings and credit associations (roscas). Rosca refers to 'an association formed upon a core of participants who make regular contributions to a fund which is given in whole or in part to each contributor in turn' (Ardener 1995:1). Turkish roscas are known locally as *gün* (i.e. day) and can take various forms (see e.g. Bellér-Hann 1996, Eroğlu 2010a, Khatib-Chahidi 1995, White 1994). A number of studies, including research on *gün*s, reveal that women in poor households are less likely to participate in organisations of this nature (Bellér-Hann 1996, Burman and Lembete 1995). Scholars tend to explain (lack of) participation in terms of income size and/or regularity (Bellér-Hann 1996, Burman and Lembete 1995, Kimuyu 1999, Levenson and Besley 1996, Sterling 1995). Another group of studies however confirms the use of roscas by poor households. Kurtz (1973:49) for instance regards roscas as 'an adaptive response to a condition of poverty or relative deprivation among both peasant and urban populations'. A few of these studies demonstrate a significant investment potential for roscas organised by impoverished groups (Hospes 1995, Nelson 1995), or acknowledge their double function for both 'survival' and investment (Kimuyu 1999). Most research emphasises their instrumental role in meeting basic needs, e.g. food and medical assistance (Almedon 1995, Kurtz 1973, Mayoux and Anand 1995). Thus, *I do not expect roscas organised by poor households to possess a significant potential for asset acquisition* (Hypothesis V). Overall, *my hypothesis is that those households which mobilise social capital for asset acquisition are unlikely to accumulate beneficial assets* (Hypothesis W).

Another external resource which may be of use in asset acquisition refers to institutional entitlements granted to specific groups. As Buğra (1998) points out, the uncertainties surrounding urban land tenure patterns provided the Turkish State with an opportunity to create entitlements to public land in exchange for votes by legalising part of the *gecekondu* stock. These clientelist practices are claimed to contribute to the prevention of social upheaval and legitimisation of the existing social order (Buğra 1998, Öncü 1988). In particular, by the enactment of Redevelopment Law No. 2981, those *gecekondu*s built prior to 1985 were authorised to become part of the urban stock and the owners of these *gecekondu*s were given the right to build apartment blocks of up to four storeys (Leitmann and Baharoğlu 1998, Şenyapılı 1998, Yönder 1998). The *gecekondu* rights obtained are thus likely to have a positive impact upon poverty. In fact, a recent study by Başlevent and Dayıoğlu (2005) demonstrates the corrective effects of squatter housing on income distribution in Turkey. Nevertheless, it should be borne in mind that the owners of post-1985 built *gecekondu*s lack entitlements to redevelopment and not all *gecekondu* owners with such entitlements benefit significantly from the redevelopment process since, as discussed earlier, returns to *gecekondu* land depend on several factors, such as land size and location. A case study of an atypical *gecekondu* settlement in Turkey concludes that early rural-to-urban migrants are less likely than newcomers to suffer from poverty (Işık and Pınarcıoğlu 2001, Pınarcıoğlu and Işık 2001). This simplistic association between the year of migration and poverty does not move beyond reinstating the self-evident fact that early occupants of *gecekondu* land were more likely to reap the benefits of the authorisation and redevelopment processes. This case study thus provides no insight into what factors enabled or constrained access to *gecekondu* land by early rural-to-urban migrants. Moreover, it reduces poverty to land market behaviour, a limitation also addressed by Şengül and Ersoy (UPL 2001). Thus, *I do not anticipate that year of migration will be a significant predictor of household deprivation, but nevertheless expect those with entitlements to gecekondu redevelopment to experience lower levels of deprivation than those without* (Hypothesis X).

To conclude, poor households may possess resources, but this does not necessarily enhance their capacity to adapt to worsening conditions of economic decline, or help them maintain a decent life. Hence, I agree with Gonzales de la Rocha (2001b:127) that the 'much-heralded resilience of the poor has its limits'. As I have sought to emphasise throughout this review, structural factors such as the adverse conditions of the labour market and economic crisis are likely to impose overwhelming constraints on the benefit delivery capacity of the resources available to poor households. Thus, *in contrast to scholars who draw the logical conclusion that access to a larger number of resources reduces deprivation* (see e.g. Piachaud 2002), *I do not expect this to make a significant difference* (Hypothesis Y). As for my expectations about change in deprivation, *assuming that structural conditions restricting poor households' resource capacity are unlikely to improve over the six months period between my first and second visits to the field, I anticipate that the majority of households will be unable to move out of poverty* (Hypothesis Z).

**Conclusion**

This chapter has sought to develop a sound basis for explaining household responses to poverty and to set out hypotheses for field research. The model advanced here was shown to extend the resource-based approach in order to provide a theoretically more sophisticated framework with greater empirical applicability. The major points of improvement are discussed later in Chapter 11. The chapter has also provided an overview of previous findings to set out hypotheses for field research. The chapter outlined a set of hypothesized influences on household deprivation, which are summarised in Table 3.1.

**Table 3.1 Independent variables and their hypothesised effects on deprivation**

---

**Variables expected to reduce deprivation**

| | |
|---|---|
| Greater participation in the formal labour market | (Hypothesis E) |
| Greater accumulation of formal cultural capital | (Hypothesis G) |
| Collective income distribution | (Hypothesis Q) |
| Access to *gecekondu* entitlements | (Hypothesis X) |
| Access to strong ties in job search | (Hypothesis K) |

**Variables expected to have no effect**

| | |
|---|---|
| Range of resources mobilised for income generation | (Hypotheses A, Y) |
| Dependency ratio | (Hypothesis D) |
| Volume of social capital | (Hypothesis I) |
| Access to clientelist ties in job search | (Hypothesis J) |
| Use of economic capital in income generation | (Hypotheses F, L, M) |
| Direct use of social capital in income generation | (Hypothesis N) |
| Use of institutional entitlements in income generation | (Hypothesis O) |
| System of financial management | (Hypothesis Q) |
| System of financial control | (Hypothesis Q) |
| Secret kitty possession | (Hypothesis S) |
| Range of non-commodified expenditure areas participated | (Hypothesis T) |
| Range of resources mobilised for non-commodified consumption | (Hypotheses T, Y) |
| Year of migration to the city | (Hypothesis X) |
| Range of resources mobilised for asset acquisition | (Hypotheses X, Y) |
| The use of social capital in asset acquisition | (Hypothesis W) |

---

Chapter 4

# Researching Poor *Gecekondu* Households:
# The Method, Setting and Respondents

This chapter outlines the research design and techniques used in sample selection and data collection and analysis. It also presents a description of the setting and the sample, placing them within a wider context of *gecekondu* settlements and dwellers in the Turkish capital.

**Research Design and Method**

The book draws on a short-term longitudinal study of 17 low-income households living in a *gecekondu* settlement in Ankara. The study involved two visits to the field: one in April 2002 and the other in October 2002. Longitudinal design was chosen because it comprises a robust research base for identifying causal processes, and collecting high quality data. The choice of design helped enhance data quality especially through allowing time for building rapport. Field visits were set six months apart because although there is no perfect time for longitudinal research, shorter studies are less susceptible to external shocks and sample attrition. This study was indeed able to avoid both risks. The six month gap proved adequate for exploring household plans and whether they were realised.

*Sample Selection*

The eligible households had to have: a) an average monthly income below US$370; b) four members; c) nuclear structure; d) one child at or above the age of 15; and e) *Sünni* or *Alevi* religious backgrounds. The reasons for introducing the eligibility criteria were as follows. The income threshold was used in place of the FWID to identify poor households – an inevitable substitution to obviate the need to collect exhaustive data prior to main interviews. The chosen threshold took a middle ground between the TÜRK-İŞ (The Confederation of Turkish Labour Trade Unions) Starvation and Poverty Lines[1], and represented approximately the bottom 15 per cent of the Ankara population and 30 per cent of the population in Turkey (Sönmez 2001). Four member nuclear families were selected to reflect

---

1   The respective lines represent the monthly income needed for the basic food-and-non-food needs of four member households. These were US$234 and US$712 in March 2002 (Bağdadıoğlu 2002a).

the typical characteristics of urban households, including *gecekondu* dwellers (Doğan 1993, Kandiyoti 1982), and to eliminate the possible effects of variation in household size and structure. The age restriction was imposed on one child to control for the life-cycle stage. Finally, the religion criterion was included to capture the two largest Islamic sects in Turkey, which tend to differ in their religious observations, political viewpoints, life-styles and their approach to women (Ayata 1997, Shankland 1996). Such differences were assumed to give rise to variation in household resources and behaviour patterns.

In principle, eligible households could have been randomly sampled across the city or from multiple settlements. However, the research was conducted within a single *mahalle²*, based on the presumption that this would encourage the building of trust required to minimise sample attrition and to enhance data quality. The study indeed benefited from the extended time spent in one location as building rapport proved to be a gradual process. The research setting was selected to increase the likelihood of finding households that met the eligibility criteria. It was thus considered more preferable to concentrate on a *gecekondu* settlement where *Alevi*s, the second largest sect, comprised roughly 25 per cent of the population. The focus was restricted to *gecekondu* areas due to their higher incidence of poverty (Bulutay 1998) and the heterogeneity in their inhabitants' levels of poverty. Such *gecekondu* features made it possible to meet the research aims through a study of a single locality.

The ideal would have been to randomly select the setting from an up-to-date database showing the distribution of *gecekondu mahalle*s. In the absence of such information, the selection had to be made at the district level. Out of the eight districts within the boundaries of the Metropolitan Municipality of Ankara (MMA), the Mamak District was chosen firstly because with 8.6 per cent, it had the greatest share within the 1990 Ankara population subjected to amelioration (or improvement) plans, prepared by the district municipalities to enable the implementation of the laws that authorise *gecekondu* redevelopment (MMDPB 2000). The total percentage of Ankara population affected by the amelioration plans was 31.3 per cent in 1990 (MMDPB 2000). Secondly, the *gecekondu* settlements within the Mamak district have been relatively less affected by the redevelopment process. Thirdly, the district had a rather balanced distribution of *Alevi*s and *Sünni*s. This may partially be evidenced from the 1999 local election results where more than half of the votes were shared between Republican People's Party (RPP) and Welfare Party (WP), i.e. 26.1 and 26.3 per cent respectively (MMA 2002). The *Alevi* population generally supports the social democratic RPP, whereas conservative segments of the *Sünni* population tend to favour WP, the Islamic party of the time. Finally, Mamak was typical of Ankara *gecekondu* settlements populated with low-income early migrant families who came from the

---

2    *Mahalle* refers to the smallest unit within the Turkish urban administrative system, governed by an elected local representative called a *muhtar*. A district is made up of several *mahalle*s.

rural parts of Central Anatolia through chain migration (Alpar and Yener 1991, Güvenç 2001) and who were *Alevi* or *Sünni* by background. These settlements also reflected the common characteristics of the wider *gecekondu* population in Turkey which can however vary in terms of rural origin.

In selecting the *mahalle*, the study drew on Güvenç's (2001) 'income-status' map of Ankara, indicating a greater concentration of poverty within the South-Eastern part of Mamak situated between the railway and the ring road. This part of the district contained 19 *mahalles* among which only six matched the desired population distribution. One *mahalle* was randomly selected from the six but access to information was denied by the *muhtar*. The adjacent settlement within the sample also had to be dropped to make a fresh start. Of the remaining four, Ege Mahallesi was selected and then access was obtained through developing strong links with insiders.

The sample was obtained through random selection by starting from the *muhtar*'s database, which contains information on household size, structure and age of children for two areas within the same *mahalle*; the Northern part predominantly *Alevi* and the Southern part predominantly *Sünni*. The sample frame thus contained 156 out of 2005 households. Random number tables were used to select from this frame and then households with an income above US$370 were excluded during access negotiations. 49 per cent of the negotiations yielded ineligible results and 30 per cent concluded in refusal. Consequently, the sample included 17 households, i.e. three less than targeted. The main reasons for falling below the target relate to the application of multiple eligibility criteria, separate interviewing and random sampling technique.

*Data Collection and Analysis*

The data was drawn from face-to-face interviews, participant observation and document collection. The interviews were performed with both partners jointly as well as separately. Joint interviews were based on a highly structured questionnaire applied once in April during access negotiations to elicit information as to their members' demographic, socio-economic and housing status. Separate interviews drew on semi-structured guides and a fixed choice questionnaire. Four guides were designed for male and female spousal interviews in April and October. Each guide was divided into sections on employment, financial management and consumption, and contained questions about the actual levels of deprivation and social support. A certain degree of overlap was built into the design of male and female interviews to cross-check their accounts on sensitive topics such as money management, savings and debts. In all but one household, semi-structured interviews were conducted separately with both partners on both occasions; resulting in a total of 67 interviews. All interviews were tape-recorded and transcribed in full. The average interview duration was 47 minutes for men and 60 minutes for women. Fixed choice interviews were used exclusively to administer the subjective deprivation questionnaire designed to assess the extent to which respondents perceived the 'objectively' selected items as necessities of life. Except for two males, the questionnaire was applied to both partners once in October; yielding 32 cases in total (see also Appendix A).

In addition to interviews, participant observation was performed over a three month period, during the stages of sampling and interviewing where I spent most of my time staying with a family from the studied *mahalle*. My frequent stays in the field made me gradually assume the role of 'observer as participant' which helped obtain 'objective data' and a better understanding of the respondents' perspective (Hammersley and Atkinson 1983). Observational data was collected e.g. on living arrangements of households visited during access negotiations and interviews, daily life situations of the inhabitants and relationships between them.

Finally, documents were collected from private and public sources. Respondents were requested to keep personal diaries for the next six months in order to aid recall particularly on receipt of social support and changes in consumption, employment and financial status. A hand-made diary was distributed to each spouse but the decision to make joint or separate entries was left to the couple. Illiteracy was not considered a great obstacle as the household eligibility criteria ensured that at least one child either had completed or was still in compulsory education. The non-response rate was 47 per cent (8 out of 17). Moreover, only 29 per cent (5 out of 17) recorded information on a fairly regular basis. Due to the lack of researcher control over diary keeping, the data produced proved partially or wholly irrelevant and/or superficial. Nonetheless, regularly kept diaries provided useful work-related data in scoring the FWID. Furthermore, various public documents were surveyed primarily to collect information about the research setting and its stage in the *gecekondu* redevelopment process. These documents included newspaper cuttings, plan reports, environmental risk surveys and official records concerning the legal status of the Northern *gecekondu*s.

The data was analysed both quantitatively and qualitatively to answer separate research questions and to validate quantitative results. Statistical analysis of the entire sample was performed to explain why some households were more successful in reducing their deprivation than others. One could have explored this question on a larger sample, but this would have meant superficial data. Here the sample size was kept small in order to meet the detailed data requirements of this study as well as to generate valid data. The statistical analyses drew on techniques that are relatively safer to apply on a small sample. These include descriptive statistics (e.g. frequencies and cross-tabulations) and statistical tests such as Pearson's correlation, Spearman's non-parametric test and one-way ANOVA. The qualitative data and theoretical knowledge accumulated through the literature review were used as a basis for casual inferences drawn from the observed correlations and tabulations.

In addition, three case studies were conducted to examine how households responded to poverty and whether they were able to realise their plans in the next six months. The cases were selected to represent one household from each deprivation group, i.e. better off, moderately deprived and worse off. How these categories were formed is explained in the next chapter.

## Research Setting: Ege Mahallesi at a Glance

**Figure 4.1    A panorama from Northern to Southern Ege**

Ege Mahallesi is located in the South-East of Ankara, 15 km from the city centre of Kızılay. The settlement had one recently built school and was served by two medical centres situated in the adjacent *mahalles*. It was also well-connected to the centres of Ulus and Kızılay through bus and minibus links offering frequent services. The area was supplied with water, electricity, sewage and telephone networks, reported to adequately serve the current population (Kentkur 2002:20). According to the muhtar's database[3], the *mahalle* population consisted of 8067 people in 2005 households living mostly in one or two storey *gecekondu* dwellings.

At the time of research, amelioration plans for the area were completed, and yet there was some ambiguity around the choice of transformation (or redevelopment) model. The most likely and conventional option was to use the existing amelioration plans to transform the *gecekondus* gradually into four-storey apartment blocks on a plot basis through individual agreements between small-scale land developers and the legal owners of *gecekondu* land. The other involved rapid redevelopment of the entire area by means of large-scale private firms or Mass Housing Authority. It appears that Ege inhabitants would be unequally affected from these planning options due to variation in their entitlements to *gecekondu* house/land. The key differences are explained below in relation to the North-South division mentioned earlier.

*Northern Ege* contained 253 *gecekondus*[4] the majority of which were built after 1985. This meant that they were unauthorised and ineligible for redevelopment.[5]

---

3    These figures might not be fully accurate because some inhabitants avoid registering with *muhtarlık* so as to be able to vote in their hometowns. Nevertheless, the *muhtar* estimates that the database covers at least 95 per cent of the population.

4    The Kentkur (2002) figure is 310 but I counted 253 *gecekondus* in the municipal records.

5    Unless stated otherwise, information regarding the planning process of Northern Ege is obtained and synthesised from the official documents and reports which belong to

These *gecekondu*s were built on a former solid waste dump, and due to the threats it posed to the health and safety of the dwellers, the construction plan of 1993 recommended that the area should be cleared of human settlements. The independent expert reports confirm the presence of serious environmental risks, and not surprisingly, converge in their support for the plan (Hacettepe University 1994, TMMOB 1993, TTB 1994).[6] Subsequently, the *gecekondu*s concerned were bought out by the MMA through compulsory purchase, meaning that the dwellers lost all legal ground to stand up against evacuation and were left to their own means to resettle themselves in any future evacuation.

In pursuit of a solution to the resettlement problem, applications were made to the Mamak (District) Municipality and Ministry of Public Works and Housing, which resulted in the decision to allocate cheap land for housing co-operatives. Out of five co-operatives established, S.S. Ege-Mutlu Konut Yapı Kooperatifi covered Northern Ege inhabitants, but for unknown reasons 63 of them were excluded. Moreover, sizeable drop-outs were recorded since the establishment of the co-operatives. From an interview with an administrative board member of the S.S. Ege-Mutlu Konut Yapı Kooperatifi, it appeared that due to a chronic inability to keep up with the inflationary monthly instalments and quarterly lump-sum payments, at least 25 per cent of the members from Northern Ege had to hand over their rights to third parties. To give an idea, since the beginning of the construction in 1995, monthly instalments had risen from 2.5 million TL to 200 million TL, i.e. above the net minimum monthly wage in April 2002 (164 million TL).[7] For these reasons, a substantial number of Northern Ege inhabitants were faced with a high risk of evacuation.

As a matter of fact, in September 2000, the MMA attempted to demolish the *gecekondu*s on the grounds that the state had exhausted all possibilities provided in law to mitigate the vulnerability of the inhabitants. The inhabitants reacted to this with a series of demonstrations.[8] These protests did not yield a final resolution, but led the MMA to postpone the enforcement of the demolition decision indefinitely.

*Southern Ege* covered 1230 *gecekondu*s, of which 704 were authorised in accordance with laws no. 2981 and 3290, and the rest declared illegal (Kentkur 2002:23). The average land size for authorised *gecekondu*s in the area was 272 m², corresponding to more than half of the maximum allowed by the law (i.e. 400 m²) (Kentkur 2002:23). The land rights of their owners were protected by both redevelopment plans. The plight of the illegal occupiers was however considered

---

the MMA. I am grateful to the staff of the MMA Nationalisation Department for facilitating my access to the 'Mamak Former Dump Area' file.

6 Two of these reports attracted media interest when they were first published. See e.g. Günçiner (1993), Cumhuriyet (1994) and Sabah (1994).

7 In 2005 six digits were dropped from Turkish Lira, i.e. TL renamed as YTL (New Turkish Lira). The monetary figures reported in this study are in old currency.

8 For media interpretations of the demolition attempt see Evrensel (2000a, 2000b), Sabah (2000a, 2000b), Zaman, (2000), Akşam (2000) and Güneş (2000).

only within the second plan, which proposes to loan this group of dwellers a flat in the new blocks on special terms and conditions (Kentkur 2002). This constitutes the least likely plan and even if it was put into action, their homeownership cannot be guaranteed as they remain vulnerable to the risk of displacement for reasons similar to those that led Northern Ege inhabitants to withdraw their co-operative housing membership.[9]

### Respondents: A Socio-demographic Profile

As explained earlier, the sample households were chosen controlling for their size, structure and stage in the life-cycle. In all households, couples were married with two children. The majority were in the consolidation phase of their life-cycle.[10] Some however were in transition between stages. 29 per cent (5 out of 17) were between expansion and consolidation, and 18 per cent (3 out of 17) were between consolidation and dispersion. Over the six month period, neither the size nor the structure of the respondent households had changed. The age and gender distribution of their members was as follows: the age of the female partners varied between 33 and 52 [mean = 40] whereas that of male partners lay between 36 and 57 [mean = 43]. Among a total of 34 children, there were only 12 females. The ages of younger children ranged from 9 to 20 [mean = 16] whereas those of the elder from 15 to 21 [mean = 19].

Among the sample households, 65 per cent (11 out of 17) were *Alevi* and the rest were *Sünni*. There was no inter-marriage between the two groups. All the male partners were first-generation rural migrants who had moved to Ankara between 1972 and 1989 through chain migration and 88 per cent (15 out of 17) were from different parts of Central Anatolia. All female partners were also rural migrants by background, but three of them were second-generation migrants. Among them, 82 per cent (11 out of 14) were first generation migrants who had moved to the city between 1972 and 1989, following the same type of chain migration as their husbands. Marriage appeared as the main cause of female migration to the city, given that the post-marriage migration rate among first generation female migrants

---

9   For further cases of *gecekondu* displacement in Ankara see Dündar (2001), Türker-Devecigil (2005) and Uzun (2005).

10   This study draws Gonzales de la Rocha's (1994) definition for the life-cycle stages. She identifies three main stages, namely expansion, consolidation and dispersion. Expansion refers to the stage that begins with the formation of a unit either through marriage or co-habitation and lasts up until the female partner reaches the age of 40. Consolidation starts when the female partner reaches the end of her fertility. This phase is sometimes called 'equilibrium phase' as children begin to participate in the labour market. Finally, dispersion denotes the period which begins when the children leave parental home to set up a separate home.

was 71 per cent (10 out of 14). As for hometown, 94 per cent of female partners (16 out of 17) were from Central Anatolia.

The sample reflects the typical features of the population living in the *gecekondu* areas of Ankara in terms of household size and structure as well as the origin, year and type of migration. According to Alpar and Yener (1991), male migrants from Central Anatolia accounted for 73 per cent of the *gecekondu* population in Ankara. They also show that 72 per cent of these men had been in the city for 1 to 20 years. Equivalent figures for the year 2002 would be 12 to 31 years, matching exactly the duration of stay among all spouses in the sample. In reading these figures, one should however bear in mind that the dynamic process of *gecekondu* transformation might have changed the demographic character of the residents within the past 11 years since Alpar and Yener's study was published. Economic and educational profiles of the respondent households will be examined in the following chapter.

**Conclusion**

This chapter has explained the research design along with the sampling, data collection and analysis techniques used in this study and outlined the key characteristics of the research setting and respondent households. Figure 4.2 summarises the links between dependent and explanatory variables. The next six chapters present the findings from this research, starting with three chapters which look at the entire sample.

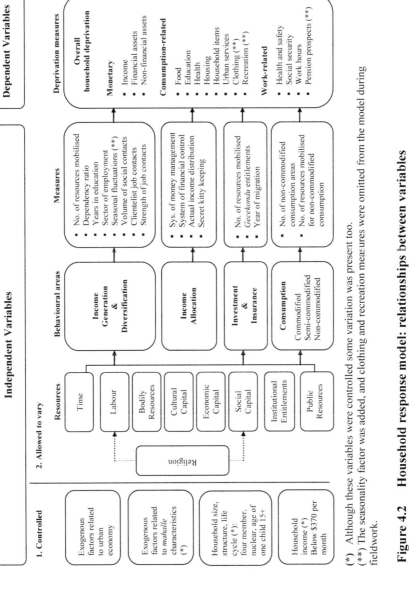

**Independent Variables**

**Dependent Variables**

**1. Controlled**

**2. Allowed to vary**

| Resources | Behavioural areas | Measures |
| --- | --- | --- |

Time

Labour

Bodily Resources

Cultural Capital

Economic Capital

Social Capital

Institutional Entitlements

Public Resources

Religion

Exogenous factors related to urban economy

Exogenous factors related to *mahalle* characteristics (*)

Household size, structure, life cycle (*): four member, nuclear, age of one child 15+

Household income (*): Below $370 per month

**Income Generation & Diversification**

**Income Allocation**

**Investment & Insurance**

**Consumption**
Commodified
Semi-commodified
Non-commodified

- No. of resources mobilised
- Dependency ratio
- Years in education
- Sector of employment
- Seasonal fluctuations (**)
- Volume of social contacts
- Clientelist job contacts
- Strength of job contacts

- Sys. of money management
- System of financial control
- Actual income distribution
- Secret kitty keeping

- No. of resources mobilised
- *Gecekondu* entitlements
- Year of migration

- No. of non-commodified consumption areas
- No. of resources mobilised for non-commodified consumption

**Deprivation measures**

**Overall household deprivation**

**Monetary**
- Income
- Financial assets
- Non-financial assets

**Consumption-related**
- Food
- Education
- Health
- Housing
- Household items
- Urban services
- Clothing (**)
- Recreation (**)

**Work-related**
- Health and safety
- Social security
- Work hours
- Pension prospects (**)

(*) Although these variables were controlled some variation was present too.
(**) The seasonality factor was added, and clothing and recreation measures were omitted from the model during fieldwork.

**Figure 4.2    Household response model: relationships between variables**

# Chapter 5

# Income Generation and Diversification

The aim of this chapter is to uncover why some households are more successful in reducing deprivation by income generation activities. Is the answer, as claimed by earlier studies, engagement in a more diversified set of cash-generating activities, having more earners or having a greater volume or range of resources? The chapter explores these questions through a focus on the likely constraints on the labour and non-labour resources used by sample households to obtain an income. The analysis starts with an exploration of the relationship between household income and deprivation, and then turns to examine the possible determinants of success or failure.

## Overall Relationship between Income and Deprivation

The average monthly household incomes ranged between 133 and 500 million TL, which amount to $75 and $365 respectively. Figure 5.1 demonstrates the household income distribution in April [mean = 361 m TL, std. deviation = 99 m TL].[1] Within the sample 35 per cent (6 out of 17) had an income below 320 million TL ($181); 35 per cent (6 out of 17) earned between 320 and 410 million TL ($181-$231], and the rest above 410 million TL ($231).

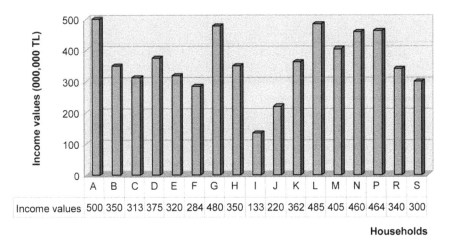

| Income values | A | B | C | D | E | F | G | H | I | J | K | L | M | N | P | R | S |
|---|---|---|---|---|---|---|---|---|---|---|---|---|---|---|---|---|---|
| | 500 | 350 | 313 | 375 | 320 | 284 | 480 | 350 | 133 | 220 | 362 | 485 | 405 | 460 | 464 | 340 | 300 |

Households

**Figure 5.1    April distribution of monthly household incomes**

---

1    For some of the households, the average monthly income and April income values differ due to the seasonal nature of their employment.

As for the household deprivation levels, Figure 5.2 presents the results obtained from the FWID where higher scores imply lower deprivation [mean = 22.20, std. deviation = 4.57].[2] Based on the cut-off points derived from the aggregate scores, through the use of SPSS frequency facility, the sample was divided into three deprivation groups. According to this classification, *worse off* households represented 35 per cent of the total (6 out of 17), *moderately deprived* households made up 30 per cent (5 out of 17), and the remaining 35 per cent was comprised of *better off* households.

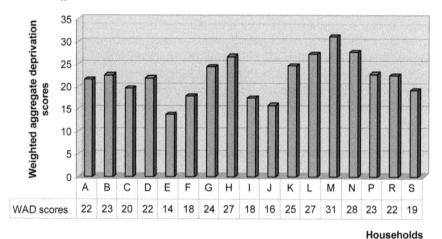

| WAD scores | 22 | 23 | 20 | 22 | 14 | 18 | 24 | 27 | 18 | 16 | 25 | 27 | 31 | 28 | 23 | 22 | 19 |

**Households**

**Figure 5.2     April distribution of household deprivation levels**

In order to determine whether deprivation categories differed significantly, a one-way analysis of variance (ANOVA) was performed comparing mean weighted aggregate deprivation scores between groups [worse off = 17.35 (2.19); moderate = 22.27 (0.52), better off = 26.98 (2.46)]. The results indicated a significant difference [$F (2, 14) = 35.25$; $p < 0.01$], which may well be due to significant variation in the composition of household resource portfolios and behavioural responses devised against poverty.

Since the average monthly household income was used as a substitute for the FWID to initially identify the poor households to be included in the study, it is interesting to examine the correlation between these two measures. The results of the Pearson correlation test conducted to this end revealed that income was strongly predictive of deprivation [$r = 0.64$; $p < 0.01$]. But nevertheless, this outcome still suggests that poverty cannot simply be understood in terms of earning below a certain level of income. Therefore, both the use of an income proxy and a multi-dimensional poverty instrument appears justified.

---

2   These scores were determined by grouping the interval data according to the cut off points obtained for April data only. For more information regarding the calculation of April scores see Appendix A.

**Does Having a More Diversified Income Bring Success?**

The aim here is to explore whether households with more diversified incomes were more successful than others in reducing their deprivation. Here income diversification is understood as the range of cash-generating activities and measured by summing up the number of primary resources used in dissimilar activities of this kind. Here, each labour deployment was given a separate score regardless of whether it was undertaken by a different member or not, and the resources deployed simultaneously with labour resources (e.g. cultural capital and time) were excluded from the calculations. The observed levels of income diversification are presented in Figure 5.3 [mean = 2.47; std. deviation = 0.94].

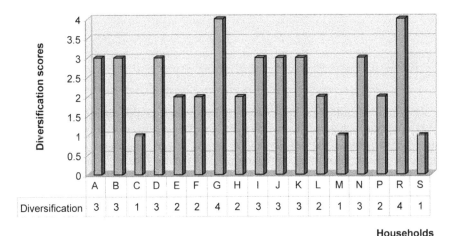

| | A | B | C | D | E | F | G | H | I | J | K | L | M | N | P | R | S |
|---|---|---|---|---|---|---|---|---|---|---|---|---|---|---|---|---|---|
| Diversification | 3 | 3 | 1 | 3 | 2 | 2 | 4 | 2 | 3 | 3 | 3 | 2 | 1 | 3 | 2 | 4 | 1 |

**Households**

**Figure 5.3    April distribution of household income diversification levels**

It appears from the figure that 18 per cent (3 out of 17) mobilised only one resource, 29 per cent (5 out of 17) two resources; 42 per cent (7 out of 17) three resources; and the remaining 12 per cent (2 out of 17) used four resources in separate income-generating activities. The types of resources employed in these activities were as follows. All households were found to depend on their labour resources. For 65 per cent (11 out of 17) labour constituted the only resource for income generation whereas the remaining 35 per cent (6 out of 17) deployed both their labour and non-labour resources. Among the users of non-labour resources, 29 per cent (5 out 17) drew on different kinds of institutional entitlements while 12 per cent (2 out of 17) either used their social or economic capital resources. This picture is thus congruent with the prevailing findings, demonstrating extensive/ intensive use of labour resources by poor households for income generation purposes.

In order to examine whether the degree of income diversification had a significant effect on success, the scores presented in Figure 5.3 were subjected to two Pearson correlation tests with a) average monthly household incomes (see Figure 5.1) and b) weighted aggregate deprivation scores (see Figure 5.2). Neither of the test results revealed a significant association [r (a) = 0.09 and r (b) = −0.03]. This is also evident from Table 5.1, showing a lack of variation between deprivation groups in terms of the degree of income diversification.

**Table 5.1     Household income diversification level by deprivation category**

| Income diversification | Deprivation category | | | Total |
|---|---|---|---|---|
| | Worse off | Moderate | Better off | |
| 1 (Lowest) | 2 | – | 1 | 3 |
| 2 | 2 | 1 | 2 | 5 |
| 3 | 2 | 3 | 2 | 7 |
| 4 (Highest) | – | 1 | 1 | 2 |
| Total | 6 | 5 | 6 | 17 |

Bearing in mind that any causal relationship could run from income diversification behaviour to deprivation and *vice versa*, one conclusion that can be drawn from these results is that the use of a greater range of resources in income generation may not necessarily lead to success – a conclusion congruent with my hypothesis. In what follows, the reasons behind this are explored in relation to the labour and non-labour resources mobilised across the sample.

**The Use of Labour Resources: Does Having Fewer Dependants Bring Success?**

As shown above, the income generation practices of the respondent households were largely dependent upon the use of labour resources. This section examines their contribution to success, starting with a description of households' labour market behaviour.

At the time of April interviews, on average, households had two labour resources mobilised for income generation [mean = 2.06; std. deviation = 0.83]. In 88 per cent of households (15 out of 17) working member(s) participated in a single labour market activity while the rest had a member involved in two separate activities. Table 5.2 summarises the employment status of household members in their main occupation.

**Table 5.2      Employment situation of household members by status in the main job**

| Household members | Employment status* | | | | Total |
|---|---|---|---|---|---|
| | Regular employee | Casual employee | Self-employed | Unpaid family labour | |
| Female spouse | 2 | 2 | 4 | – | 8 |
| Male spouse | 5 | 8 | 3 | – | 16 |
| Female children | 2 | – | – | – | 2 |
| Male children | 5 | 3 | – | 1 | 9 |
| Total | 14 | 13 | 7 | 1 | 35 |

*Note*: *The criteria used for defining regular employment were two-fold: a) to have a fixed employer and b) to earn a salary. Also note that some of the male spouses had dual employment status as casual worker and self-employed, which varied depending on the type of job contracted. Here they were classified according to their most common work pattern.

As can be seen from the table, at 40 per cent (14 out of 35) the percentage of regular employees was the highest; the casual employees followed this at 37 per cent (12 out of 35); the self-employed were represented at 20 per cent (7 out of 35) and finally, the unpaid family labour at 3 per cent (1 out of 35). The age and gender distribution of the working population was as follows. Female spouses were found to undertake 23 per cent of the main labour market activities (8 out of 35), amounting to only half of the contributions made by the male spouses (16 out of 35). At 31 per cent (11 out of 35), the children's contribution was also higher than that of the female spouses. The figure increases to 48 per cent when 11 children who were below working age are excluded.

Across the sample, economically active female spouses represented 47 per cent (8 out of 17), of whom 25 per cent (2 out of 8) were regular employees; one worked as a housekeeper and the other as a cleaner in the refectory of a textile factory. A further 25 per cent (2 out of 8) were employed on a casual basis; one as a home-based piecemeal worker, doing lacework on demand for people who supply the material for the desired design, and the other as a day-cleaner in two separate homes. The remaining 50 per cent (4 out of 8) were self-employed, two were engaged in the home-based production and sale of various handcrafts, such as bootees and embroidered trimmings, while the other two were occupied with home-based commerce, selling either ready-made shoes or socks.

By contrast, all male spouses actively participated in the labour market, except for one man who had retired early due to a work-related accident. Of these men, 31 per cent (5 out of 16) were regular employees: a cleaner at a university, a driver for a construction company, a welder at a medium scale factory, a security guard in a university hospital and a salesman in a bidding shop. A further 50 per cent

(8 out of 16) were casual employees: five were construction workers (two were master plasterers, two were master tile installers and one had no specialisation), and the others were a porter, a cleaner at a construction site and a taxi driver. Finally, 19 per cent (3 out of 16) were self-employed: one sold fruit and vegetables in different bazaars; a second ran a *simit* (sesame roll) bakery and a third was an electrician contracted to small-scale projects.

As for children, only 17 per cent of females (2 out of 12) as opposed to 41 per cent of males (9 out of 22) contributed to labour market activities. This is supportive of my observation that households were inclined not to send girls to work outside the home unless the family had complete trust in the work environment. However, the difference might be reflective of the age distribution of female and male children. As a matter of fact, 80 per cent (8 out of 10) of the females who were economically inactive in April were at the age of compulsory education. Furthermore, with one exception, none of the under age children was involved in the labour market, implying a tendency for households to avoid using child labour. However, in three households, at least one of the under age children was found to have had a casual job during the summer vacation prior to the April interviews.

Among the economically active children, all females were regular employees: one was a cashier in a café and the other one was making eye-glass cases at a small-scale workshop. Among the male children, 50 per cent (5 out of 9) were employed on a regular basis: a worker in a medium-scale factory producing and fixing suspended ceilings, a caretaker in a privately owned school canteen, a worker doing errands and small deeds in an auto garage, and two sales assistants (one in a pharmacy and the other in a supermarket). A further 20 per cent (3 out of 9) were employed on a casual basis: a bellboy in a sport club, earning tips, a construction worker, and a technician repairing computers and installing electrical networks for friends and neighbours. The last male child was an unpaid family worker in his father's bakery.

Turning to describe the employment status of household members in their second occupation, only 13 per cent of male spouses (2 out of 16) were actively engaged in another job in April. One of them did extra cleaning for a private company over the period when language classes were organised at the university where his main work was based. The other sold pens to horse race punters while working in a bidding shop. There were other men who occasionally participated in an additional labour market activity but they were inactive at the time of April interviews. To illustrate, over the previous season, the company driver earned money by selling the fruit he was allowed to collect freely from the farm of his employer to the bazaar vendors. The welder also did odd welding jobs on request from his social contacts and the security guard worked as a porter and wall-painter over his last annual leave.

Concerning the intra-household distribution of labour market activities, let us have a look at household dependency ratios, which refer to the total number of dependants divided by the total number of working members [mean = 1.35; std. deviation = 0.98]. Across the sample, 18 per cent (3 out of 17) had only one dependant (i.e. three working members); 59 per cent (10 out of 17) had two dependants (i.e. two working members); and the rest had three dependants (i.e. only one working member). The distribution of household dependency ratios is presented in Figure 5.4.

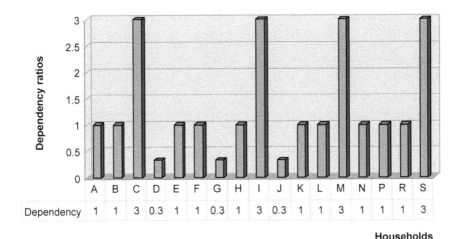

**Figure 5.4    April distribution of household dependency ratios**

Similar to those who view income diversification as a route to success, some scholars claim that the lower the dependency ratio the more likely the households are to be better off (Hackenberg et al. 1984, Kalaycıoğlu and Rittersberg-Tılıç 2002, Selby et al. 1990). This proposition seems to draw on a rather straightforward logical association between household income and the number of working household members. A Pearson correlation test was performed to investigate whether household income levels presented in Figure 5.1 differed significantly according to household dependency ratios. The results indicated a moderate inverse relationship [r = −0.38]. However, a much weaker relationship was obtained when the test was repeated between household dependency ratios and weighted aggregate deprivation scores (see Figure 5.2) [r = 0.09]. Table 5.3 also confirms this by demonstrating the lack of a significant variation between deprivation groups in terms of household dependency ratios.

Overall, it was found that despite its moderate effects on income, deployment of a greater number of labour resources did not bring significant success, since poverty means more than earning below a certain income level. As far as multi-dimensional poverty is concerned, the straightforward association established earlier between success and lower dependency rates thus appears not applicable. The reasons for this are explored below in relation to demand and supply side influences restricting the benefit delivery capacity of the labour resources mobilised across the sample.

**Table 5.3  Household dependency ratio by deprivation category**

| Dependency ratio | Deprivation category | | | Total |
|---|---|---|---|---|
| | Worse off | Moderate | Better off | |
| 0.33 (low) | 1 | 1 | 1 | 3 |
| 1.00 | 2 | 4 | 4 | 10 |
| 3.00 (high) | 3 | - | 1 | 4 |
| Total | 6 | 5 | 6 | 17 |

*Demand Side Labour Market Forces*

Demand side factors refer to those labour market influences which arise from the demand for labour from employers and self-employment. Through a focus on two major influences, it will be shown that variation in deprivation was depended upon a) the sector of employment and b) seasonal fluctuations in the labour market.

*Does informality matter?*  This sub-section examines the possible impact of the sectoral division within the labour market on household success by income generation activities. The distribution of working population by sector of employment is summarised in Table 5.4.

**Table 5.4  Sectoral distribution of working household members**

| Household members | Sector of employment | | Total |
|---|---|---|---|
| | Formal sector | Informal sector | |
| Female spouse | 1 | 7 | 8 |
| Male spouse | 10 | 6 | 16 |
| Female children | 2 | - | 2 |
| Male children | 6 | 3 | 9 |
| Total | 19 | 16 | 35 |

According to this table, almost half of the working population within the sample deployed their labour in the informal sector.[3] The overall percentage of formal

---

  3 One way to identify informal sector workers involves looking at whether they have social insurance in their current employment or not. Here, the lack of tax registration was instead taken as a basis in order to capture the extent of labour rights violations occurring within the tax regulated parts of the private sector. Also note that some of the casual workers

sector participants was 54 per cent (19 out of 35). Male spouses constituted the highest percentage of formal sector participants at 29 per cent (10 out of 35), and the children followed this at 23 per cent (8 out of 35). The formal sector participation of female spouses was particularly low at only 3 per cent (1 out of 35).

To demonstrate the sectoral distribution of working members within each household, the household formal sector participation (FSP) ratios were calculated by dividing the total number of members working in the formal sector by the total number of working household members. Figure 5.5 demonstrates the observed ratios [mean = 0.53; std. deviation = 0.42].

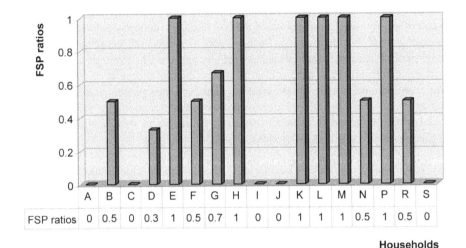

| FSP ratios | 0 | 0.5 | 0 | 0.3 | 1 | 0.5 | 0.7 | 1 | 0 | 0 | 1 | 1 | 1 | 0.5 | 1 | 0.5 | 0 |

**Households**

**Figure 5.5    April distribution of household formal sector participation ratios**

From the figure, it appears that 29 per cent (5 out of 17) of the sample had no formal sector participants. In 12 per cent (2 out of 17) one out of three; in 23 per cent (6 out of 17) one out of two and in 12 per cent (2 out of 17) two out of three working members consisted of formal sector participants. Only in the remaining 12 per cent did all working members participate in this sector of the labour market.

Did the sector of employment have a significant effect on household deprivation? In exploring this, a Pearson correlation test was performed between the household FSP ratios and weighted aggregate deprivation scores (see Figure 5.2). The results indicated a fairly strong positive correlation between the two variables [$r = 0.51$; $p < 0.05$]. This can also be seen from Table 5.5 which demonstrates a greater tendency for working members in better-off households to participate in the formal sector than those in worse-off households.

---

had a tendency to participate in both sectors of the labour market but were counted here as informal unless at the time of interview they were employed by a tax paying company.

**Table 5.5    Household formal sector participation by deprivation category**

| FSP ratio | Deprivation category | | | Total |
|---|---|---|---|---|
| | Worse off | Moderate | Better off | |
| 0.00–0.50 | 5 | 4 | 1 | 10 |
| 0.51–1.00 | 1 | 1 | 5 | 7 |
| Total | 6 | 5 | 6 | 17 |

The result of this analysis thus supports my hypothesis that the greater the extent of informal sector participation the less likely the households are to achieve success in reducing deprivation. So how does the informal sector obstruct the attainment of success? The following sections explore this through a focus on working conditions (e.g. pay, social insurance, health and safety), interrelated with five deprivation areas upon which the sector of employment is likely to have had an effect. These include: a) average household hourly earnings; b) household social insurance ratio; c) pension prospects; d) access to state healthcare; and e) occupational health and safety risks.

*Pay conditions*    In order to understand the extent to which pay conditions differed by sector of employment, two bivariate tests were performed. Firstly, the household FSP ratios (see Figure 5.5) were subjected to a Pearson correlation test with an FWID measure i.e. weighted average hourly household income rates.[4] In calculating the rates, first, the monthly earnings of each member were multiplied with the total number of hours (s)he spent to earn this money. The values obtained were then added up and divided by the total number of work hours spent by all working members in the household. Figure 5.6 demonstrates the observed averages [mean = 2.18 million TL; median = 1.87 million TL; std. deviation = 0.99] whose purchasing power proved very low given that a standard return bus ticket cost 1.20 million TL in April. The results of the Pearson test suggested a weak association [r = 0.20], indicating that there was no significant association between the hourly earnings of households with greater and lower rates of formal sector participation.

Secondly, a Spearman test was performed between the sector of male employees and their average hourly earnings [mean = 1.38 million TL; std. deviation = 0.65]. This time slightly higher rates were observed among informal sector employees, but the nature of the relationship proved rather weak [r = 0.27]. Consequently, given the weakness of both correlations, it can be suggested that pay conditions were rather unfavourable whichever sector of the market households deployed their labour resources.

---

4    Weighted averages were used in the FWID to avoid the bias likely to result from the large differences between members' income contributions.

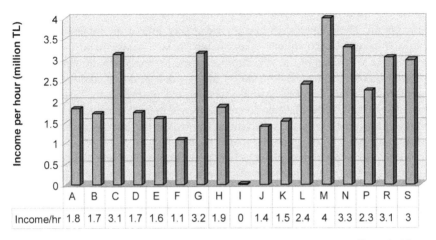

| Income/hr | A | B | C | D | E | F | G | H | I | J | K | L | M | N | P | R | S |
|-----------|-----|-----|-----|-----|-----|-----|-----|-----|---|-----|-----|-----|---|-----|-----|-----|---|
| | 1.8 | 1.7 | 3.1 | 1.7 | 1.6 | 1.1 | 3.2 | 1.9 | 0 | 1.4 | 1.5 | 2.4 | 4 | 3.3 | 2.3 | 3.1 | 3 |

**Households**

**Figure 5.6    April distribution of weighted average household income per hour**

*Access to social security*    In contrast to its weak relationship with hourly income rates, the sector of employment was strongly associated with having social insurance through current work. The results of a Pearson test performed between the household FSP (see Figure 5.5) and social insurance ratios confirm this [$r = 0.59$; $p < 0.05$]. However, it appears from the results that a considerable number of formal sector workers in the sample also lacked social insurance. Let us first describe the social insurance status of the working population in the sample before exploring why and how this might have happened.

At the time of the April interviews, there were three major social insurance schemes, allowing access to state pensions and healthcare on specific terms and conditions: a) Retirement Fund (ES) set up for civil servants, b) Social Security Institution (SSK) for other employees, and b) Independent Workers Institution (BAĞ-KUR) for the self-employed. Regular premium payments were necessary to keep active membership of these schemes, the first two of which required both the employer and the employee to make a contribution.

Among formal sector participants, only 47 per cent (9 out of 19) had social insurance; 78 per cent (7 out of 9) of which were registered with the SSK and 22 per cent (2 out of 9) with the ES. As expected, none of the informal sector participants had social insurance, except one casual employee who contributed to an optional SSK scheme which, at the time of research, allowed its members to pay towards a state pension without any contribution by the employer.

Evidently, the distinction between formal and informal sector participants in access to social insurance was rather blurred, the reasons for which are explored below in relation to the market conditions faced by the self-employed and employees. Within the former group, only 14 per cent (1 out of 7) had a formal status. They tended to own small-scale businesses, built on limited or no economic capital at all. These enterprises hence yielded very little or no profits, and were highly vulnerable to conditions of economic crisis. This seems to be a major reason as to why none of the self-employed were currently able to contribute to BAĞ-KUR. To illustrate, the *simit* bakery owner was unable to accumulate enough surplus to buy a license for his business let alone pay the premiums. Likewise, the fruit and vegetable seller made no contributions within the last one and a half years as he was also unable to make sufficient profits to clear the growing debts he owed to the wholesalers for the goods he sold in the bazaar.

Within the group of employees, 93 per cent (25 out 27) worked in the private sector. In contrast to public sector employees all of whom had social insurance, 72 per cent of private sector employees (18 out 25) were without social insurance among whom 50 per cent (9 out of 18) participated in the formal, tax-regulated, sector.

The factors restricting their access to social insurance are multiple, an exhaustive analysis of which is beyond the scope of this book. However, most fundamental forces relate those which a) cause failures in the enforcement of the regulation put in place to protect labour rights and b) reduce the ability of employees to bargain and/or claim their rights. The relevant influences hence extend from corruption, inefficiencies of the inspection and judicial mechanisms to processes that led to increased unemployment and a decline in trade-union organisation.[5] Some of these influences are evident within the following extract from an interview with a casual plasterer:

| | |
|---|---|
| Interviewer: | Have you discussed your entitlements to social insurance with your employer? |
| DY:[6] | If you discussed it with him, he wouldn't give you the job; it is impossible. He says 'I'll tell you what will happen to your social insurance' he says 'fuck off' as clearly as that. [...] He says 'fuck off, what are you talking about; you found the job and now are making a fuss about the insurance'. Nobody, I mean there are 500 workers there; not even one can mention insurance. Do you know what he [the employer] also does? He gets his mum registered; gets his father registered; gets his sibling registered; gets his uncle's son registered. It is compulsory. Let's say in the workplace, it [the law] obliges you to have 10 people [with |

---

5    According to the official figures based on a narrow definition, the unemployment rate in Turkey increased from 8.4 per cent in 2001 to 10.3 per cent in 2002, and the respective figures for urban areas were 11.6 and 14.2 per cent (TURKSTAT 2003c). Furthermore, the trade-unionisation rates had fallen from 67 to 58 per cent between January 1996 and 2002 (MLSS 2003). Also note that none of the working population in the sample had union membership.

6    The letter X refers to female interviewees and Y to males.

social insurance registration]. He doesn't get registered those who work there but does his brother or father; whoever he has in his mind.

Interviewer:  Can the workers not say anything at all?

DY:  Who to?

Interviewer:  I don't know, perhaps to the inspectors.

DY:  They're in a sham fight. Otherwise aren't they [the inspectors] able to sneak in and ask whether you [the workers] have insurance?

The above mentioned influences are likely to have had an impact on the terms of 'agreements' between the private sector employers and employees concerning premium payments. Three distinct types of arrangements were in evidence. The first one compelled the employees to work without any employer contribution to premiums – a common practice observed among 66 per cent (18 out of 25) of the private sector employees in the sample.

In another set up, employers made illegal arrangements to pay premiums at a reduced rate, which meant that employees had to settle for less than what they were entitled to by law. Among private sector employees in the sample, 29 per cent (2 out of 7) suffered from such arrangements. A female cleaner in the refectory of a medium scale textile factory had no choice but to sign the wage slips where she appeared to earn the net minimum wage; yet in reality, she earned 18 per cent less than the minimum wage. The amount deducted illegally from her net wage was used to pay towards the employer's share of the premiums. A male welder who worked at a medium scale company had to give consent to a more common arrangement. He 'agreed' to sign the wage slip where he also appeared to earn a minimum wage, although in reality, his earnings were above the threshold set by the law to calculate the lowest premium requirement for the employer. This way, his employer saved 20.5 per cent of the difference between his real earnings and the threshold every month, while restricting the size of his future pension.

In a third form of 'agreement', the employer bypassed the SSK and paid the premiums (s)he become liable for directly to the employee to avoid redundancy compensation. None of the private sector employees had such an arrangement, except for a self-employed technician and sometimes a casual worker, who received cash in lieu of the premiums he earned after April. Despite its appeal to employees who are desperate for instant cash, this type of arrangement can also work against them as it entails the relinquishment of certain labour and welfare rights.

Consequently, it was ultimately the employees whose rights were violated in any of the arrangements made. It was partly through such violations that the labour market induced deprivation on informal, and to a lesser extent, formal sector participants as they meant restricted access e.g. to state pensions and healthcare, which are explored next.

*Pension prospects*   This section explores the possible effects of informal employment on male pension prospects only. Female spouses were excluded from the analysis since there was no significant variation between the amounts of premiums they contributed to date. The observed amounts were either very limited or non-existent, meaning low pension prospects for all. The likelihood of men's access to *full* pension was predicted on the basis of the male spouse's current social insurance status and retirement conditions set out within the 1999 Social Security Reform Law No. 4447, amended soon after the fieldwork by law no. 4759.[7] Retirement conditions for men differed across the three schemes. ES members had to meet the minimum age requirement and have 25 years completed in service. SSK members had to fulfil the minimum age and contribution size criteria and to have registered with the scheme for 25 years. Finally, BAĞ-KUR members had to be above a certain age and have paid 25 years' worth of premiums. The age thresholds for the respective schemes were made to vary according to years remaining in service, time following registration and time remaining for premium payments. Table 5.6 presents the social insurance details of male spouses, age and premium requirements of the scheme they belonged to and their pension prospects.

Across the sample, 47 per cent (8 out of 17) of male spouses were found to have low; 18 per cent (3 out of 17) to have medium and the remaining 35 per cent (6 out 17) to have high pension prospects. These pension categories were subjected to a Spearman test in order to explore the possible effects of the sector of male employment.[8] The results revealed a strong association, meaning that informal sector participants are less likely to secure a pension [r = −0.59; p < 0.01]. This can also be seen from the cross-tabulation presented in Table 5.7.

Whilst confirming our hypothesis, the results also demonstrate that at 46 per cent (5 out of 11), a considerable portion of formal sector participants had low to medium pension prospects. So, why were some men's pension futures more restricted? This question is explored below in relation to the conditions faced by the SSK employees as they comprised the majority of men with low pension prospects.

One likely explanation concerns the time spent outside the labour market due to unemployment and/or involvement in precarious work (casual/seasonal) in the past and, or present job(s). The relevance of this explanation was investigated here through a focus on current employment status, which appears to be a good predictor of men's employment history given their tendency to stay in the same area of work since the initial social insurance registration.

---

   7   Since this research was conducted, the conditions for access to state pensions and healthcare have been rearranged by the Social Security and General Health Insurance Law No. 5510 enacted on the 1st of October 2008. Potential implications of the new law for the respondent households are briefly discussed in Appendix B.

   8   This variable takes into the status in both current and last employment before retirement.

**Table 5.6    Men's social insurance status, full pension requirements and prospects**

| | Social insurance details | | | Full pension conditions^ | | | |
|---|---|---|---|---|---|---|---|
| | Social insurance scheme | Registration year | Age | Premiums (days) or years served to date* | Min. age | Min. premiums (days) or years in service | Pension prospects |
| AY | SSK (optional) | 1977 | 39 | 2200 | 44 | 5000 | Low |
| BY | BAĞ-KUR | 1999 | 41 | 550 | 60 | 25 years | Low |
| CY | SSK | 1984 | 36 | 2088- | 48 | 5225 | Low |
| DY | SSK | 1968 | 42 | 1500+ | 44 | 5000 | Low |
| EY | SSK | 1974 | 57 | 1500+ | 44 | 5000 | Low |
| FY | SSK | 1982 | 37 | 2000+ | 46 | 5075 | Low |
| GY | ES (active) | 1979 | 47 | 23 years | 44 | 25 years | High |
| HY | SSK (active) | 1981 | 39 | 6000+ | 46 | 5075 | High |
| IY | SSK | 1976 | 44 | 3910 | 44 | 5000 | Medium |
| JY | SSK | 1987 | 43 | 1578 | 50 | 5375 | Low |
| KY | SSKʸ | 1972 | 53 | 4689 | 44 | 5000 | High |
| LY | SSK | 1972 | 53 | 3651 | 44 | 5000 | Medium |
| MY | SSK (active) | 1981 | 38 | 6000+ | 46 | 5075 | High |
| NY | ES (active) | 1987 | 39 | 15 years | 50 | 25 years | High |
| PY | SSK | 1978 | 43 | 3500 | 46 | 5000 | Medium |
| RY | SSK (active) | 1978 | 43 | 3908- | 44 | 5000 | High |
| SY | SSK | 1987 | 40 | 2200 | 50 | 5375 | Low |

*Notes*: *The plus and minuses are used where respondents provided an approximate value for their premium contributions to date in order to indicate that the exact value can be slightly higher and lower than reported. ʸHe is a work injury pension recipient. ^The size of full pension can differ between and within schemes.

**Table 5.7    Sector of male employment by pension prospects**

| Male sector of employment | Male pension prospects | | | Total |
|---|---|---|---|---|
| | Low | Medium | High | |
| Formal | 3 | 2 | 6 | 11 |
| Informal | 5 | 1 | 0 | 6 |
| Total | 8 | 3 | 6 | 17 |

The Spearman test performed to see whether seasonal/casual employment had a significant effect on men's pension prospects revealed a very strong relationship [$r = -0.90$; $p < 0.01$]. This meant that seasonal/casual workers had a lower chance of securing a full pension in the future. However, the reason for this was not simply that they worked fewer days than those with regular or more stable employment. From the accounts of seasonal employees in the sample, it appears that on average, seven years' worth of their work life went unrecorded in the social security books.

How could this have happened? Let us re-examine the employee and employer behaviour to find answers to this. Employers were shown to engage in illegal practices to minimise their share of premium payments. These practices include employing people without recording them in the books, and doctoring the records to make them look as though the employees earned less or left the job. On the other hand, employees were reported to delay registration due to suspicions about the consequences of having social insurance. This does not represent the behaviour of men in the sample, but was observed by a respondent who came across construction workers reluctant to supply identity details for registration. The reluctance of employees may have to do with limited awareness of social insurance schemes and their welfare implications. However, employee behaviour seems to be of secondary relevance since ultimately it is the employer who is legally responsible for providing information and keeping correct records of their employees. Instead of doing this, employers appear to have benefited from the less educated character of their employees which can make them more vulnerable to manipulation and less able to monitor social security records.

Those working without social insurance appear to have had little opportunity to increase their pension prospects by means of optional schemes which allowed their members to pay towards a lower pension without any contribution by the employer. Out of 10 employees without social insurance, 90 per cent were unable to make any optional payment. A casual plasterer who had a work life of 20 years explains why:

> Interviewer:   Have you got social insurance?
> FY:           No.
> Interviewer:   Not at all?
> FY:           Had some paid through construction work but they're only worth one and a half years in total. Apart from that, I optionally paid a further one and a half years' worth of premium by saving from my own earnings, but I was unable to continue any longer. Where can I find the money if there is no work? Three years' worth of premium, that's all... 50 million TL [monthly premium rate] may not appear a lot but we can't stretch our income given the local shop [food expenses], given the electricity, water [bills]...

Overall, in addition to engagement in precarious and low-paid jobs, the violations of labour rights appear to be a major factor in restricting men's pension futures.

*Access to state healthcare*    At the time of research, access to the Turkish social security system, which combined state pensions and healthcare, was heavily dependent on labour-based contributions. Thus, demand side influences found to reduce men's pension prospects are likely to have led to an exclusion from state healthcare (i.e. free hospital treatment and subsidised medicine) unless the households had alternative coverage through the green card and unemployment insurance. Also during this period, the green card entitled those below a certain income with no assets or social insurance to free hospital treatment but denied access to subsidised medicine (Ministry of Health 2001). The latter, in accordance with law no. 4447, provided those made redundant through no fault of their own with a basic income and state healthcare on the condition that, within the last three years before their redundancy, the employee has to accumulate 600 days' worth of premiums; 120 days of which had to be uninterrupted. Let us now see how far these benefits helped bridge the social security gap created by the labour market through a focus on the effects of sectoral division on two FWID measures, i.e. the number of household members benefited from a) subsidised medicine and b) hospital treatment.[9]

The subsidised medicine variable was subjected first to a Pearson correlation test with the household FSP ratios (see Figure 5.5) and then to a Spearman test with the sector of male employment. Both results indicated a strong relationship which imply a greater tendency for formal sector participants to have access to subsidised medicine [r (a) = 0.55, p < 0.05; r (b) = −0.83, p < 0.01]. The discrepancy between the two results was due to the following reasons. First, while the dependants of workers with social insurance were allowed access to state healthcare, male children above the age of 18 outside education were not considered a dependant even if they lived with their parents. This condition affected two households where both children were employed without social insurance. One of them, however, due to being a pharmacy salesman, had some access to free medicine through his clients' entitlements. Secondly, a certain amount of premiums had to be paid before dependants could become entitled to state healthcare. This requirement affected one household where the male spouse started a new job after a period of unemployment. Finally, although working male children with social insurance were allowed to register their parents as dependants, none of the three eligible households used this opportunity due to a lack of time to deal with the paperwork and because the dependency of male spouse meant relinquishment of the premiums paid to date and hence any future claims to a state pension.

---

9    At the time of research, access to university and public (i.e. SSK and State) hospitals and hence the quality of healthcare obtained by active members varied across social insurance schemes (See also Appendix B).

Conversely, the results from a Spearman correlation test indicated a fairly weak relationship between the sector of male employment and access to free hospital treatment [r = −0.32]. This meant that some of the households whose male spouses worked without social insurance were able to find alternative ways to get free treatment for some or all of their members. However, only in 27 per cent (3 out of 11), all members had coverage through the green card while the remaining 73 per cent either had only one child covered through work/higher education or no coverage at all. Their exclusion from the green card seems to do with tight eligibility criteria, which disregard the fact that not all assets have a significant potential for income generation.

Moreover, none of those with dormant accounts were eligible for unemployment insurance, although the great majority of casual workers were virtually unemployed due to conditions of economic crisis strongly felt in the construction sector. [10] This was also to do with the application of tight eligibility criteria. As a matter of fact, 80 per cent of the working population in the sample (28 out of 35) was either kept outside the scope of the scheme, or failed to meet the strict premium conditions.

Consequently, it appears that the gap created by the labour market in access to state healthcare was neither successfully bridged by the green card nor unemployment insurance. Poor households were therefore allowed to fall through the social security net despite their greater need for protection given their impoverished living and working conditions. Let us now explore how far they were exposed to risks at work.

*Occupational health and safety*  The level of health and safety risks faced by working household members were determined using the SSK premium tariff for occupational illnesses and accidents grading jobs on a risk scale of 1 to 12, i.e. from lowest to highest (Social Security Institution 1981). Adjustments were made to the grades where the observed jobs were considered to impose less or greater risk than suggested by the tariff. The grades corresponding to working household member(s) were added up and divided by their total number to obtain the average grades presented in Figure 5.7 [mean = 2.6; std. deviation = 1.3].

The household risk grades were subjected to a Pearson test with household FSP ratios (see Figure 5.5) in order to explore the possible effects of sectoral division within the labour market. The results indicated a weak association, implying that households with greater informal sector participation were disposed only to a slightly higher level of occupational risk [r = −0.25]. Regarding the risk grades of working members across the sample, they ranged between one and five [mean = 2.46; std. deviation = 1.69]. The reason for their scoring towards the lower end of the SSK risk scale is the lack of participation in occupations such as ammunition production, mining and shipping. The male spouses had a greater tendency to take on employment imposing higher risks given that 53 per cent

---

10   The rate of contraction in the sector was 3.6 per cent in the last quarter of 2001 (TURKSTAT 2002a).

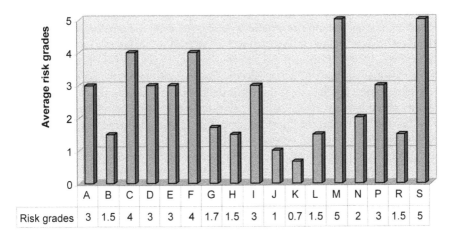

| Risk grades | A | B | C | D | E | F | G | H | I | J | K | L | M | N | P | R | S |
|---|---|---|---|---|---|---|---|---|---|---|---|---|---|---|---|---|---|
| | 3 | 1.5 | 4 | 3 | 3 | 4 | 1.7 | 1.5 | 3 | 1 | 0.7 | 1.5 | 5 | 2 | 3 | 1.5 | 5 |

**Households**

**Figure 5.7    April distribution of mean household occupational risk grades**

(9 out of 17) of them worked in jobs graded above four while none of the female jobs exceeded the risk grade two. The high risk group mainly involved those working in construction, manufacturing and transportation sectors. All but one man from this group worked informally without social insurance, which meant that in the event of an accident or illness they would not be able to receive state healthcare, accident compensation, disability pension, etc. As shown earlier, some of these conditions also applied to a considerable number of employees working in the tax-regulated sector.

Overall, it was shown here that households are rather unlikely to achieve success in a labour market environment restricting access to the social security system where employment status, to a large extent, determined who should benefit from state pensions and healthcare. Despite the introduction of the green card and unemployment insurance schemes, it was found that a considerable number of households were left to their own means to meet their medical needs, had little chance to obtain a full pension, and remained unprotected against occupational risks. Violations of labour rights and the prevalent conditions of economic crisis were shown to have played a significant role in their failure. These forces were influential within both formal and informal sectors of the labour market but it was the informal sector participants who suffered the most from their consequences.

*Does seasonality matter?*    Although no hypothesis was advanced concerning the impact of seasonal labour market fluctuations on household deprivation, this sub-section will focus on seasonality which was found to be of particular importance to the lives of most respondent households.

Across the sample, 37 per cent (13 out of 35) of the working population was subject to seasonal market fluctuations in various ways. The nature of seasonal effects is shown below with reference to branch of economic activity. The construction sector constituted the branch of activity for 61 per cent (8 out of 13) of the seasonal workers, of whom, except for one self-employed, all participants were employees. The length of the construction season was highly dependent on weather conditions. At times of frost and rain, construction activities tended not to be carried out unless the construction company (subcontractor etc.) used new technology. The majority of construction sector participants in the sample worked casually for small scale enterprises which lacked such technology. This, in turn, shortened the period within which they could generate an income. At best the construction season lasted around eight months; starting mid-March and ending mid-November.

The other branches of economic activity in which seasonality was observed include commerce, manufacturing and transportation. Among the seasonal workers, 15 per cent (2 out of 13) were employees in commerce and transportation; one was a caretaker at a school canteen open during term times, and the other was a porter carrying household items door-to-door; hence his work was contingent upon the peak season for house-moves which fell between spring and autumn. The remaining 24 per cent (3 out of 13) were self-employed in a branch outside construction. One of them was running a bakery, distributing *simit* to street vendors. His sales fluctuated according to changes in the level of outdoor activity and hence tended to be higher between spring and autumn. The other was a fruit and vegetable seller whose earnings were dependent on the seasonal changes in food prices. Given that three of the four bazaars he had were based in poor neighbourhoods of Ankara, his sales tended to be higher between spring and autumn when the fruit and vegetable prices are relatively cheaper. Evidently, for most seasonal workers the period between spring and autumn constituted the high season during which they generated most of their annual income.

To demonstrate the intra-household distribution of working members affected from seasonal fluctuations, household seasonality ratios were calculated by dividing the total number of seasonal workers by the total number of working members in the household. Figure 5.8 presents the ratios obtained. The majority of households had at least one working member exposed to seasonal market fluctuations [mean = 0.42; median = 0.50; std. deviation = 0.37]. In 35 per cent (6 out of 17), no working members were affected by seasonality; in 41 per cent (7 out of 17), one out of two working members and in 6 per cent (1 out of 17), two out of three working members were subject to such influences. In the remaining 18 per cent (3 out of 17), seasonality affected all working members in the households.

In order to investigate whether seasonality had a significant effect on household deprivation, a Pearson correlation test was conducted between the household seasonality ratios (see Figure 5.8) and weighted aggregate deprivation scores (see Figure 5.2). The test results suggested a very strong inverse association

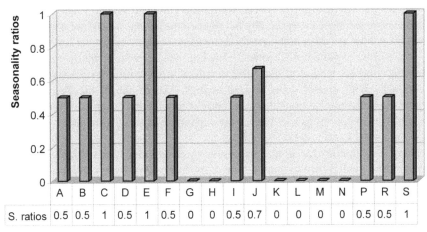

**Figure 5.8     April distribution of household seasonality ratios**

$[r = -0.83; p < 0.01]$. This implies that households with greater rates of participation in seasonal work were more likely to display higher levels of deprivation. This relationship can also be seen from Table 5.8 where household seasonality ratios are cross-tabulated with deprivation groups.

**Table 5.8     Household seasonality ratio by deprivation category**

| Seasonality ratio | Deprivation category | | | Total |
|---|---|---|---|---|
| | Worse off | Moderate | Better off | |
| 0.00–0.50 | 2 | 5 | 6 | 13 |
| 0.51–1.00 | 4 | – | – | 4 |
| Total | 6 | 5 | 6 | 17 |

In contrast to better off households where none of the working members were subject to seasonal market fluctuations, worse off households had at least one working member who suffered from the consequences of seasonality. The question then is: how did seasonal influences lead to household failure? Such influences are likely to restrict the benefit delivery capacity of their labour resources not by limiting the earnings of seasonal workers but also the social insurance premiums they could accumulate. As the latter was explored earlier, the focus will mainly be on income and other two aspects of monetary deprivation i.e. savings and debts.

To be able to cope with income decline during the low season, the households with seasonal earners needed to accumulate savings by the end of the high season. They considered winter food stock as a kind of savings which helped them cope with seasonal fluctuations. However, winter food preparation was found not to be an exclusive response to seasonality but rather a traditional way of securing cheap food for winter. Whether adequate food stocks were obtained for the forthcoming winter will be explored in Chapter 7. The households predominantly containing seasonal workers tended to enter the month of April with less income but not necessarily with greater debts or less savings. The results of the Pearson test where the household seasonality ratios correlated with the variables of household monthly income, savings and debts, were supportive of this [r (income) = −0.42, r (savings) = 0.14 and r (debts) = 0.27].

One explanation for greater deprivation in income terms might have to do with the availability of time as the April interviews were conducted at the beginning of the high work season where heavy showers caused interruptions in construction activity. However, the time factor seems to be of less importance as compared to the labour market conditions worsened by the economic crisis in 2001. A few macro-economic indicators indicate the severity of the crisis. In the last quarter of 2001, the GNP relative to previous year was −12.3 per cent but varied from one branch of activity to another. For example, it was −3.6 per cent in the construction sector; −14.4 per cent in the commercial sector; −10.7 per cent in the manufacturing industry; and finally, −3.7 per cent in the transportation and communications sector (TURKSTAT 2002a). The dramatic decline in growth rates were also manifested in unemployment rates which increased from 11.6 in 2001 to 14.2 per cent in 2002 in urban areas (TURKSTAT 2003c), and also in the annual rate of inflation that reached 65.1 per cent in April 2002 (TURKSTAT 2002b). These conditions were highly likely to have caused a decline in the real earnings and purchasing power of all households to varying extents and seasonal workers are particularly likely to have become affected. The effects of these conditions are further explored in Chapter 7 looking at change in deprivation.

Overall, it was shown that adding labour into the market to reduce the number of dependants was not a straightforward recipe for success. So far the reasons behind this were explored by reference to demand-side influences such as informality and seasonality. These influences were found to restrict the benefit delivery capacity of labour resources especially through reducing workers' ability to generate a sizeable income, and preventing their access to social insurance (hence state pensions and healthcare) and/or leaving them unprotected against occupational risks. It was also demonstrated that the tax-regulated sector of the labour market did not necessarily offer more decent working conditions. The following sections will explore the role of supply-side influences in household success.

*Supply Side Labour Market Forces*

Supply side forces refer to those affecting the supply of labour to the market. One set factors includes those likely to determine the number and nature of labour resources available (e.g. household size, life-cycle stage, attitudes to work, domestic and caring responsibilities) while another influences the position labour resources occupy within the market (e.g. cultural and social capital). The main focus of this section is on the latter group of forces given their particular relevance to our central question: why does low dependency not always lead to success? Before examining this question, the hypothesised relationship between religion and female labour participation will be explored.

*The role of religion in female labour market participation*    The aim here is not to provide a full account of why female labour participation rates turned out rather low, but to test whether my initial assumption that *Alevi* women are more likely to take part in market activities proved to be correct. As discussed earlier, this assumption was based on the idea that *Alevi*s tend to hold more progressive ideas about women's involvement in the public sphere than *Sünni*s.

Within the sample, 23 per cent (8 out of 35) of the main income generating activities involved using female labour. This means that 47 per cent (8 out of 17) of female spouses were involved in labour market activities of some sort. Nevertheless, 63 per cent (5 out of 8) of these activities were home-based, requiring limited interaction with urban life beyond the *mahalle* boundaries. Current employment status thus proved to be a poor indicator of women's public sphere involvement. Therefore, the variable of post-marriage work experience outside home was instead compared with religious affiliation. The cross-tabulation presented in Table 5.9 is indicative of a strong relationship, confirming our initial assumption. According to this table, 64 per cent (7 out of 11) of *Alevi* female spouses worked outside home either in the past or present; compared with only 16 per cent (1 out of 6) of *Sünni*s. Likewise, of women with a history of work outside home, 88 per cent (7 out of 8) were *Alevi* by background.

Table 5.9    Female work history outside home by religious affiliation

| Religious affiliation | Female work history outside home | | Total |
| | Work outside | No work outside | |
| --- | --- | --- | --- |
| *Alevi* | 7 | 4 | 11 |
| *Sünni* | 1 | 5 | 6 |
| Total | 8 | 9 | 17 |

The labour market participation of married *Alevi* women proved to be higher than that of *Sünni* women; and yet, my overall impression was that, irrespective of religious affiliation, most male spouses, if not all, held patriarchal values in their attitudes to female work outside home. Some of the reasons for their not wanting women to work outside was linked to masculine pride. Female labour participation seemed to pose a threat to masculinity in two respects. Firstly, men tended to take pride in being the sole provider; therefore, women's work made some feel a failure or appear so in the eyes of others. Secondly, protecting a woman's virtue is also a matter of masculine pride; therefore, by keeping their wives at home men sought to avoid any rumours or accusations of sexual misconduct and to protect them against possible sexual harassment on the workplace. Unfavourable work conditions were found to contribute to the rationalisation of such patriarchal values, as is evident from the account of a 32 year old *Alevi* woman:

| | |
|---|---|
| Interviewer: | Are you currently looking for work? |
| IX: | My partner doesn't give permission. He said the wages of [cleaning] companies were very little. They select men for work via acquaintances; they wait for money [bribery]…That's why we couldn't enter anywhere like that. My partner says companies are disgraceful, though; he says lots of dirty things happen there… As he is suspicious of things like assaults against women, he doesn't want to send [me to work]. As we hear also a lot of this happening in house cleaning, he doesn't want it. |
| Interviewer: | What do you say to this? |
| IX: | I tell (him) but my partner doesn't trust the companies. I want to enter into cleaning kind of job; for instance, to do cooking or clean the bureaus of companies and so on. […] He says 'no'. He says 'it isn't worth your kids becoming wrecked unless it is a trustworthy place'. He says 'the minimum wage you'll receive would come to nothing; it would be spent away on the roads'. |

Patriarchal pressures are highly likely to have militated against female labour participation. However, I agree with Ecevit (1995) that too much emphasis on patriarchy might disguise other pressures preventing women from participating in the labour market. As shown in the above extract, influences on the market side can also put women off work. It seems that by making women's labour market involvement a rather worthless exercise, poor work conditions let patriarchal values prevail.

However imposed or maintained, patriarchal values dominated the attitudes of most male spouses to female work outside home. Nevertheless, *Alevi* men tended to be more flexible in this matter, and agreed to their wives working outside home, especially when the household is desperate for money. Among *Alevi* men and women who internalised these values, female work outside was perceived as a last resort. Within the worse off household category, five households had an *Alevi* background, and in 60 per cent (3 out of 5) of these, female spouses were actively searching for a job, while the rest was willing but not permitted to do so.

On the other hand, within the six *Sünni* households, no women were currently seeking a job. One of these households was worse off, another was moderately deprived, and the other four were better off. One can turn the argument round and claim that *Sünni* women did not have to go out to work because most were relatively well-off. Nevertheless, even at times of desperation, it seemed rather unlikely for traditional *Sünni* men to give consent to their wives' working outside home. Of moderate to better off *Sünni* households, four were highly religious and traditional households where male authority was very strong, and two men from these households clearly stated that under no circumstances should married women be allowed to work outside home. This rule seemed less strict for their unmarried daughters.

Consequently, despite the differences observed between *Alevi* and *Sünni* women in their history of work outside home, these religious groups proved similar in that men's attitudes to female employment was very much based on traditional values of patriarchy. Therefore, most men were ultimately in favour of keeping their wives at home. The attitudes (and behaviour) of male spouses however tended to differ at times of destitution: when desperate for money, *Alevi* men were more likely to accept their wives working outside home, whereas for *Sünni* men the subject was hardly negotiable; in the event of increased hardship, they were rather inclined to make intensive use of male labour.

*The role of cultural capital in labour market participation*   By virtue of its role in job attainment, cultural capital can affect the benefit delivery capacity of labour resources and hence household success in reducing deprivation. Due to its quantifiable character, this section explores only the possible effects of formal cultural capital (FCC) presented in Table 5.10.

Starting with female spouses, 40 per cent (7 out of 17) were without a primary-school diploma and 17 per cent (3 out of 17) were illiterate. This group included women with no primary schooling, primary school drop-outs and literacy certificate holders. With 54 per cent (9 out of 17), primary school graduates constituted the largest group and the smallest group was composed of junior school graduates, represented by 6 per cent (1 out of 17). As for the educational status of male spouses, primary school graduates constituted the majority with 82 per cent (14 out of 17), and junior high school graduates comprised 12 per cent (2 out of 17). The remaining 6 per cent (1 out of 17) had no primary schooling and was illiterate. None of the male spouses had a high school diploma; only one was a high school drop-out.

Regarding the children's educational background, 62 per cent (21 out of 34) were currently in education: 67 per cent (8 out of 12) of girls and 59 per cent (13 out of 22) of boys. Within the group of students, 48 per cent (10 out of 21) were in compulsory education; a further 48 per cent (10 out of 21) were in a high or vocational school, and the remaining 4 per cent (1 out of 21) was in university education. The group of graduates including the drop-outs constituted 38 per cent (13 out of 34), of whom 23 per cent (3 out of 13) were graduates of primary school, 46 per cent (6 out of 13) were of secondary school and the rest were of *lise* or its equivalent vocational schools.

**Table 5.10 Formal cultural capital status of household members**

| FCC status* | | Household members | | | | Total |
|---|---|---|---|---|---|---|
| | | Female partner | Male partner | Female children | Male children | |
| Illiterate | | 3 | 1 | – | – | 4 |
| Literate | | 4 | – | – | – | 4 |
| Primary school | Student | – | – | 1 | 2 | 3 |
| | Graduate | 9 | 14 | 2 | 1 | 26 |
| Junior high school | Student | – | – | 3 | 4 | 7 |
| | Graduate | 1 | 2 | – | 6 | 9 |
| High school (i.e. *lise*) | Student | – | – | 4 | 4 | 8 |
| | Graduate | – | – | 1 | – | 1 |
| Vocational school | Student | – | – | – | 2 | 2 |
| | Graduate | – | – | 1 | 2 | 3 |
| Higher education | Student | – | – | – | 1 | 1 |
| | Graduate | – | – | – | – | – |
| Total | | 17 | 17 | 12 | 22 | 68 |

*Note*: *During the spouses' time of schooling, pre-higher education used to be divided into primary school (5 years), junior high school (3 years) and high school, i.e. *lise* or its equivalent vocational schools (3 years) and primary schooling used to form the compulsory part of national education. However, primary and junior high schools has then been merged to comprise the compulsory education, which lasts eight years in total.

Among the children who were at the age of higher education (i.e. around 17 and above), 93 per cent (14 out of 15) lacked access to university. The majority of children had very low prospects of attending higher education for reasons discussed below. Entry to universities in Turkey is through a national exam for which private coaching has virtually become a requirement. Of 43 per cent (6 out of 14) who were eligible for the national exam, 83 per cent were neither able to afford private exam coaching nor had the time for it as they were working on a regular basis. The exceptional case was able to attend a private course since a teacher acquaintance of her family who taught in the same place helped her get registered at half price. The remaining 57 per cent (8 out of 14) were ineligible for the exam since they dropped out the education system either (or both) due to income constraints, which often led to their becoming part of the family workforce, or due to their own negative attitudes towards education. Some children – mostly male – were reported to have made their own mind about leaving school. Parental attitudes towards education were found to have no adverse effect. Despite some disbelief in the value of higher education, given the high rates of unemployment among university graduates[11], parents across the sample were of the view that 'let our children become educated so that they shall not suffer like we do'. This reflected the attitude of both *Alevi* and *Sünni* parents in relation to the education of either gender. However, the realities of their financial situation appear to have caused a conflict between what they thought and what they were actually able to achieve.

So how far did the existing FCC resources of households contribute to success? This question was explored through a focus on the household FCC scores which represent the average number of years that working members of each household had spent in formal education. The average scores presented in Figure 5.9 [mean = 6.37 years; std. deviation = 1.97].

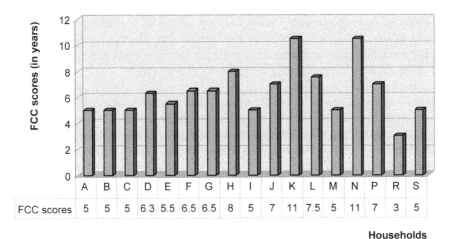

**Figure 5.9** **April distribution of average formal cultural capital accumulations of household workforce**

The FCC scores were then subjected to a Pearson correlation test with the weighted aggregate deprivation scores to determine whether household deprivation varied significantly according to the FCC resources of working members. The test results suggest a moderate relationship [r = 0.35]. The limited FCC effects can be explained in different ways. First of all, from the FCC accumulations of individual working members, it can be seen that years spent in formal education ranged from 0 to 11 [mean = 6.40; std. deviation = 3.10]. In other words, the educational background of working members varied between having no schooling and high school education. Hence it may be suggested that having a primary or a high school qualification made no significant difference to job attainment – all of these qualifications are likely to have churned labour resources at the lower end

---

11   As a matter of interest, between 2001 and 2002, the unemployment rate among university graduates has increased by 38 per cent (i.e. from 157,000 to 255,000 people) (TURKSTAT 2003a).

of the market. Or equally, it is probable that the FCC accumulations were of little relevance to the type of jobs performed. In fact, most of the observed jobs involved using skills acquired informally through personal life experience. Working females had a tendency to deploy their traditional – and mostly rural – housekeeping skills (e.g. bread-making, cleaning and lacework), and men to apply skills they acquired by themselves throughout their work life (e.g. baking, brick laying, driving and tiling). Their informal skills might have helped them manoeuvre within the low end of the market but do not lend themselves to a quantitative analysis of their effects on poverty.

Overall, the range of FCC possessed was found to be limited in its capacity to shift labour resources towards the upper echelons of the market. Therefore, contrary to our expectations, households with greater FCC accumulations were found not to display lower levels of deprivation. The findings are nevertheless congruent with our general working hypothesis that deployment of a greater range of resources does not necessarily lead to reduced deprivation.

*The role of social capital in labour market participation*    Like cultural capital, social capital stock of households can potentially affect household success through its role in determining the market position of labour resources and their capacity to deliver benefits. This section examines whether social capital use in job attainment makes a significant difference.

Households were found to make extensive use of their social capital resources in order to attain or maintain a status in the labour market. As a matter of fact, 97 per cent (34 out of 35) of the working members mobilised their stocks of social capital for this purpose. Their use of social capital differed according to employment status and specific requirements of the work being sought. All employees used it for seeking a job either on a one-off or continuous basis, depending on whether they had regular or casual/seasonal employment. Furthermore, all the self-employed made use of social capital to find customers, or to a lesser extent, to obtain loans for their businesses. Since the overwhelming majority of households were dependent on social capital, we are unable to explore whether the levels of household deprivation differed significantly between users and non-users. Yet there is room for exploring which features of social capital are more likely to ensure attainment of a better job. In what follows, this question was examined through a focus on the extent (volume) of social contacts and contact status, both of which attracted considerable attention in the social capital and social network literatures.

The social capital volumes were determined by counting the number of social contacts which were reported in either interview to be helpful or unhelpful but present in April and expected to remain so in the foreseeable future. Information about social contacts was elicited through asking situational questions concerning various forms of social support. The observed volumes ranged between 30 and 128 contacts [mean = 68.94; std. deviation 23.30]. Despite concerted efforts to determine the precise volumes, the values obtained are unlikely to reflect the totality of their contacts. Therefore, instead of using the actual scores, households were rank-ordered into groups with low, medium and high volume of social capital, using cut-off points obtained through the SPSS frequency facility. According to this, 29 per cent (5 out 17) had low, 41 per cent (7 out of 17) medium, and the remaining 29 per cent (5 out of 17) had a high level of social capital.

These household categories were then subjected to three Spearman correlation tests to see whether the volume of social capital is associated with a) weighted aggregate deprivation scores (see Figure 5.2), b) weighted work-related deprivation scores [12] and c) income obtained from labour market activities. As can also be seen from Table 5.11, the first two sets of results revealed no significant association [r (a) = 0.14; r (b) =0.03], which means that those with a greater stock of social capital were not necessarily less deprived at work or in general.

**Table 5.11    Household social capital volume by deprivation category**

| Social capital (volume) | Deprivation category | | | Total |
|---|---|---|---|---|
| | Worse off | Moderate | Better off | |
| Low | 3 | - | 2 | 5 |
| Medium | 2 | 2 | 3 | 7 |
| High | 1 | 3 | 1 | 5 |
| Total | 6 | 5 | 6 | 17 |

The final set of results was indicative of a moderate relationship [r(c) = 0.36], suggesting that households with higher levels of social capital are slightly more likely to earn higher amounts. However, none of the results is strong enough to conclude that the volume of social capital made a significant difference to success in reducing deprivation or attaining a better position in the labour market.

So how about the status of the contact person used in job finding? Does it significantly increase one's chances of acquiring a better status? Multiple characteristics of the contact person can potentially affect one's job chances (e.g. occupational and educational status). The job search experiences of the studied households revealed that the contact person's location of work can sometimes play a more important role than his or her occupational status. To illustrate, one of the female spouses reported to have found a regular job as a domestic worker through the help of her relatives who happened to work as concierges in military blocks located in an affluent part of the city. In what follows, the possible effects of the contact person on job attainment are explored with a particular focus on clientelist ties likely to connect poor households with people in positions of power.

---

12    See Table A.2 in Appendix A for the list of work-related deprivation measures.

In 41 per cent of the households studied (7 out of 17), at least one working member, often the male spouse, entered into patron-client relationships to find regular or casual work. The urban patrons they came into contact with were owners of small or medium-scale businesses in the formal or informal sector (e.g. taxi, betting shop and removal company owners), and to a much lesser extent, professionals in the public or private sector (e.g. civil engineers and doctors). The clientelist transactions that took place between the two parties were based on trust and hence middle to long-term acquaintance. The clients gave their loyalty in return for employment and other past or future benefits (e.g. advance payments, second hand goods and loans). The patrons also benefited from the loyalty of their clients which often meant commitment to getting the job done properly and/or undertaking errands outside their job description.

It is clear that patron-client relationships provided some households with an opportunity for employment. However, whether the users of clientelist job ties were better off than the non-users is another matter. In exploring this, the variable grouping households into users and non-users were subjected to a Spearman correlation test with a) weighted aggregate deprivation scores (see Figure 5.2), b) weighted work-related deprivation scores and c) income obtained from labour market activities. Only the results from the second analysis reached statistical significance [r(a) = 0.34, r(b) = 0.45 $p < 0.05$; r(c) = −0.12]. This meant that the use of clientelist job ties is unlikely to make a difference to the levels of household earnings and deprivation, but could lead to less work-related deprivation. However, only 44 per cent of the users displayed lowest levels of work-related deprivation compared with 25 per cent of the non-users. Hence, a considerable number of households with or without clientelist job ties remained to have moderate to high levels of work-related deprivation.

Such limited effects might be due to the diversity of urban patrons with varying control over valuable resources (see also Nelson 1979). Indeed, a few of the patrons to which household members were connected through work were reported to be equally impoverished. However, in my view, this explains only part of the picture. Other influences are linked to a) the majority of patrons being of employer status in the private sector, and b) the increased desperation for work in circumstances of economic crisis, high levels of unemployment and saturation in the informal labour market. These influences can reduce the patron's incentive to deliver favours whilst compelling his clients to accept unfavourable conditions of work in the hope of keeping their current employment or obtaining future work. This meant that it was the subordinates who incurred the costs of clientelist transactions. An extract from an interview with an employee of a medium-sized metal factory illustrates some of the costs involved:

MY:         We [I] bent our [my] neck [debased myself] to everything, and came to work for them once again. Our neck is bent to everything even if they beat or swear. We don't calculate our five, ten minutes or one hour. If we stop working at 5:30 or 7:30,

> we [work] until 7:45 and sometimes half an hour or an hour
> more, when necessary. He says 'this task is urgent'. We don't
> say 'but we have our break', I mean.

Clientelist ties were however established not only with employers but also with professionals who mediated access to a public sector job or a project contract. These contacts proved more beneficial but were available only to the lucky few. Given these considerations, having connections with urban patrons may provide a marginal group of households with relatively better job opportunities. However, it does not necessarily follow that the users of clientelist ties will less deprived than those who simply rely on their reciprocal contacts in the job search.

So far we have explored the effects of social capital, i.e. contacts that are relatively durable in nature. Let us now focus on transient contacts that are of particular interest in terms of their implications for the weak ties argument (Granovetter 1973, 1982). With 29 per cent (5 out of 17), a considerable number of households were found to use transient contacts to attain or maintain a position in the labour market. The tendency to use such contacts proved to be particularly strong among those whose working members were on constant search for jobs or customers. While 71 per cent of these households (5 out of 7) used transient contacts on a frequent basis, none of the households without a constant job search pattern (0 out of 10) were found to rely on such contacts. The proponents of the weak ties argument might claim that the likelihood of attaining a better labour market position is higher for the users of transient contacts as they are more likely to come into contact with dissimilar people. However, quite a different picture was obtained from the results of the Spearman correlation tests performed between the variable dividing households into users and non-users of transient contacts and the following three variables: a) weighted aggregate deprivation scores (see Figure 5.2), b) weighted work-related deprivation scores and c) income obtained from labour market activities [$r(a) = 0.55$ $p < 0.05$; $r(b) = 0.57$ $p < 0.05$; $r(c) = 0.42$ $p < 0.05$]. The results suggest that those reliant on transient contacts are more likely to generate less income and experience greater levels of work-related and overall deprivation.

How can we make sense of this? Most users of transient contacts were casual/seasonal workers whose job search experience was more contingent on chance. This is probably why the labour market, where those who work on a daily wage basis gather to search for jobs, was named by its participants as '*düşeş*'. The term *düşeş* is Arabic in origin and means double six. It denotes the best possible dice combination in backgammon; allowing the player to move his or her stones four times six. For the labour market participants, throwing *düşeş* means meeting the right contact who can provide them with a job or customers.

The daily struggle of job or customer seeking was however not as random as it appears in backgammon. In addition to the conditions of economic crisis which further restrict job availability and customer's purchasing ability, two influences appear to have militated against the random operation of *düşeş* factor. The first concerns the tendency for job transactions to operate by verbal contract and hence to require a strong trust basis. Given the weaker basis of trust within a web of transient links, those reliant on such links are likely to have had a reduced chance of throwing *düşeş*. The second factor relates to the principles of social exchange which dominated the job search process. The prevalence of such informal rules meant that people are more likely to provide work first for those whom they feel close to or who provided for them in the past and work their way towards transient contacts. This also reduces the likelihood of those reliant on transient contacts to throw *düşeş* in the labour market. For these reasons, in an economic crisis environment, weak ties or transient contacts are unlikely to bring success to those dependent upon them for job search.

The last two sections have focussed on two supply side influences in order to ascertain the extent to which cultural and social capital affected household success by virtue of their role in job attainment. Formal cultural capital accumulations of household members were found to remain rather limited in their capacity to help them attain favourable positions in the labour market. This was also the case as far as three characteristics of social capital were concerned: neither having an extensive web of relatively durable contacts nor being connected to urban patrons nor having transient ties with dissimilar people was shown to bring success. The successful allocation of labour resources rather seems to depend on being linked to the right person in the right place and time. Especially in circumstances of economic crisis, such contingent factors seem to have become increasingly decisive in determining who succeeds or fails.

## The Use of Non-Labour Resources

The previous sections have explored the effects of demand and supply side forces on household success by labour market activities. What follows examines the extent to which non-labour resources contribute to household income, with a view to concluding our quest as to why greater income diversification did not necessarily bring success.

Across the sample, only 35 per cent (6 out of 17) were found to use at least one non-labour resource for income generation purposes. The type of resources mobilised and the amount of income accruing from these resources are presented in Table 5.12. Three tendencies seem to emerge with regard to the use of non-labour resources. First, the number of households reliant on non-labour resources was rather limited. As a matter of fact, only 6 per cent of households (1 out of 17) derived income directly from economic capital (i.e. rent from a flat located in the adjacent neighbourhood), 6 per cent (1 out of 17) from social capital (i.e. household allowance and pocket money for children's schooling needs), and finally, 29 per cent (5 out of 17) from different institutional entitlements (i.e. entitlements to a work injury pension and municipal and charitable bursaries). Second, the income contributions of non-labour resources were small in size. The

**Table 5.12** Household income generated from non-labour resources (000,000 TL)

| Case | Income from non-labour resources | | | | Total household income | Deprivation category |
|------|------------------|---------------|--------------|-------|------------------|------------|
|      | Economic capital | Social capital | Entitlements | Total |                  |            |
| A    | 100              | –             | –            | 100   | 500              | Moderate   |
| B    | –                | –             | 40           | 40    | 350              | Moderate   |
| I    | –                | 110           | 20           | 130   | 133              | Worse off  |
| K    | –                | –             | 52           | 52    | 362              | Better off |
| N    | –                | –             | 10           | 10    | 460              | Better off |
| R    | –                | –             | 10           | 10    | 340              | Moderate   |

mean income obtained from non-labour resources, i.e. 57 million TL, amounted to one sixth of the average monthly household income. Third, except for a rentable flat and entitlements to a work injury pension, none of the non-labour resources acted as a constant source of income.

Let us now discuss some of the influences contributing to these tendencies by reference to the observed non-labour resources. Starting with economic capital, one might presume that the great majority possessed no assets. This assumption is however incorrect. As will be explored in detail within the next chapter, households owned assets of some sort, but the majority of them could not be used as a source of income firstly because most assets were of little value, and secondly because those with some potential (e.g. *gecekondu*) were used to meet other needs such as shelter. In fact only 24 (4 out of 17) per cent of households had sizeable financial or non-financial assets available for income generation. While one of the households realised this potential by renting out the flat, the others chose to keep their savings for future emergencies. Thus, for the majority, economic capital proved to be a rather unfruitful resource for income generation.

Likewise, social capital was found to be of little help in raising an income. The reasons for this are far more complex than construed by those who attach importance to the extent (volume) of social contacts. The key factors affecting the flow of monetary as well as non-monetary support are discussed below from the viewpoint of parties situated on either end of a potential exchange transaction; i.e. providers and recipients.

On the side of providers, major constraints were linked to the limited economic capacity of social contacts, extended family backgrounds, self-interest and doubts about the creditworthiness of the needy. The bulk of the social capital resources owned by the sample households were composed of people in similar economic circumstances to themselves, and hence had a limited capacity to provide benefits. The severe conditions of economic crisis may have further weakened this capacity.

Having an extended family background, which was the case with either or both spouses across the sample, appears to have further restricted the flow of benefits by making it impractical for the few financially well-off contacts to support all the needy kin located at an equal social distance. In some cases, the limited availability of financial means led to the selective provision of support, e.g. where priority was given to the most impoverished, whereas in others, it resulted in the withdrawal of support. The latter response is evident from the following extract taken from an interview with a male spouse:

> Interviewer:   Are you in touch with your sister in Germany?
>
> DY:            She's rich but we're poor so she doesn't approach... Maybe if she approaches a little more, one of my siblings would say 'I'm hungry'; the other would say 'I'm thirsty'; another would say 'I don't have coal', and another would say 'I don't have wood'... on top of them, a mother and a father [to support]. Her in-laws circle is also poor... They stay away, I mean; they stay away from everybody.

In addition, concerns about self-interest and creditworthiness of the needy also seem to have constrained the flow of support. These were at play especially when the type of support needed had an economic aspect to it. Paradoxically, the worse off households who were most in need of such support tended to be more affected since they had the least economic ability to reciprocate. This is well illustrated by the following two extracts taken from the interviews with female partners of two worse off households:

> Interviewer:   Is there anyone else whom we have not talked about so far but who helped you since our first interview?
>
> JX:            I swear there was no one... He [her husband] went to his uncle's son to say 'come and become a shareholder of the bakery or I shall give it to you'. The guy didn't agree. [...]
>
> Interviewer:   Why not?
>
> JX:            One of those things. He said 'I know nothing about the business; my money is enough for me'.

> Interviewer:   Is there anyone else whom we haven't talked about so far but who helped you since our first interview?
>
> EX:            No one got any job done for me; my children did though when they had any money.
>
> Interviewer:   How about neighbours and the like?
>
> EX:            We didn't get anything from them. They don't help because we don't have anyone working. They used to help before when you [I] wanted but now they don't as we don't have any security.

On the side of recipients, the limited economic ability to reciprocate, and concerns for pride and independence were found to constrain the benefit delivery capacity of social capital. Of particular importance was the lack of economic capacity which posed a constraint by evoking the fear of not being able to reciprocate on an 'equal' footing and hence becoming dependent on others. This is evident from the following extract from an interview with the female spouse of a worse off household:

| | |
|---|---|
| Interviewer: | Do you ask for help from anyone like your neighbours? |
| SX: | Not really. |
| Interviewer: | Why not? |
| SX: | Well, I can't make the necessary return... That might be why, for instance...today let's say I need tea or oil or one day I don't happen to have any tomato paste... That's all we could do with neighbours, we can't do much else. |

The limited economic ability of households to reciprocate either led them to stop seeking support or to engage mostly in balanced reciprocal exchanges especially when help was being asked of friends and neighbours. For poor households, involvement in such exchanges meant a restricted flow of benefits since what they gained was virtually confined to what they could offer within the limited means available to them. This was however not necessarily the case with the generalised reciprocal exchanges occurring predominantly among close relatives. However, most close relatives were also reported to have a limited economic capacity to provide support. This is well illustrated by the common response to my enquiries about the receipt of social support: 'everybody is just about able to look after themselves'.

Furthermore, concerns for pride also restricted the flow of benefits in the following ways. While men tended to take pride in their role as the main provider, the self-sufficiency of the family unit was a matter of pride for both spouses. That is why the very act of asking for help was often perceived as a threat to masculine and/or family pride, and as shown in the following extracts, had an adverse effect on support-seeking behaviour. The first is an excerpt from an interview with the female spouse of a worse off household:

| | |
|---|---|
| Interviewer: | Can you afford the medicine you have to pay for? |
| CX: | Well on many occasions we couldn't. |
| Interviewer: | Anyone help you with it at all? |
| CX: | You can't ask anyone, 'can you buy me medicine?' It is a matter of pride... |

The other is extracted from an interview with the male spouse of a better off household, but where the female spouse was also present:

| Interviewer: | What do your neighbours do in return for the help you provide? |
| HX: | Nothing... |
| HY: | Nothing because we wouldn't say anything. |
| HX: | I don't like at all telling my neighbours 'give this or that to me'. I'd rather buy it on credit from the local shop. I can't go and ask for it from a neighbour. |
| HY: | Neighbours do come to me and ask for money, or ask for a loan. Let's say I'll go to Ulus [market] and I don't have money for the minibus in my pocket. I'd rather go on foot but wouldn't go and ask for it. I have such a character. |
| HX: | We don't like showing our home situation to other people. Even if I'm hungry, I wouldn't say that I don't have bread at our home. |

It is clear from the above excerpts that pride discouraged some households from seeking and accepting support even in cases of extreme need. As shown later in a case study, another response was to seek support from selected sources where the perceived risk of refusal was minimal. Paradoxically, financially well off contacts tended to be perceived as a high-risk group, since they were thought to lack empathy for the impoverished conditions of the potential recipient. Either way, pride seems to have restrained the flow of benefits.

Further constraints related to both the potential providers and recipients, and included a) competitive attitudes largely directed against those perceived as equally well off or better off, and b) personal and familial conflicts, in particular, those occurring between in-laws. Competitive and conflictual influences within one's social environment often led to negative reciprocal transactions, which not only hampered the flow of benefits but also involved deliberate attempts at undermining the well-being of the parties involved. This is illustrated later within the case studies. Overall, for reasons outlined above, social capital resources of the majority proved rather unfruitful in terms of allowing access to various forms of social support including those of monetary kind.

Finally, turning to institutional entitlements, despite being a more frequently used source of income than economic and social capital, this resource type also tended to allow access to small amounts of income on a short-term and/or irregular basis. With the exception of conditional rights to a work injury pension, access to all the observed entitlements was means-tested. The municipal and charitable entitlements to a one-year bursary were granted to households ranging from the least to the most deprived. This raises questions as to why the remaining 71 per cent (10 out of 14) of households with schooled children were denied access. Their lack of access can be explained by the means-testing criteria being either not based on an objective set of standards or applied in a discretionary fashion. This especially made the granting of municipal entitlements susceptible to clientelist purposes, which often meant the exclusion of those reluctant to enter such relationships of subordination or those who are (known as) non-supporters of the party in power even if they met the eligibility criteria. It also meant that the ineligible households could be granted access.

Overall, non-labour resources, such as social capital and entitlements to cash benefits, were found to provide a minority of households with a limited and sporadic income. Structural (e.g. labour market-related) constraints upon households' economic ability to acquire beneficial assets and observe the principles of social exchange, along with the lack of generous state support and standardised access to cash benefits, were shown to play a role in this.

## Conclusion

This chapter has sought to uncover what lies behind household success by income generation activities. Does it depend on engagement in a more diversified set of cash-generating activities, having fewer dependants or mobilising a greater range of labour and non-labour resources? The above analysis appears to confirm the general argument I advanced against these three postulates by demonstrating that no matter how diversified an income or greater the number of labour market participants or varied the type of resources mobilised, households can still suffer from increased deprivation unless the mobilised resources are free from forces restraining their capacity to deliver benefits.

Chapter 6

# Income Allocation, Investment and Consumption

The previous chapter examined the role of income generation activities in household success with a focus on the likely influences relating to both demand and supply sides of the labour market. This chapter continues to discuss the forces behind household success through a respective exploration of income allocation, investment and consumption behaviour. The analyses presented below make use of April data.

## Income Allocation: Overt and Covert Mechanisms

This section focuses on overt and covert mechanisms of income allocation in order to understand the extent to which respondent households were able to avoid 'secondary poverty' (see Chapter 3). It begins with an analysis of the ways in which income is managed, distributed and controlled within the household and then turns to explore women's secret kitties.

### Income Management, Distribution and Control

The income management systems adopted by the sample households resembled three of the types used by Pahl (1983) and Vogler (1994). The most common system, employed by 47 per cent (8 out of 17), was the 'female-whole wage' where women took responsibility for managing the total income. The 'female-managed pool', wherein both spouses shared responsibility for managing this common pot but the female responsibility was greater, was used by 29 per cent (5 out of 17). Finally, a system similar to the 'housekeeping allowance' model was adopted by 24 per cent (4 out of 17) of households where men had access to the main source of income and only allowed their spouses to have access to a small and often unfixed portion for certain areas of household expenditure (e.g. food). Nil households were found in the categories of male whole-wage, male-managed pool and joint-pool.

Did the observed systems of financial management make a significant difference to household success? In exploring this, the FWID was modified first to exclude income and work-related items in order to increase its sensitivity to the effects of income allocation. It should however be noted here that the modified index captures overall household deprivation rather than differences between members. Figure 6.1 demonstrates the weighted management-related deprivation scores obtained [mean = 15.66; std. deviation = 2.81].

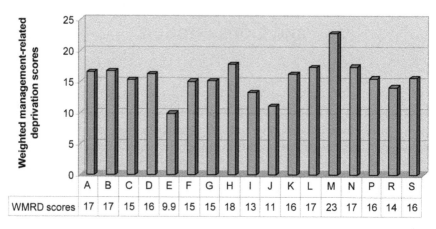

| WMRD scores | 17 | 17 | 15 | 16 | 9.9 | 15 | 15 | 18 | 13 | 11 | 16 | 17 | 23 | 17 | 16 | 14 | 16 |

**Households**

**Figure 6.1    April distribution of management-related deprivation levels**

A one-way ANOVA was then performed to compare the mean deprivation scores across the adopted management systems. The test results indicate no significant difference between the two variables [$F_{(2, 14)}$ = 1.86; mean (housekeeping allowance) = 16.76; mean (female whole-wage) = 14.34; mean (female-managed pool) = 16.90]. In interpreting these results, one should to bear in mind that a) the selection of households ensured that all households were experiencing deprivation, b) any relationship could run from deprivation to management system or *vice versa*, c) the sample size is small and the distribution of households into financial management groups is uneven. Nonetheless, a couple of inferences can be drawn here. One interpretation could be that systems of housekeeping allowance and female-managed pool were likely to generate less deprivation than that of female whole-wage. However, given the small differences in mean scores, I am inclined to conclude that the choice of management system made no significant difference to overall household deprivation. This may be attributed to the previously discussed limitations of the typologies created by Pahl (1983) and Vogler (1994). Fundamentally, these typologies do not provide a consistent measure of actual income distribution. To illustrate, within the system of independent management, partners are construed to have no access to each other's income. However, this gives no indication as to how their actual incomes are distributed between the needs of the overall household and 'fair' and 'controversial' areas of personal spending.

The way forward for our analysis was to explore the poverty effects of actual income distribution through a focus on the portion of total income allocated to areas of personal spending deemed controversial by either spouse in terms of their contribution to the 'collective good' (e.g. alcohol, tobacco, leisurely coffee house visits and small scale gambling). Two categories were hence formed: a) 'more collective' households, where controversial personal spending is either non-existent or sporadic and minimal in size, and b) 'less collective' households where a greater portion of income is allocated to controversial areas on a fairly regular basis. 'More collective' households where neither spouse made controversial personal spending constituted 24 per cent (4 out of 17). The remaining 76 per cent (13 out of 17) comprised 'less collective' households, of which 39 per cent (5 out of 13) represented the traditional pattern where only men's personal spending included controversial elements. In the rest, both spouses spent money on controversial items such as cigarettes.

The (rank-ordered) household categories and management-related deprivation scores were then subjected to a Spearman correlation test in order to investigate whether levels of overall household deprivation varied significantly according to the actual distribution of income. The results indicated a fairly weak inverse relationship [$r = -0.34$]. Bearing in mind that any association could run from poverty to income allocation or *vice versa*, the results can be interpreted in two ways. First, poorer household may have shown greater concern for the 'collective good' in allocating income between different areas of spending. Second, the observed patterns of income distribution are likely to have caused little increase in overall household deprivation and possibly in intra-household deprivation due to the limited share of controversial personal spending in total income. To illustrate, a daily packet of cigarettes which comprised the most common example of such expenditure cost around £4.50 per month, and this corresponded to 5 per cent of the mean monthly household income in April. Consequently, a display of concern by both spouses for the 'collective good' in their income allocation decisions seems to have minimised further experience of deprivation by the overall household and its individual members. From my observations, this is probable given the male tendency to take a pride in being the provider for their families.

Turning to financial control, it was found that while the responsibility for income management fell mostly on women, men were more likely to be in control of household finances. Table 6.1 demonstrates that in 65 per cent of the households (11 out of 17), finances were controlled predominantly by men, whereas the rest adopted female or joint control. Furthermore, although in 76 per cent of the households (13 out of 17), women played a dominant role in income management, only 44 per cent of the 'female managers' (6 out of 13) had some control over household finances.

In order to explore the possible effects of financial control on overall household deprivation, a Pearson correlation test was performed between the dichotomous financial control variable and weighted management-related deprivation scores. The results indicated a moderate inverse relationship [$r = -0.37$], from which it appears that households with male-controlled finances tended to be less deprived. This tendency contradicts the dominant view but is far from being conclusive. Therefore, I am inclined suggest that the choice of financial control system had no significant bearing upon overall household deprivation.

**Table 6.1    Financial management system by gender in control of household finances**

| Financial management system | Financial control | | Total |
|---|---|---|---|
| | Male-dominant | Joint or female dominant | |
| Housekeeping allowance (male) | 4 | – | 4 |
| Female whole-wage | 4 | 4 | 8 |
| Female-managed pool | 3 | 2 | 5 |
| Total | 11 | 6 | 17 |

Overall, the findings about overt mechanisms support the hypotheses set out earlier. While confirming the prevalence of management and control systems that are typical of low-income households, they suggest that such systems may be of less significance to poverty than how income is distributed in practice.

*Women's Secret Kitties*

The above analysis sought to explore the effects of overt mechanisms on overall household deprivation. This section focuses on women's secret kitties order to investigate how and why women created them and what they meant for deprivation.

Across the sample, 41 per cent of women (7 out of 17) had a secret kitty at the time of April interviews. If those who used to keep one in the past but currently did not either due to severe conditions of impoverishment or due to their kitties being discovered are included, then the figure increases to 59 per cent (10 out of 17). It appears from women's accounts of their past experiences and from the rumours about the kitties owned by other female neighbours that concealed savings can reach a considerable size. However, none of the women in the sample reported having a sizeable kitty. The kitty sizes ranged between 1.4 and 5.6 per cent of the mean household income for April [mean= 360 million TL].

So where did the kitty money come from? Women's own earnings appear not to be the only source, given the balanced distribution of kitty ownership between working and non-working women. As can be seen from Table 6.2, 38 per cent of the female workers (3 out of 8) and 44 per cent of the non-workers (4 out of 9) owned a secret kitty. The kitty money was drawn from personal income and/or earnings of other household members and often through the use of manipulative techniques. The ways women obtained the money are illustrated in case studies but in general involved a) cutting back on claimed personal expenditure, b) inflating reported household expenditure, c) keeping the money saved from household shopping, and d) keeping the difference between home-made substitutes and their market equivalents.

**Table 6.2    Secret kitty ownership by female labour participation**

| Female employment | Secret kitty ownership | | Total |
| --- | --- | --- | --- |
| | Owner | Non-owner | |
| Working | 3 | 5 | 8 |
| Non-working | 4 | 5 | 9 |
| Total | 7 | 10 | 17 |

Perhaps a more important question concerns why women felt the need to keep a secret kitty? I shall start by discussing why certain motives are less likely. Given the observed tendency for women to spend the kitty money on food staples, household items (cutlery, plates, glass, curtain etc.), underwear for themselves and the children, presents for relatives, pocket money for kids, and trousseaus for unmarried children, it seems rather unlikely that the motivation was to reserve more money for personal spending *per se*.

If secret kitties were not strictly aimed at personal spending, what was women's rationale for keeping them? The results from two cross-tabulations may shed some light on this. The first indicates a significantly greater tendency for women to own a secret kitty in male-managed systems than in female-managed ones. Table 6.3 shows that 75 per cent of the women in male-managed systems (3 out of 4) had ownership, whereas the figure was 31 per cent (4 out of 13) for households where finances were predominantly managed by women.

**Table 6.3    Secret kitty ownership by financial management system**

| Financial management system | Secret kitty ownership | | Total |
| --- | --- | --- | --- |
| | Owner | Non-owner | |
| Predominantly male-managed | 3 | 1 | 4 |
| Predominantly female-managed | 4 | 9 | 13 |
| Total | 7 | 10 | 17 |

In fact, women were found to perceive income management as burdensome due to a) the stress involved in having to stretch a tight budget and b) the strict male supervision of the actual management process. This is evident from the following extracts taken from interviews with two female managers of the entire income. The first interviewee did not have a kitty at the time of research but very rarely kept one:

Interviewer:    Do you come across any problems due to the fact that you manage the household income or not?

RX:             I'm not happy with it at all. I'm telling him 'spend the money yourself, use it yourself'. I'm experiencing an incredible amount of difficulties with it. You believe it or not, I sometimes ask myself whether I dropped the money or lost it. I look at the thing I purchased and then the money withered away in my hand. I get shocked [...]. He [her husband] says 'come my dear, let's put it on paper what you've purchased'. It turns out all was spent; all money was used up.

The other respondent however currently owned a kitty:

Interviewer:    So you mean the entire task of managing money is left to you?

DX:             Our folk [household members] don't have a clue about shopping-bazaar business. My husband wouldn't know a thing, but my brother-in-law would do. When the bills arrive, he puts them in his pocket and when he goes downtown, he pays them off; he goes and buys food for breakfast for instance; therefore his wife is much relaxed. She didn't shoulder the responsibility but I did... It's like a big thing on me. If you buy it is a problem; if you don't, it's another problem. I'm thinking what if he gets angry; what if he asks 'I have given you that much money. What have you done with it? Where did you spend it?'

Secret kitty keeping is by no means a remedy for problems associated with handling a tight budget. Nevertheless, it seems to provide women with a small financial domain free from male supervision and any charge of money 'misuse'. It follows from this that women are likely to keep secret kitties to gain an increased sense of financial agency. The results from the other cross-tabulation substantiate this idea by demonstrating a moderate tendency for women to use secret kitties in households where finances were predominantly controlled by men. As shown in Table 6.4, while 55 per cent of the women in predominantly male-controlled systems (6 out of 11) had a secret kitty; kitty ownership was as low as 17 per cent (1 out of 6) in systems controlled either by both partners or predominantly by women. It should be noted here that among households whose finances were controlled by men, there were some women who displayed an interest in keeping a secret kitty but who were unable to do so e.g. due to the tight income, strict male supervision over the actual management process or because their kitties came to light. If this subgroup of women had been counted within the figures, a stronger relationship would have been observed between financial control and secret kitty keeping.

**Table 6.4      Secret kitty ownership by gender in control of household finances**

| Financial control | Secret kitty | | Total |
| --- | --- | --- | --- |
| | Owner | Non-owner | |
| Male-dominant | 6 | 5 | 11 |
| Joint or female-dominant | 1 | 5 | 6 |
| Total | 7 | 10 | 17 |

Qualitative evidence also confirms that women's motives for kitty keeping represent an aspect of enhancing their level of financial agency. The two excerpts below are highly illustrative of this. The first is from an interview with a female respondent who was given an unfixed housekeeping allowance:

Interviewer:    Why do you feel the need to keep it a secret?

LX:             If [he knew that] I've money in my hand; he'd take it from me. He'd take it from my hand saying 'let it [her need] wait a while, we can buy it another time'. Yes, another time but when? The time of beans, potato and onion arrives. Tomato paste, pickles need to be made. If you don't buy them now when can you buy them? […] He wouldn't know such subtle issues. We [women] decide on it instead. […]

Interviewer:    What happens if you asked him money for these needs?

LX:             He'd of course give. His gas bottle needs filling up; at the end of the day he also needs to have food at home. He'd give but we don't ask him much. He's also upset about things… There's no money, I mean. He'll say 'how I can give you that money'; he'll say 'try to get by'. How will you manage it then? You'll manage it this way [using a secret kitty]. Also it would cause a fight while we're having our peace and quiet.

Interviewer:    Why?

LX:             What will happen when he says no? Everything stems from that 'no'. He'll say 'no'; you [I] will say you find money for going out but can't find for this and this will carry on back and forth. He doesn't smoke; drink or gamble though, but when he goes to the coffeehouse he needs to have enough to drink a glass of tea with his mates.

The other is extracted from an interview with a female who had greater responsibility for managing the pooled income:

| Interviewer: | Why did you feel the need to create such a kitty? |
| FX: | So that we'll take it out in our rainy days, when he [her husband] has no work to do. |
| Interviewer: | What happens if you let him hear about the kitty? |
| FX: | I wouldn't let him know. |
| Interviewer: | Why? |
| FX: | I might buy things concealed from him. |
| Interviewer: | What sort of things? |
| FX: | What would women buy? Underwear, teaspoon, glass, plate kind of things. [...] |
| Interviewer: | What happens if you discuss these needs with him? |
| FX: | Men don't attach importance to subtle things. Let's say our curtain got torn apart. You'll need to save up to buy this. He says 'leave it for god sake; we're already poor, let sun shine in'. If I asked for net curtains he'd buy a thick one. As he doesn't know [what to buy], we're compelled to do it. |
| Interviewer: | So this is why you don't ask him? |
| FX: | He might not say anything against it if I did. He'd buy but I'd also buy, I mean. |

From the evidence presented so far, it appears that women can create secret kitties for the following reasons. One is to have an increased ability to make, as well as execute, financial decisions according to one's own values, principles and priorities. A second is to channel men's earnings in a way to reduce the likelihood of men spending on personal areas that women found controversial due to their disregard for the 'collective good'.

A third motive is to avoid the need to seek permission and money from men for an intended expenditure, and thereby eliminate the risk of refusal. If permission were sought, the refusal rate would be high because nearly all areas on which women spent their kitty money comprised a potential source of disagreement between spouses. Disagreements were generally centred on the importance and urgency of the intended expenditure, or whether they served a good purpose, and resulted from the differences in spouses' principles (e.g. on parenting) as well as awareness of household needs and obligations attached to social relationships and traditional observances (e.g. weddings). Unsurprisingly, women often displayed a better knowledge of such 'subtle' needs and obligations and how to meet them. They were, for instance, better informed about seasonal variations in food prices. By secret kitty keeping, women were able to meet some of the needs to which they attached importance, hoping that their purchases would escape men's notice. However, even if they were discovered, men tended to interpret them as a frugal management of income, as long as they were kept to an acceptable minimum.

A fourth reason for secret kitty keeping appears to be to reduce financial accountability to men, and thereby escape any accusation of mismanagement. A fifth motive seems to concern the pure desire to acquire financial autonomy, given that women can keep secret kitties even when overt mechanisms allow their access to the same area of expenditure. Finally, women also seem to use secret kitties in order to avoid financial conflicts likely to result in verbal arguments or domestic violence. The potential sources of conflict were varied and the above-mentioned disagreements constitute one obvious example. In a rather less obvious way, men's inability to meet their spouses' financial demands appears to have caused conflict and upset as men were inclined to perceive such demands as a threat to their masculine authority and pride derived from their role as the main provider. Thus, while seeking to maintain a 'peaceful' family atmosphere through secret kitty keeping, women either intentionally or unintentionally protected their spouses' masculine pride.

Consequently, in my view, it can be suggested that secret kitties act as a covert mechanism whereby women indirectly challenge men's financial authority in order to enhance their own agency through limited but exclusive exercise of discretionary power over a hidden sum of money. This seems also true for the working women whose secondary role as income earners is unlikely to have given them sufficient powers to confront male domination in an overt fashion. The reasons for women's failure to do so are however not restricted to their income and employment status, and can include fears of domestic violence, threats to masculine pride, etc. Whatever the reason, their belief in the futility of an overt confrontation seem to have led women to seek an alternative way to influence decisions and practices of income allocation, which had to be covert and often involved manipulation. That is why I believe secret kitty keeping fits in well with a particular way of 'bargaining with patriarchy' known as 'traditional defiance' (Bolak, 1997; see also section 3). The likely outcomes of this bargaining process might not be ideal but seem significant enough to encourage women to continue keeping secret kitties.

Turning to explore their likely effects on deprivation, here the key concerns are under what circumstances women withdrew money from the total income and how they spent the money accrued. Women in worse-off households with very tight budgets tended to avoid secret kitty keeping. However, given that all households fell below a certain poverty threshold, one might expect any withdrawal to increase the deprivation of the overall household and/or other members. Yet, the evidence presented above seems to defy this straightforward expectation. Although the kitty money was spent on areas to which they attached greater importance, and which tended to give rise to disagreements between spouses, it was generally used to meet the needs of the household and the children and hence in one way or another contributed to the 'collective good'. Thus, assuming that the money transferred to secret kitties was diverted from areas of spending that would also have served 'the collective good', it may be concluded that secret kitties did at least not increase deprivation. However, another conclusion is also likely if we take into account the motive to minimise the risk of men's controversial personal spending. It remains unknown whether the risk was only perceived, or actual. Yet, where this risk was genuine, women's secret kitties are likely to have increased the inflow of money that can be put to 'better' use, and hence had a positive effect on deprivation.

To conclude, the above analysis lent some support to the hypotheses set out earlier with regard to income allocation. The analysis confirmed the well-documented tendency for women in low-income households to manage income single-handedly while men retain control over processes of financial decision-making. However, contrary to the dominant view which associates male management and control with increased poverty, it revealed no significant difference between male or female managed and controlled systems. This was attributed to the general concern by spouses for the 'collective good' in the actual distribution of total income. It was hence argued that how income is distributed in practice may be of greater relevance to poverty than systems of management and control. Furthermore, women were shown to create secret kitties more to gain greater financial agency than to reduce male-induced deprivation. However, where there is an actual risk of men's controversial spending, these kitties are likely to have reduced 'secondary poverty' given the family-oriented character of women's spending. Nevertheless, on balance, all sample households had considerable success in avoiding severe forms of 'secondary poverty'.

## Investment, Insurance and Credit Use

This section examines the main sources of success in asset acquisition. It first evaluates the financial and non-financial asset portfolios of the respondent households in terms of their capacity to a) generate income, b) promote further asset accumulation and c) ensure future security. It then explores how these assets were obtained, and whether some of the resources used in the process were more effective than others in allowing access to beneficial assets.

The household portfolios were found to contain one or a combination of the following non-financial assets: *gecekondu* house/land being occupied, a house/ plot/land located in other urban, semi-urban or rural areas, work space/supplies/ equipment and vehicles (mainly cars). Some might categorise cars as a consumption item, but as shown below, most owners could not afford to make everyday use of their cars. For them, cars symbolised an investment in status, and hence were considered here as part of non-financial assets. By contrast, household items were excluded from the asset portfolio since the general tendency was to perceive them as objects with a symbolic meaning for the unity and self-sufficiency of the household. Their sale almost meant dispersion of the family. This contradicts Hoodfar's (1996) study where Egyptian households were reported to accumulate such items for their exchange value.

Turning to financial assets, they were reported to include one or a combination of the following elements: savings kept in a bank, under the pillow or in rotating saving and credit associations (roscas) and contributions to social insurance schemes. Table 6.5 demonstrates the number of financial and non-financial assets possessed by the households from each deprivation category.

**Table 6.5     Household asset portfolio by deprivation category**

| Non-financial assets | Deprivation groups | | | Total |
| --- | --- | --- | --- | --- |
|  | Worse off | Moderate | Better off |  |
| *Gecekondu* house occupied | 5 | 5 | 5 | 15 |
| *Gecekondu* land occupied | – | – | 3 | 3 |
| Other urban/semi-urban house/plot | 3 | 1 | – | 4 |
| Rural land | 3 | 2 | 3 | 8 |
| Rural house/plot | 1 | – | 2 | 3 |
| Work plot or equipment | 2 | 2 | 1 | 5 |
| Car | 1 | 2 | 3 | 6 |
| **Financial assets** | | | | |
| Deposit savings | 1 | – | 2 | 3 |
| Home savings | – | 2 | 1 | 3 |
| Rosca savings | 1 | 3 | 5 | 9 |
| Social insurance contributions | – | 3 | 5 | 8 |
| Mean asset ownership | 2.83 | 3.80 | 4.00 | 3.53 |
| Number of households | 6 | 5 | 6 | 17 |

*Note*: The scores were calculated by giving households a point for each asset they possessed and can for instance be read as three worse off households had rural land.

The results are discussed in the next two sections where the benefit delivery capacity of each listed asset is evaluated, starting with the category of non-financial assets.

*Non-financial Assets*

The observed non-financial assets were of five main types. The first concerns the house currently occupied. All sample households lived in *gecekondu* housing which displayed variation in terms of tenure type: 70 per cent (12 out of 17) were owner-occupiers of an unauthorised *gecekondu*; 18 per cent (3 out of 17) were owner-occupiers of a legal *gecekondu*, and the rest were tenants. Within the first group, 92 per cent (11 out of 12) were residents of Northern Ege who, for reasons explained in Chapter 4, neither legally owned the house nor the land on which it was built, and were faced with high risk of evacuation. Their *gecekondu*s hence provided no housing security but still held some potential for being rented out or even being sold. In fact, one *gecekondu* from Northern Ege was sold at the time of fieldwork. The monthly rent charged for Northern *gecekondu*s was similar to that of their legal counterparts within the *mahalle* (around 75–100 million TL per month). However, both the possibility of their sale and the sale price they were likely to fetch were lower. Besides, the majority of the sample households from Northern Ege were neither in a position to sell nor rent out their *gecekondu* since they had nowhere else to go. None were current members of the housing cooperative established to alleviate their vulnerability against demolition. In event of demolition, only 36 per cent (4 out of 11) had another asset to fall back on.

The last illegal owner-occupier was a household from Southern Ege whose housing situation was more favourable in that despite lacking legal ownership of *gecekondu* land and hence entitlements to redevelopment, the household still had possession of the house itself and hence enjoyed some housing security. Furthermore, at the time of interview, this group of occupants was being considered within an alternative transformation plan which might allow them to buy a flat in the new development on special terms and conditions. Despite concerns around affordability, this planning option could possibly mean increased returns from the *gecekondu* occupied.

All three tenants were Southern Ege inhabitants who, similar to the illegal owner-occupiers from Northern Ege, had no ownership of the *gecekondu* house or land. Nevertheless, they had greater housing security due to their close social connections with their landlords and the long time needed before the redevelopment of the area.

Finally, the last three households were comprised of legal owner-occupiers from Southern Ege (i.e. right-holders) who had the most secure housing and potentially the highest returns from the *gecekondu* they occupied. As owners of houses built prior to 1985 (or appeared so in the official records), they were not only entitled to authorised housing but also had rights to transform their land into an apartment block. This meant an increase in the current value of their *gecekondu* as well as the future returns to be obtained from it, though the latter depends on several other factors, such as the land size after municipal deductions, rent potential of the location, and agreement between the right-holder and land developer. The right-holders within the sample had 250–270 m$^2$ land left at their disposal. So should the area be transformed according to the current amelioration plan, they can, quite optimistically, obtain 2 to 2.5 flats in the new blocks.

The second asset type concerns urban/semi-urban houses and plots. Assets of this kind were owned by 24 per cent (4 out of 17), all of which were from Northern Ege. One was a rental flat located in the adjacent neighbourhood. The flat neither generated significantly higher rent than that obtained from the *gecekondu*s nearby, nor offered greater housing security given the sizeable debts created for its purchase. Nonetheless, it potentially had a higher sale price than that of those located in an urban-rural interface. Another asset was a self-help house being built on the periphery but still unfinished due to the monetary costs involved. The last two were plots also situated on the periphery. Due to a lack of economic capital, no houses were built upon them. Although potential returns from the sale of the last three assets were considerable, they offered limited housing security and opportunity for rental. The limited ownership of such assets suggests that not all *gecekondu* owners can be treated as land speculators. Perhaps, if it had not been for the demolition threat, these households would have been unlikely to have made risky investments that they could barely afford.

The third asset type refers to a rural house and plot. Across the sample, 47 per cent (8 out 17) possessed rural land of different sizes and 18 per cent (3 out of 17) had a small plot of sufficient size to build a house. The land sizes varied between 15–50 *dönüm*, i.e. 3.75–12.5 acres approximately. The rural land was of little value both in terms of income generation or investment. The land size appears not to change the picture given the shortage of demand. The reasons for this are beyond the realm of this research. Nevertheless, they may relate to a) labour scarcity due to youth migration from rural to urban areas, b) increasing cost of agricultural production, c) land fragmentation through inheritance, and d) abolition of certain agricultural subsidies (e.g. direct purchase). However, returns to rural land could increase, following the enactment of a recent agricultural subsidy policy which entitles rural land owners to direct income support (i.e. 10 million TL for each *dönüm*). In fact, some of the households who owned rural land but no longer engaged in agricultural activity were seeking to benefit from these subsidies. Given the inadequacies of title deed registrations, they had a real chance of succeeding.[1] Concerning their capacity to provide future security, rural assets were indeed perceived by some as a safety net to fall back on in case things went wrong in the city. However, given the decline in agricultural revenues, they are unlikely to provide security for those without regular earnings or a future pension. This meant that only those owned by 36 per cent (4 out of 11) had some potential to act as a safety net.

The fourth type concerns work-related assets (e.g. work space, supplies or equipment) owned by 29 per cent (5 out of 17). Two households possessed assets linked to their private businesses; i.e. four bazaar stands in different districts of Ankara, and bakery equipment. The possibility to charge rent on these assets was low, and also the amount that can be obtained was limited. However, potential revenues from the sale of bazaar stands were five times as much as those for bakery equipment. Yet, neither asset was as source of future security since their owners lacked the economic capital to stabilise their businesses in an economic crisis environment. Further two households had assets they used in wage-based work; i.e. a welding machine and saw to cut tiles and wood. The last household owned work supplies, an oxygen bottle, which could never be used due to the lack of sufficient economic capital to set up the business. The last three assets held little value for sale or as rental, and provided no other security for their owners.

---

1 For a detailed discussion of the shortcomings of this policy see Yükseler (1999).

The final asset type involves vehicles possessed by 35 per cent (6 out of 17). One of these vehicles was a truck and the rest were cars. None of the cars were used for income generation or daily transportation. In fact, one household bought a car for work purposes but as the work did not go as planned the car became idle. Almost all owners used their cars only for special occasions so as to reduce expenses. The cars in their possession were old models of limited value. The newest car in the sample was a 1994 registration Lada. Overall, most vehicles proved unprofitable as they provided no significant returns or future security for their owners. Hence, by purchasing cars, households seem to have made a symbolic investment in their status, rather than responding to a consumption need.

So far the focus has been on the non-financial assets owned across the sample. I shall next evaluate the benefit delivery capacity of the observed financial assets.

*Financial Assets*

Two main types of financial asset were in evidence: savings and social insurance contributions. Across the sample, 71 per cent (12 out of 17) had savings at least in one of the following three forms. *Deposit savings* were kept by 18 per cent (3 out of 17) only. The mean size of deposit savings was 2.92 billion TL, which equalled eight times the mean household income for April. According to TURKSTAT (2002c), the monthly rate of real returns from a deposit account for April was around 1.8 per cent in April. Thus, after inflation[2] was allowed for, the average monthly interest accrued on the deposit savings of the three households amounted to 53 million TL, i.e. 15 per cent of the mean household income for April. Despite the favourable conditions in the Turkish financial market, with banks offering annual interest rates reaching up to 48 per cent, the deposit account proved an unfavourable means of financial investment as far as the poor households were concerned, since only a few with regular incomes had an account and those with an account were unable to obtain significant returns due to the limited size of the savings they deposited.

As for *home savings*, 18 per cent of the sample households (3 out of 17) kept under the pillow some savings in gold or a foreign currency with an aim to obtain real returns in an inflationary environment. The mean size of home savings was 91 million TL, which equalled 25 per cent of the mean household income. According to TURKSTAT (2002c), the respective monthly rates for real returns from dollar, euro and gold were – 4.7 per cent, – 3.6 per cent and – 1.6 per cent. The negative rates meant a negligible loss of value on the observed home savings given their limited size.

*Rosca savings* proved more popular with 53 per cent (9 out of 17). In general terms, rosca refers to a form of informal financial organisation composed of members who make periodic payments to a fund which is given to each contributor in turn (Ardener 1964, 1995). The term 'rotation' indicates each member's turn to receive the fund or lump-sum. Members are expected to continue for at least

---

2  As a reminder, the monthly rate of inflation was 2.1 per cent in April 2002 (TURKSTAT 2002b).

a 'round' of rotations, i.e. until each member's turn has been served. After the completion of a round, they can decide whether to continue, disband or quit the rosca. Like roscas across the world, Turkish roscas also differ in form but are given the generic name *gün* (i.e. day) to indicate each member's turn.

The *gün*s in which the sample households participated were of three types; i.e. *şeker günü* (i.e. sugar day), *altın günü* (i.e. gold day) and *dolar günü* (i.e. dollar day) which had the following features in common. First, all of them were based on a verbal contract. Second, none of them required a specific person to be assigned the role of organiser, as in roscas observed in other parts of the world (see Ardener 1964). Third, the number of members was fixed for one round. Fourth, the order of rotations was determined by drawing lots. Fifth, *gün* payments or contributions at each rotation were the same for all members. Last, either the contributions or the lump-sum was fixed to a medium whose value could be protected against inflation during the life of the *gün*. On the other hand, the most distinctive difference among these *gün*s was in the medium of the contributions or the lump-sum, according to which they were labelled. There were also variations in terms of membership size and rotation frequency but these features were not specific to any particular type. The main features of the observed *gün*s are presented in Table 6.6.

**Table 6.6    Distribution and characteristics of the *gün*s observed in April**

| Case | Type of *gün* | No. of members | No. of rotations per month | Size of lump-sum per rotation | Size of member contribution at April rotation(s) |
|------|------|------|------|------|------|
| A | Dollar | 3 | Once | $150 | $50 |
| B | Sugar | 8 | Twice | 50 kg sugar: 53 m TL ($40) | 13.3 m TL ($10) |
| G | Sugar | 8 | Twice | 50 kg sugar: 53 m TL ($40) | 13.3 m TL ($10) |
| H | Gold | 10 | Once | 10 gold coins ($152) | 1 gold coin ($17) |
| J | Gold | 8 | Once | 8 gold coins ($122) | 1 gold coin ($17) |
| K | Sugar | 11 | Once | 100 kg sugar: 106 m TL ($80) | 9.6 m TL ($7.2) |
| L(a) | Sugar | 11 | Once | 100 kg sugar: 106 m TL ($80) | 9.6 m TL ($7.2) |
| L(b) | Gold | 11 | Once | 11 gold coins ($167) | 1 gold coin ($17) |
| N | Gold | 10 | Once | 10 gold coins ($167) | 1 gold coin ($17) |
| P | Sugar | 12 | Twice | 50 kg sugar: 53 m TL ($40) | 8.8 m TL ($6.6) |

The working principles of the three *gün* types were as follows. Starting with *şeker günü,* the lump-sum here was in Turkish Lira but based on the wholesale price of 50 or 100 kg of sugar. At each rotation, the price was obtained from a certain dealer and divided by the number of members to determine the size of contributions. This allowed price increases to be accommodated; thereby giving members an equal chance to buy the same amount of sugar. In *altın günü,* the lump-sum was composed of quarter gold coins. In every rotation, each member contributed a small gold coin, known as *çeyrek* (i.e. quarter), to a fund which was then given to the member whose turn was due. Thereby, all members were able to acquire the same amount of coins despite changes in the price of gold. Finally, *dolar günü* was based on similar working principles as *altın günü,* the key difference being that the contributions were fixed to the US dollar (e.g. \$50 per member at each rotation). The lump-sum was equal to the fixed amount multiplied by the number of members. This meant that members had the opportunity to obtain an equal amount of US dollars despite possible fluctuations in exchange rates.

Of the three types, *şeker günü* was most popular and *dolar günü* least. Among the participant households, 56 per cent (5 out of 9) were members of a *şeker günü* whereas the respective figures for *altın* and *dolar günü* memberships were 44 per cent (4 out of 9) and 11 per cent (1 out of 9). At the time of April interviews, *şeker günü* members either used or had plans to use their lump-sum to buy food and/or cleaning supplies in bulk. The others were planning to make emergency savings or service part of the loans obtained for investment. Although the majority were able to realise their plans, the capacity of their *gün* savings to generate income, promote asset accumulation or provide future security was highly restricted for two reasons. First, the size of savings obtained from a single round was often very small, as compared with the amount of debts incurred on large-scale assets. Second, most members were unable to sustain membership beyond the first round due to income constraints such as precarious or seasonal work conditions which appear to have been worsened by the economic crisis in 2001 (For an extended analysis of *gün*s organised by poor households see Eroğlu 2010a).

Turning to explore insurance contributions, only those paid to the state schemes were in evidence. As shown in Chapter 5, 35 per cent (6 out of 17) of male partners had active membership with a social insurance scheme. Five of them made contributions through work with a percentage paid towards them by the employer, whereas the sixth one, who was an optional scheme member, received no contribution from an employer. This scheme was also open to the remaining 11 men with a dormant social insurance registration but none of them were able to afford the monthly premiums. As mentioned before, access to a state pension was dependent on upon age, year of registration, and premium contributions to date. According to these requirements, only 35 per cent (6 out of 17) had high pension prospects; 18 per cent had moderate and 47 per cent had a low chance of having a pension in the future. The premiums men accumulated to date offered no opportunity for income generation. Neither did they have a significant scope for asset accumulation given their limited size (see Chapter 5). Moreover, the conditions applied to these schemes made the option to cash in past premiums unrealistic. Also, the majority of male partners appeared rather uninterested in this option with the hope of making future contributions through employment. However, given the severe violation of workers' rights in the labour market, their expectations are rather unlikely to come true. It is thus clear that insurance type of assets proved beneficial only for the minority.

Overall, the last two sections have provided an evaluation of the household asset portfolios households. Through this evaluation, it was shown that most of the observed assets had a rather limited capacity to promote asset accumulation, income generation and/or provide a safety net for the future. Nonetheless, a legally owned *gecekondu* and contributions to a social insurance scheme are shown to offer significant benefits to their owners. However, such assets were available only to a small number of households.

*The Use of Resources in Asset Acquisition*

This section seeks to examine the role of resources mobilised for asset acquisition in household success. The analysis once again revolves around the question of whether it is the range or type of resources used is more crucial for success. It is shown here that the latter is of greater significance.

In building their current asset portfolio, the respondent households were found to use three main types of resources. These include economic capital (i.e. income, financial and non-financial assets), social capital and institutional entitlements. The analysis below focuses on the last two resources so as to understand the degree to which they were effective in removing the pressure on income and/ or existing assets. All households made use of their social capital in one way or another. However, as far as current entitlements were concerned, the proportion of households fell to 65 per cent (11 out of 17), of which 42 per cent (7 out of 11) had entitlements to a *gecekondu* house or urban/semi-urban land (re)development; 42 per cent (7 out of 11) had labour-based entitlements; and 6 per cent (1 out of 11) had entitlements to formal credit.

Did the range of resources used in asset acquisition affect household success? To answer this, firstly, household resource diversification levels were determined by summing up the number of resources mobilised in the process. Here, the types of entitlements outlined above were treated as separate resource categories. Figure 6.2 shows the distribution of resource diversification scores across the sample [mean = 2; std. deviation = 0.94]. According to this figure, 35 per cent (6 out of 17) relied on a single resource, another 35 per cent (6 out of 17) on two resources; 24 per cent (4 out of 17) on three, and finally, 6 per cent (1 out of 17) employed four different types of resources in building their asset portfolios.

*Beyond the Resources of Poverty*

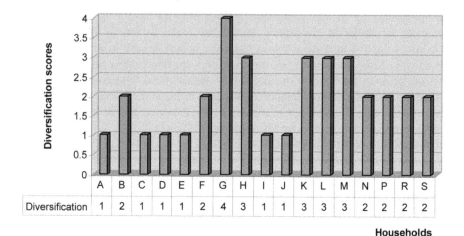

**Households**

**Figure 6.2    April distribution of household resource diversification levels in asset acquisition**

Secondly, the FWID was modified to exclude the following items in order to increase its sensitivity to the effects of asset acquisition: income/work hours, household social insurance ratio and mean household occupational risk grades. The scores obtained from the modified index are presented in Figure 6.3.

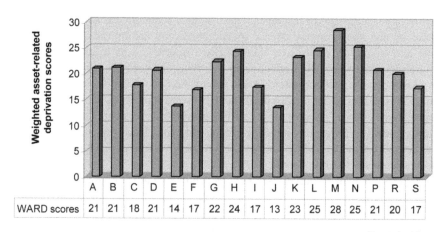

**Households**

**Figure 6.3    April distribution of asset-related deprivation levels**

The above variables were then subjected to a Pearson correlation test to assess whether deprivation levels varied significantly according to the range of resources used in asset acquisition. The test results were indicative of a very strong positive relationship [$r = 0.68$; $p < 0.01$]. This implies that those who deployed a broader range of resources proved more successful – a result which seems to negate my hypothesis. However, before concluding the discussion, attention needs to be drawn to the results from the second Pearson correlation test performed, this time using a dichotomous variable where households were grouped according to whether or not they employed any form of entitlements in building their asset portfolio. The results proved very interesting not only because of their level of significance, but also because of their closeness to the previous ones [$r = 0.59$; $p < 0.05$]. From these results, it appears that greater levels of success were associated with the use of a particular resource type, i.e. institutional entitlements. This lends support to my overall argument that the benefit delivery capacity of mobilised resources matters more to success than the range.

Consequently, institutional entitlements appear to have had a greater capacity to promote asset accumulation. The following sections explore in what ways institutional entitlements proved more beneficial than social capital, starting with an analysis of the particular role played by the latter.

*The role of social capital in asset acquisition* The households studied were found to use their social capital resources in a variety of ways: For 65 per cent (11 out of 17), they proved useful in the direct supply of the asset (e.g. through inheritance), for 53 per cent (9 out of 17) in the organisation of *güns*, for 47 per cent (8 out of 17) in access to information on asset availability and conditions of purchase, for 41 per cent (7 out of 17) in the supply of loans, for 24 per cent (4 out 17) in the provision of labour and material support for the actual making of the asset (e.g. *gecekondu*), and finally, for 12 per cent (2 out of 17) in the supply of monetary gifts towards an asset.

Despite the variety of their contributions to asset acquisition, social capital resources were of limited help in the following respects. Potentially, the process of asset acquisition can pressure households to create an income surplus and/or cash in their existing assets. Such pressure is most likely to be eliminated or considerably reduced when assets are supplied for free, or when monetary contributions are made towards their purchase. A large number of the sample households were indeed supplied assets mostly passed on through inheritance. However, the majority of assets obtained in this way consisted of rural land, to which 56 per cent of the spouses attached little value in terms of reducing deprivation. This is no surprise given the lack of demand for this type of land and its limited potential for profit (see also above). Only 12 per cent (2 out of 17) were directly supplied assets of considerable value. One of these households inherited four work stands and a truck from the father of the male spouse, and the other bought a semi-urban rural land from a relative well below the market price.

Likewise, the percentage of households which were given monetary gifts was restricted to 12 per cent (2 out of 4). The assets bought in this way were comprised of *gecekondu*s located in either part of the *mahalle*, and hence were of variable but significant value. Thus, only the social capital resources of a minority provided an opportunity to obtain beneficial assets without putting income or assets under significant pressure.

The other observed uses of social capital seem to offer less of an opportunity, despite their frequent occurrence. This can be illustrated by two common uses relating to *gün* organisation and informal borrowing. Social capital resources were frequently used in setting up neighbourhood-based *gün*s, which disciplined their members into making regular savings. However, member households still had to bear the brunt of having to create an income surplus for *gün* payments. Moreover, as shown earlier, the savings made through *gün* participation were of limited size.

Social capital resources were also used widely to obtain loans for an asset. As a matter of fact, 86 per cent of the households (6 out of 7) which still had asset-related debts in April borrowed the money from their relatives, neighbours and friends. Most of these debts were considerable in size, ranging from US$201 to US$4191 (i.e. 268 million to 5.6 billion old Turkish Liras). The mean asset-related debts were US$1647 (i.e. 2.2 billion old Turkish Liras), amounting to six times the mean household income for April.

It might be true that social capital made asset ownership possible for those denied access to formal credit institutions due to factors affecting their credit rating (e.g. limited/irregular income), and for those who avoided them, fearing that their earnings might not allow them to keep up with the repayments. As a matter of fact, only two households where both male partners worked as a civil servant had access to formal credit. However, social capital borrowing tended to leave households with a considerable pressure to make the necessary repayments. Social capital might have been of some help in spreading the pressure over time but it appears from the agreed repayment schedules that households were not necessarily given the flexibility they required. This may explain why some had to resort to what I call 'debt chaining'. This response involved borrowing from one contact in order pay the debts to a previous contact. Debt chaining is a rather ineffective way of managing debts because the debts essentially remain unpaid. There were also limits to this activity due to concerns over the creditworthiness of poor households in the eyes of their social contacts (see also Chapter 5).

Overall, despite being used extensively in asset acquisition, social capital resources of the majority neither had a capacity to provide access to 'beneficial assets' nor to remove pressure on income and/or existing assets.

*The role of entitlements in asset acquisition*    By contrast, some of the institutional entitlements used in asset acquisition tended to be fruitful in either respects. In terms of allowing access to beneficial assets, rights to *gecekondu* redevelopment and labour-based entitlements proved most helpful. However, only 18 per cent (3 out of 17) were covered by the *Gecekondu* Redevelopment Law No. 2981. Should the area be transformed according to the current amelioration plan, these households would be able to obtain 2 to 2.5 flats. Further 18 per cent (3 out 17) had entitlements to land development, allowing their claimants to build a self-help house in a semi-urban location. Thus, as compared with entitlements to *gecekondu* redevelopment, their potential to deliver valuable assets was restricted.

Besides, 65 per cent (11 out of 17) used to have entitlements to co-operative housing development on cheap land allocated in accordance with the *Gecekondu* Law No. 775. Yet, none of them managed to convert this right into a housing asset. The majority sold their rights to third parties early in the development. The main reason for drop-out was the failure to afford the ever increasing monthly instalments. Two households were an exception to this rule; one of them left due to their son's suicide and the other due to disbelief in the future of the co-operative. Moreover, the majority failed to make significant gains from the right transfers as they used the money to clear their arrears; only 27 per cent (3 out of 11) were able to sustain their membership longer than others and hence to obtain higher returns from the transaction.

Similarly, labour-based entitlements had the potential to deliver beneficial assets as they enhanced their claimants' chances of obtaining a state pension. However, only 29 per cent of the male partners (5 out of 17) had high pension prospects.

The same types of entitlements also proved beneficial in terms of removing pressure on income and/or existing assets. Those with rights to *gecekondu* redevelopment were in fact struggling to make the four monthly payments for their legal title deeds which in total amounted to two or three billion TL. However, the size of payments was rather negligible as compared to the potential value of the assets to which they became entitled. In contrast, those with former entitlements to co-operative housing development had to pay a much higher amount towards a flat. Faced by greater income pressure, all eligible households from the sample eventually lost their rights. The same could happen to the owners of unauthorised *gecekondu*s in Southern Ege if given the right to buy a flat in the new blocks.

Labour-based entitlements, which were found to release considerable income pressure, were of two types. One concerns rights to redundancy pay. Across the sample, 24 per cent (4 out of 17) had assets, a sizeable portion of which was drawn from this payment. The other relates to social security membership which enabled access to welfare benefits on the condition that 14.5 per cent of the premiums were paid by the employee and the remaining 20.5 per cent by the employer. This meant reduced income pressure on the part of the employee. The above condition was however inapplicable to members of the optional scheme. Given that only 10 per cent of eligible men (1 out of 10) had membership, the majority were unable to cope with the pressure to pay the premiums. Finally, a number of households were found to use formal credit entitlements to purchase assets. However, for reasons discussed earlier in relation to social capital borrowings, this type of entitlements had little capacity to reduce income pressure.

Consequently, the rights to *gecekondu* redevelopment and labour-based entitlements were found to comprise the most beneficial resources given their capacity a) to allow access to more valuable assets and b) to bring relief to income and/or existing assets. Ultimately, the former was a product of the policy decision to authorise and redevelop the *gecekondu* stock built before 1985. Likewise, as shown earlier, access to the latter entitlements is highly contingent on employer behaviour. It can hence be concluded that structural forces were a significant determinant of household success in reducing deprivation by investment practices.

## *Gecekondu Acquisition and Clientelism*

This section focuses on the process of *gecekondu* acquisition to assess validity of findings from a recent Turkish poverty study and to explore the role of clientelist relationships in this particular process.

The poverty research concerned was conducted by Işık and Pınarcıoğlu (2001) in Sultanbeyli, an atypical *gecekondu* settlement in İstanbul, predominantly occupied by fundamentalist Islamic groups (see also Pınarcıoğlu and Işık 2001). I have the following reservations against the theoretical underpinnings of this work. First of all, the study reduces so-called survival strategies to housing market processes. Secondly, it construes *gecekondu* acquisition as a strategic act poor households devise to move out of poverty. I consider such conception to be simplistic in that it overlooks the differences between *gecekondu* owner-occupiers in access to *gecekondu* redevelopment rights and their divergent outcomes for success in reducing poverty. Given the greater chance of success by right-holders than occupants with no rights, the actions of occupants who bought or built their *gecekondu*s prior to the enactment of the law authorising the stock built prior to 1985 cannot be seen as a strategic move to escape poverty since they are unlikely to have considered the possibility of future redevelopment rights. These dwellers were more likely to have acquired a *gecekondu* to meet an immediate need for shelter. However, the actions of the following overlapping groups might be of strategic value: a) those who built more than one *gecekondu* with plans to rent them out, b) those who built *gecekondu*s after the enactment of the redevelopment law, hoping that another amnesty could be granted in the future, and c) those who bought a *gecekondu*(s) from the authorised stock. The study by Işık and Pınarcıoğlu, however, fails to reflect such complexity in the housing behaviour of *gecekondu* dwellers.

The empirical part of this study drew attention to two main influences on poverty. The first concerns the migration behaviour of the urban poor. The study reveals that early migrants were better off than the late comers as they took more opportunities in the *gecekondu* housing and land market. This conclusion was inferred from a bi-variate correlation between migration year and a poverty index containing the measures of housing, urban land, and a set of household items. The results from this correlation indicated increased poverty among those who migrated in and after the period of 1983–1988.

To examine this hypothesis against my own data, I categorised male partners according to their year of migration, using 1983 as a cut-off point. This grouping revealed that 71 per cent of male partners (12 out of 17) moved to Ankara in or before 1983. The dichotomous variable of male migration year was then subjected to a Pearson correlation test with a) the weighted aggregate deprivation scores and b) a composite weighted variable including the measures of *gecekondu*, urban plot and second urban/semi-urban house ownership. The test results revealed no significant difference between the deprivation levels of earlier and later migrants [r (a) = −0.10, r (b) = 0.14]. This can also be seen from Table 6.7, which demonstrates equal distribution of pre-1983 male migrants across the three deprivation groups. The table also indicates that 41 per cent (4 out of 12) of those who migrated in or before 1983, and 40 per cent (2 out of 5) of post-1983 migrants remained within the worse off category.

Table 6.7    Year of male migration by deprivation category

| Year of migration | Deprivation category | | | Total |
| --- | --- | --- | --- | --- |
| | Worse off | Moderate | Better off | |
| 1983 or before | 4 | 4 | 4 | 12 |
| Post-1983 | 2 | 1 | 2 | 5 |
| Total | 6 | 5 | 6 | 17 |

The above results are hence incompatible with the idea that early migrants are more successful due the abundance of opportunities present in the *gecekondu* market at the time of their arrival. I believe these results to be of some significance because, unlike the work of Işık and Pınarcıoğlu (2001), the study sought to reflect the typical characteristics of the *gecekondu* population. However, it should be kept in mind that a) the sample was drawn from a much smaller population, and b) the selected households fell below a certain income threshold. Moreover, from the tenure types and the ways in which *gecekondu*s were obtained across the sample, it appears that some past or current *gecekondu* house/land owners have generated an income and/or made speculative profits e.g. by renting out their (additional) *gecekondu*s, parcelling out the land illegally for sale, or selling their (additional) ready-built *gecekondu*s. The decision to select households below a certain income level might have excluded those who benefited from these processes most.

Hence, it remains possible that some households succeeded in moving out of poverty through urban land speculation. Their early migration to the city might have helped with this. However, in my view, what matters more to success is whether they were able to join the process of *gecekondu* acquisition prior to 1985. This is so because the benefit delivery capacity of an authorised *gecekondu* is incomparably higher provided that the land is of a considerable size and located in a rentable part of the city. The majority of the sample households failed to join this process in time despite having migrated to the city earlier. Some of the reasons for this include a) lack of economic capital to purchase land or ready-made *gecekondu* from the legal stock, b) lack of information regarding the legal status of the land occupied, and c) urgent need for sheltering a newly formed or moved family.

However, their current lack of access to *gecekondu* redevelopment does not mean that this channel is forever closed to the illegal occupiers. This leads us to another shortcoming of Işık and Pınarcıoğlu's study. The researchers anticipate that latecomers are not presented with the same opportunities as the new comers to move out of poverty since there is no further land to be occupied and therefore we should expect to see the emergence of Turkish underclass. The possibility for large-scale urban land speculation might have diminished, but nevertheless I very much doubt that there exists a real land scarcity. I also believe their quick conclusion is rather blind to the future opportunities clientelist party politics can provide for current and perhaps future illegal occupiers. As a matter of fact, the fourth article of a recent draft proposal which suggests the sale of treasury land within the boundaries of the municipality primarily to their occupiers indicates that a new amnesty is not improbable.[3]

The second influence emphasised by Işık and Pınarcıoğlu (2001) relates to the clientelist relationships existing within the *Sünni cemaat* (community). The researchers claim that these relationships play a significant role in *gecekondu* acquisition and are in turn reflected in the distribution of poverty. The poverty distribution presented in this study draws on a three layer pyramid, denoting differences in terms of access to urban housing, land and a set of household items. However, the study provides no substantial evidence to prove the connection between the pyramid and the political activism of *Sünni cemaat* in Sultanbeyli. It uses the hometown of *gecekondu* dwellers as an indication of clientelist activity, which, in my view, lacks validity. Moreover, it fails to explain how clientelism impacted upon *gecekondu* acquisition in the area. For these reasons, their claim as to the significance of clientelism, in my view, remains unsubstantiated and hence rather speculative.

However, this is not to suggest that clientelism plays no part in *gecekondu* processes. From my findings, it appears that clientelist relationships tended not to occur during the actual acquisition of the *gecekondu* house or land as this was rather based on an informal market exchange. These relationships seem to come into play at the stages of *gecekondu* legalisation and in the granting of (re) development rights. There is no evidence to confirm that the owners of authorised *gecekondu*s within the sample voted or promised to vote for the party of the time which proposed to legalise the *gecekondu* stock. Regardless of whether they were actively involved or not, these households benefited from the clientelist party politics aimed at winning over *gecekondu* votes in the 1980s (Buğra 1998).

Conversely, the illegal occupiers of Northern Ege *gecekondu*s appear to have actively engaged in clientelist relationships. The occupiers were predominantly *Alevi* by background, as was the mayor of Mamak District who was in power at the time. Faced with pressure from those affected by the evacuation decision, the mayor took steps to obtain an allocation of cheap land. The elected board of the

---

3   For detailed information on this see Chamber of City Planners of Turkey (2003).

Ege-Mutlu Housing Co-operative was then given the administrative responsibility for land development.

The housing co-operative, however, proved to be a failure. At the time of field research, the apartment blocks had not yet been completed despite the seven years since the start of construction. Moreover, the promise to produce low-cost housing remained unmet. Some of the respondents provided interesting accounts regarding the fraudulent activity on the part of the administrative board. One of them pointed to the sudden change in the wealth of board members and their close relatives. Board members were claimed to make their monthly payments from the interest accrued on the payments of other co-operative members, as well as the commission they sought from the subcontracts granted to construction companies. The same issue was raised also by another respondent who claimed to have discovered their fraudulent activities in a one-to one conversation. While the board members found secure ways of making monthly payments, which had increased 80 times in nominal value since the construction launched in 1995, the low-income groups found it very difficult to maintain their membership. All cooperative members in the sample dropped out at different stages of the construction, selling their rights to third parties. This was indeed a common occurrence. By the end of seven years, the portion of co-operative members liable to evacuation declined from 344 to 161. The failure of the housing project seems to have led the clientelist relationships between the mayor and the *Alevi* occupants to unravel. Some of the respondent households reported that nobody in the area voted for the mayor in the next elections. Mamak is a district where local politics is sensitive to slight changes in the voting behaviour of *Alevi* and *Sünni* groups since the district population is rather equally distributed between them. The resentment of 344 *gecekondu*s, or roughly 750 votes, might well have tipped the power balances against the mayor, contributing to his party losing the next election.

To conclude, it was shown here that asset ownership may not guarantee success as it all depends on the benefit delivery capacity of the assets possessed. The majority of households were found to own assets with a limited capacity to ensure a) further asset formation, b) income generation and/or c) future financial security. The claimants of rights to *gecekondu* redevelopment and labour-based entitlements were considered successful as these resources had a significant capacity to a) provide access to beneficial assets and b) release some pressure on income and/or existing assets. On the other hand, despite their widespread use in asset acquisition, social capital resources were found to have a limited benefit delivery capacity. Finally, it was shown that what matters to success more than the migration year is whether *gecekondu* occupants have entitlements to redevelopment. It was then argued that policies devised in the 1980s with clientelist intentions paved the way for some *gecekondu* owners to enjoy speculative profits. Such clientelist channels still seem to operate in *gecekondu* areas. These channels might now be accessible to a smaller population than they did in the 1980s and deliver benefits restricted in capacity, but one of their characteristics appears unchanged; they continue to create their own winners and losers.

## Consumption and Borrowing

This part of the chapter seeks to explore household success in reducing deprivation by consumption behaviour with a particular emphasis on legal and illegal practices whereby households obtain free or subsidised access to goods and services – i.e. activities extending from non-to-semi-commodified areas of consumption. Commodified aspects of consumption are excluded because, as discussed earlier, they are least likely to counteract income shortfalls without inducing deprivation.

### Non-and-semi-commodified Consumption

This section starts with a description of non-and-semi-commodified consumption practices observed in selected areas of expenditure. In the area of food, all households had different ways of obtaining food for free, which included borrowing, collecting certain plants and receiving support from formal and informal sources. The scope for food support was however rather restricted. For example, 29 per cent (5 out of 17) obtained municipal aid delivering 52 kg worth food staples on more or less a six month basis, with no guarantee for the next round, and 59 per cent (10 out of 17) had food sent over from their villages. However, the amount of support received was significant only for four households. The figures may be indicative of a drastic decline in a source of support that previously brought significant relief to household income. This is evident from the account of 51 year-old female interviewee:

> Interviewer:    Has anyone provided you with food support lately?
> KX:             We borrow and lend; other than this no… Obviously, we give it back when we borrow. But in the past we used to say 'just take it' but not anymore… I can't resent anyone; everybody is like how I am. Also the *gecekondu* environment is a poor environment. […] We're all the same; people frying by their own oil [just about to look after themselves], what can you expect from others? You can borrow and lend only. There's now no one who'd say 'I'll give a plate from the food my husband brought from village'.
> Interviewer:    How was it in the past then?
> KX:             We used to be so different towards each other; I used to go to the village to bring some; the other also goes and brings some; we would it give it to each other; we wouldn't know what borrowing did mean. […]
> Interviewer:    So you mean there used to be a lot more [food] coming from the village?
> KX:             It used to be a lot. Now, the villages stopped it. Had we ever used to pay for the bulgur wheat in the past? We used to go to the village to make and bring some. Not any longer though.

> There are some who still do; those who are deeply rooted in
> their village; those with mothers and very close relatives in the
> village. Since we don't have any, who would do it for us?

Concerning free state-run healthcare, both within and between household differences were discernible with respect to access to hospital treatment, type of hospital and hence the quality of service being received. This was also true for state-subsidised medicine. In 76 per cent of households (13 out of 17), at least one member benefited from free hospital treatment, whereas in 47 per cent (8 out of 17), all members were entitled to such service. As far as access to subsidised medicine is concerned, the respective percentages fell to 53 per cent (9 out of 17) and 24 per cent (4 out of 17). Among those with partial or no access to state healthcare, 54 per cent (6 out of 11) obtained free medicine either from social contacts or charitable organisations. However, in all but one household where the male child who worked as an apprentice in a pharmacy made use of the social insurance entitlements of his clients, the use of social or charitable contacts provided only limited and irregular access to free medicine.

In the area of education, 59 per cent (10 out of 17) were exempt from the term-based contributory fees for one of their children; yet some managed to avoid also paying for the second. At the start of the new school year, five households obtained 30 million TL and some stationery as part of World Bank aid distributed via school administrations. Only 23 per cent (4 out of 17) had at least one member attending free training courses in sports, literacy, university exam preparation etc. In the area of housing, 88 per cent (15 out of 17) had rent-free *gecekondu* accommodation. The rest were tenants also in *gecekondu* type housing. With regard to utilities including electricity, telephone, water and fuel, 88 per cent (15 out of 17) had free access to at least one of these utilities; 23 per cent (4 out of 17) illegally used electricity; 82 per cent (14 out of 17) had access to wood and 29 per cent (5 out of 17) to coal free of charge. Regarding house repairs, 12 per cent (2 out of 17) had free access to some construction material through their work. As for household items, 94 per cent (16 out of 17) acquired some of the items for free; but the number of items obtained in this way varied across the sample. With regards to transportation, 82 per cent (12 out of 17) had free or subsidised access to public and/or private transport facilities; yet there were variations within each household. Among them, at least one member was entitled to travel at a 33 per cent discount price due to being disabled or a student. In 23 per cent (4 out of 17), at least one working member was entitled to bus service provided by their workplace. Only in 12 per cent (2 out of 17) did at least one member benefit from free private arrangements (e.g. lift). As for clothing, 76 per cent (13 out of 17) had some free access to first or second hand clothes and occasionally to knitting material.

In exploring the poverty outcomes of the above practices, firstly, the number of expenditure areas in which households had free/subsidised access to goods and services were counted to determine the household non/semi-commodification levels presented in Figure 6.4 [mean = 6.71; std. deviation = 1.16].

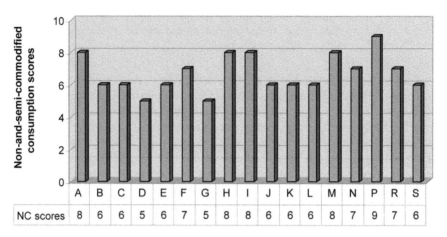

**Figure 6.4**    **April   distribution   of   household   non/semi-commodified**
**consumption levels**

Secondly, the FWID was modified to exclude the following items in order to increase its sensitivity to the effects of consumption behaviour: mean household income/work ratio, mean household social insurance ratio, pension prospects and mean occupational risk grades. The weighted consumption-related deprivation scores obtained from the modified index are presented in Figure 6.5.

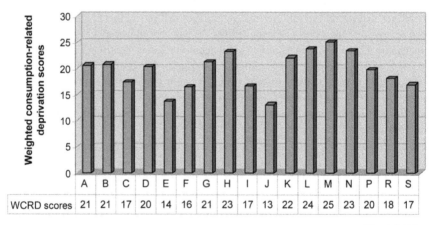

**Figure 6.5**    **April   distribution   of   household   consumption-related**
**deprivation levels**

The two variables were then subjected to a Pearson correlation test in order to investigate whether household deprivation levels varied significantly according to the degree of non/semi-commodified consumption. The results revealed a weak association [$r = 0.19$]. In interpreting these results, it should be kept in mind that the level of detail presented here neither reflects intra-household variation within each area of expenditure nor takes into account the value of the practices involved. It may nevertheless be suggested that greater involvement in these spheres of consumption does not necessarily bring success.

*The Use of Resources in Non-and-semi-commodified Consumption*

This section explores the type of resources used in non-and-semi-commodified consumption in order to understand their implications for deprivation. The resource type is crucial for our analysis since the benefit delivery capacity of the resources deployed in the process is likely vary between households. Table 6.8 demonstrates the type of resources which directly or indirectly enabled access to free/subsidised goods and services in nine selected areas of expenditure.

**Table 6.8    Distribution of mobilised resources across selected areas of expenditure**

| Expenditure areas | Resource Types[*] | | | | |
| --- | --- | --- | --- | --- | --- |
| | Institutional entitlements | Social capital | Transient contacts | Public resources[†] | Cultural capital |
| Food | 7 | 14 | 2 | 6 | – |
| Clothing | – | 13 | 1 | – | – |
| Health | 12 | 5 | 2 | – | 3 |
| Education | 10 | 7 | 1 | – | – |
| Housing | 3 | 1 | – | 12 | – |
| Utilities | 2 | 9 | 3 | 10 | – |
| Household items | 4 | 13 | 3 | – | – |
| House repairs | – | 2 | – | – | – |
| Transportation | 13 | 2 | – | – | – |

*Notes*: [*]Labour and skills kind of resources used in self-provisioning are excluded from the analysis as they were accessible to all households in one way or another. [†]There is some ambiguity concerning the ownership of the populare trees used by the households to produce logs for winter. Here they were considered as publicly owned natural resources.

The case studies shed light on how these resources were mobilised for non-and-semi-commodified consumption. In what follows, the poverty effects of the range of resources used for such purposes are examined based on the following method designed to determine the levels of resource diversification. One point was given to each resource which directly or indirectly a) enabled access to free and/or subsidised goods and services or b) gave households the right to use them. In cases where more than one resource was mobilised to obtain a single item or service, only those considered equally significant were given a separate score. For instance, if a household gained access to subsidised medicine using other people's entitlements to social insurance, one point was given for the use of social capital and another for cultural capital (i.e. hustling skills).

In addition, some of the resource types and expenditure areas were further differentiated to capture as much detail as possible. The resource types subjected to this treatment concern institutional entitlements and those allowing free access to goods and services. For example, instead of using a broad category of 'educational entitlements' and giving it a score of one, entitlements were divided into sub-categories of educational aid, contributory fee reductions etc., and then each eligible household member was scored individually. For instance, if only two members benefited from free state-run healthcare, their hospital treatment score was calculated as two. Likewise, the following expenditure areas were either itemised or divided into sub-categories: a) food (urban and rural food support), b) health (hospital treatment and medicine), c) selected household items, and finally, d) utilities (e.g. electricity and fuel). The resource(s) used in each area were scored separately. The scores obtained in this way are presented in Figure 6.6 [mean = 15.77; std. deviation = 4.82].

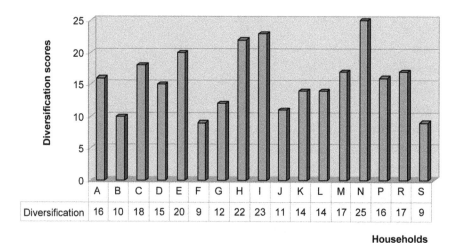

| Diversification | 16 | 10 | 18 | 15 | 20 | 9 | 12 | 22 | 23 | 11 | 14 | 14 | 17 | 25 | 16 | 17 | 9 |

**Households**

**Figure 6.6    April distribution of household resource diversification levels in non/semi-commodified consumption**

In order to see whether the range of resources mobilised for non-and-semi-commodified consumption had a significant effect on household success, the resource diversification scores were subjected to a Pearson correlation test with the modified deprivation scores (see Figure 6.5). The results were indicative of a weak association [r = 0.21]. Before interpreting the test result, let us have a look at the mean diversification scores for each deprivation group [mean (worse off) = 15; mean (moderately deprived) = 14.8; mean (better off) = 17.3]. The mean scores revealed a higher level of resource use by better off households, which could explain their marginally greater achievements in non/semi-commodified consumption. However, the differences between deprivation groups appear rather weak to conclude that the range of resources made a significant difference to household success.

Their limited contribution is also apparent from the outstanding debts households incurred to meet their consumption needs by April. Figure 6.7 demonstrates the amount of consumption-related debts created [mean = 418.12 million TL; std. deviation = 332.36].[4] Most of these loans were borrowed from social contacts; there were in fact only two households which used a credit card for consumption purposes.

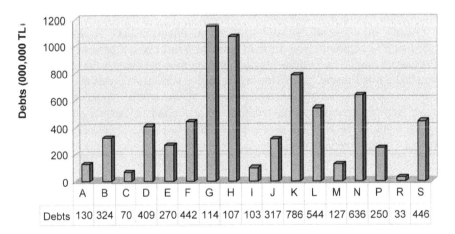

| Debts | 130 | 324 | 70 | 409 | 270 | 442 | 114 | 107 | 103 | 317 | 786 | 544 | 127 | 636 | 250 | 33 | 446 |

**Households**

**Figure 6.7    April distribution of household consumption-related debts**

The debt scores were subjected to two subsequent Pearson tests in order to explore whether they varied according to the levels of a) non/semi-commodified

4    The outstanding consumption-related debts that belonged to Household E amounted to a total of 2,843 million TL. However, approximately 90 per cent of these debts were created by their son's 'friends' who used his credit card and disappeared without paying, and hence were excluded from the analysis of consumption.

consumption and b) resource diversification. The results from the first analysis indicated a fairly weak inverse correlation [r (a) = − 0.30]. This might mean that those with greater involvement in non/semi-commodified consumption were slightly less in need of borrowing to counteract their income deficit. However, given the weak nature of the relationship, I am rather inclined to conclude that such practices were of little value in terms of reducing the need for commodified consumption and hence borrowing. Yet, I am aware that the results may have been affected by a) the limited level of detail presented here, b) differences in household incomes and c) the types of commodified practices undertaken. For instance, the practices of using cheap purchasing methods, cutting down on or going without certain goods and services could well have contributed to keeping debts at a low level.

The second analysis revealed a very weak inverse relationship between the size of outstanding debts and the range of resources used for non/semi-commodified consumption [r (b) = −0.06]. It may follow from this that most of these resources were rather unbeneficial in terms of lifting income pressure. The types of beneficial resources are explored later in the case studies. However, in brief, they were found to include public land and labour-based entitlements, which brought sizeable as well as consistent income relief by allowing access to rent-free accommodation, free hospital treatment and subsidised medicine.

Overall, the observed non-and-semi-commodified practices of consumption were found to contribute very little to household success, not because the range of resources mobilised for these practices was narrow, but because the majority of them had a low capacity to provide access to free/subsidised goods and services, and/or to remove substantial income pressure. However, these conclusions were drawn from an analysis which remains rather limited in capturing the extent and the value of the practices concerned. Further research is therefore needed to provide a higher level of detail.

## Conclusion

This chapter has sought to examine the determinants of household success by income allocation, investment and consumption behaviour, and revealed results congruent with my hypotheses. By the analysis of income allocation behaviour, it was shown that how income is managed or controlled within the household had a little bearing on overall household deprivation. This was explained by the general tendency for both spouses to display concern for the collective good when allocating income between different areas of household and personal spending. The analysis thus lends some support to the idea that households can act collectively at times of hardship. It was also shown that women tend to keep secret kitties to counteract male financial authority without inducing 'secondary poverty'.

The analysis of investment behaviour revealed a tendency for households to own assets with a low capacity to a) promote asset accumulation, b) generate income, and/or c) ensure future security. Among the main resource types used in asset acquisition, institutional entitlements tended to have a greater capacity than social capital to allow access to beneficial assets and reduce pressure on income and/or existing assets. Of particular significance were rights to *gecekondu* development and labour-based entitlements access to both of which were structurally determined. It was hence argued that structural factors such as housing policy and labour market conditions are likely to determine who fails or succeeds in the making of an asset portfolio.

The final analysis focused on consumption practices which allowed access to free/subsidised goods and services. Success in reducing deprivation was claimed to depend on the type rather than the range of resources used in these practices. The beneficial resource types are explored in detail by the case studies, following the analysis of short-term change presented in the next chapter.

# Chapter 7

# Understanding Short-term
# Change in Deprivation

The data at one point in time does not reveal whether the sample households were experiencing short or long spells of poverty. This chapter seeks to explore this through a focus on short-term change in deprivation between the April and October interviews. The chapter starts with a depiction of the change trends, followed by a further examination of the possible causes of household success or failure in reducing deprivation.

## Describing Change in Deprivation

The changes in household deprivation observed over the six months varied both in degree and direction. This is evident from Figure 7.1, displaying the weighted aggregate change scores[1] [mean = 0.55, std. deviation = 1.48].

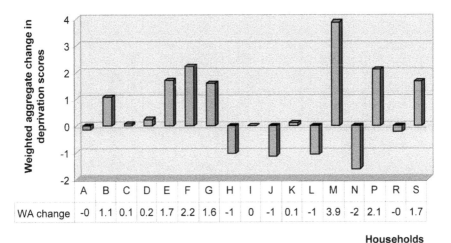

| | A | B | C | D | E | F | G | H | I | J | K | L | M | N | P | R | S |
|---|---|---|---|---|---|---|---|---|---|---|---|---|---|---|---|---|---|
| WA change | -0 | 1.1 | 0.1 | 0.2 | 1.7 | 2.2 | 1.6 | -1 | 0 | -1 | 0.1 | -1 | 3.9 | -2 | 2.1 | -0 | 1.7 |

Households

**Figure 7.1**    **Change in household deprivation levels**

---

1    Refer to Appendix A for details regarding the calculation of weighted aggregate change in deprivation scores.

Three change groups appear to emerge from the aggregate scores: The first group (24 per cent) experienced negative change (Households H, J, L and N); the second group (35 per cent) had no change (Households A, C, D, I, K and R), and the last group (41 per cent) displayed positive change (Households B, E, F, G, M, P and S). In order to determine whether the change groups were significantly different from each other, a one-way ANOVA test was performed, comparing their means [mean (negative change) = $-1.22$ (0.27); mean (no change) = 0.00 (0.17); mean (positive change) = 2.04 (0.90)]. The results suggested a significant difference [$F (2, 14) = 40.45$; $p < 0.01$].

However, it cannot be inferred from this classification that those who displayed positive change succeeded in moving out of poverty. This leaves us with the question of whether the results were also significant in absolute terms. One way to identify those households which moved out of poverty was to use a cut-off point obtained from the weighted aggregate change scores as a threshold. However, this would increase the arbitrariness of the analysis. Hence, an alternative approach was taken here employing an externally defined income threshold; i.e. half of the TÜRK-İŞ poverty line. The threshold was used earlier in sample selection, but this time was readjusted to 536 million TL since between April and October the TÜRK-İŞ poverty line had risen from 987 to 1,072 million TL (Bağdadıoğlu 2002b, 2002c). Let us now examine the nominal household incomes in October presented in Figure 7.2 in order to see whether any of the respondents households were able to move out of poverty.

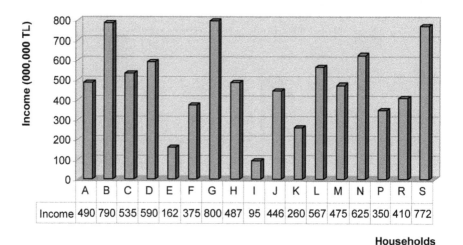

| | A | B | C | D | E | F | G | H | I | J | K | L | M | N | P | R | S |
|---|---|---|---|---|---|---|---|---|---|---|---|---|---|---|---|---|---|
| Income | 490 | 790 | 535 | 590 | 162 | 375 | 800 | 487 | 95 | 446 | 260 | 567 | 475 | 625 | 350 | 410 | 772 |

**Households**

**Figure 7.2    October distribution of household nominal incomes**

Across the sample, only 36 per cent (6 out of 17) had an income above 536 million TL, while 6 per cent (1 out of 17) remained on the borderline and the rest 58 per cent (10 out of 17) fell below the threshold. However, given the seasonal effects, not all households above the threshold can be assumed to have moved out of poverty on a permanent basis. Among those who were on or above the threshold, 57 per cent (4 out of 7) contained at least one seasonal worker, which could well mean that their movement out of poverty would be short-lived given the dramatic seasonal decline in the jobs available in the four or five months after October. There were only three households above the threshold, whose incomes were not severely exposed to seasonal effects. Yet we cannot presume that their achievements were of a permanent nature either. This was particularly true for Household L where the male partner's loss of job as a taxi driver was temporarily compensated by the additional job their son had taken until starting military service. Thus, for the majority of households, changes that had occurred in their deprivation within the six months period had little significance beyond being fluctuations around a poverty threshold.

In order to explore whether households who were better off in April improved their situation further, and those who were worse off became even worse, two bi-variate tests were conducted. Firstly, the weighted aggregate change scores were subjected to a Pearson correlation test with the weighted aggregate deprivation scores for April. To improve the consistency of measurement, the latter had to be recalculated, using interval data regrouped according to the cut off points obtained for merged April and October data (see also Appendix). The new scores are presented in Figure 7.3.

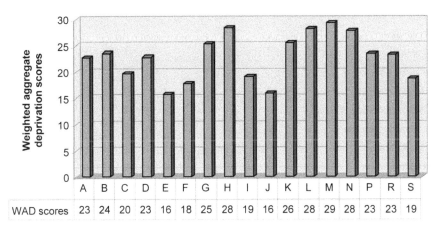

**Figure 7.3    April distribution of household deprivation levels (version 2)**

The results indicated no relationship between the two variables [r = −0.10]. The analysis was then repeated, applying a non-parametric correlation (Spearman) test between the change groups and the same deprivation scores. The results were indicative of a fairly weak relationship [r = −0. 26]. From these analyses, it appears that households which fared better in April were not necessarily more able to improve their situation over the six months. In fact, evidence of an inverse correlation seems to suggest a weak tendency of change against better off households. Consequently, the weakness of the association seems to imply that the respondent households operated on such slippery ground that any success was only temporary in nature.

Turning to describe the change trends according to the three dimensions of deprivation (i.e. monetary, consumption and work-related), the descriptions below are based on grouped data instead of actual interval data so as to keep this part of the analysis compatible with the rest, although this might disguise some of the sizeable changes. Table 7.1 sums up the course of change within each dimension.

**Table 7.1    Change trends within three dimensions of deprivation**

| Areas of deprivation | Direction of change | | |
|---|---|---|---|
| | Negative change | No change | Positive change |
| *Monetary* | | | |
| Disposable real household income | 2 | 7 | 8 |
| Housing tenure security | – | 17 | – |
| Urban plot ownership | – | 17 | – |
| Second urban house ownership | – | 17 | – |
| Real household savings | 1 | 13 | 3 |
| Real household debts | 2 | 13 | 2 |
| *Consumption* | | | |
| Furniture | – | 17 | – |
| Electrical appliances | 1 | 16 | – |
| Age of furniture | – | 17 | – |
| Age of electrical appliances | – | 17 | – |
| Optimum house size | – | 17 | – |
| Private bedroom | – | 17 | – |
| Utilities | – | 16 | 1 |
| Heating | 16 | 1 | – |
| Medicine | 2 | 13 | 2 |
| Quality of medical service | – | 16 | 1 |
| Children's school attendance | – | 16 | 1 |
| Monthly average meat consumption | 6 | 10 | 1 |
| Winter food stock | 6 | 7 | 4 |
| *Work* | | | |
| Household income/work hours | 2 | 10 | 5 |
| Household mean social insurance ratio | 1 | 11 | 5 |
| Pension prospects | – | 16 | 1 |
| Mean occupational risk grades | 5 | 10 | 2 |
| Weighted aggregate change | 4 | 6 | 7 |

In the field of monetary deprivation, 59 per cent (10 out of 17) experienced changes in their disposable real incomes to varying extents. 80 per cent of these households (8 out of 10) had an increase in real income, which seems not to result from a wage increase but from the seasonality factor. In contrast, no change was discernible in the non-financial asset portfolio of the households. None of the households bought or sold a house or plot between April and October. However, there were some changes in non-financial asset ownership, though not captured by the FWID. One of the households bought a car by using bank credit, and two households sold some or all of their work-related assets, either to pay back their debts or meet some of their consumption needs such as education. As opposed to stagnation in ownership of non-financial assets, certain changes took place in the financial asset portfolio of the households. Table 7.1 demonstrates that 18 per cent (3 out of 17) managed to increase their savings, whereas 6 per cent (1 out of 17) experienced a decline. However, the use of grouped data in measuring deprivation disguises the sizeable increases in the savings of those with the highest levels of savings in April. The actual values of April and October real savings are hence provided in Figure 7.4.

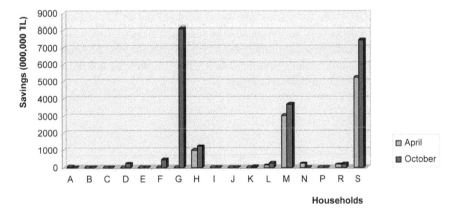

**Figure 7.4    April and October distribution of household savings**

The figure demonstrates that for 53 per cent (9 out of 17) the level of real savings was higher in October. The amount of increase was however significant only for 12 per cent (2 out of 17). These households had more than two billion TL worth increase in their real savings, which equals 4.6 times as much the mean October household real income, i.e. 439 million TL [std. deviation = 191 million TL]. Household G attained increased deposit savings after receipt of male partner's retirement gratuity. Household S, on the other hand, increased their deposit savings by putting aside a considerable portion of their seasonal earnings. There were two more households, i.e. Households H and M, with a deposit account. However, the amounts of increase in their real savings remained relatively small. The remaining five households had a small amount of home-savings in gold, foreign exchange or Turkish lira. Within the sample, the 35 per cent (6 out of 17) which experienced no change in their real savings were composed of those who had no savings in the first place. Evidently, the majority of households either had no or very limited savings on both occasions, although financial markets offered highly favourable investment opportunities. According to the official figures (TURKSTAT 2002d), the six monthly rate of real return between April and October was 10.6 per cent for deposit accounts; 11.8 per cent for US dollar; 23.9 per cent for Euro and 16.9 per cent for gold (ingot).

Such means of investment did indeed deliver favours to some who were able to find considerable amounts of money to invest; yet the majority of the respondent households were not among them. It appears that they were not only excluded from favourable investment opportunities, but also adversely affected by the conditions of the financial market given their tendency to accumulate debts in foreign exchange or gold. In April, all households had debts of varying sizes [mean April debts = 1,810 million TL (std. deviation = 1,626 million TL); median April debts = 1, 460 million TL] and 76 per cent (13 out of 17) owed money in the form of bank loan, foreign exchange or gold [mean April debts in given forms = 1,510 million TL (std. deviation = 1,678 million TL); median April debts in given forms = 597 million TL]. Evidently, the money borrowed in any of the above forms was of significant size. Table 7.1 shows that 76 per cent (13 out of 17) had no change in the amount of debts they accumulated between April and October, while 12 per cent (2 out of 17) cleared some of their debts and the rest accumulated more debts by October. The actual values presented in Figure 7.5 provide a more detailed picture of change in household debt levels.

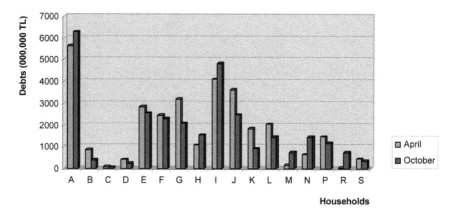

**Figure 7.5    April and October distribution household debts**

As can be seen from the figure, by October 59 per cent (10 out of 17) managed to reduce the level of their debts whereas the rest accumulated further debts. Although some were successful in managing their debts, 59 per cent (10 out of 17) still had a significant amount of unpaid debts, i.e. above one billion TL; that is,

2.3 times the mean household real income for October. Among them, 80 per cent (8 out of 10) owed money in the form of bank loan, foreign exchange or gold and 72 per cent (7 out of 10) avoided borrowing sizeable amounts after April. Therefore, it can be argued that as well as the factors constraining household incomes, the conditions of the financial market also appear responsible for the inability of households to clear their debts by October.

Within the field of consumption, there was very little change to the stock of household goods. With two exceptions[2], none of the households bought or sold any of the selected household items[3]. Likewise, their house size and private bedroom availability remained unchanged given that no one undertook large-scale extension tasks or moved house. In all but one household which obtained a private electricity account, access to utilities also remained the same. However, certain changes occurred in the area of heating. According to Table 7.1, 94 per cent (16 out of 17) experienced a decline mainly due to their failure to build up a coal stock for winter. The results may have been affected by the timing of the interviews; however, given the fact that coal prices increase towards winter, their inability to buy coal in advance, which they tended to prefer to do, meant paying more, doing with less or going without.

The area of health was also subject to a few changes, which particularly affected access to state-subsidised medicine. Table 7.1 demonstrates that in 12 per cent of the households (2 out of 17), some members lost access whereas another 12 per cent (2 out of 17) had improved access. These changes mainly resulted from household members' movement in and out of social insurance entitlements. For instance, while households with male children over 18 lost their son's right to subsidised medicine, the dependants of the male partners who uninterruptedly paid a premium for 120 days in a new job earned an entitlement. In the area of education, no change was discernible except in one household which managed to send their elder son to high school after a year's drop out. Finally, food was also one of the areas where significant changes took place. The monthly average meat consumption of 59 per cent (10 out of 17) remained unchanged, whereas 35 per cent (6 out of 17) cut down on their consumption considerably. As for winter food stock, 41 per cent (7 out of 17) made preparations of similar size and content in comparison to last year, while 35 per cent (6 out of 17) had to reduce their winter stock in size and/or content.

Finally, in the field of work, some of the observed changes appear positive in character. Table 7.1 shows that the mean hourly income increased for 29 per cent (5 out of 17) and remained the same for 59 per cent (10 out of 17). Likewise, 29 per cent (5 out of 17) had an increase in their mean social insurance ratio whereas the rest experienced no change. There was also very little change in men's pension prospects. With one exception, none of the households was able

---

2    The consumption behaviour of one of these households was not captured by the FWID due to the use of grouped data.

3    Refer to Table A.2 for the full list of the selected household items.

to enhance their likelihood of obtaining a pension in the future. Finally, mean occupational risks increased for 29 per cent (5 out of 17), but remained unchanged for 59 per cent (10 out of 17). One should, however, be careful in interpreting these results since the majority of measures used to assess working conditions were average household ratios. For this reason, not all positive change can be regarded as actual improvements in working conditions. Some of these changes are pseudo-improvements, for instance, resulting from household members with unfavourable working conditions leaving their jobs after April.

## Explaining Change in Deprivation

From the trends presented above, it appears that major changes in household deprivation are most likely to be associated with the behavioural areas of income generation, income allocation and consumption. Through a re-examination of household behaviour in April, this part of the chapter seeks to identify the correlates of the observed changes and thereby uncover some of the likely forces affecting success or failure.

### Income Generation and Change in Deprivation

By revisiting selected April variables, this section examines the degree to which income diversification levels and labour market influences on the supply and demand side help explain change in household deprivation.

In order to explore whether change levels were significantly affected by the degree of income diversification, a Pearson correlation test was performed between the income diversification (see Figure 5.3) and change scores (see Figure 7.1). The results indicated a moderate inverse relationship between the two variables [$r = -0.40$], implying that those with less diversified incomes are more likely to have improved their situation over the six months. This can also be seen from the cross-tabulation presented in Table 7.2.

**Table 7.2    Household income diversification level by change category**

| Income diversification | Change category | | | Total |
|---|---|---|---|---|
| | Negative change | No change | Positive change | |
| 1 (Lowest) | – | 1 | 2 | 3 |
| 2 | 2 | – | 3 | 5 |
| 3 | 2 | 4 | 1 | 7 |
| 4 (Highest) | – | 1 | 1 | 2 |
| Total | 4 | 6 | 7 | 17 |

Hence, both results seem supportive of my hypothesis that greater income diversification does not always equate with success, since what leads to success is not the range of resources used but whether they have the capacity to provide access to a sizeable income and decent working conditions. It may follow from this that households with a more diversified income may have failed to improve their situation because the resources they mobilised for income generation were of limited benefit delivery capacity.

So, which factors were influential in determining their capacity? In April analysis, labour power was found to comprise the most extensively used resource type. Therefore, the analysis below will have a labour market focus, exploring whether demand and supply side forces which were previously found to affect the benefit delivery capacity of labour resources were still relevant. Starting with the supply side influences, the analysis will examine the effects of a) household dependency ratio, b) formal cultural capital (FCC) accumulations and finally, c) volume of social capital.

In order to determine whether households with a greater number of workers fared better over the six months, a Pearson test was conducted between the household dependency ratios (see Figure 5.4) and change scores (see Figure 7.1). The results revealed a fairly weak relationship between the two variables [r = 0.32]. This is also evident from Table 7.3 where dependency ratios are cross-tabulated with change groups.

**Table 7.3    Household dependency ratio by change category**

| Dependency ratio | Change category | | | Total |
|---|---|---|---|---|
| | Negative change | No change | Positive change | |
| 0.33 | 1 | 1 | 1 | 3 |
| 1.00 | 3 | 3 | 4 | 10 |
| 3.00 | – | 2 | 2 | 4 |
| Total | 4 | 6 | 7 | 17 |

The association proved weak but stronger than it was in the April analysis, suggesting that those households with fewer dependants tended be rather more successful over the next six months. This difference is likely to have resulted from the changes in income levels as well as working conditions. However, it has to be borne in mind that some of the improvements in working conditions were pseudo in nature. Therefore, given the timing of research which coincided with the peak work season, it may be argued that having more workers is likely to have enabled the flow of more income into the household, but have helped little in terms of improving working conditions of the household members; particularly when their social insurance status is concerned. As a result, despite the more pronounced positive effect of low dependency ratio on change, the results remained rather weak, confirming my hypothesis that increased labour market participation does not always explain success.

How far did the formal cultural capital (FCC) accumulations of the households have an impact on the benefit delivery capacity of household labour resources? To address this question, the household FCC ratios (see Figure 5.9) were subjected to a Pearson correlation test with the change scores (see Figure 7.1). The test results suggested a moderate inverse relationship between the two variables [$r = -0.38$], implying that those households with relatively better educated workers were inclined to be less successful in the second round. The results obtained from the analysis of April and change data both proved similar in terms of the significance of the association between the variables but differed in terms of its direction. Despite the difference, the results remain supportive of two inferences made earlier: First of all, given the low level and narrow range of the FCC possessed, having a few more years in education are unlikely to have made a difference to the labour market position of the working members; perhaps the majority were positioned towards the lower end of the market where the working conditions were particularly unfavourable. Secondly, given the extensive use of informal cultural capital in employment, the amount of FFC accumulated may have been of little relevance to the type of work undertaken. Both interpretations, however, converge on the idea that their FCC accumulations are rather limited in their capacity to move household labour resources to upper echelons of the labour market. Let us now see whether their social capital resources enabled such an upward movement.

To explore this, a non-parametric (Spearman) correlation test was performed between the two variables measuring the volume of social capital and change levels (see Figure 7.1). The results suggested no relationship between them [$r = -0.09$]. This is also apparent from the cross-tabulation presented in Table 7.4.

**Table 7.4    Household social capital volume by change category**

| Social capital (volume) | Change category | | | Total |
| --- | --- | --- | --- | --- |
| | Negative change | No change | Positive change | |
| Low | 1 | 2 | 2 | 5 |
| Medium | 1 | 3 | 3 | 7 |
| High | 2 | 1 | 2 | 5 |
| Total | 4 | 6 | 7 | 17 |

The table demonstrates that the change levels were hardly affected by the volume of social capital possessed. This appears congruent with my earlier findings and hence the general line of argument that mobilisation of a greater range of resources does not necessarily lead to success. However, this does not mean that social capital resources were unhelpful in finding jobs. As a matter of fact, all household members who were in search of employment after April on a continuous or one-off basis made use of their social contacts. However, the extent of their achievements varied;

only three households succeeded in finding a secure formal job for one of their members. In their job search, these households used relatively durable contacts which were either of employer or professional status. Success in employment thus seems more contingent upon the person, with whom the households were linked, than on the volume of social contacts. Especially those with strong ties to people better placed within the urban opportunity structure seem to stand more chance to attain a relatively favourable position in the labour market.

Turning to explore the demand side influences on change, the analysis below focuses on the effect of a) household formal sector participation (FSP) ratios and b) household seasonality ratios. In order to see whether levels of change in household deprivation varied significantly according to the extent of formal sector participation, a Pearson correlation test was conducted between the household FSP ratios (see Figure 5.5) and change scores (see Figure 7.1). The results were indicative of a weak relationship between the two variables [$r = 0.26$]. This is also evident from the cross-tabulation displayed in Table 7.5.

**Table 7.5    Household formal sector participation by change category**

| FSP ratio | Change category | | | Total |
|---|---|---|---|---|
| | Negative change | No change | Positive change | |
| 0.00–0.50 | 2 | 5 | 3 | 6 |
| 0.51–1.00 | 2 | 1 | 4 | 7 |
| Total | 4 | 6 | 7 | 17 |

Thus, it seems that households with greater formal sector participation performed only slightly better than those with one or more informal sector participants. Although the change analysis indicated a much weaker association than that found in our April analysis, this is not incompatible with my earlier argument. On the contrary, it seems to justify my reservations regarding the existence of a firm line between formal and informal sectors of the labour market particularly where employment conditions are concerned. Since the pay and working conditions offered for either sector workers tended not to differ significantly, it seems probable that having a greater number of formal sector participants did not make much difference to success. The differences could well be blurred, as both sectors were exposed to the same severe conditions of economic crisis and to violation of labour rights. This could, for instance, mean that some formal sector participants were also deprived of entitlements to social insurance, and/or earned a similar income to an informal sector participant. It was nevertheless shown earlier that some sectoral differences still existed in access to social insurance (hence state pensions and healthcare). However, since the social security conditions for informal sector participants are unlikely to have improved over the six months, it is possible to suggest that employment conditions have remained pretty much the same for both groups. Therefore, changes in household deprivation cannot be attributed to the sector of employment. If this is the case then how can we make sense of the increase in income levels? Let us now see whether the increase has to do with seasonal effects.

In exploring this, a Pearson test was performed between the household seasonality ratios (see Figure 5.8) and change scores (see Figure 7.1). The results suggest a very weak relationship between the two variables [r = 0.16], implying that households with a greater number of seasonal workers were not necessarily able to improve their situation. Table 7.6 also demonstrates the weakness of the association.

Table 7.6    Household seasonality ratio by change category

| Seasonality ratio | Change category | | | Total |
|---|---|---|---|---|
| | Negative change | No change | Positive change | |
| 0.00–0.50 | 3 | 5 | 5 | 13 |
| 0.51–1.00 | 1 | 1 | 2 | 4 |
| Total | 4 | 6 | 7 | 17 |

These results proved different from the April analysis, where a very strong tendency towards increased deprivation was found for households predominantly composed of seasonal workers. Nevertheless, the results of change analysis make sense given the timing of research. The first round of interviews was conducted towards the end of the low work season whereas the period between the first and second round of interviews coincided with the peak season. Therefore, the seasonal workers are likely to have had the time to bridge the income gap between their households and those less affected by seasonality. Over the work season, some of the seasonal workers were able to earn an income equal to or perhaps more than those unaffected by seasonal fluctuations, but the majority of them failed to earn significantly higher amounts. This seems bad news for households with seasonal workers as the income generated may not suffice to cover the forthcoming winter days without any work.

Overall, neither households with a more diversified income nor a greater number of workers were found to perform significantly better over the six month period. The supply and demand side labour market forces were shown to play a significant role in this. Most fundamentally, the wider conditions of economic crisis as well as labour right violations seem to have continued to create unfavourable pay and working conditions both for formal and informal sector workers. Both social and cultural capital accumulations of the majority were unable to ensure a movement towards the echelons of the labour market where conditions were more favourable. Consequently, from April to October not much seems to have changed in respect of the elimination of the influences constraining the benefit delivery capacity of household labour resources. What has changed, however, was the removal of the adverse effect of seasonality, enabling most seasonal workers to earn a higher income; yet not enough to stretch over winter days without work.

*Income Allocation and Change in Deprivation*

This section aims to explore the possible impact of income allocation mechanisms upon the levels of change in household deprivation. The analysis revisits three variables used in the April analysis: a) financial management models, b) financial control systems and c) actual income distribution, and examines their effects, based on a modified version of the change scores, which excludes the differences in the April and October scores of disposable real household income, mean household income/work hours, mean household social insurance ratio, pension prospects and mean household occupational risk grades, in order to improve the relevance of measurement to income allocation behaviour. Figure 7.6 presents the new scores [mean = 0.09; std. deviation = 1.45].

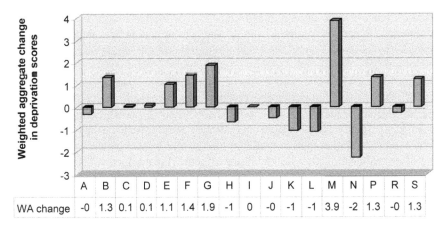

| | A | B | C | D | E | F | G | H | I | J | K | L | M | N | P | R | S |
|---|---|---|---|---|---|---|---|---|---|---|---|---|---|---|---|---|---|
| WA change | -0 | 1.3 | 0.1 | 0.1 | 1.1 | 1.4 | 1.9 | -1 | 0 | -0 | -1 | -1 | 3.9 | -2 | 1.3 | -0 | 1.3 |

**Households**

**Figure 7.6    Change in household deprivation levels (version 2)**

In order to see whether change levels differed significantly according to the adopted models of financial management, a one way ANOVA was performed, comparing the mean change scores across the models [mean (housekeeping allowance) = −0.34 (1.08); mean (female whole-wage) = 0.05 (0.35) and mean (female-managed pool) = 0.50 (1.68)]. The mean differences revealed that predominantly female-managed systems fared slightly better than the male-managed systems (i.e. housekeeping allowance system). However, the results were only indicative of a weak association [F (2, 14) = 0.35]. Thus, they appear congruent with my hypothesis that how money is managed is less likely to be of relevance to poverty than the actual distribution of income. However, the validity of these findings remain questionable given the small sample size, unequal distribution of households into financial management categories and limited sensitivity of the poverty instrument to differences between members. Nevertheless, I have some confidence in the findings as the results of the change analysis proved congruent with those in April.

In investigating the possible effects of financial control mechanisms, a Pearson correlation test was performed between the dichotomous variable of financial control variable (see Table 6.1) and the modified change scores (see Figure 7.6). No significant relationship was however found between the two variables $[r = -0.05]$. Although the observed association turned out to be much weaker than it did in the April analysis, the results from either analysis proved too weak to be of any significance. It may follow from this that who controlled the finances did not significantly affect the levels of change in household deprivation. Both analyses are hence confirmatory of my hypothesis; yet it should be noted that the above mentioned limitations of the sample size and the poverty instrument still apply.

Is it likely that the actual distribution of total income overrode the effects of financial management and control mechanisms? In order to explore this, a non-parametric (Spearman) correlation test was performed between the modified change scores (see Figure 7.6) and the rank-ordered household categories measuring the degree of collectiveness in actual income distribution (see Chapter 6). A fairly weak relationship between the two variables was obtained $[r = 0.28]$. Despite the similarities between the April and change analysis in terms of the degree of the association, the former indicated an inverse relationship. How can we make sense of these seemingly contradictory results? Perhaps they can be said to be compatible rather than contradictory as the relationship between deprivation and income allocation may well be bi-directional. This means that the former can determine household decisions as to how to allocate the total income between different spheres of household and (fair or controversial) personal spending. It also means that the outcomes of these decisions can determine the extent to which households avoid or experience 'secondary poverty'. Consequently, the weakness of the association seem to reinforce my earlier conclusion that even less collective households were distributing their total income in a way that prevented them from experiencing severe forms of 'secondary poverty'.

Overall, in keeping with the April findings and hypothesis, the results of this change analysis suggest that how household finances are managed or controlled may be of less relevance to poverty than the actual distribution of income. Given the small share of controversial personal spending among the observed patterns of income distribution, the results also lend support to the argument that poor households can act collectively to alleviate some effects of their impoverishment.

*Consumption and Change in Deprivation*

The final section explores consumption-related effects on change through a focus on practices that allow access to free and subsidised goods and services. In what follows, the effects of two variables measuring non/semi-commodification and resource diversification levels are examined, based on a modified version of the change scores which excludes the differences in the April and October scores of household income/work hours, mean household social insurance ratio, pension prospects and mean household occupational risk grades in order to improve the relevance of measurement to consumption behaviour. The new scores are presented in Figure 7.7 [mean = 0.37; std. deviation = 1.43].

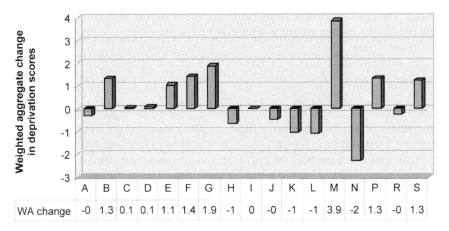

| | A | B | C | D | E | F | G | H | I | J | K | L | M | N | P | R | S |
|---|---|---|---|---|---|---|---|---|---|---|---|---|---|---|---|---|---|
| WA change | -0 | 1.3 | 0.1 | 0.1 | 1.1 | 1.4 | 1.9 | -1 | 0 | -0 | -1 | -1 | 3.9 | -2 | 1.3 | -0 | 1.3 |

**Households**

**Figure 7.7    Change in household deprivation levels (version 3)**

In order to see whether the extent of involvement in activities that allow access to free or subsidised goods and services had a significant effect on household success over the six months, a Pearson correlation test was conducted between the non/semi-commodified consumption variable (see Figure 6.4) and the modified change scores (see Figure 7.7). The results revealed no significant relationship [r = 0.13]. Despite limitations in the level of detail presented here, the consistency of these results with those for April provides some assurance as to their validity. Thus, it may still be suggested that greater participation in practices of non/semi-commodified consumption does not lead to significant success. The depictions of change trends also confirm the limited contribution of these practices by demonstrating a tendency for households to cut back on items such as heating, meat and winter food stock.

Could the narrow range of resources used be responsible for their failure? This was examined through a Person correlation test performed between the variable of resource diversification (see Figure 6.6) and the modified change scores (see Figure 7.7). The results indicated a moderate inverse relationship [r = −0.39], implying less improvement among those with a greater number of resources. This picture contradicts the one portrayed in April where the association turned out weaker but had a positive direction. So how can we make sense of these results? One interpretation is that over the six months period, households may have lost control over some of the resources they initially had access to. Another interpretation is that they may have employed resources that were of limited capacity to provide *regular* access to *sizeable* free/subsidised goods and services and hence lift substantial income pressure. These interpretations are not mutually exclusive; meaning that households may have undergone both processes.

Consequently, the results from both analyses lend some support to my overall argument that success is more likely to depend on the benefit delivery capacity of resources available than their range. So which resource types were more beneficial? The case studies presented in the subsequent three chapters throw light on this.

## Conclusion

This chapter has sought to examine whether households experienced short or long spells of poverty through a focus on short-term change over the period between April and October interviews. It was shown that although nearly half of the households have been able to reduce their overall deprivation levels, the majority were unable to move out of poverty. This was so despite the removal of seasonal effects and substantial success achieved in avoiding 'secondary poverty', since structural factors relating to the labour and financial markets as well as wider conditions of economic crisis remained to have a restrictive effect on the benefit delivery capacity of the resources available to them. Moreover, the minority who were able to rise above the poverty threshold are most likely to have experienced short-lived success due to the subsequent winter decline in labour market opportunities.

Chapter 8

# The Ayhans: A Relatively
# Better Off Household

Unlike Chapters 5 to 7 which refer to all the households, Chapters 8 to 10 are based on case studies of three individual households belonging to different categories of deprivation. The case studies illustrate in detail how poor households responded to their conditions of impoverishment and whether they have been able to realise their plans for the next six months. Thereby, they shed light on some of the forces that lead to household success or failure. This chapter depicts the responses of a *Sünni* family, the Ayhans, which entered the month of April as the most successful household in the sample, and had fared well over the six month period.[1,2] The case study starts with an overview of the household's socio-demographic background, followed by an examination of its responses to poverty in relation to four key types of behaviour.

## A Socio-demographic Profile

İmdat and Zarife were a married couple with two children. İmdat was 38 and Zarife, his wife, was 42 years old. They were both primary school graduates and first generation migrants. The couple's move to the city fits the pattern of chain migration. İmdat came to Ankara earlier than Zarife and until his military service, he stayed with his brother and started working in a small workshop as a welder. İmdat's urban life became more established after completing his military service. In 1985, İmdat got married to Zarife from his hometown. Six months after their marriage, Zarife left the village to live with her husband in a *gecekondu* he rented in Ankara. Their first son, Burak, was born in this house in 1986. Two years later, the family bought a ready-built *gecekondu* and have not moved house since then. Their second son Samed was born there in 1990.

In April, the Ayhans had already entered the consolidation phase, although their sons had not yet taken their place in the family workforce. At that time, both Burak and Samed were attending school: The younger son was a first year student in compulsory education. The elder brother was in the first year of industrial vocational training.

---

1   The Ayhans had a weighted aggregate deprivation score of 31.18 in April. Their weighted aggregate change score was 3.88.

2   All the names and surnames used across the case studies are pseudonyms.

## Income Generation and Diversification

The Ayhans generated income using their time, labour and cultural capital only. The following three sub-sections explore the labour market behaviour of the female and male spouses and their children respectively between April and October.

### Zarife's Labour

Zarife was a housewife. In April, she had neither a regular nor an irregular job either at or outside home. Nonetheless, she sometimes made bread for money. Bread-making required certain skills which Zarife acquired informally in her village where she spent 25 years of her life. It was a casual, informal job for which she was paid a daily wage, and was performed usually in spring and/or autumn to prepare a stock. It involved a team of three to five women working together usually from 7:00 am to pm until the whole sack(s) of flour was used up. The daily wage was around 10 million TL, which came to 830,000 TL per hour (i.e. 62 US cents). However, Zarife earned nothing from bread-making this year. Presumably, in the face of economic crisis conditions, those in 'employer' positions either gave up on home-made bread or found alternative way of producing it, e.g. by setting up a reciprocal team where members exchange their labour free of charge. For Zarife, this meant an end to this source of income.

In April, Zarife gave the impression that she had some work-related plans: "We're [I am] looking for a job, we'll work but I'm disabled so I can't work. I'd like to do cleaning of some place yet here are kids studying; I'm a lone housewife [have nobody to help with housework]; as I don't have support at home, I can't go." In October, it became evident that Zarife had made no effort to look for a job. Thus, her idea of working as a cleaner seems more wishful thinking than a real plan. Nonetheless, it involved a realistic evaluation of what the labour market could offer a primary school graduate with no previous work experience. Zarife mentioned a few supply-side pressures which prevented her from taking a job: the traditional division of labour, which placed the responsibility of daily chores and child-care on Zarife's shoulders. Zarife seemed to have preferred caring for her kids and making sure that their focus was on their studies to working in a low paid cleaning job. Moreover, Zarife limped due to a problem with her hip bone and this disability slowed down her movements to some extent.

Zarife's reasons for staying at home sound perfectly plausible. Nevertheless, there was a tendency among my female respondents to make a list of reasons which sounds convincing but are rather peripheral to those which actually prevented them from working outside. Zarife's disability seems to illustrate this well. The amount of hard work she did at home made it less convincing that her disability impeded her taking a job. In fact, the family did not feel desperate for Zarife's labour. Even if they did, it is doubtful whether İmdat would have let his wife work outside the home. Zarife said nothing to help reveal her husband's attitude on this matter. In fact, İmdat once stated that it was he who taught Zarife how to orient herself in the city, and that he was now pleased to see her coping with the unknown outside the *mahalle* so that he would not need to take time off from work. Nevertheless, working outside is rather different to her one-off interactions with outsiders, in particular with men. The Ayhans were a typically patriarchal family with strict adherence to Islamic practices, which was evident from Zarife's religious scarf wearing. Men from traditional families tend to take pride in protecting their wives' virtue/honour, and being the provider for the family. For such reasons, Zarife could well have been disallowed from working beyond the *mahalle* boundaries.

*İmdat's Labour*

İmdat was a welder. He received no formal training but had mastered welding skills through 22 years of on-the-job-experience. In April, İmdat had been working in a medium scale factory for a month or so. This was his first regular job after being made redundant from Total Gas when the factory closed down due to economic crisis. During the eight month period of his redundancy, İmdat did casual welding jobs here and there, and even went to work in another city.

The way İmdat found this job was quite a coincidence: "I worked at their [the directors'] place in 1980. [...] Regarding this job, they had an advert in the newspaper so I went there to fill a form [without knowing it was them]. I couldn't find the address either; I was on the mobile, phoning them and suddenly they came in the car, stopped near me and asked 'İmdat, what are you doing there?'" That was it; İmdat was immediately given the job because the factory directors knew him as a person and also because they knew that they could trust his loyalty. İmdat and his employers had no formal contractual relationship. They instead had an informal contract based on the principle of clientelism whereby İmdat agreed to submit his loyalty to his patrons in return for their past favours and probably, in the hope of future favours. Yet, there was a downside to this agreement. İmdat worked for them several times without claiming the true price of his labour. This meant that their clientelist bond was a mild and subtle form of exploitation to which İmdat 'chose' to give consent.

Relatively speaking, İmdat's working conditions were not so severe. Yet, İmdat had to work extremely long hours to earn his salary. In April, he worked seven days a week: between 8:00 am and 7:30 pm on weekdays, and between 8:00 am and 5:30 pm at the weekend. His weekly working hours came to 73, of which 23 were paid overtime. Compared with the time İmdat spent at work, his earnings were rather low. In April, he earned 200 million TL from his usual work hours, and 150 million TL from overtime. His hourly pay was therefore 4 and 6.5 million TL (i.e. 3 and 4.9 US dollars) respectively. In addition, the company granted one month's wage as a gratuity twice a year, and paid 55 million TL to cover his bus fares. In total, his income amounted to 405 million TL in April.

The degree of risk associated with welding was five on a scale of 1 to 12 listed in the social insurance premium tariff; higher grades indicating greater risk (Social Security Institution 1981). In spite of this, İmdat claimed that his job did not pose any threat to his health and safety. There was air conditioning in the factory, which was hardly on but the smoke did not interfere as the ceilings were quite high. İmdat's entitlements to social insurance were nevertheless quite sufficient in terms of covering the risks involved in his job. İmdat was an active SSK member, and in case of an accident or illness he could benefit from SSK hospitals since his current employers regularly contributed to his premiums. However, it appeared that they made premium contributions at the lowest possible rate, although İmdat earned at least three times as much as the minimum wage (i.e. 163,563,537 TL in April 2002). For İmdat, the consequences of his employers' behaviour were serious: he would receive a smaller state pension. The fear of losing his job in the face of high unemployment, the lack of a trade union and the loyalty agreement with his patrons seem to have made him accept his employers' behaviour. Despite the violation of his labour rights in his current job, his pension prospects were quite good since he had been registered with SSK scheme since 1981 and had so far accumulated 6000 days premiums. This meant he had already met the minimum premium requirement for retirement. All İmdat needed was to work five more years to become entitled to a pension. However, İmdat, as a new entrant, was not sure about the future of his job. His prospects were mainly contingent upon how well the enterprise performed in attracting new contracts in an environment of economic crisis. If it failed, İmdat would be among those who would be shown the door first. This implied that in their clientelist contract it was İmdat who was expected to bear the costs involved rather than his patrons.

Although İmdat was aware of the redundancy risk, in April he had no sound alternative job plan simply because there was severe unemployment outside the factory door. İmdat's hope was to go back to his job at Total Gas since it had relatively better working conditions: an established trade union, which meant better pay for workers, paid holidays, regular social insurance contributions, etc. His expectation was, however, rather difficult to realise as there was little his social contacts could do to help him avoid the fierce competition for the job. İmdat nevertheless had some chance due to his skills and experience. In October, it appeared that İmdat was not in the list of winners since the enterprise selected workers according to the principle of maximum skills-minimum staff. Nonetheless, İmdat managed to hang on to his welding job at the family enterprise. Yet, the risk continued; İmdat still did not know what would follow the contract Turkish Ground Forces Headquarters awarded to the company. There were however a few changes in his work conditions. As the workload of the company lessened, he no longer worked on Sundays. Together with his overtime and transport costs, the nominal value of his October income amounted to 475 million TL. However, his real hourly pay rose only by 260.000 TL, which was in October equal to the price of a loaf of bread in the local shop.

Apart from his main job, İmdat did some additional work. In some households, men take a second job instead of the women being sent to work, which seems to appeal particularly to *Sünni* families. His second job was again to do with welding. İmdat kept a welding machine at home and used it to do free-lance small welding jobs usually for his neighbours. Between April and October, only on one occasion did he earn money in this fashion. There were two reasons for this: First of all, his time was very limited, and secondly, even if he did find time, he refused to get involved with neighbours whom he found unappreciative of his help:

İmdat: You can't cosy up to this circle. I [do this job] neither for money nor pocket money. If (s)he [an undefined neighbour] said 'come, I'll give you 100 million, I wouldn't do it either because we have such people that they go too far. Today, (s)he'd say 'come and get my job done'; I'd go and get it done for free; (s)he'd gossip behind me; therefore, I don't want to get any job done for this *mahalle*. There are; there are in fact a lot of jobs but I don't want to do any. (S)he says one word, breaks one's back, I mean. I moved here in the year 1987 or 88; since then they [neighbours] were envious of me, I mean. When I first came, oh let's not be in trouble with the neighbours, we're ultimately neighbours so we ended up doing whatever they wanted; we went and helped with their construction so on so forth, and yet we couldn't cosy up to [them]. I've now stopped it [welding for others] completely. I have my own welding job here; I'm making windows and doors. They make a complaint against me, saying that 'he's using illegal electricity; he's using illegal I don't know what'! The other day, they [officers] came from TEK [Turkish Electricity Institution]; they checked everywhere; could find nothing. I asked 'brother, who made a complaint against me?' He said 'I don't know, brother, somebody informed us; made a complaint; he said 'we came upon complaint'. If they revealed the name, we'd at least know our friends and enemies. He searched everywhere; could find nothing.

Interviewer: So you say they are more of an impediment than of help…

İmdat: Exactly, like that.

İmdat's 'second job' was based on the principle of reciprocity. He earned money in the process but, at the same time, helped out his neighbours by letting them decide how much to pay him. İmdat however reduced the amount of welding work he did for his neighbours as he had suffered adversely from their envious eyes. It is highly likely that being a better off family made the Ayhans an object of jealousy among their neighbours. This would have impeded any improvement to the Ayhans' well-being not only by eroding the flow of support but also by leading some of their social contacts to deliberately undermine the 'wealth' they possessed. The prevalence of a competitive spirit clearly shows that social capital can operate on the principle of 'negative reciprocity', and act more as a source of impediment than of help.

*Burak and Samed's Labour*

İmdat could afford to give up his second job to avoid envy as well as to show his resentfulness. The Ayhans were also able to keep their children in education without having to make them work. Samed, Zarife believed, was too young to earn money. Burak, however, had a brief work history as a hairdresser assistant. The previous year, Zarife dropped into a men's hairdresser and asked if there was any need for an assistant. As his earnings proved unworthy of the effort, Zarife was reluctant to send Burak to work again. Thus, between April and October, neither child was out working. The Ayhans generated income mainly by using the male spouse's labour and skills. Let us now explore how the total income was allocated.

## Income Allocation: Overt and Covert Mechanisms

As the sole provider and a responsible father and husband, İmdat brought all the income he earned into the family. When money came through the house door, the responsibility of managing the entire income landed on Zarife's shoulders.

> Interviewer:    In whose hands is your income accumulated?
> İmdat:          At my wife's... Now, I bring [it], my wife says we'll give this
>                 here and there. I take my bus fare. And [say] take this [the rest
>                 of the income] and distribute it where you have credits to and
>                 keep the remaining. In that matter [managing money] my wife is
>                 very conscientious [frugal]. She wouldn't say 'I shall squander,
>                 I shall buy this, I shall wear this'.

İmdat sounded very pleased and proud of Zarife's 'frugal nature' as it enabled them to get by with a limited income: "I spare my bus fare; I give the rest to her and she uses [it] in a thrifty manner. While handing over the money, I say, 'use it economically', so she spends it accordingly. I mean, money wouldn't last if she weren't frugal... She's very frugal... If she were someone else, we could neither develop nor get by with this money". This helps explain why Zarife acted as the 'whole-wage' manager of the house. İmdat's comment however raises the question as to whether Zarife was forced into frugality. When talking about their finances, Zarife, like many other respondents, showed her frustration with their tight income. She also pointed to another problem, rendering it likely that her frugality was partly enforced:

> Interviewer:    Have you got any problems regarding the fact that you look after
>                 the money?
> Zarife:         Of course I do... We can't buy what we want... We go to the
>                 bazaar; buy half a kilo not a kilo... We can't go most of the time,

for instance. Whatever Allah gave us here; good or bad… If I did
buy everything I wanted, nothing would remain in my hand.

Interviewer:     Any other problems at all?

Zarife:          I have the fear that the money won't stretch. […] Will I be able
                 to make this money stretch for my husband or not?

It appears that the management style adopted within the household exposed
Zarife to pressures from two directions. One was tight income and the other was
patriarchal authority. The question for Zarife was not simply whether the money
would stretch until the next pay day, but also whether she would be able to meet
her husband's expectations.

İmdat's comments and expectations were not the only manifestation of his
control over household finances. In practice Zarife was responsible for managing
income but she had to 'consult' her husband when she needed to buy anything. As
İmdat put it, "[w]ithout letting me know, she'd buy nothing; she'd consult me. If
my budget allows so, or I did a [welding] job so there will be some money coming
up, I'd say OK, we will get that much money from there so go and buy whatever
you like, I mean. But if I don't have any security from anywhere, I'd say this
month, you wait". These 'consultations' helped İmdat control household finances.
His strict control was evident in the way that financial decisions were finalised:

Interviewer:     Who makes the final decision in financial matters?

Zarife:          Your uncle İmdat does…

Interviewer:     Oh really?

Zarife:          Ultimately, head is tied to head; head is [then] tied to sultan. If
                 I have money in my hands, I'd look at it [the situation]; I'd buy
                 it if it was suitable. In fact, I wouldn't buy it; I'd consult him in
                 the evening. I'd say this is like that. Is it economical or not? He,
                 too if there's something that sticks in his mind; he'd consult me
                 about whether we should do this or buy this.

Interviewer:     Who ties the final knot?

Zarife:          We do it together. İmdat does it more often, though. For
                 instance, he works; money comes from him. It is he who knows
                 how money is earned. If I decided, I wouldn't know the value of
                 money.

As Zarife made no contribution to the family income, in any case of conflict, she
had no power to overtly challenge the 'sultan's' authority in the house:

Interviewer:     Who makes the final decision in financial matters?

İmdat:           We think twice; we come together; we say let's do it like this; we
                 say OK or we say let's think again.

Interviewer:     What if there is a conflict?

| İmdat: | Nothing like that happens. Whatever she decides, she buys; but if there is something that I like most, I say this [the one she liked] is not nice; let's buy that instead so she agrees to my idea, I mean. |
|---|---|

The couple seems to have taken part in a discussion when deciding what was to be purchased. This might sound egalitarian; yet it seems that the final decision was up to İmdat. Zarife simply obeyed his final decision to avoid conflict. Zarife avoided challenging patriarchy overtly, but in the past she had resorted to some covert ways: she used to keep a secret kitty. Zarife tells us her story of creating the kitty: "I saved small gold coins, you know. We're eating [shopping] from the local shop then [on credit]. If I ate five, I said ten [to her husband]. This way, I saved eight gold coins. I was telling him 'buy me a washing machine' but he didn't. I phoned his aunt's son; told him this and that, let's make use of this [savings]. He then told me 'let's buy you a washing machine' [...] and I then asked him 'shall we, shall we?' 'No...', but we convinced him; took the coins with us and went." When İmdat found out about the kitty, he initially felt quite proud of his wife's frugality:

| Interviewer: | What did your husband say when he saw the coins for the washing machine? |
|---|---|
| Zarife: | He didn't say much... How happy he was then, it was like ready-to-spend, I mean. He immediately paid for the first instalment. If I had [money] in my hands now, I'd say, I found it from somebody else but I don't have any in my hands... It doesn't prove fruitful that way, though. I don't like it, I mean. Your brother İmdat doesn't like it either; he says 'don't tell a lie, tell the truth'. |

The washing machine incident was however her first and last attempt to create a secret kitty:

| Interviewer: | Do you currently have a little separate kitty? |
|---|---|
| Zarife: | No, never... With us, all together, all together... |
| Interviewer: | Some women do for instance accumulate the left over from the bread-money. |
| Zarife: | Yes, they do but my husband says appear at the door if you have money, don't appear if you don't have money... Besides, I can't tell a lie. I can't manage this. I can't say I today gave this here; I got this from there.' |
| Interviewer: | What about the washing machine incident? |
| Zarife: | It happened once. |
| Interviewer: | Not ever again? |
| Zarife: | No, no... I don't. |

Interviewer:     Why?

Zarife:     I don't know... all together, there shan't be restlessness at home and also I can't tell a lie. [...] Ultimately, saying 'I bought two instead of one' is a lie and I can't accept this as right.

Perhaps Zarife gave up on the kitty because she needed to restore trust and unity within the family which was shaken by the lies she told to create her kitty. However, despite what she said, the fact that she did not want to live a lie seems to have played less of a role. From her accounts, we can understand that Zarife would like to carry on keeping secret savings if she were given the chance. It is likely that İmdat's current strict control over household finances restricted her movements. However, my observations suggest that women could be highly creative in working out ways to quietly get round such control mechanisms. It is therefore probable that Zarife chose to adhere to her husband's advice. Several reasons can be suggested for this. Firstly, as she had already been discovered once, any further attempts, if found out, might cause overt conflict or 'restlessness' in the house. Zarife certainly did not want to face this. Why did Zarife, like many other women, want to avoid overt confrontation? We do not have enough evidence to say for sure but perhaps her total dependence on İmdat's wage and property or social pressures against widowhood make divorce a less likely option for her. Secondly, by going for a sizeable household item, Zarife pushed the 'legitimate' boundaries within which husbands allowed their wives to operate; thereby shaking İmdat's patriarchal authority. It is therefore likely that she gave up on her concealed budget to consolidate his authority.

Obviously, the way in which money was controlled within the Ayhans was not so egalitarian. This meant that İmdat had more financial power to dictate his consumption preferences. Nevertheless, the adopted system of control appears not to have made Zarife or the children significantly more deprived than him. This may be due to the general concern by both spouses for the 'collective good' in their decisions about income allocation. İmdat was typical of a patriarchal male figure which had the final say over financial decisions. However, he brought his entire income home without keeping any pocket money except his bus fares for work. Zarife was the same:

Interviewer:     What does your husband keep for himself?

Zarife:     He takes his bus fare... He doesn't have [smoke] cigarettes. And gives the rest to me and I wouldn't spend it. I'd stretch my feet according to my duvet.

Interviewer:     Do you have any personal needs at all?

Zarife:     I do but money [our income] doesn't stretch that far... It doesn't stretch, we wait till the pay day, I mean. The guy [her husband] says 'look, spend this money in a thrifty manner; this money shall last till next pay day'.

Personal spending meant little for Zarife perhaps due to her being a typical self-sacrificing mother figure and leading a house-bound life-style. Moreover, despite their relatively sizeable income, they had little room for choice. In the face of more pressing needs, neither İmdat nor Zarife prioritised their personal needs. In addition, Zarife was a highly frugal person likely to limit her personal needs to bare essentials. Also, the fear of failure to stretch the income and hence to obey her husband's instructions may have put her off from spending some money on her own needs. For whatever reasons, İmdat and Zarife were both making an effort to allocate the household income in the most collective manner possible. This way, they were able to avoid 'secondary poverty'. Having explored the financial arrangements made within the household, we will next consider the Ayhans' asset portfolio and how it was formed.

### Investment, Insurance and Credit Use

The Ayhans's portfolio contained both financial and non-financial assets. Beginning with their financial assets, they had some savings, most of which were probably deposited in a Turkish bank. Both İmdat and Zarife constantly denied having a bank account, about which their neighbours were gossiping, but they failed to explain what happened to part of İmdat's 5 billion TL worth redundancy compensation from the Total Gas job. Presumably, the family still had at least 2.5 billion TL deposited in a bank in April, and kept it there for the following six months[3]. If we assume that this money was deposited in *Ziraat Bankası*, a popular Turkish bank, for a six month term; the interest rate would be 49 per cent and their savings in October would amount to 3,111,123,100 TL. If we exclude the effect of the 11.5 per cent increase in inflation between April and October, their real savings would be 2,753,343,940 TL. It is thus likely that their real gain in six months was around 300 million TL, which was very small. Consequently, although Turkish banks might offer extremely favourable interest rates, as İmdat's case showed, the interest that low income families accrued on their savings is limited. This meant that the route out of poverty via saving was closed to poorer segments of the population.

In addition to their bank deposits, the Ayhans collected some gold coins to protect the value of their savings against high inflation. Both in April and October, the Ayhans held two coins. In the free gold market, these coins were worth approx 42,320,000 TL in April and 59,973,332 TL in October; real return was 11,467,742 TL. In between, the Ayhans saved at least four more gold coins which were given away at occasions such as circumcision ceremonies and weddings. The gold coins were not simply regarded as a present; they also fulfilled obligations of a rather 'balanced' reciprocal transaction. This can be viewed as a form of rosca with the

---

3   Unaccounted savings are included in scoring their deprivation level.

term of rotation spread across a life time. Apart from this, neither İmdat nor Zarife belonged to any well-defined rosca due to a lack of trust in their social 'circle'.

With regard to their non-financial assets, the *gecekondu* they currently occupied was potentially their most profitable asset. In 1988, İmdat purchased this ready-built *gecekondu* in Southern Ege. As the *gecekondu* was built before 1985, the Redevelopment Law No. 2981 secured their housing tenure and entitled them to redevelopment. Yet, we do not know whether İmdat was aware of what he was becoming entitled to at the time of purchase. We cannot therefore tell whether his investment was strategically planned. Either made consciously or unconsciously, it carried a great potential for moving out of poverty. Before the amelioration plan, İmdat had 362 m² land. With the implementation of the plan, his land was reduced to 253 m² since 30 per cent of the land was confiscated by the municipality to be used for public services. Potentially the remaining plot allowed him to obtain at least two flats after redevelopment. İmdat's plan was to also purchase the municipal share on his land to increase the number of prospective flats. If necessary, he was prepared to sell his car for this purpose. In April İmdat had already applied to the municipality but the lists had not yet been opened. In October this poverty escape plan was still unrealised since the revision implementation plans had still not been completed.

Another non-financial asset they possessed was a 1994 registration KARTAL SLX, a Turkish car. The story behind the purchase of this car is very interesting in that it reveals the 'favourable' work conditions İmdat was exposed to at his previous work-place: "We acquired this at the place which closed down. I entered Total Gas in the year 1990 ... I worked for five months or so. They sacked those they employed recently. Of course, they gave us a compensation, I then got some money around 400 million [TL], though. We bought a TV, book shelf, a stereo and so on. A week later they called me back; I worked one and a half years or so; they sacked me again in the period of collective negotiations. They don't touch those who had worked there for five to ten years; instead they sacked recent employees. [The company owner] says how much would their [recent employees'] compensation cost? He says I'd give one billion or 500 million and call them back later after collective negotiations ended. They'll later re-employ from minimum wage. That time, they sacked us again, and gave our compensation, of course... That time, I got something like 14 million TL and bought a MURAT 124 [a Turkish car brand] for 16 million. My aunt's son helped me then; lent me some Marks [DM]. We'd got on [used] that car for three years. I said we got on but I mean it stayed at home. Then they called me back again. Thanks to that place, we became a car owner. After this, I'd worked there for nine years. Our salary got increased; we didn't have any debts so what should we do; lets enhance our car. We joined a *gün* [rosca] among work-mates. Some [money] came also from there. [...] We then exchanged the MURAT 124 for a MURAT 131, paying 400 million towards it. Of course then another collective negotiation period arrived; we had a quite good increase in our salary and in our social rights; in our gratuity and coal aid etc. There used to be saving encouragement fund; we got 200 million TL from there; we also saved some dollar-mark by trimming our salary. This way we sold the MURAT 131 and got this one in return."

For the Ayhans, the car was more a symbolic investment in their status than an item of consumption since İmdat could rarely afford to move the car out of the drive. For the Ayhans, the car was a false investment in several respects: First of all, due to the high price of petrol, İmdat was unable to afford to drive the car. Secondly, there were the road tax and insurance cost to be met. In April, İmdat had already postponed the payments for the car insurance and road tax, which in total cost 100 million TL. This was a lot of money in the eyes of the Ayhans; in fact, it was equal to 40 per cent of his earnings from usual work hours. İmdat managed to pay these delayed bills by October, but due to the interest charges, he had to pay more. Thirdly, the KARTAL SLX was an old car and needed more maintenance. Finally, each year the car depreciated in value. Despite everything, in April İmdat had no plans regarding the KARTAL SLX.

Finally, the Ayhans had rural assets inherited from their parents. However, the legal status of these assets was dubious. On Zarife's side, there was around 42 acres of arable land to be shared between seven sisters including her. Yet, currently none of the sisters had any legal rights to sell, rent out or use the land, due to the conflict between the sisters regarding how the land should be shared and used. The case was taken to court to resolve the conflict. İmdat also supposedly owned a much smaller plot in the village. However, rivalries between him and his brothers not only prevented him from building a house on the plot but also caused him to lose out on the building materials he had purchased. In October, it appeared that İmdat decided to use the material to build on a new plot to be bought from the *muhtar* of the village at a very low price. This section depicted components of the Ayhans' asset portfolio, and explained how this portfolio was created. The final section focuses on the household's consumption behaviour.

## Consumption and Borrowing

The consumption practices undertaken by the Ayhans to counteract their income deficit took place in different spheres ranging from commodified to semi-and-non-commodified. How successful were these activities in terms of lifting income pressure and enhancing household well-being? We will now examine this in relation to nine selected areas of expenditure: food, health, education, housing, home-maintenance, household items, fuel-utilities, transportation and clothing.

### Non-commodified Consumption

Starting with food, the Ayhans' access to free food was very limited. In spring, Zarife collected various types of edible plants, which she rarely exchanged with her neighbours. The Ayhans also had free access to the left-over fruits and vegetables that Zarife's sister obtained from the supermarket where her son worked in April but such support was cut off after he was made redundant. The Ayhans received no food staples from their village since İmdat was not on good terms with his two brothers there. Even if he had been, it is doubtful whether he would have obtained food support since his brothers were farming on a small scale. Zarife explains why she was no longer able to receive food support from the village either: "Not many relatives remained as such. In the village, everyone buys and sells for themselves, I mean. I had one sister who died; it [food] would come from her. She had a garden; we used to go there in the summer. We used to make our tomato paste, bulgur wheat from there. She used to help me a little. I have one more sister in the village but she just about gets by… On the other hand, there is this grief [probably the conflict]… We wouldn't ask from her, I mean." The conflict over land also led the Ayhans' food support to cease over the years. Other forces concern those leading to erosion in the capacity of agricultural workforce to support their large families living in urban areas, e.g. the flux of migration to the cities, fragmentation of land through inheritance and increase in cost of agricultural production. In these circumstances the agricultural producers became more concerned about sustaining the lives of their rural families first.

Failing to obtain sufficient food support from their social contacts, the Ayhans applied to the Greater Municipality for food and coal aid, but their application was turned down for a number of reasons. First of all, Zarife's degree of disability was found not severe enough to warrant either aid. Secondly, the Ayhans possessed a car, and so failed to meet the means-test criteria. Evidently, despite their *Sünni* background, the Ayhans were unable to find the right man to circumvent on-the-spot checks conducted to see whether the applicant had made a true statement regarding their means. Moreover, one of their 'envious' neighbours informed the officer during the checks that '*their situation is good*'. It was true that the Ayhans had a car and were relatively better off. It is nevertheless interesting to see how reliant a supposedly formal aid distribution process was on local people's subjective opinion. The assumption that some kind of communal justice exists in the given locality seems to underlie the food distribution, but such justice does not necessarily apply in reality. The internal conflict between local agents could well lead to an unjust distribution of resources.

Regarding access to health services, the Ayhans were in a highly favourable position. Since İmdat's SSK premiums were paid on a regular basis at his current job, İmdat became entitled to free treatment in SSK hospitals. These hospitals however offered a lower quality service than State and University Hospitals. By October, having paid 120 working days of premiums at his new job İmdat had already met this condition, Zarife and the kids also became eligible for the same service. Before this, on one occasion after April, Zarife obtained free medicine from other sources. When Zarife fell severely ill due to making bread two days in a row, she was given some pain killers by her neighbour whose pharmacist son ingeniously made use of his client's entitlements to obtain medicine for free.

As for education, access to Turkish national education is supposedly free. Yet due to an under resourcing of the service, schools have introduced fees under the name of 'charitable contribution'. This might sound optional but a lot of pressure was put on families and their kids to pay such fees each term. The Ayhans however neither paid registration nor contributory fees. However, most educational expenses had to be taken care of by the family because, in the new school year, except for a pair of boots given to Burak, none of the kids received any educational aid.

In terms of access to housing the Ayhans were in a favourable position. The ready-built *gecekondu* they owned freed them from rent. As for house repairs Zarife's sister's brother-in-law, a tile installer gave them second hand tiles free of charge. Regarding household items, the Ayhans were given a mini-oven by their ex-landlady for free. They hardly borrowed household items from anyone either due to their being well-equipped or due to rivalries present in their social 'circle'. As for utilities, the Ayhans obtained a ton of wood from the three of their poplar trees cut last year. Moreover, Zarife collected some sticks and twigs from the İmrahor Valley to use in bread-making. The Ayhans had individual subscription to water, telephone and electricity. The neighbourly rumours were that the Ayhans used electricity illegally. The big electrical heater standing in the middle of the front room was supportive of such rumours. Nevertheless, the electricians from Turkish Electricity Company who came in response a complaint from a neighbour found no sign of illegal use.

Regarding clothing, Zarife's house cleaner sisters sometimes brought clothes their employers no longer wanted. Zarife then adjusted them to her kids' size. Nevertheless, Zarife received no help of this nature after April because the number of houses her sisters looked after had fallen as their employers began to recruit cleaners on a monthly salary.

On the whole, the Ayhans' non-commodified practices proved fairly fruitful in terms of their effects on the household income and well-being. How did the family achieve this? Evidently, the path to free goods and services via social support was almost closed to the Ayhans. This may be because the benefit delivery capacity of their 'useful' contacts was limited. Their contacts certainly had urgent survival needs of their own to attend to, and were hence unable to provide any help for others. Moreover, the competitive spirit, which dominated the Ayhans' social environment, seems to have had an undermining effect. Given the lack of support, how were the Ayhans then able to achieve some success in their non-commodified practices? The answer mainly lies in their entitlements. It is true that the Ayhan's food claims were a failure and their access to educational aid was limited in scope but some significant contributions were achieved in the areas of health and housing, since the amount of pressure their land and labour-based entitlements took off their income was consistent and potentially sizeable. What made their practices more successful was the security that these entitlements provided; even though some risk of redundancy was evident in İmdat's current job.

*Semi-commodified Consumption*

In this sphere of consumption, most activities that the Ayhans conducted were of the self-provisioning type. Regarding food acquisition, two distinct self provisioning activities were carried out at their home. The first was food-processing. Like many first-generation migrant women, Zarife possessed the skills necessary to process food in various different ways. Some of the food processing activities were undertaken on a daily or weekly basis. For example, Zarife did home-cooking and bought five kilos of milk on credit from the distributor-on-wheels to make home-made yoghurt. Some others, such as bread-making, were performed at certain times of the year. In April and October Zarife made bread for the summer and the winter. Home-made bread worked out cheaper for the Ayhans as Zarife belonged to a bread-making team of five people: Zarife, her sister and three neighbours. Zarife reported no rivalries between the members, which may have to do with the reciprocity principle underpinning the way team operated. The team acted as a rotating credit association where labour was exchanged in highly balanced terms. The bread-makers called this transaction 'borrowing'. Each member 'borrowed' the other team members' labour until she paid back all her dues in the successive turns. In this way, the team members managed to avoid the monetary cost of labour and could follow their traditional diet.

The other food processing activity took place on an annual basis during preparations for the winter food stock. It started in spring, when fruit and vegetable prices were low. Stocking food was a rural tradition, and certainly proved a cheaper way of acquiring food for winter. The Ayhans' stock for the forthcoming winter contained the following items processed at home: two kilos of sour cherry jam left over from last year, home-made pasta left over from those Zarife prepared last year with the help of her sister and her sister's daughter and daughter-in-law, bottles of tomato paste and sauce that Zarife made out of cheap tomatoes she purchased from the supermarket wholesale, and a good quantity of vegetables such as green beans, pepper and aubergines she bought from the local bazaar over summer to keep in her new freezer. The second type of food provisioning activity was growing fruit and vegetables in the garden where Zarife grew mint and spring onions and kept various fruit trees of their own *gecekondu*. Their fruit yield was usually considerable, but the scope for vegetable growing was limited due to the water bill. Otherwise, there was a lot of space in their garden. That summer, the yield on the trees was also negligible, which obstructed the fruit-processing tasks she used to perform. Because of seasonality, the size of their winter stock proved smaller than the previous year.

In the area of health, the family benefited significantly from İmdat's labour-based entitlements, but 120 days' worth premiums had to be paid before his wife and children were granted access. In contrast, their semi-commodified activities in the field of education were limited: Burak was entitled to the school lunches subsidised by the municipality. As for housing, the Ayhans performed large scale home-maintenance tasks. Between April and October, as planned, they insulated the ceilings of two rooms, plastered and painted them together with the walls. İmdat had the skills to do the metal work but was not as adept at wood work so he called on his neighbour, Kadir, to learn how to install the plywood on the ceiling. Zarife's sister, her daughter and son also came to help. The second maintenance task involved renovation of the kitchen, and Zarife's sister's family, their neighbour and İmdat's aunt's journalist son provided him with labour help. Zarife's sister's brother-in-law gave them second hand tiles for free. İmdat's metal work skills were also of use in the self-provisioning of some household items; İmdat made a dinner table, a shelf and a couple of coffee tables by himself. But the Ayhans did not follow some *gecekondu* dwellers that produced fuel by mixing manure and plaster or coal dust.

Regarding transportation, as students Burak and Samed received 33 per cent concession on the municipal bus and underground services. Being disabled, Zarife was also entitled to the same benefit. The final area was clothing. Zarife was not skilled at lacework but she knew how to knit. She quite often knitted socks, jumpers, cardigans etc for herself and the family members, sometimes by recycling the threads available.

How far did the Ayhans' semi-commodified activities contribute to reducing their deprivation through lifting income pressure? These practices proved helpful mainly in the areas of food, health and home-maintenance. They provided the family with a good food stock, access to subsidised medicine, a better insulated house and a more pleasant kitchen. Besides this, the support they received from social contacts helped them save on labour costs and thereby take off some income pressure. Moreover, working out cheaper ways of buying food and construction materials also reduced the pressure to some extent. Their successes in the areas of education were nevertheless limited as, unlike health their educational entitlements delivered limited and unreliable benefits. The Ayhans' self-provisioning activities encompassed many areas of expenditure. However, self-provisioning was inapplicable to some of the areas to which the Ayhans allocated the biggest share from their budget, e.g. utilities. Consequently, their semi-commodified consumption practices were only of partial help in reducing income pressure and meeting their basic needs. Considerable involvement in the commodified sphere was thus inevitable for the Ayhans.

*Commodified Consumption*

The Ayhans engaged in various commodified consumption practices, ranging from working out cheaper ways of purchasing goods and services to doing completely without. Starting with the methods that the Ayhans used to access certain items cheaply, they purchased fruit and vegetables from the local bazaar set up on a weekly basis. Zarife's visits to the bazaar were more frequent over summer when fruits and vegetables were considerably reduced in price. Due to a lack of ready cash, the Ayhans were less able to purchase wholesale food. After April, the only occasion where they were able to do so was when Zarife bought cases of supermarket tomatoes on offer. Regarding education, the Ayhans had some cheap access to text books. Zarife purchased some books second hand, and where possible sold those from the previous years but had to purchase some brand new.

The Ayhans obtained cheaper deals for the materials used in home repairs. In building the roof over the veranda İmdat paid the labour costs of a former building worker neighbour whose workmanship he trusted. This was an expensive solution yet İmdat believed that it was worthwhile because his neighbour '*worked on the roof as if he had been working on his own*'. Nevertheless, the roof still worked out cheaper as the tiles and wood were purchased second hand from the warehouse owner whom İmdat had known since he moved there. Also when renovating the kitchen, İmdat's aunt's other son sold him the kitchen cupboards at a discount price. Regarding the purchase of household items, the Ayhans found some cheaper solutions as well. The children's beds were bought on sale from a workshop in Siteler, where İmdat worked for a couple of months. Due to his brief acquaintance with the workshop owner, the employer gave him a further 4 million TL discount for each bed. They bought cheap and hence low quality mattresses for the beds, after long searches among the workshops for the cheapest offer. As for clothing, a similar method was used. The Ayhans purchased their clothes from the cheap and low quality markets in Ulus. This had not happened very often since the Ayhans had not always had ready cash for their clothing needs.

Due to their limited income, the Ayhans were neither able to buy in bulk to get wholesale prices nor to buy expensive items for cash. Therefore, they used some flexible payment arrangements such as payments on credit and/or in instalments. These arrangements were a kind of cashless borrowing based on acquaintance and trust. The Ayhans applied this method to a broad range of expenditure areas: Zarife had a credit account with various food distributors-on-wheels, and paid in instalments. She sometimes opened up an account with the textile distributor as well, but during the time of my research she had none. This method was also used for purchasing the text books and school equipment kids needed. For urgent needs, İmdat borrowed the credit card of his aunt's son whom he regarded as much closer than his full brothers and sisters. Similarly, building material, such as the plywood and second hand roof tiles, were purchased based on a flexible schedule from the warehouse owner whom İmdat had known for years. Furthermore, his aunt's other son also let him pay for the kitchen cupboard in instalments. A flexible payment method was also used to purchase coal. The previous year the Ayhans had bought two tons of coal from the municipality in instalments. Zarife got Samed's school teacher to act as a guarantor since, although the family had civil servant relatives whom the municipality would regard as creditworthy, Zarife was unable to find anyone closer to do her a favour. Finally, the Ayhans purchased most of the household items from the shops on flexible terms of payment.

The Ayhans *gecekondu* was well-equipped with electrical appliances and furniture. They possessed a TV, stereo, fridge-freezer, hob, mini-oven, washing machine, vacuum cleaner and computer. Some of these appliances were fairly new. Their mean age was around seven years old. The Ayhans owned a dinner table with six chairs, a corner settee in the front room, five sofas, three beds, a study unit for kids, and two wardrobes. Except for the dinner table, all the pieces of furniture had been purchased within the last year or so. The mean age for these items was also around seven years. When İmdat was asked whether he had sold any household items since April, he said he hoped that *Allah* would not make him do so. The Ayhans by no means perceived them as assets for sale. In their eyes, these items had a use value as well as being a symbol of 'wealth'. This partly explains why the Ayhans chose to channel their spending onto their house to be redeveloped soon after the plans have been approved.

Their home-based activities involved a trade-off. This was evident in İmdat's evaluation of their economic situation in October: "We're hard up for our economic situation. We can't overcome this till the Ramadan, I suppose... It [the hardship] stems from the home-maintenance. We can neither buy food properly nor meat nor anything else. More correctly, we're skimping on food. It [insulation] was also a need; otherwise, [...] it would remain freezing cold inside. We guaranteed this not to happen; we thought rather than using two buckets of coal, we could then use one. We said let's not eat or drink but get the house done." Such a trade-off may sound perfectly rational; yet it was not the insulation of the ceilings with plywood which cost the Ayhans most money but the renovation of the kitchen and the roof over the veranda. This reinforces the idea that the Ayhans placed their spending priority on items which visibly manifested their 'wealth'. It then makes sense why food consumption was less of a priority for the Ayhans. The clothing items were also a target. This might at first sight appear contradictory as clothing items were indeed visible by others but fashion was not a great concern particularly to older generations as long as clothes were clean and neat.

Consequently, flexible payment arrangements are in general regarded as an expensive consumption method since the term of payment is usually rather long. In an inflationary environment, such arrangements might have turned to the Ayhans' advantage. Nevertheless, it is difficult to know exactly since we have no information regarding the initial price, the duration of credit or the price of the item if purchased for cash. However, this method seemed to have served their interest considerably in the purchase of the kitchen cupboards and in case of the coal where the Ayhans obtained help from their social contacts. Examples of such help were however very limited.

Besides these methods, the Ayhans cut down or went completely without certain items of necessity. Their local bazaar attendance was by no means regular; especially in winter when the frequency of their bazaar shopping fell even further. This meant cutting down or sometimes doing without certain fresh fruit and vegetables. The Ayhans' monthly meat consumption was also limited. It was only during the Eid celebrations that the family members were able to consume a good quantity of red meat. During Eid, the Ayhans sacrificed sheep or a cow to observe Islamic rituals and joined a group to share the price of the sacrifice. In the last Eid before April, there were four families in the group: the Ayhans, İmdat's aunt's son, the father-in law of his aunt's son and a neighbour of his father-in-law. The cost and the meat were equally divided among the parties. After the stock ended, the Ayhans were able to purchase minced meat, chicken or fish. Their total meat consumption varied from month to month. Between April and October, the average amount of meat consumed per month had fallen from three and a half to one or two kilos. Their meat consumption was well below the 6kg per month recommended by dieticians for a four member family (Baysal 1993). Every member of the Ayhan family had three meals a day, but this tells us little about the content of their diet. Their meals were in fact rather high in carbohydrate.

The Ayhans had adopted similar practices in the areas of education, utilities and transportation. The family economised on kids' pocket money. The elder son was given a daily allowance and a bus fare. His allowance was not more than one million TL, whereas the younger son had to go without it as the school was within walking distance. As for utilities, although the couple had bought two tons of coal the previous year, they were very careful with the amount consumed. Their *gecekondu* was over 100 m², including four rooms and a large entrance hall. This was costly in terms of heating. There was no central heating to warm up the entire space. The only source of heat was from the stove in their sitting room next to the children's bedroom. The couple slept in the sitting room, sacrificing their privacy for less fuel consumption. Thereby, they saved a ton of coal for the forthcoming winter. The Ayhans were also very careful with the use of gas, telephone and water. The Ayhans had a water boiler. Nevertheless, they maximised the use of the stove by boiling water or heating the food on it, which in turn helped them economise on gas. The Ayhans cut down on their phone usage most. In order to save on her unsuccessful attempts to drop an appointment, Zarife even avoided calling the hospital. Zarife used the rinse water from the washing machine to water the garden. Finally, the Ayhans cut down on their transport expenses in various ways. They did most of their food shopping from distributors on wheels, the local bazaar and the supermarkets nearby; cut down on their visits to their relatives living in distant parts of the city or in the village; reserved their visits to the SSK hospital for very serious illnesses; and restricted the use of their car to very rare occasions such as monthly market shopping, picnics with relatives, funerals and weddings. Furthermore, İmdat walked the distance between his house and the bus stop for Batıkent buses to save a portion of his transport allowance. In good weather, Burak also walked more than an hour to school.

How far did the Ayhans' commodified practices contribute to success? The use of cheaper and flexible methods might have lifted some pressure off their income. However, most of the cheaper methods used sacrificed the quality of the consumption item and hence adversely affected their well-being. Moreover, these methods were unable to prevent them from cutting down on or going without certain items of necessity such as food. Their decision to divert their spending to items visibly manifesting their 'wealth' together with their inclination to save contributed to this result. These practices allowed the Ayhans only to save a golden coin per month (i.e. 21 million TL in April).

Concerning the overall effect of the Ayhans' consumption practices, let us have a closer look at their consumption-related debts in April:

| 100 million TL | as car insurance and road tax |
| 15 million TL | to the food distributor on wheels |
| 12 million TL | as waste disposal tax. |

The consumption activities they engaged in as well as their access to regular and relatively sizeable income and redundancy compensation are likely to have played a role in keeping the debt level rather low. However, the household's involvement in different consumption spheres can be said to be of limited help in counteracting income shortfalls, given the increase in their consumption-related debts by October:

| 340 million TL | to İmdat's aunt's other son for the cupboard |
| 200 million TL | as advance payment from İmdat's patron |
| 130 million TL | as textile instalment |
| 89 million TL | to various food distributors on wheels |
| 50 million TL | unpaid utility bill. |

Most of their debt repayments were scheduled flexibly. Therefore, the household was able to spread the pressure on their monthly income. However, the 200 million TL constituted a significant source of pressure. Consequently, the consumption practices adopted were not successful enough to help the Ayhans balance out their income and consumption without having to borrow or sacrifice the size and quality of the items consumed.

## Conclusion

The Ayhans were the most successful household in April. Although they did not have many plans and some of their plans went unrealised, the Ayhans managed to further reduce their deprivation over the next six months. The forces which contributed to their relative success are summarised below with reference to four main types of behaviour. Starting with income generation, within the April-October period the Ayhans' income diversification level remained low; income was raised mainly through mobilising the male spouse's labour and his informal cultural capital. Their dependency ratio thus remained high. Three household members were dependent on a single income. So if it is not to their engagement in a diversified set of cash generating activities or deployment of a greater number or range of resources in such activities, what did the Ayhans owe their success to? The formal cultural capital stock of their working members is unlikely to have made a significant contribution since it was very limited and had little relevance to the kind of jobs undertaken. Some manoeuvrability in the labour market was rather achieved through deployment of informal cultural capital. Of greater importance are their strong clientelist ties and the luck factor which led to the attainment of a fairly secure job in part of the formal sector where labour rights were violated to a lesser extent, and seasonal fluctuations did not occur.

Concerning income allocation, the Ayhans followed the typical pattern for low-income households; i.e. they adopted the 'female whole-wage' system with the household finances remaining under strict male control. Nevertheless, they avoided 'secondary poverty' through a collective distribution of actual income where both spouses avoided controversial personal spending and made sacrifices on their own needs.

With regard to investment, in April the Ayhans had an asset portfolio containing a *gecekondu* (house and land), car, deposit savings and social insurance. Except for the small interest accrued on their savings, the content of their portfolio remained more or less unchanged over the six months. In particular, two of their assets (i.e. *gecekondu* and social insurance) were beneficial in terms of a) providing future security, b) generating income or c) promoting further asset acquisition. Both assets were obtained through the use of institutional entitlements without putting significant pressure on income or existing assets.

Regarding consumption, the Ayhans engaged in various activities of a commodified, semi and non-commodified nature. Their consumption practices had a considerable non-market focus but brought significant benefits only in the areas of health and housing. The land and labour-based entitlements secured their access to rent-free accommodation and free healthcare, which removed considerable income pressure. Their semi-commodified activities, especially those performed in the areas of food and home-maintenance, also brought some relief to income. Besides the Ayhans' own labour and skills, the provision of free labour, skills, and to a lesser extent material acquired via their social capital contributed to this. Despite these achievements, the Ayhans still had to trade off some of their basic needs or borrow money for consumption purposes in order to counteract income shortfalls. This might be firstly because their income level was low, and secondly because the benefit delivery capacity of the most resources they mobilised for consumption was rather limited.

Consequently, the Ayhans made skilful use of their resources, and collectively shared the responsibility of coping with impoverishment. However, these activities were by no means the key sources of their relative success. They rather owed it to the labour market conditions and state *gecekondu* policies which allowed them to enjoy a relatively higher and more stable pay, rights to social insurance, secure and rent-free accommodation and future returns from *gecekondu* redevelopment.

Chapter 9

# The Hikmets: A Moderately Deprived Household

This chapter focuses on the Hikmets who entered the month of April as a moderately deprived household and managed to maintain their position within the April-October period.[1] It examines in what ways the Hikmets differ in their responses to poverty, and follows up their plans for the next six months. The chapter is structured in the same way as the previous one.

## A Socio-demographic Profile

Tahir and Zühre were a married couple with two children. Tahir was born in 1963, and his wife was born in 1965. Both were primary school graduates and first generation migrants. Both spouses migrated to the city following a chain of relatives but their migration experience does not fit the usual pattern where the marriage precedes the woman's move to the city. From 1975, Tahir visited Ankara intermittently to work casually in construction sites and stayed at his brother's *gecekondu* during the work season. His builder brother and a *hemşehri* of theirs helped him find his first job as a cleaner in a construction company. Tahir settled in the city after marriage. Zühre, on the other hand, moved to Ankara in 1982 for good. Coming to Ankara was not Zühre's idea; it was a decision made by her stepmother. She was sent to Ankara to live with her brother and his wife who was also his aunt's daughter. Zühre stayed in their *gecekondu* for about three to four years, until her arranged marriage with Tahir. After marriage, the couple moved to a *gecekondu* in Northern Ege they built on land purchased from a woman who illegally appropriated the plot. Their son, Özgür, was the first born there in 1987 and their daughter, Zeynep, two years later. In April, both their children were attending school and it was Özgür's first year in *lise*. Zeynep on the other hand was in her seventh year of compulsory education. The Hikmets were about to enter the consolidation phase of the domestic cycle.

---

1    The Hikmets had a weighted aggregate deprivation score of 21.54 in April, and their weighted aggregate change score was −0.16.

**Income Generation and Diversification**

The Hikmets generated income using both labour and non-labour resources. I shall
now describe how they mobilised these resources within the April-October period,
and explore whether they succeeded in their work plans.

*The Use of Labour Resources*

The following analysis begins by exploring Zühre's labour market behaviour and
then moves on to analyse the role of Tahir and finally that of the children.

*Zühre's labour*    In April, Zühre described herself as a housewife because she did
not have a regular job outside the home. In fact, she had no work history of this
kind. It had only been in the last three years that she started doing embroidered
edgings and lacework at home in order to earn money. Her work was causal,
free-lance, informal and very small in scale. It involved selling her labour and
skills. No economic capital was invested in the job; the material necessary for
the lacework was supplied by whoever demanded the product. Zühre was taught
how to do lacework when she was 13. Traditionally, knitting and lacework skills
are assumed to be the basic skills young girls need to learn before they reach the
age of marriage.

   Zühre's job prospects were contingent upon two main influences, i.e. market
conditions and her social contacts. The market in which Zühre operated seemed
fragile because lacework is considered to be a luxury item. It is therefore something
which people dispense with in times of economic crisis. Moreover, the market
appeared to have become saturated since lacework is an easy-to-enter job option
for women who were brought up with such skills. Consequently, market conditions
were rather unfavourable for Zühre. Zühre's social contacts were not so effective
in enhancing her job prospects either. She said that: "I know one or two people.
One or two people get their children's trousseau done and I don't know anybody
else. People who know me like you do, if they know that I'm doing lacework, and
go and tell their friends and acquaintances; or a working woman get lacework
done for her daughter or for herself, I then do lacework; otherwise I don't... .
A person like you will tell me that my daughter or son will get married and only
then it might be available by chance. Because I'm a housewife, because I don't
go anywhere, who do I get to know? How shall I find lacework?" Evidently, her
house-bound life-style had an indirect influence on her job chances by preventing
her from establishing new job contacts.

   Despite such influences, in April Zühre was 'lucky' to have a lace tablecloth
order from a teacher. She found the job through her neighbour and *hemşehri*,
Nazife, whom she 'had said hello' to for 15 years. Nazife was also their *hemşehri*.
Zühre got to know the teacher via Nazife's sister whom she had also worked for in
the past and who was living in the same building with the teacher. The agreement
was that Zühre would be paid 50 million TL per ball of lace thread. As she could

finish approximately two balls per month, her monthly income amounted to 100 million TL. Zühre usually spent six hours daily on the work, including the weekends. Zühre did not see the work as a burden since she enjoyed doing it. This might be why Zühre overlooked the fact that her earnings were only 560,000 TL per hour (i.e. 42 US cents). The constant strain on her eyes was also not a problem for Zühre although the green card was the only form of social security available to her, which meant that she had no pension whatsoever.

Zühre had no idea as to what would follow the lace table-cloth order and had no plans to work outside home for the next six months, saying that this would enable her to keep the house and look after the children more effectively Zühre's reasoning for not wanting to work outside home indicates her awareness of supply-side pressures. Other supply-side pressures in Zühre's 'choice' were as follows. First of all, Zühre had no work experience outside home. She hardly interacted with the rest of the city beyond Ege Mahallesi. Even when she needed to do shopping in Ulus, the old centre of Ankara, Zühre did not feel confident enough to go on her own and thus usually asked for her neighbour İnci's company. Secondly, Zühre was under patriarchal pressure both in her family and social environment, where concerns for preserving women's virtues were very strong. In fact, Tahir had never explicitly objected to the idea of Zühre working outside home but the traditional gender division of labour was prevalent within the family. This way, Zühre was trapped at home but her virtue remained intact. Zühre seemed to have internalised patriarchal ideology. This was evident in the way she perceived women's work outside home i.e. as a last resort. The patriarchal pressures did not end at her doorstep. There was the risk of being subject to slanderous gossip about some working women, which I have personally witnessed circulating in the neighbourhood. Under these pressures it is not surprising that Zühre needed to find a trustworthy employer – somebody who would neither abuse her inexperience nor expose her to accusations of sexual misconduct. The supply-side reasons as to why Zühre, like many other women in the *mahalle*, was caught up in a house-bound life style are indeed extensive. The traditional division of labour which leaves the responsibility of household chores on women's shoulders, the lack of education, and the lack of money in the face of increasing travel expenses can be added to the list.

Certain demand-side pressures also influenced Zühre's decision to stay at home. The job options available to a female primary school graduate were restricted to low paid housework, cleaning work or maybe childcare. Although she never said so, Zühre may well have considered the earnings from this type of work as not worth leaving children at home on their own for. In April a cleaning job paid an average monthly income of 186 million TL. Working in a job of this nature became even less worthwhile when transport costs are added on – a minimum of 24 million TL. Moreover, often cleaning companies did not register their employees with the SSK scheme. In these circumstances, her casual home-based job might well have become an appealing 'option' for Zühre.

After April, Zühre had worked on the tablecloth for a month or so. In May, Zühre noted in her diary that she did five pieces of embroidered edgings for 5 million TL each. These were orders from a neighbour of hers, Nurhan, whom Zühre had known for 15 years. The orders were made on the occasion of her daughter's wedding; Zühre and Zeynep thus completed two more embroidered edgings as a gift. After this, Zühre waited for an order to turn up but by October none had come. This led to changes in her work plans:

| | |
|---|---|
| Interviewer: | In our first interview, I remember you saying that you had no work-related plans? |
| Zühre: | Yes, indeed but now I do. You'll ask why: my husband couldn't work regularly; we've too many pressuring debts; we couldn't pay any back. If my husband couldn't work in winter and my kid goes to school, my kid will need pocket money; the needs of this house must be met... |
| Interviewer: | What does your husband think about your intention to work? |
| Zühre: | He never really said anything against it... Only 'I have my youth, why shan't I work but let you work' kind of thing, you know... He used to say 'raise your children; if you be a good mother for your kids and keep the house clean, I'd be more than happy'. But he saw that he couldn't find jobs; you know that Turkey has been in crisis for the last two or three years; my husband's job [hunting] became much more difficult. Sometimes he works; earns some money; sometimes he can't find work. What he earns goes to roads [on travelling to work]. He hardly meets his own needs so I have to work. |
| Interviewer: | What kind of job are you looking for? |
| Zühre: | I don't look for it myself. I told two or three women to ask in their work places in case... You know Gülcan from Amasya; she said to me that I should have said earlier; a doctor was then looking for somebody to get her kid looked after. |

Zühre now found herself being forced into a hunt for a regular job outside home. After our second interview, her brother-in-law, Samim, informed Zühre that the doctor of the cleaning company where he had just started to work was looking for a female child-carer. Zühre went to see this doctor couple. They offered her 150 million TL including transportation costs, and no social insurance. She was expected not only to care for the child but also to cook, wash the dishes, iron and do extensive house-cleaning on Saturdays. Zühre said no to the couple, telling them that the money they were offering was below the minimum wage of the time. They simply smiled at her. My searches also proved unsuccessful. I had my mother, a retired history teacher, ask her friends whether they were looking for a house cleaner: some already had one and others asked for a reference to make sure she was trustworthy. Unfortunately, we could not provide her with a reference. Zühre was still unemployed when I said goodbye to her in October. A few months later, my mother said to me that Zühre called and told her that she was really depressed and urgently needed a job. Unfortunately none of us could be of help.

*Tahir's labour*   Tahir was a master plasterer with 25 years' experience. He acquired the necessary skills informally through working on construction sites. His job was seasonal: the construction season, if weather conditions permitted, ran from late March to mid-November, so he had only seven months to make enough money to cover the whole year. Tahir's work was also free-lance, most usually he sold his labour and master skills by the day. He worked casually; his jobs lasted from one day to 20 days in a month.

The sector of the market where Tahir constantly had to search for jobs was depressed. The construction industry was in serious decline. TURKSTAT figures indicated a corresponding decline in the number of construction workers. However, Tahir as well as other workers I interviewed claimed that the flux of newcomers continued to enter the market as no formal skills were required for the job. They said that most newcomers were Kurdish people, who had flocked into big cities especially in the early 1990s. Others were from rural areas, coming to work on a temporary basis after harvest time, as the profits from agricultural production had become insufficient to make ends meet. Perhaps TURKSTAT failed to capture the flux of new informal workers in their figures. Sectoral decline as well as saturation of the labour market seemed to have seriously restricted Tahir's chances of finding jobs.

| Interviewer: | How do you find jobs? |
|---|---|
| Tahir: | We sit in the coffeehouse; I know you as my close villager, I call you when a job drops. |
| Interviewer: | Whom do you usually call? |
| Tahir: | İsmet for instance; his brother Halil, plus there's Remzi, from my village, my uncle's son, Kemal, my father's aunt's grandsons, Vural and Mehmet; these are the people I know; I establish the rest of the circle [contacts] myself. We also have a coffeehouse, plus there's *düşeş* [job station] in Ulus. We wait there standing; if no job comes up, we go and sit in the coffeehouse. Either a subcontractor, or a master builder or a supervisor of a construction company or the contractor himself, if he hasn't got a circle, comes there with his car and picks up some men from there. We go [to work] under these conditions... There's been no proper job for the last two years, though. One person comes, 30-40 people gather around him; 100 people gather around him with the hope of finding work. This man has no proper income; he only knows this job; he doesn't have any capital even if he knows [how to do] other jobs. |

Tahir used two distinct methods for seeking work. The first was to wait for the calls from his job contacts. He and his contacts reciprocally informed each other when work was available. The second was to attend the labour market in Ulus, which the workers waiting there called *düşeş*. The Ulus job market was very much like it – the hunt for jobs being highly contingent upon luck. The fact that almost all his job contacts were subject to the same gloomy and uncertain conditions at *düşeş* limited Tahir's job prospects even further. With one exception, none of them had access to a third source of jobs, subcontracted construction projects, which tend to be bigger in scale. This person was his *hemşehri*, İbrahim Çavuş, "[a] subcontractor; he gets hold of such jobs, had built a circle. How shall we say, he was doing the construction work of Public Bank; got to know the general director of the bank, they got on well and he was awarded another contract. He later went abroad and got contracts from Russia". It was İbrahim who had previously sent Tahir to Russia to work illegally. This was a solution companies used to reduce their costs: the company which was awarded a contract passed it on to a subcontractor, who then selected the workers by bypassing the Turkish Employment Institution. The selected workers had to request a tourist visa from the relevant embassy. This shortcut meant not only a loss of tax for the State but also a violation of labour rights, as the employees had signed no written contract with their employer.

This was not the only time that Tahir had been in the illegal list of workers sent off to Russia; he had already been there several times. Due to the illegal nature of the work, Tahir's adventures in Russia were full of incidents where he did not get paid the right amount or where there were long delays in the payments. Despite the high risk of working unpaid, Tahir's April plan was to try his luck again in Russia or anywhere abroad since the payment was much better. Illegal work abroad was more appealing due to being paid in a foreign currency. As a matter of fact, despite all the work which had yet been unpaid, his illegal years in Russia were the time when he earned most. This however came at a price of 10 to 12 work hours per day. In October, however the news was not so good, as the Russia plan had failed. The person who worked for the company that planned to send him had not done so as Tahir had not paid $200 to be put on the list of workers.

Failing to realise his plans, Tahir had no choice but to face whatever conditions the *düşeş* offered. Because of the wet weather conditions in March, Tahir had to wait until April to start searching for jobs. His first job in April was plastering work of a new *Cemevi*, an *Alevi* sanctuary. It was subcontracted to Tahir by a member of his *Alevi* circle: a *hemşehri* or a relative, probably with a similar job. It was not the usual type of job for Tahir as he generally worked on a daily wage basis. The payment was 250 million TL for the entire project, regardless of the number of work days he put in. Due to the scarcity of jobs, as well as his desperation for more income, Tahir avoided employing anyone else from his circle so as to keep all the profit to himself although additional labour was required. He instead worked hard, once resorting to his son's unpaid labour. Tahir's decision suggests that worsening labour market conditions may lead workers to rely less on reciprocity.

Subsequently, while standing at the *düşeş* he was offered another plastering job by İbrahim Çopur, a tile worker. Tahir completed two days of work for him and was paid 20 million TL per day. Having liked Tahir's work, İbrahim Çopur put him in contact with Kerem Bey, owner of a small-scale construction company. Tahir worked for him on-and-off for a total of 40.5 days. The daily pay was this time 17.5 million TL since, despite standstills, the job was regarded as 'regular' and 'long-term'. Tahir found three workers for Kerem Bey among his 'friends'; one of them was his elder brother's undergraduate son, Haşim, who needed to fund his education. The other two were his *hemşehri*s, Orhan and Halil. Tahir explained why he chose them: "We'd worked together before. We know each other, I mean. I know you better; I know that you are reliable and trustworthy; I know you could do the job well. I'd therefore recommend you". The trust basis of their relationship was crucial since it allowed the team to act together like a mini trade union, defending their rights against any mistreatment by the employer, for instance when their wages went unpaid. In the standstills, Tahir did a two-to-three-day plastering job, which Fahri Çelik, his brother-in-law and his colleague, offered Tahir to do together for a daily wage of 20 million TL. İbrahim Çopur made two more offers; a total of three days' work with the same daily payment.

After this, Tahir was unable to find another job for a good month or so but then a neighbour, *hemşehri* and colleague of his, Hüsnü found him a ten-day work in Dikmen park construction where he had also worked and got paid 18 million TL per day. After the park, Tahir plastered the *gecekondu* of his neighbour in two days for 20 million TL per day. Then, Tahir worked for his *hemşehri*, Ali Şimşir who contracted a façade painting job. Tahir this time was paid the 25 million TL he wanted; yet he worked all day for approximately ten hours to finish the entire façade of the seven storey building. Tahir was however not too concerned about his overtime since those hours were invested in the reciprocal relationship with his *hemşehri*. After the façade work, Ali Şimşir found Tahir a three-day plastering job for a daily payment of 20 million TL. Two days after the interview, upon information from Zühre's *hemşehri*, Selim Yordan a building worker, Tahir travelled to İzmit hoping to work for two months but he came back after only 15 days' work.

This season, Tahir was paid for all the hours he worked. In contrast, he was still expecting 175 million TL from a last year employer who had disappeared. The decline in the construction sector and a corresponding increase in unemployment seem to have made it very difficult for Tahir to negotiate either his pay conditions or work hours or entitlements to social insurance. Thus, the decline in real wages could not be helped. Tahir's hourly real pay fell from 2.34 million TL in April (i.e. US$ 1.75) to 1.99 million TL in October (i.e. US$ 1.20). For the same reason, Tahir had little control over his work hours and had to work unpaid overtime. Also his social insurance (SSK) account was inactive over the April-October period.

In addition, Tahir's work continued to threaten his health and safety. His occupational risk grade was five. A few years previously, he had fallen off the scaffolding and broken a tooth. Now in April, he fell seriously ill because he had continued working in the drizzling rain. The four days in bed meant days without an income. His social security entitlements provided little protection against the risks involved in his job. Like Zühre, he only held a green card. If Tahir became seriously disabled at work, he would have nowhere to turn for compensation.

Looking further into the future, Tahir worked in such physically harsh conditions that he looked over 50 instead of 39. Most probably, this man will have to continue working in such conditions at his later ages – if he can – because Tahir had little prospects for receiving full state pension at 55. Some of the reasons for this related to the irregular and seasonal nature of his work and his employer's reluctance to contribute towards his premiums. In order to avoid contributing to his premiums, some of his past employers doctored the dates of his job entry and exit. In the books, Tahir appeared to have left the job when he was in reality there. Some others refused to activate his account for the time he worked for them. As a result, his total premiums since his first registered with SSK in 1977 only came to 1315 days. Tahir managed to top them up to 2200 days by April by contributing to the optional SSK scheme, and by paying the lump-sum in respect of the days served in the army. By October, he had a total of 2310 days premiums. However, he was no longer able to make voluntary contributions. Consequently, Tahir's prospects for receiving a full pension were bleak. Alternatively, he could retire at 55 if he accumulated 3600 days and had been registered with the SSK for 15 years. However, this would mean settling for a lower pension.

*Zeynep and Özgür's labour*   Neither child was working in April or in October since Tahir and Zühre had given priority to their education. Besides this, they found the outer world dangerous, in particular for their daughter: "We could send her if there's work nearby; with relatives or acquaintances but we wouldn't send her anywhere we don't trust. The milieu has become even more messed up, and she's really young as well. What kind of job can a 13 year old girl do?" For the last two years, Özgür however had been earning a few 'bob' over his summer vacations. When he first brought home money Özgür was 14, only a year older than her sister. Özgür was allowed to work since he was the male child.

In the summer of 2002, Özgür did errands in one of the companies where his father worked. Tahir did not want to take him to the site because of the harsh work conditions there. Zühre looked for jobs for her son in the supermarkets nearby but with no success so he went with his father as a last resort. It was not only desperation which made the couple let their son work. Tahir was fearful that Özgür was hanging around too much with his leftist friends from the public house and might end up in confrontation with the police. A black mark on his name could undo what he had so far invested in his son's education. Over the three-month vacation, Özgür only worked for a month or so, six days a week from 8:00 am to 7:00 pm. At the end of this period, he had made 140 million TL, but the money left to him was 100 million TL after the cost of his bus ticket and sometimes lunch was deducted. Özgür had no SSK registration because he was below the legal minimum age to become entitled to social insurance as an apprentice.

*The Use of Non-labour Resources*

The Hikmets' only regular income was from the rent from their (Tahir's) two-bedroom flat in an authorised high-rise apartment in an adjacent *mahalle*. After his last trip to Russia, Tahir had bought the apartment in order to make sure his family had somewhere to go in case of demolition. Meanwhile, they chose to live in their one-bedroom *gecekondu*. The rent for an average size *gecekondu* at that time was 75 million TL, whereas they rented out the flat last February for 110 million TL and the rent had remained the same since then. This left them 100 million TL because 10 million TL went on maintenance. By their decision, the Hikmets obtained 25 million TL more rent but had to compromise on their comfort and, to some extent, their children's education. Özgür once showed me their flat, saying that he could have concentrated on his studies better there. Özgür and Zeynep usually studied in the front room but had nowhere to escape when visitors arrived especially in winter when the kitchen was freezing cold. What made it worse was the frequency of these visits.

Though not as regular and sizeable as the returns from the flat, Tahir also obtained some revenue from his village plot. After his father's death, Tahir and his seven siblings inherited around four acres of land each. Two cultivated the land and lived on the yield. The last harvest time before April, Tahir received 50 million TL as a return for the use of his share of land. This year, Tahir received no revenue from the land. This was mainly due to the increasing costs in agriculture. This meant his brothers could make use of only a very small part of the land and hardly covered their costs. That was why one of his brothers had to come to Ankara for work.

There were a few other odd ways in which the Hikmets raised a small income after April. As in a Maupassant story, Zühre sold her hair for 3 million TL, and Özgür sold some of his books from the previous years. The Hikmets generated income, using both their labour and non-labour resources, but how was the total income allocated? The next section explores this question.

## Income Allocation: Overt and Covert Mechanisms

Although Tahir was thus no longer the sole provider of the family, he remained the main provider, which helped him keep his powerful position intact. Tahir's patriarchal authority had also been consolidated by the way in which finances were arranged within the household. Zühre handed all of her earnings to Tahir without keeping a single *kuruş* (1/100 TL) for her personal needs:

| | |
|---|---|
| Interviewer: | Who keeps your earnings? |
| Zühre: | I bring and give all my earnings to my husband. |
| Interviewer: | Do you keep any money for your personal needs? |
| Zühre: | No… |
| Interviewer: | Why is that? |

Zühre:          Because I don't do make up; don't go to a hairdresser but if I
                had to get my hair cut once in two or three months' time, I tell
                my husband that I'll go to the hairdresser, give me two million...
                Other than that, as Tahir also said, I buy myself a dress or a
                skirt once in ten years; wear it three or four years. I got this
                [showing her cardigan] knitted ages ago in 1990. 'Cause I don't
                have needless expenses...

The term 'personal spending' made little sense to Zühre for several reasons which
are also supported by my own observations. Owing to her house-bound style and/
or nature as a self-sacrificing mother, Zühre seems to have become completely
identified with her family life that she neglected her own needs as a woman.

Zühre handed in her income directly to her husband whereas Özgür gave more
than half of his earnings to his mother; she then let Tahir know about the amount
she was given. This way, Tahir and Özgür avoided the 'embarrassing incident'
which would otherwise crudely show that Tahir alone was no longer able to support
his family. Also in this way, Tahir's masculine pride was not compromised. Özgür
kept the rest of his income with the hope of buying the boots he saw in a shop
window, but later he lent it to his mother too.

Tahir did pretty much the same with Zühre. He brought his entire income
home, including the rent; yet he spared some money for his personal spending
some of which was necessary. As Zühre reported, Tahir took some money for the
bus and the tea he had to drink in the coffeehouse at the *düşeş*. Buying tea for his
work-mates was deemed necessary to meet the conventions of his work. Tahir also
spent some money on games of chance. For him, this was also necessary because
it was hopefully to save his family's future. Tahir had however some unnecessary
expenses:

Interviewer:    Do you spare some money for your personal needs?
Tahir:          No, I don't have personal needs. I've been wearing the same
                thing for 16 years. Thanks to Allah I have no needs or habits like
                that. There couldn't be.... Why; I've never had a lot of money to
                spend.
Zeynep:         But you have your lotteries...
Tahir:          Well, it is a luck thing... it is different.
Interviewer:    Coffee, tea at work, for instance?
Tahir:          My main personal need is fag; unnecessary. I don't smoke a
                posh cigarette, though; 700.000 TL per day. It burns money...
                I wouldn't smoke even that but I get angry; these conditions,
                unemployment...

On the whole, the Hikmets had a fairly collective distribution of income which
inflicted 'secondary poverty' to a lesser extent. It was true that Tahir approximately
spent 21 million TL on cigarettes that month, equal to Özgür's monthly school bus

fares. Tahir's spending on his personal needs thus certainly had an effect on the impoverishment of his family. Yet, the effect was not so devastating since his controversial expenses were far from extensive.

The Hikmets' managed their finances based on the system of the 'female-managed pool'. Tahir and Zühre both had access to the entire income. Tahir took some part in the actual management of that income, but ultimately Zühre was in charge: it was usually her who knew what was to be bought for the house, and yet, each time Zühre needed anything she had to discuss with Tahir regardless of the nature of the item to be bought. Even for a sack of potatoes, she 'consulted' her husband: "As my husband is a man, he wouldn't know: I tell him Tahir, we have this to buy; he'd say OK. No matter what, I couldn't reach any decision without asking my husband. I'd consult him. I decide by looking at him. Tahir, we'll buy shoes for Özgür; OK my dear let's do. For instance, I now need some bed sheets; if we're quite tight or we can't make ends meet, I can't buy it on my own; yet I can't buy anything without consulting him; even if I did ask, he wouldn't give me permission because there's no money... If he had [some money] in his hands, he'd say 'here is your 20, 30 million my dear go and buy some bed sheets, for instance. As we have no money what shall I tell him? Why shall I break his heart and make myself restless?" By these 'consultations' Tahir maintained complete control over household spending. Tahir also had the final word to say in defining the expenditure priorities:

> Interviewer: Who has the final say in financial matters?
> Tahir: I do.
> Interviewer: Oh, so you do?
> Tahir: Both my wife and I do; on an equal basis... Let's say the budget is insufficient. There's 50 million at hand. What can you buy with it; a sack of flour. I instead say the kids are going to school; the bazaar shopping has to be done. What do I say; may your flour stay.

Obviously, Tahir had money for his cigarettes but Zühre never held this against him. Zühre never challenged his authority either covertly or overtly. Unlike some women in the *mahalle*, Zühre did not have a secret kitty of her own. Why not? Was it because keeping a secret budget sounded like betraying Tahir who brought most of his income home and discussed with her how to spend it? Possibly; it might well be that like Tahir, Zühre also perceived these 'discussions' as egalitarian. Or, was it because she did not want to live a lie? This is a possibility yet Zühre had never as much. From her reports, what is certain is that the traditional environment in which Zühre was brought up caused her to internalise patriarchal authority: "Because I saw the same thing [system of financial management] from my family; from my father and brother, it does not bother me at all." Zühre might therefore have remained quite reluctant to seek the secret alternative. Her October reports suggested that their tight income as well as Tahir's strict control over household finances may have also restricted her moves:

| | |
|---|---|
| Interviewer: | Do you have a kitty separate from your husband? |
| Zühre: | [Laughs] No. I don't. |
| Interviewer: | Never? |
| Zühre: | I suppose, it doesn't happen because his earnings are insufficient. How could you save? He should give you 5 million and shouldn't ask what happened to it so you could save, couldn't you? Last night he gave me 40 million; he took 5 million of it back as his pocket money, gave 6 million of it to our son; I went to the bazaar twice. Whatever I spend is in front of [his] eyes. How can I set money aside? |

Zühre was hence unable to create a secret kitty. Was there another kitty to secure the Hikmets' future? This is explored in the next section.


**Investment, Insurance and Credit Use**

The Hikmets' portfolio included both financial and non-financial assets. Starting with their financial assets, the family had no savings deposited in a bank account in April. In fact, Tahir saved some money as a result of his trip to Russia, but his bank book showed that they were all used up within a year because after he came back, he could not find enough jobs partly due to the seasonal nature of his work: when he arrived, it was already late summer and most jobs were gone. Then, the two subsequent economic crises hit the market. As a quick way of making money, Tahir also took a risk in buying $3000 worth bonds in the stock market, but lost all but $500 worth.

The family was thus not part of any formal saving scheme in April but Zühre had already been a *gün* (rosca) member with her husband's knowledge. The working of their *gün* was simple. Once a month, on a fixed date, members contributed $50 to a common pot to be granted to the member who came up that month in the draw. This continued until the member who came last received the lump-sum. The draw took place at the very outset so that every member would know their turn in advance. Their choice of US Dollar was to protect the value of lump-sums received by each member. The number of *gün* members was unusually small. There were Zühre, and two of her neighbours, İnci and İnci's daughter. With at least two lump sums Zühre was expecting to receive between April and October, she was planning to pay off some of their debts. In October, it appeared that her plans were unrealised because, due to the lack of regular and sufficient income, Zühre had been unable to keep up with her monthly contributions. She thus became indebted to the member(s) to maintain her membership. The other *gün* she participated in after April had however proved more successful. In this *gün*, other than Zühre, there were six people all of whom were her neighbours. Every month two members shared equally the lump-sum based on the wholesale price of two sacks of sugar (100 kg). How to use the lump-sum was the member's own business. Yet, Zühre bought a sack of sugar (50 kg) with hers. Zühre was this time able to cope well as more members meant reduced contributions.

Why did Zühre join these *gün*s? Could she not have made the same savings on her own? Probably not. The monthly contributions were perceived as a form of loan; therefore, *gün* membership was a test of credibility, in which pride is also invested. Failure to repay debts would therefore be costly. It might not only jeopardize the future flow of benefits that might accrue from the contacts who heard about their reputation but also wound their pride. To prevent this, members with a tight income had to make the extra effort to set aside some money, which could otherwise easily be spent on other pressing needs. *Gün*s hence acted as a motivating force for people on a low income to save.

Turning to the Hikmets' non-financial 'assets', as mentioned earlier, they owned an apartment which Tahir bought when the Northern Ege *gecekondu*s were on the verge of demolition in September 2000. Owing to the dwellers' strong resistance, the Hikmets managed to keep their *gecekondu* for the time being. If it was not for the flat, the family would otherwise have nowhere else to go. The housing co-operative was no longer an option because Tahir had already sold his rights to a third party, due to being no longer able to keep up with the regular and gradually increasing nature of the instalments. He used 250–300 million TL proceeds to clear the debts incurred to pay the instalments. Tahir invested in the flat, using the dollars he saved after his fruitful trip to Russia; but this was insufficient to cover the whole price. Therefore, Tahir was very hopeful that another trip would come up anyway in the future, chose to borrow from their 'circle'. Given their irregular and limited earnings, their contacts were the only source of credit offering flexible terms of repayment: "All those [referring to people whom he borrowed money] are the friends I know of. You [they] know that I have nothing; you [they] are already working and make do; and if I tell them not to pressurise me; they'd understand; because they know; they know that I'll repay when there's [money]. We manage each other like that." In April, the debts on the flat were:

$1725  to Tahir's brother [building worker]
$750   to Zühre's step sister's husband [building worker]
$500   to Zühre's 'close villager' [building worker]
$300   to Zühre's uncle's grandson [small-scale company owner]
$250   to Zühre's uncle's son-in-law [building worker]
$200   to Nazife, neighbour-*hemşehri* [husband – rubbish collector]
$150   to Tahir's uncle's son [municipal worker]
$100   to Zühre's aunt's son [building worker]
DM200  to Zühre's sister's husband [now unemployed].

The list of debts indicates that most of the creditors were relatives on Zühre's side. Zühre never said so, but I heard other women saying that it was mostly them who got involved in debt transactions in order to save their husbands' pride. This might be one reason; or it might simply be that the Hikmets were closer to Zühre's relatives. What is certain here is that the creditors were carefully chosen to minimise the risk of refusal. This principle was important for Tahir to protect his pride from getting hurt in the very act of asking for a loan:

| | |
|---|---|
| Interviewer: | [Referring to Zühre's uncle's grandson] How about his economic situation? |
| Tahir: | Yes, his is very well; set up a company in partnership of his brother. |
| Interviewer: | Can you call on these people for help in the future? |
| Tahir: | No... Currently it's because of unemployment... You can't ask help of everybody. |
| Interviewer: | Why is that? |
| Tahir: | The full stomach would know nothing of the empty stomach... He'd say there are jobs, he could well work and earn money. Also when people are inclined towards making capital; they'd say I shall make six *kuruş* out of three *kuruş*; then ten billion out of this. There's such ambition for money. Even if he gave, I wouldn't demand myself... |

[...]

| | |
|---|---|
| Interviewer: | Can you call on the others then? |
| Tahir: | As we did when they had it [money]. Among the people from whom we borrowed, we can both borrow from them as well as we can lend to them... If there were any [money]... If there weren't, what of theirs can we borrow; nothing. |
| Interviewer: | You said you wouldn't from one person? |
| Tahir: | Out of all [creditors], only from that one... everybody has their own temperament. He'd give, though – if I asked but I have a principle. I should get it hundred percent from the person I asked for. If I didn't, then my pride would get hurt. I don't want to get my pride hurt. |

Yet, it was not only Tahir whose pride would get hurt in the process:

| | |
|---|---|
| Interviewer: | Is he [aunt's son] somebody whom you can call for help in the future? |
| Zühre: | He would; why should I deny but I've never asked. |
| Interviewer: | Why is that? |
| Zühre: | Because he wouldn't tolerate our whim. |

Interviewer: Why not?

Zühre: I don't know. We do ask for help from anybody but I don't have the habit of asking from him, neither does my husband. He'd swagger, I mean... so we don't want to swoop. Full of themselves, you know... She [his wife] has golden bracelets on her arm, if you go and ask, she'd say I can't or I don't know. I'd then feel offended; my pride would get hurt. I'd rather ask from someone else. I ask from the one who would tolerate my whim. You tolerate it so I'd ask from you; he's son of my aunt; but I wouldn't.

The risk seemed to have been minimised by borrowing from the reciprocal contacts a) for whom the Hikmets had done favours in the past, and/or b) who were of similar socio-economic status. For Tahir, the risk of refusal was higher with people of higher status as they tend to be less sympathetic to the predicament of the worse off. It also seems that better off people are less likely to have interest in fulfilling the reciprocity obligations, simply because they are less in need of the support of others and hence might find it less difficult to turn down the requests for help. As I have observed in two other cases, it might also be that the better off members might have the willingness to help, but helping one might trigger a request from another. If the other calls for help were turned down, this might cause gossip and resentment. The better off might thus choose to help none. The list of reasons could well be extended but what is also important here is that such dynamics can cause a growing isolation between the better and worse off, leaving the worse off people like Tahir in a paradoxical situation: To borrow money, the people Tahir ended up having to turn to were less likely to have an excess of money to offer, or more likely to have accumulated it with great difficulty. Thus, in times of sheer desperation, Tahir could not avoid turning to his better off contacts for help and hence facing a higher risk of refusal.

In April, Zühre and Tahir had no plans to sell the flat as it was their only regular source of income. They were instead expecting to clear their debt by Tahir's working abroad. The collapse of the Russia plan had a series of consequences. Firstly, Zühre's rosca plan failed. Thus, the family had been unable to clear any of their flat debts in the next six months. The size of their real debts rose from 5,564,043,000 to 6,873,250,000 TL. This indicates that borrowing can be unfavourable even in a highly inflationary environment. Failing to realise their initial plan, the Hikmets resorted to a common tactic which I refer to as 'debt-chaining', i.e. becoming indebted to new creditors to repay earlier ones. Tahir and Zühre devised this tactic when they started sensing that their reciprocal contacts were no longer able to '*tolerate their whim*'. Using the debt-chaining tactic, the Hikmets were managing to hold on to their flat.

Apart from the flat, the Hikmets owned four acres of rural land Tahir inherited after his father's death. The benefit delivery capacity of the plot was very limited. Tahir would neither be able to rent it out nor sell it as it was – or at least used to be – his brothers' source of subsistence. Yet, Tahir perceived those four acres as a form of family insurance to fall back on in case 'things went wrong' in the city and hence his plan was to keep it as it was but given the decline in agricultural profits, a return to the village would seem unlikely unless Tahir received a pension. However, as shown earlier, Tahir's likelihood of receiving a pension was very low.

### Consumption and Borrowing

In order to counteract their income deficit, the Hikmets adopted various practices in different consumption spheres ranging from commodified to semi-and-non-commodified. How far did their activities contribute to releasing income pressure and reducing deprivation? The following three sub-sections explore this in relation to nine selected areas of expenditure, i.e. food, health, education, housing, home maintenance, household items, fuel-utilities, transportation and clothing.

*Non-commodified Consumption*

Starting with food, the Hikmets obtained little free food. Zühre collected wild spring plants as part of their traditional Central Anatolian cuisine and their social contacts sometimes supplied free food. Her neighbour, İnci, let her collect the wild plants in her garden since coming from Black Sea Region, her dietary habits were rather different. She also gave them a sack of potatoes, and for some time had shared three of her eight-loaf daily bread allowance granted by the municipality. The bread support, however, had to be withdrawn after new members joined İnci's household. Zühre's comments on her granddaughter's educational failures are also likely to have led İnci to withdraw her support. In addition, a *hemşehri*-neighbour, Pembe, brought some fruit and vegetables once last winter when Zühre was unable to afford the local bazaar shopping. Mainly Pembe and, to a lesser extent, İnci provided the family with food left in the saucepan after dinner or with food in whose preparation Zühre was of help. The Hikmets also had cooked meals at certain neighbours and relatives' homes as part of socialising. Most food exchange was governed by the rule of reciprocity. Thus Zühre made similar returns. This was all the free food support the Hikmets had access to. Tahir's brothers had sent no food from the village as there was no surplus.

Failing to obtain sufficient food support from their social circle, the Hikmets applied for municipal food (and coal) aid but without success. It is likely that the ways in which such aid was distributed played a role in their failure. The aid was distributed in at least two distinct ways. One was by direct application to the municipality with four official documents: a) a written statement from the *muhtarlık*, providing family evidence and a brief description of their predicament, b) a document from the deed office, proving that none of the members possess any non-financial assets, c) a document from the tax office, declaring that none of the members own a car or run a business, and d) records from the offices of three social insurance schemes, indicating that the applicant had no entitlements. The application was assessed by the municipal officers but it was believed that if the applicant could find 'the right gatekeeper' to influence the assessment he would guarantee the aid. The right man could be anybody; a *hemşehri*, a friend of a *hemşehri*, a relative, a party member etc. With the help of the gatekeeper, even on-the-spot-checks could be circumvented. The Hikmets had however no contact with such gatekeepers. Another reported method bypassed the above procedure. The Greater Municipality was said to allocate a quota for their party members and previous voters to consolidate their loyalty and to assign a neighbourhood representative to identify these people. However, the Hikmets, due to their *Alevi* background, would evidently not appear on any list prepared by members of a *Sünni* Islamic Party either.

In terms of access to healthcare, the family was in quite a favourable position. All family members held green cards, although they should have failed the means-test due to their possession of a flat. The green card enabled the members to benefit from the State and University hospitals which offered a high quality medical service. However, the Hikmets lacked access to state-subsidised medicine, which rendered their eligibility for hospital treatment less worthwhile. Similarly, the Hikmets could hardly meet the children's educational needs by their non-commodified activities. When Özgür first started *lise*, he borrowed his uncle Samim's black jacket until Zühre could afford to buy him one. In September, Zeynep won a prize (e.g. note-books, pencils and a school bag) from a radio program.

The Hikmets lived in a rent free *gecekondu* in Northern Ege, which was liable to evacuation[2]. The *gecekondu* was occupied illegally but Tahir saw this as a self-endorsement of his right to shelter. The Hikmets did not perform any non-commodified activities to maintain their *gecekondu*. The family did not have much free access to household items either. Despite this, their *gecekondu* was well-equipped with white electrical appliances and furniture. They had a TV, video, small stereo, fridge, vacuum cleaner, hob set and mini-oven. Their mean age was seven years. As for furniture, they owned a table with six chairs, three sofas, two of which were the beds for the children, one double bed, wardrobe, and carpets for the front room and the kitchen. The average furniture age was ten years. For the Hikmets, these items symbolised status, and perhaps the unity and self-sufficiency of the household. Some items were borrowed from the neighbours; for instance, an oven to bake something that did not fit in theirs. This was however a rare occurrence as it either imposed costs on the party who lent the item or ran the risk of the item being broken in the process.

Regarding utilities, the Hikmets had an individual subscription to electricity, telephone and water services and unlike some neighbours who made illegal connections to the main electricity lines or manipulated the meter, the Hikmets paid for the service. As for fuel, they used wood and coal in the stove only to heat the front-room and had free access to wood, which came from different

---

2   The reasons underlying the evacuation decision are explained in Chapter 4.

sources. During the previous winter, Tahir cut down two trees and for this winter, Fahri, Zühre's brother, a security guard in a construction site, brought them old wood pieces from his workplace. By October, the coal had however not yet been sorted out. Zühre applied for the municipal coal aid again but the results were yet unknown.

Overall, their non-commodified practices were rather limited in terms of their effects on the household income and well-being. The most significant contributions were achieved in the areas of health and housing since their access to green card entitlements and public land brought consistent and potentially sizeable relief to their household income. Yet, their access was insecure. The family was faced with the high risk of being evacuated from their *gecekondu* and their green cards being taken away. Moreover, the limitations of their social capital also restricted their success. It seemed that most of the people from whom the Hikmets received free goods and services had limited capacity to deliver benefits. As Tahir pointed out, "[w]hat can I say to anyone? Everybody is in the same situation [...]. For this reason, you'd neither feel offended nor get upset with it; everybody uses whatever opportunities there exist in their hands. You can't do anything beyond this; even if you wanted to do so. Today, you're smoking a cigarette; you're asking for one from me. I have one cigarette; what can I do; I could only give half of this to you; half is yours; the other half is mine. I can only do this can I do anything else? In the end, everything is tied to this. Only those who have the opportunities use it. [...] Yet, with us, the opportunities are limited". For these reasons, the flow of free goods and services from their contacts remained rather restricted.

*Semi-commodified Consumption*

Most of the Hikmets' semi-commodified activities were of the self-provisioning type. Two main food-provisioning activities were performed at home. The first was food-processing. Zühre had the skills to process food in all sorts of different ways: baking, drying, preserving, pickling etc. Some of these were performed on a weekly basis such as yogurt-making. Others took place annually, generally in autumn. Preparing a winter stock was not a response confined to families with seasonal workers; it was in fact a rural tradition maintained by most urban migrants. It was of particular importance to the Hikmets as a safety net for long winter days with no work. By October, Zühre's winter stock was complete and included more food than the previous year as her husband had earned relatively more. A large portion of the stock was composed of processed food: a total nine kg of apricot, peach and quince jam, 25 kg of garlic, chilli pepper, cucumber and tomato pickles; 30 kg of dried vegetables including aubergine, green beans, okra and pepper; ten kg of pickled vine leaves and 20 kg of home-made macaroni. Zühre prepared most of it herself; sometimes Zeynep helped her mother. Pembe came to help with the macaroni only and Zühre helped her in return. The second food-provisioning activity was fruit and vegetable growing in the garden but Zühre grew only spring onions, cress and parsley, and kept a walnut tree in her garden. This was because the soil was not fertile enough; it therefore demanded more water, which in turn put a strain on the water bill. Moreover, the size of their garden was rather small.

The Hikmets' semi-commodified involvement in the other expenditure areas such health, education, home-maintenance, household items, transportation and clothing was quite extensive but of rather low value. Starting with health, the Hikmets were granted a green card but they still had to pay for prescribed medicine. Seeing Zühre going without her anti-depressant pills, İnci, a pensioner, tried to get the pills prescribed on her social insurance card but failed. Later Zühre called on help from Melike, a neighbour whose son was working in a pharmacy. Her son got hold of the pills for which Zühre only had to make 20 per cent contribution. Melike's son managed this by finding a doctor who agreed to prescribe the pill on his father's social insurance card.

In the area of education, the Hikmets used various methods to avoid both the registration and contributory fees. Zühre, with the help of a neighbour, managed to get reductions on the arbitrary fees to be paid to get registered with a supposedly free state high school:

Interviewer:   Have you come across any problems when getting your son registered, then?

Zühre:         They didn't first accept him. We found the [right] man and got our kid registered with money. First I insisted; she [the senior director] was an acquaintance, the daughter of my neighbours' sister-in-law. She said 'no we can't accept him'; I then took my neighbour with me and said no way would my son remain outside. She said their cadre [capacity] was full. How come full? She then mentioned money. OK but then don't tell us that the cadre is full. We found dollars, exchanged it and took it to the school.

[...]

Interviewer:   How much did you pay?
Zühre:         One hundred million.
Interviewer:   Was it the asking price?
Zühre:         No, they first asked for 250 million. I said I couldn't possibly pay this. They then said you'd give 150 million, and I said I couldn't even pay 50; my husband was a plasterer; we had green card; I was doing lacework. I didn't have any means at all but I'd find this money just for my son not to remain outside school. They, then, settled for 100 million and gave me a receipt.

Her neighbour's mediation ensured Özgür's attendance at a school which, in their view, delivered better quality education, yet proved unsuccessful in removing the fee altogether, as Zühre had expected. In fact, their neighbours Göksel and

Cansel were able to get their daughter registered with the same school without paying a single *kuruş*, perhaps because the person whom they got in touch with via one of Cansel's brothers occupied a more powerful position in the administrative hierarchy of the school. Regarding the contributory fees paid each term, the family had two children at school, which meant that the request Zühre sent to the director of Özgür's school to be exempt from one fee was accepted. She also refused paying Zeynep's fees and confronted the school director, saying that he was 'welcome' to terminate Zeynep's studies. Obviously, this would not have happened because her access to national education is guaranteed by law but it was a cause of tension in the family and humiliation for Zeynep in the class when she was pointed out as one of those who were unable to pay the fees.

In the area of housing, the Hikmets engaged in several maintenance activities helped by Tahir's building skills. Tahir did most of the small-scale electrical repairs himself but sometimes called on his neighbour Nuri for help. The plumbing repairs were done free of charge by a *hemşehri*-colleague for whom Tahir did some plastering in return. After April, though unplanned, Tahir carried out two main maintenance tasks in the house. Firstly, he insulated, plastered and repainted the ceiling himself. A neighbour, Göksel who was a driver in a construction company supplied the material cheaply and delivered it free in the company car. Secondly, Tahir added a roof over the veranda, for which he also received some support. Hamdi, the tile worker *hemşehri* and neighbour, obtained cheap second hand roof tiles. In return, Tahir supervised him while he was installing bathroom tiles, and did some plastering for their *gecekondu* at a discount price. As for household items, the curtains, mats and sofa covers were made by Zühre with the help from Pembe. Most material was purchased but the curtains were recycled from curtains which a transient employer of Tahir had given him a few years previously. The coffee tables were produced by Tahir, mostly by recycling the material available at home. The carpets were exchanged with tokens that Tahir accumulated from a newspaper he purchased for this reason. With regard to transportation, as students, Özgür and Zeynep were entitled to 33 per cent concession on the municipal buses and the underground. In the field of utilities, no semi-commodified activities were carried out. A final area was clothing. Zühre knew how to do knitting and sewing. In April, she was knitting a jumper for Zeynep, which was quite a rare activity because the increasing cost of material made knitting less worthwhile. Cheaper alternatives were available in Ulus, and Sıhhiye clothing markets and in the local bazaar.

On the whole, how far did the Hikmets' semi-commodified practices prove successful? The greatest benefits were in the areas of food and home-maintenance; they had now at least a good food stock and a better insulated house for the forthcoming winter. The labour support received perhaps brought some relief to the household income. Also the use of certain methods to find cheaper offers is likely to have taken off some income pressure. Their achievements particularly in the areas of health and education were however small mainly due to their lack of access to beneficial entitlements. Moreover, no self-provisioning activities were undertaken in areas, such as utilities, to which a significant portion of their income was allocated, and some others e.g. making clothes did not save any money. Their semi-commodified practices remained rather restricted in reducing income pressure and meeting basic needs. This meant that most of their basic consumption needs had to be met through the market.

*Commodified Consumption*

In this sphere of consumption, the Hikmets performed various practices ranging from finding cheaper alternatives to going completely without certain items. The Hikmets used a number of methods for purchasing goods and services more cheaply. Starting with food, from mid-spring to the end of autumn, Zühre did most of her food shopping in the weekly local bazaar where the prices were cheaper. She often went there in the early evening when prices were even lower; yet this was when the sellers usually introduced their low quality product and hence created a false economy. Sometimes, Tahir bought food for breakfast from the market in Ulus which was also cheaper. In October, Zühre stopped buying the bread from the local shop on credit. Instead she started queuing up at 5:00 am in front of the municipal kiosk for cheap but low quality bread. While preparing the winter stock, Zühre bought a sack of sugar from a wholesaler and ordered lentils and various sorts of wheat from the village. The price was the same as those in food distributors-on-wheels. And yet, her order worked out cheaper because, as Zühre reckoned, the quality of rural food was much better. Regarding education, Zühre paid less for her children's school uniforms as she bought them from the markets in Ulus and Sıhhiye where clothing was also cheap but once again low quality; the children were expected to wear these uniforms throughout their three-year education. A final area where such methods were applied was home-maintenance. With the help of his two neighbours, Tahir obtained one lot of construction material at wholesale price and another at second hand price.

Owing to the irregular and limited nature of their earnings, the Hikmets were unable to buy in bulk at wholesale prices or to buy expensive items. They therefore had to make flexible repayment arrangements to purchase certain goods (e.g. food, gas bottles and household items). These arrangements included buying on credit and paying for by instalments, and were usually made with local shops and distributors-on-wheels, who knew and trusted Tahir and Zühre. A written contract and a guarantor were required where the trust element was weak. Flexible repayment was in general assumed to be an expensive solution but inflationary environment might have made it an advantage. Yet, since we do not have enough knowledge of the initial price and duration of credit, we cannot tell for certain.

The above methods did not prevent the Hikmets from cutting down or going without some items of necessity. In winter, Zühre was unable to afford regular shopping even in the local bazaar. Most of the time, they relied on their food stock, and rarely ate fresh fruit and vegetables. Zühre purchased apples and oranges, but 'luxury' fruits such as bananas entered their house once or twice a year. In summer, her bazaar shopping became more frequent and varied as fruit and vegetable prices were lower. For the last two years, Zühre was unable to include home-made bread in her winter stock as she had to cut down on the flour. Their meat consumption was also limited. Each month Zühre could only afford four kilos of chicken thighs, two thirds of what is recommended by dieticians for a four member family to have a balanced diet. The family members had three to four meals per day. This nevertheless tells us little about the content of their diet, which was rather high in carbohydrates.

Similar practices were also used in the areas of education, health and transportation. The children's pocket money was a target for such practices. Özgür was sometimes only given his bus fare; Zeynep's school was within reach. Four days a week she thus came home for lunch. Only on Fridays was she given a small amount so that she would not feel excluded when her mates were buying food from the school canteen. Transportation was a great burden on the family budget. Other than Tahir's *dolmuş* fare to work and Özgür's bus fare to school, all transportation costs were minimised: Zühre used nearby options for shopping such as the bazaar, the distributors on wheels, or Tahir bought some food on his way home from work. The family reserved their visits to SSK hospitals only for very serious illnesses as getting there meant paying a double fare. Similar practices were performed in the area of health. Zühre had to stop before completing a six-month course of her medication.

In brief, their commodified practices were also limited in their contribution to household success. The methods used for buying items cheaply and flexibly might have helped remove some income pressure. Yet the quality of these items was often compromised. Moreover, the family had to cut down on or go without some of the basic consumption items. Their commodified practices thus proved rather insufficient in terms of counteracting income shortfalls without inducing deprivation.

This was also the case with the Hikmets' consumption practices as a whole, given the extent of their borrowing. The insufficient and irregular nature of their earnings compelled the Hikmets to borrow from their social contacts constantly and on a short-term basis. Zühre's note-book contained the following list of consumption-related debts in April:

| | |
|---|---|
| 60 million TL | to the local shop |
| 35 million TL | Pembe-Cemal [transporting goods] |
| 30 million TL | to Gülcan- Nuri [child-carer, regular worker in a factory] |
| 5 million TL | to Fatma [her husband, civil servant]. |

The 'debt-chaining' tactic was also used in repayment of these debts. All creditors were neighbours who were relatively more able to afford money lending. There occurred no significant change to their borrowing pattern within the next six months:

| 22.5 million TL | to the gas bottle distributor |
|---|---|
| 12.5 million TL | to the flour wholesaler |
| 50 million TL | to the local shop |
| 35 million TL | to Gülcan |
| 10 million TL | to Pembe-Cemal. |

Consequently, the Hikmets' consumption practices failed to allow them to balance out their income and consumption needs without having to borrow or sacrifice their well-being. This is due to their limited earnings and the low benefit delivery capacity of the resources mobilised for consumption purposes.

**Conclusion**

The Hikmets were moderately deprived when they entered the month of April. Even though most of their plans failed, they managed to preserve their position over the next six months. The factors which rendered them less successful than the Ayhans are discussed below in relation to four areas of behaviour. Beginning with income generation, the Hikmets' income in April was relatively more diversified. They raised income using both their labour and non-labour resources. Their dependency ratio was relatively low: only two members were reliant on household income. By October, their income became less diversified and the number of dependants increased to three. However, at both times, the Hikmets remained moderately deprived. The formal cultural capital accumulation of their labour force is also unlikely to have caused this because it was equally low and less relevant to the type of labour market activities carried out. The Hikmets also appear to have achieved some manoeuvrability in the labour market through mobilising their informal skills and social capital resources. However, like cultural capital, the latter was also of little help in terms of attainment of a better job. Thus, the working members of the family remained caught up in the informal sector where labour rights were completely unprotected and seasonal fluctuations were strongly felt. Although the working conditions offered in the informal sector had not improved significantly over the six months, the removal of the seasonal influences after April enabled the male spouse to earn more. This is likely to have counterbalanced the effect of the wife's job loss but proved insufficient in preparing them for the forthcoming winter. The Hikmets were indeed unable to accumulate any savings other than the winter food stock.

With regard to income allocation, the Hikmets used the 'female-managed pool' system. The household finances were strictly controlled by the male spouse who had privileged access to a few controversial areas of personal spending. Nevertheless, their actual distribution of income remained fairly collective in nature. Thus, the Hikmets also managed to avoid 'secondary poverty' to a considerable extent.

Concerning investment, the Hikmets possessed an asset portfolio which consisted of a flat, 10 *dönüm* rural land and a *de facto gecekondu* house that they managed to hold on to over the six month period. However, apart from the flat, none of these assets had a high benefit delivery capacity. Their social capital rendered the purchase of the flat possible, but was incapable of lifting the pressure on the Hikmets' income and existing assets since the increasing real returns to foreign currency within the April-October period turned social capital borrowing to their disadvantage. Moreover, their lack of access to *gecekondu* and labour-based entitlements also made them less successful.

Finally, the Hikmets adopted various consumption practices of a commodified, semi-and-non-commodified nature. Their non-commodified activities took place in eight expenditure areas among which the value of their practices were most significant in the areas of health and housing. The members' entitlement to green card and *de facto* occupation of public land for shelter helped remove considerable income pressure, but left them exposed to insecure housing. Their semi-commodified activities were of similar significance particularly in the fields of food and home-repairs. The use of family labour and skills as well as those freely available through their social capital helped lessen some income pressure. In the commodified sphere, the use of cheap and flexible purchasing methods failed to prevent the Hikmets from having to cut back or go without basic goods and services or borrow money. Overall, their consumption activities were hence rather unsuccessful in counterbalancing income shortfalls. This results both from the limited and irregular character of their income and the low benefit delivery capacity of the resources deployed in these activities.

Like the Ayhans, the Hikmets were an enterprising family, skilfully using whatever resources were available, and acting in a fairly collective manner to cope with their impoverishment. However, such efforts meant very little success on their own. The Hikmets proved less successful than the Ayhans due to being faced with informal and seasonal labour market conditions and exclusion from state *gecekondu* policies. They were hence denied the opportunity to obtain a higher and more stable income, access to social insurance through work, secure accommodation and returns from *gecekondu* redevelopment.

# Chapter 10

# The Cansevers: A Relatively Worse Off Household

This chapter examines the case of the Cansevers which proved to be one of the most deprived households in April and whose situation had worsened by October.[1] It seeks to understand how they differed in their responses to poverty and why their plans failed to bring about any improvement. The chapter follows the same structure as the previous case studies.

## A Socio-demographic Profile

Cemal and Süreyya were a married couple with two children. Cemal was 43 years old, and his wife was two years younger. Both were primary school graduates and were first-generation migrants. Cemal's move to the city was typical of chain migration. He migrated to Ankara at the age of 12, and initially worked with his uncle's son as a street vendor. Cemal then worked and literally lived in other people's bakeries until he got married in 1984. Süreyya moved to Ankara after their marriage, but whether she was abducted by or agreed to flee with Cemal remains unclear. Since then, they have lived in several rental *gecekondu*s.

Their son, Umut was born in 1985 and their daughter, Nazlı, four years later. In April, the Cansevers were in the consolidation phase of their domestic cycle: Süreyya's fertile years were behind her; their children were grown up; Nazlı was in the seventh year of compulsory education. Umut was working for his father and at the same time studying electronics at a vocational school. That year was his final year but in April, Süreyya said he dropped out for financial reasons; otherwise he was really a keen student. Nevertheless, the school administration recalled him so he was able to complete his vocational training by October. His parents were however unable to afford his further education. Currently, Umut was neither being coached privately nor able to find the time to prepare himself for the university entrance exam, as he was busy earning an income.

---

1 The Cansevers' weighted aggregate deprivation score in April was 15.88 and their weighted aggregate change score was −1.14.

## Income Generation and Diversification

The Cansevers raised an income, using their labour and cultural capital resources only. The next three sub-sections portray how the family mobilised these resources, and follow up their work plans. The focus is first on Süreyya's labour market behaviour, and then on the contributions of Cemal, and finally, those of the children.

*Süreyya's Labour*

In April, Süreyya described herself as a housewife because she did not have a regular job outside the home. She had never had any regular jobs but worked outside home as a cleaner. For the previous 18 years, Süreyya had made bootees, embroidery edgings and bread to earn an income. She had learnt these skills in the village during her childhood. Since then she improved her skills either through personal effort or help from her uncle's daughter, who lived nearby and did the same work.

Her bootee and embroidery work was casual, free-lance and small in scale. Süreyya devised two different methods of work. Firstly, she sold her labour and skills on order. The person who made the order supplied the material required for the desired design. Secondly, she produced a variety of bootees and embroidered edgings in advance. Therefore she needed a small amount of capital which came from her previous sales. She then either waited for demand to rise, or showed the product to potential clients. Süreyya had several entry points to seek clients. One was a web of neighbours, which Süreyya presumably broadened by participating in the religious *mahalle* meetings (i.e. *tarikat*). She was secretive about these illegal gatherings. However, a close neighbour of hers knew for certain that she attended meetings of this kind – at least – in the past. Süreyya had at least five entry points outside the *mahalle*. She usually took her bag full of various bootees and embroidered edgings to her sister, to two daughter-in-laws of her sister-in-law, to her former employer, and finally to her former landlady. In this way, Süreyya sought to increase her chances of finding clients. Süreyya's job chances were subject to the same influences as Zühre's. Both their chances were dependent on labour market conditions and social contacts. In contrast to Zühre, Süreyya had access to a wider network of potential clients perhaps due to her work history. Having worked outside home must have also given her some strength to interact with urban life beyond the *mahalle*. However, both were faced with fierce competition in a saturated market. The current conditions of economic crisis had indeed caused a decline in Süreyya's sales.

In April, Süreyya sold her bootees and embroidered edgings for 3 million TL each. Her monthly earnings generally varied between 10-40 million TL. April was one of her 'lucky' months; she was waiting for 40 million TL to arrive, which included the cost of the raw material. To produce a pair of bootees, Süreyya had to work around 15 hours. Her hourly pay rate thus came to 200.000 TL (i.e. 15 US cents). This was more or less equal to the April price of the bread sold in the municipal buffets. Most days, Süreyya spent around 10 hours on these hand-made products. Whilst knitting, the strain she put on her eyes, back and shoulders was constant. Despite such risks to her health and safety, she had no social insurance whatsoever. This meant that Süreyya neither had health coverage nor pension prospects.

In spite of her poor work conditions and declining sales, Süreyya had no option but to continue with her current work: "I don't have any work plans. I'll carry on like this till I die. [...] What other type of job could I possibly do?" Süreyya was evidently aware of the limited options the labour market could offer to someone with primary school education. Her 'choices' were restricted to low paid jobs such as child care and cleaning. Süreyya also believed that she was getting too old for such demanding work. There might be other supply-side pressures that we are unaware of. Nevertheless, religion and patriarchy seem to have had a less restrictive effect on Süreyya's work plans. In fact, Süreyya once said Cemal had become less domineering over the years. The influences likely to have weakened his authority will be discussed later.

Süreyya was hopeful that more of her bootees would be sold over the summer. However, the October interview revealed that her expectations had been rather optimistic:

| | |
|---|---|
| Interviewer: | How many bootees have you sold after me [our first interview]? |
| Süreyya: | None... Not even a pair. |
| Interviewer: | Oh really? |
| Süreyya: | I swear... Look, it [the products] remains in the bag as the way it was. I shall bring the bag if you'd like to have a look. |
| Interviewer: | Not even a single pair? |
| Süreyya: | I sold not even a pair. |
| Interviewer: | How were your sales within the six months before April? |
| Süreyya: | It was OK; I had sales then. |
| Interviewer: | Why do you think this happened? |
| Süreyya: | I don't know everybody is like me... Due to crisis, no one [could afford]. After you left, I didn't sell even one; my embroidery edgings are resting too. |
| Interviewer: | You had several clients? |
| Süreyya: | There were; there were lots of people I knew. There were indeed and yet everybody hardly get by. They can't afford to buy; how shall they buy? |
| Interviewer: | Did you take them [the products] here and there? |
| Süreyya: | Wouldn't I do that? Of course I did. I took it [the bag] to my villagers; I took it to places my sister was acquainted with; took it to Mamak. The daughter-in-law[s] of my sister-in-law lives there. I took it to Dikmen [ex-landlady], I couldn't sell [any]; I came back without even selling one. It wasn't worth the travel fares I paid. |

The conditions of economic crisis seem to have had an initially small but progressively increasing effect on Süreyya's sales. It was evident that Süreyya was in contact with people whose economic status was more vulnerable to economic shocks. After the crisis broke, the purchasing power of her contacts must have declined to an alarming level, forcing them to omit Süreyya's bootees and embroidery edgings from their list of spending. Thus, although Süreyya kept the prices same, she could not sell anything. This was a victory of structure over her resources as an agent. Despite having a wider web of contacts, Süreyya was unable to counteract the structural forces.

To lessen the effect of her loss, Süreyya made bread for money as she did every autumn. What was different this autumn was the type of people she made bread for. She usually worked for ten or fifteen neighbours, and five or six relatives. Out of principle, Süreyya avoided going to a stranger's door. That autumn, Süreyya however abandoned this principle since no demand arose from her usual 'circle'. Süreyya found her first 'employer' by chance, whilst queuing up for municipal bread. Her skill at dough rolling was well appreciated by this person, which enabled her to find four more people to make bread for.

The conditions of bread-making were rather tough. To earn a 10 million TL daily wage, Süreyya worked from 6:00 am to 7:00 pm, with perhaps an hour's lunch break. Her hourly pay was thus 833,000 TL (i.e. 62 US cents). Whilst rolling dough thinly, she put constant strain on her arms and back as well as risking respiratory disorder from breathing the smoke coming out of the tandoor. The difference in the temperature inside and outside the tandoor was another threat to health. It was therefore no surprise to see Süreyya feeling under the weather in the October interview. Nevertheless, due to sheer desperation for money, not for a moment did she consider cancelling her fifth bread-making appointment.

*Cemal's Labour*

Cemal was a baker. For the last two to three years he had been running a *simit* bakery, specialising in traditional sesame rolls. His *simit*s were distributed to certain street vendors working for the bakery. Cemal's involvement with *simit* went back a good 20 years; yet this was the first that time he was the boss of his own 'enterprise'. Previously, he used to sell *simit* on the streets, initially with his uncle's two sons, and work for other bakeries. Süreyya told vividly the story of how they set up the business:

| | |
|---|---|
| Interviewer: | How did he [your husband] set up the business? |
| Süreyya: | I set up that job too. The guy [her husband] didn't have a job, he was going and coming like that. He said, 'a friend is looking for a shareholder for a bakery; I'd like to become a shareholder but I don't have the money.' |
| Interviewer: | Who's that friend? |

| Süreyya: | From Erzurum; we don't know him. He said via a friend of his. After he [her husband] went to bed, I phoned up that guy and asked, are you looking for a shareholder for a bakery; he said 'yes'. I said my husband wants to become a shareholder; he said 'OK'. |
|---|---|
| Interviewer: | So that friend directed you to the person you phoned up? |
| Süreyya: | Yes... I didn't know the other one either. He's also a friend of my husband from Erzurum; both are from Erzurum. I gave him [her husband] even the bus fares so that he could go and meet him. He said 'we don't have any money'; I said we shall find it. From these jobs [bootee and bread-making], I had six or seven golden bracelets; golden coins and some dollars... At those times, gold was cheaper. The guy [from Erzurum] said OK to 1 billion 250 million [TL]. I also had some money in the bank [her private insurance]; we withdrew that; cashed in the gold. My sister lives in Topraklık. My brother in-law is something like an adviser at Vakıflar Bank. I took him too, so we opened that bakery with three shareholders. |

Including Cemal, the bakery initially had three shareholders. However, it was by no means a stable source of income. Three forces were mainly responsible for the lack of stability. The first was the seasonal fluctuations in the market. Sales were particularly low in winter due to the decline in the outdoor activities people undertake. The others were the general conditions of economic crisis and finally, the lack of economic capital to compensate for the decline in their profit margins. Thus, unable to consolidate the business, two shareholders dropped out. Yet Cemal was eager to hang on to the bakery.

To this end, Cemal had devised several responses by April. One was to purchase the shares of the other two. Since Cemal lacked economic capital, he had no choice but to become indebted. A second response was to postpone the licence application so that he could continue to avoid paying tax. The illegal character of the bakery escaped the eyes of neither the municipal police nor the tax inspectors but Cemal got away with both, by using his contacts or bribing the officers. A third response was to buy raw material on credit. This was a method of purchasing material used by self-employed people to gain time until sufficient cash has been accumulated. The debts to wholesalers were however quite large, suggesting that the tax avoidance failed to raise their revenue to a level which would suffice to run the business in a smooth fashion, despite their labour costs being low due to the use of unpaid family labour. A fourth method was to find a new shareholder. The new profit sharer had six brothers who also started street vending the *simit*s of the bakery. The new shareholder was verbally entitled to less than half of the profits as he had not contributed to the costs of setting up the business. A final response was to resort to unpaid family labour. Umut was working at the bakery with his father during the week as well as the weekend. Cemal worked from 6:30 am to 8:30 pm, two hours more than Umut as he had to take care of accounting and cleaning type errands. Despite long working hours, their profit margin was barely sufficient to pay the rent on the *gecekondu*, and their travel costs. Süreyya once said if it were not for her bootee money, they would die of hunger.

On the whole, none of these responses were helpful in stabilising the business; which was also evident in the level of debt waiting to be repaid. In April, the amount of their business-related debts and the composition of their creditors were as follows:

| | |
|---|---|
| $270 | to Nezahat, a female neighbour [housewife] |
| $100 | to Nezahat's husband [a civil cervant] |
| $100 | to Ayfer, a female neighbour [running a bus service] |
| 1 plain gold bracelet | to Hanife,a female neighbour-*hemşehri* [retired; canteen owner] |
| 1 twisted gold bracelet | to Hanife [same person as above] |
| 3 gold coins | to Süreyya's sister [housewife] |
| 1 gold coin | to Nermin, a female neighbour [cleaner, security guard] |
| 280 million TL | as a bank loan to Süreyya's brother-in-law [adviser in a bank] |
| 1.8 billion TL | to the flour and sesame wholesalers. |

The Turkish lira equivalent of their total debt was around 3,620,000,000 TL. It is clear from the list above that most of the money was lent in the form of foreign currency and gold to preserve the value of the loan against inflation. Moreover, the composition of the creditors also implies concerns for masculine pride. The great majority were either relatives from Süreyya's side, or neighbours with whom Süreyya interacted on a daily basis. It therefore seems likely that by borrowing from them, like Zühre, Süreyya aimed to help her husband to avoid the moment of encounter which would otherwise blatantly confirm his failure to provide for the family.

In April, the repayment of these debts was a priority in their list of plans. The couple was also planning to purchase the licence of the bakery. This would then allow them to start topping up Cemal's previous social insurance (SSK) premium contributions. To be able to assume worker status in the SSK, Cemal was thinking of declaring Süreyya as the owner of the bakery. Cemal registered with the SSK back in 1987. Despite his 25 to 30 years work-life, his SSK premiums amounted only to 1580 days, as most of his employers refused to contribute towards his premiums. Therefore, his chances of receiving a pension were very low. Have their plans improved his chances?

The picture in October was bleak. Despite the better season for sales, the business was still highly vulnerable to the conditions created by the economic crisis. They were no longer in a position to buy even raw material. In these circumstances, the profit sharer was the one who left first. Cemal made a final attempt to save the bakery and asked his relatively well-off uncle's son if he would like to become a shareholder. His proposal was refused. Having been turned down by the person whom he felt the closest, Cemal had no choice but to close down the business two months before the October interview. All the couple's plans followed bankruptcy: the plans to purchase the bakery licence and pay Cemal's SSK premiums went unrealised; most of their debts remained unpaid. The baking equipment that belonged to Cemal was given to the landlord in lieu of the bakery rent. In fact, Cemal was able to pay back some of the money he owed to the wholesalers. He concealed how much was left in order not to upset Süreyya any further. Süreyya however suspected that at least 750 million TL remained. Apart from this, there was no change either to the form of their debts or to the composition of creditors. Borrowing in an inflationary environment may be considered rather favourable. However, the debt situation of the Cansevers suggested the contrary. As their loans were in the form of foreign exchange and gold; the family became much worse off in October. The real value of their dollar debts rose from 627,763,490 TL in April to 702,260,090 TL in October, whereas that of their gold debts increased from 616,047,620 TL to 715,095,960 TL. As for the bank loan, Süreyya's brother-in-law paid it back so they did not know how much interest had been accrued on it. However, the failure of the Cansevers to pay the loan back on time caused the two families to fall out. This incident illustrates the erosion of social relationships in the face of increased levels of poverty.

Thus, Cemal had to find an alternative way to earn money. More or less two weeks after the bakery closed down, Cemal started working for other bakeries, since *simit*-making was the only area he specialised in. He was a master in *simit* making; he was not prepared to go and work for instance in a restaurant where he did not feel he had any competence. This took him back to where he was before he set up the bakery. Cemal's new conditions of employment turned out very similar to Tahir's. His new job was casual, free-lance, seasonal and informal in character. Cemal made *simit* for different bakeries until the owner told him to 'have a rest' the next day onwards.

Cemal used two methods to search for jobs. First was to attend the *düşeş* market. In the *düşeş*, there was also a coffeehouse(s) for the *simit* makers where the workers waited for the jobs to materialise. Thus, his job prospects became more dependent upon chance. In contrast, the second method Cemal used to hunt for jobs involved less uncertainty. Over the 25 to 30 years he had spent in the sector, Cemal had developed a large web of job contacts, including bakery owners. After work, Cemal began to visit them, and asked if any labour was needed in order to minimise periods of unemployment between jobs. Their acquaintance increased the likelihood of his being employed due to the element of trust. Yet, except for providing him with a temporary job, the bakery owners offered him no other forms of support. Moreover, the jobs they gave him were not only short-term but also low-paid, especially when the hours worked are considered. They did not provide him with social insurance either. Until October, Cemal worked on and off for at least three different bakeries. Each job lasted a week or so. In October, he was employed in another bakery on a short-term basis. He had been working there for the fifteen days before the date of our interview. When there was work to do, Cemal went to work regardless of whether it was a weekday or weekend, often between 5:00 am and 5:30 pm. In return, he only earned a daily wage of 12 million TL. Assuming that there was no lunch break, the maximum Cemal was able to earn was 960.000 TL per hour (i.e. 58 US cents). The amount was insufficient to purchase a return bus ticket the price of which had increased to 1.5 million TL by October.

*Umut and Nazlı's Labour*

Umut was the only child sent to work. This was so not only because he was older than Nazlı was but because he was the male child. Süreyya said of Nazlı: "We haven't sent her to such [work] places. She's only 13 years old. She does not even know how to get down from here. She needs direction. How would you send a 13 year old child to work? She is not a male child, she is a female child." Until the bakery closed down, Umut worked in his father's bakery without getting paid. His father nevertheless paid his travel costs and every now and then gave him a little pocket money. During the time he dropped out of school, Umut worked from 6:30 am to 6:30 pm. His being recalled by the school administration forced him to reallocate his time between work and education. After the bakery closed down, Umut also 'became unemployed' but ten days before our interview in October, he started a new job as an apprentice electrician. Umut thought that the conditions of work in his new job were much better than that of the bakery. Nevertheless, he worked six days a week from 8:00 am to 19:00 and earned 30 million TL per week. Moreover, this job provided him no entitlements to social insurance.

Umut found the job by himself. Süreyya said that no one from their social 'circle' helped him with the job search: "None... I swear, no. [...] Don't fall my dear; don't fall... The one who falls would have no friends, my dear, so don't fall... The saying goes 'if you have money, the whole world is your man [mortal in relation to Allah], if you have no money, the insane asylum is your way'. Who would do what with you after you fall?" Evidently, as they 'fell', the Cansevers gradually lost their economic capacity to fulfil their obligation to reciprocate and hence their chances of receiving support from their social 'circle'. In this section, we have explored the Cansevers' income generation behaviour. We will next consider their income allocation behaviour.

**Income Allocation: Overt and Covert Mechanisms**

Whatever income could be generated was given to Süreyya. None of the household members allocated money to personal spending, except for the essential bus fare to work. Personal spending was a remote idea for Süreyya for the same reasons that apply to Zarife and Zühre. Süreyya was also a typical self-sacrificing mother figure, trying to meet her family member's needs first with a tight income. Once she said: "I can't meet any needs of mine, I swear. I don't want anything if only their needs could be met; good or bad, I somehow manage in the house." Her house-bound life-style also seems to have restricted her personal needs. It can be claimed that their impoverishment made the Cansevers distribute their income as collectively as possible, which in turn helped them avoid 'secondary poverty'.

The Cansevers managed the household income using a 'female whole-wage' system. Süreyya was assigned to this task perhaps firstly because she spent the money frugally and skilfully and secondly because she was more aware of the household needs. Finally, it also appears that Cemal passed the responsibility to Süreyya so as to avoid the stressful exercise of stretching a very tight income. That's what Süreyya seemed sure of:

| Interviewer: | Have you got any problems regarding the fact that you look after the money? |
|---|---|
| Süreyya: | Of course I do… No teeth left in my mouth due to gritting; no hair left on my head because of anxiety… If you give [spend money], your front opens up [budget falls short]; if you don't, the kid gets upset. I wish that money didn't come to me. I tell the guy [her husband] 'you don't want to spend [manage] that money yourself to throw the stress on me'. If he took it [the responsibility of managing money] he'd buy from expensive places. A man wouldn't know; but I wander, I mean: I start from Ulucanlar; I go and buy from the wholesaler where it's ten lira cheaper. This causes a lot of grief; may Allah forbid anyone. If woman alone is made to hold the responsibility of the entire house, then… |

Contrary to the general tendency, Süreyya had the final say in financial decisions, including those pertinent to her husband's personal needs. Süreyya's control over household finances may have to do with her being under less pressure of patriarchy. Several reasons can be postulated for the strong challenge to Cemal's male authority. They include the couple's age, Süreyya's previous and current contributions to income, and Cemal's limited and perhaps diminishing capacity to provide for his family.

Although Süreyya controlled the household finances, she still felt the need to create a secret kitty. Süreyya once had two kitties of this kind. One contained sizeable savings for emergencies in the past and the other was a small budget for items such as material for her daughter's trousseau. She used to draw the money for these kitties from her own earnings. However, neither in April nor in October, was there any money in Süreyya's secret accounts. Nonetheless, the generalised manner in which she declared her opinion that all women have secret kitties implies that she had not yet given up the idea of keeping a secret kitty:

| Süreyya: | I tell you, every woman would have some savings of their own… |
|---|---|
| Interviewer: | Why do you think it is concealed from their husbands? |
| Süreyya: | It's your future… Let's say, you have a funeral, with which money I could hold the funeral? The husband isn't there… Tell me, if somebody from my close relatives died, how will I get there? I'll get there by cashing in either one of my bracelets or my dollar[s]. Where could I find my husband now for instance? Where could he find money anyway? White days [monies] are for black [rainy] days. A woman doesn't always show it to her husband. |
| Interviewer: | Why is that? |
| Süreyya: | Her husband would sit down to gamble; and ask his wife 'I have that much debt, pay it' because he knows that you have [money] on you. He'd try to take it away from you but if [he thinks] there isn't any, then he'd say 'my wife doesn't have any money' so he'd be on his guard. Do you think he'd pay me back? He'd say 'she's my family, what would she need this money for'; he'd say 'I'm bringing her [money] anyway' but he wouldn't think how the woman manages at home. Put it into your head, my girl: set aside a portion of your salary… He's at the end of the day a stranger; provide the world for him, he would forget after he leaves that door. No matter who he was… every woman has a kitty; there's no woman without one. |
| Interviewer: | What if she doesn't work? |
| Süreyya: | OK, then… One day he [the husband] leaves money for bread, the next day the milkman comes… What does she owe to the milkman: 20 million [TL]. He'd know nothing about the milkman. How much money she'll have to give him, I mean… She'd say 30 million [TL]; 10 million [TL] would be left to her… The woman would save like this if she's the woman of her house and cares about her family. Let's say I get my son married; the bride's side, for instance, wants us to attach two gold pieces; and the guy [her husband] becomes obstinate, saying that let this arrangement be violated; 'I'm no way doing this'. Would you mess up the arrangement or go and attach two of your concealed gold for the sake of your son? |

Süreyya had several motives for keeping a secret kitty. One was to provide some security against the uncertainty of future events. Another was to ensure that Cemal brought all his earnings home. Yet it is likely that the impoverished predicament of the household made him behave like this given that his discovery of her secret savings did not lead him to spare any money for controversial personal spending. Her final motive was to resolve disagreements without disturbing the peace within their home and/or social environment. As is evident in Süreyya's account, there was a possibility of her failing to resolve conflict over financial matters in an overt manner. This implies that there were limits to Süreyya's financial control. The kitty seemed to have enabled Süreyya to attain greater control in cases of conflict where overt mechanisms proved inadequate. Some issues, such as the wedding presents to be exchanged between the in-laws or the daughter's trousseau, were particular sources of conflict:

| | |
|---|---|
| Interviewer: | Have you got any debts separate from your husband? |
| Süreyya: | No... [...] You are bringing up a child. My husband wouldn't know that her kitchen set [decorative cloths] needs getting done; he wouldn't know whether cotton cloth or lace is needed for this. A woman would buy them by herself [secretly]. |
| Interviewer: | What if you discussed with him? |
| Süreyya: | You'd go down there [to the market] he'd strike up a fight, leave it there and go back; he'd say 'do I have to buy this'; he'd say 'I have other things to think about'. A man would know nothing about such subtleties.... |

Süreyya was very much in favour of the idea of keeping a secret kitty. Nevertheless, she was no longer able to create such kitties because of their tight budget. Süreyya said she could not dare set aside money for her own kitty while her children's basic needs were unmet, otherwise she did not seem affected by the fact that her secret was discovered with the purchase of the bakery. Süreyya conducted various manipulative acts to create her concealed kitties. Yet, she neither did this to deprive her family of their basic needs nor to divert money for her own personal use. On the contrary, she aimed to secure the future of her family and maintain the relations with kin which Cemal might not have thought to be of value. So far the focus has been on the allocation of income within the household. We now explore whether the Cansevers were able to create an income surplus to invest in their asset portfolio.

**Investment, Insurance and Credit Use**

The Cansevers' portfolio contained only a few financial and non-financial assets. Beginning with their financial assets, Süreyya used to have concealed savings in the form of dollars and gold as well as eight-years of private insurance contributions all of which were cashed in to set up the bakery. In April she only had some savings deposited in a rosca with which she was planning to repay some of the family debts.

The rosca she participated in had ten members, all but Süreyya were from the same *mahalle*. In fact, Süreyya only knew one of the members, the sister-in-law of her uncle's daughter, who gave her word for Süreyya's creditworthiness to allow her admission. It was known as *altın günü* and governed by the following principle: Once a month, on a fixed date, each member was expected to contribute an amount based on the selling price of the gold coin on that particular day. The choice of gold was a measure of protection against inflation. Within the April-October period, the real value of the lump-sum was preserved since the increase in the real value of gold had risen faster than inflation. The lump-sum was granted to the member whose turn came up in the draw for that month. Süreyya joined the club, relying on her bootee money. Despite her sales going down drastically, she was able to keep up with the monthly contributions but how she managed this remained a mystery. One thing we know is that she did not need to go into debt because in September, Süreyya received a lump-sum of 290 million TL she was entitled to, and exchanged it for $180. This amount fell $20 short of what she previously borrowed from her neighbour, Nezahat, in order to pay the four-month rent of their *gecekondu*.

The Cansevers were also part of a kinship network which acted like a generalised rosca, where the term of rotation spread across a life-time. In other words, it was a kind of saving scheme operating on the rule of reciprocity. In this scheme, the parties had to bring certain valuable items such as gold coins to the significant events of family life such as circumcision and wedding. The Cansevers were however unable to fulfil their obligations without becoming indebted. To pay their dues, after April Süreyya borrowed two gold coins; one from her neighbour Ayfer, and another from her sister-in-law's son.

The situation of their non-financial assets was also bleak. The Cansevers were a tenant family; the family held no legal title deed to *gecekondu* land and were hence excluded from any enjoyment of urban land speculation. They missed out on the opportunity to build their own *gecekondu* for reasons we do not exactly know. Perhaps they had no one to support them in finding the right plot ad building the house, or perhaps they lacked the economic capital required to meet the cost of building. The latter sounds more plausible because if they had had the capital, they could have well purchased a ready-built *gecekondu*. The Cansevers owned neither an urban house nor a car. Their only asset was a rural plot and some arable land sufficient to build a house and conduct small scale farming. These assets were inherited after Cemal's father's death.

In April, the plan was to keep hold of the arable land, hoping that one day they would return to the village. How realistic was this? It seemed more like wishful thinking than a sound plan since, given their low pension prospects, the Cansevers were unlikely to be able to cope with the decline in agricultural revenues in the face of increasing costs. Contrary to their initial plan, the family contacted Cemal's widowed sister, who lived on donations from the villagers, to put the land on the market with a view to clearing off their debts but no one wanted their land. Having portrayed the content of the Cansevers' asset portfolio, and how this portfolio was formed, we will now turn to their consumption practices.

## Consumption and Borrowing

The Cansevers engaged in various practices in order to counteract their income deficit. Their consumption practices took place in different spheres; ranging from commodified to semi and non-commodified. How significant were these practices in terms of removing income pressure and reducing their deprivation? This is explored by reference to nine selected areas of expenditure.

*Non-commodified Consumption*

Starting with food acquisition, the Cansevers' free access to food was quite limited. Süreyya collected some spring plants to use for culinary purposes. In April a rather socially distant neighbour let Süreyya pick up the plants growing in her garden. Further food support came from Süreyya's former landlady with whom she had been in contact for 16 years. Before April this landlady sent Süreyya some *tarhana,* a traditional foodstuff made chiefly of curds and flour and used for making soup. Süreyya in return made bootees and embroidered edgings for her three daughters. Except for these two occasions, the Cansevers received no food support from their social contacts, including those in the village.

| | |
|---|---|
| Interviewer: | Is there any [food] coming from the village? |
| Süreyya: | Beforehand, my mum used to give us some. My father was alive then. We had cows; we had everything; our field were all sown up; my mum used to come, filling [the sacks] all up. My father is dead for two years. As we've nothing left; my mum's very old; she's 80 years old now. What will come? What could you grab from the hands of an 80 year old woman? What could she do? |
| Interviewer: | I thought you said they sent cheese or so? |
| Süreyya: | I send my mother [the money]; she gives a five kg container to her neighbour. I send the money from here; if you give the money, they would then send it. |
| Interviewer: | Anything they send [for free] at all? |
| Süreyya: | No... only in cash... If you send the money, it [food] would then come. What will strangers send us? Beforehand we had a father; we used to go there to farm and bring back [food]. There emerged conflict [over land division] after he died. |

Their rural food dried up for a number of reasons. They include decline in the agricultural labourers as a result of urban migration, increasing cost of agricultural production and conflict between inheritors as to how to share the land. A more idiosyncratic reason was Süreyya's mother's lack of appreciation for the healthcare Süreyya provided for her. Süreyya was in fact the only person who took care of her mother although she had three more daughters in the same city. After her visit ended, Süreyya's mother told the people in her village that her children took all her food and kicked her out of the door. She also turned Süreyya down when she asked for a sack of flour. As a consequence, Süreyya felt offended and refused to take care of her the next time. This incident reinforces ideas about the downside of social capital.

Besides, such limited informal sources of food support, the Cansevers were granted food and coal aid by the Greater Municipality. Süreyya claimed that no one mediated their access to the aid. By the food aid, the municipality aimed to meet the two month food needs of a four member family. The aid contained 52 kilos of food, including rice, pasta, flour, margarine, tomato paste, sugar, tea, chocolate etc. However, as I have personally witnessed, the quality of food was very low. The flour, for instance, was thin and grey. The food aid was received before April and Süreyya was unsure whether there would be any subsequent deliveries.

In terms of access to health services, the Cansevers had nowhere else to turn to than *Allah* to seek protection against any illness that affected the family. Süreyya had faith, since so far *Allah* had not bestowed any serious illness on her children whom she paid particular attention to bring up in a healthy way. Süreyya hoped this condition would continue because otherwise, they would neither be able to afford hospital treatment nor medicine. They had no free access to hospital treatment other than that provided by the local medical centre due to a lack of entitlements to social security. They neither had access to social insurance nor assistance schemes such as green card. The reasons behind their exclusion from the green card are unknown to me. It seems unlikely that the family would have failed the means-test as the criteria were very similar to that of food aid: They required the applicant not to a) possess any non-financial assets, including a car; b) run a business; or c) belong to any other social security scheme. It was true that Cemal was running a bakery, but this could not be detected due to his lack of a licence. Moreover, he had a bit of rural land but this was also invisible as the land had not been officially divided between the inheritors. Thus, quite plausibly, the family might have failed to apply due to the monetary costs imposed by the application procedure.

In the field of education, the Cansevers engaged in a few non-commodified practices. Upon Süreyya's statement of hardship, the director exempted Nazlı from the registration fee for a State school. A year before the interview, a former neighbour gave Nazlı a school uniform that belonged to her daughter. Nazlı was sometimes given second hand books by her school-mates who were a year ahead of her; or exchanged her previous books with relevant ones. Last school year the school administration granted Nazlı 30 million TL and some stationery (e.g. notebooks, pencils) as part of the World Bank funded aid package. This school year, Nazlı however received no help of this kind, but made use of the pages of the notebooks which remained unused the year before.

With regard to housing, the Cansevers had no rent free access to accommodation. Two years ago, they rented a two bedroom annex of a *gecekondu* that belonged to a very close *hemşehri* of theirs. Their acquaintance secured the tenancy of the Cansevers until the day land development would begin. In the April interview, Süreyya claimed that their being acquainted with the landlord would protect them if the family failed to pay the rent on time. So far she said she paid the rent quite regularly, but by October the rent had already been increased to 100 million TL while the capacity of the Cansevers to afford the rent had declined further especially after the bakery went bankrupt. The landlord refused to reduce the rent:

| | |
|---|---|
| Interviewer: | I thought he [the landlord] was your close villager? |
| Süreyya: | So what? If you give the money, no one's better than you; if you don't, there's no one worse than you. I saw this most in my own relatives and villagers. |
| Interviewer: | Why? |
| Süreyya: | Because the money ambition takes over... The person whose eyes were taken over by such ambition turns around to find even five lira. I told you that, I bought all the paint for the doors and windows; I paid 25 million. Am I going to take these doors on my back when I leave? He never said 'give half of it my daughter and I'll give the other half'; he said nothing... He took it all. |

Süreyya associated the intolerance of her landlord with his ambition to earn more money. However, the landlord was a retired man, living with his wife on a small pension and the rent from the annex. Probably, in circumstances of economic crisis, they were also in need of money, and had to put their interest first, which in turn caused the spirit of solidarity to diminish. This extract points to another downside of social contacts. When a financial transaction is based on an informal verbal contract, as between Süreyya and the landlord, one of the parties may lose out on the rights which a formal contract is likely to provide. In this case, the losing party was the Cansevers as the landlord made them liable for the maintenance of the rental property. The Cansevers had no choice but to accept this condition.

The Cansevers had little non-commodified access to household items. Seventeen years ago, Süreyya's younger brother, a retired security guard, bought the fridge she was currently using. A former neighbour in Dikmen gave her the wooden table in the kitchen. Her former employer gave away her old carpet that Süreyya kept in the front-room. The bride of Cemal's uncle also gave them a piece of second hand carpet obtained from the floor of a governmental office. Finally, Süreyya's mother gave her a hand-knitted door mat as a present. As for utilities, the only free access the Cansever had was the 500 kilos of coal granted by the municipality. In contrast to food aid, the Cansevers were assured that a subsequent delivery would be granted but 500 kilos of coal aid only met half of their fuel needs.

Finally, the Cansevers had some access to free clothing. Every now and then, her neighbour, Nermin, who worked at private Bilkent University as a cleaner, brought Süreyya's children shoes, trousers, and jumpers that the rich students no longer wanted to keep in their wardrobes. In addition, Süreyya's sister sometimes bought small presents, such as a pair of slippers or socks. Her sister's support remained limited because, as often happened among female siblings, she was highly dependent on her husband's income.

On the whole, the Cansevers' non-commodified practices contributed very little to household success. This was firstly because they lacked access to resources with high benefit delivery capacity, such as land and labour-based entitlements. This relates to the labour market conditions the family was exposed to as well as the influences which prevented them from building a *gecekondu* before 1985, or buying a pre-1985 built one. The year of migration was evidently not one of those influences. The food, coal and educational aids that they were entitled to certainly helped the family get by in times of hardship. Nevertheless, none of these aid packages were sufficient in size, and most of them were delivered inconsistently. Secondly, certain forces restricted the flow of support between the Cansevers and their social contacts. Although the Cansevers were in contact with numerous people, they were of limited help in providing free goods and services. This may result from the fact that the benefit delivery capacity of most contacts was quite fragile. Some of their contacts seemed to have some economic capacity; and yet they chose not to help out. Perhaps, in the eyes of their self-interested contacts, the Cansevers were regarded as unreliable because their capacity to reciprocate was restricted.

*Semi-commodified Consumption*

Most of the semi-commodified activities the Cansevers adopted were of the self-provisioning type and the majority of these were performed to obtain food. Süreyya acquired food provisioning skills through dealing with every aspect of farm life. She performed two main types of food provisioning activity. One was to keep a kitchen garden near their *gecekondu*. The scale of this activity was restricted to a few herbs and vegetables such as cress, lettuce, parsley, spring onion and an apricot and cherry tree. The other was food processing. Süreyya undertook such tasks on a weekly and an annual basis. The weekly tasks included home-cooking and yoghurt making.

The rest of the food processing activities involved winter food stock preparation. The winter stock worked out cheaper because the price of fruit and vegetables was lower between spring and autumn. Süreyya made the following preparations for the forthcoming winter: She made a container full of puree using leftover tomatoes she purchased from the local bazaar vendor at a cheaper price, dried aubergines and green beans, pickled ten kilos of vine leaves and five kilos of cabbage, preserved green beans and tomato sauces in bottles. Süreyya usually made jam and beverage out of the fruits in their garden. However, this summer the yield was so limited that the stock had to do without them.

In general, while carrying out the above tasks the daughter of Süreyya's uncle who lived nearby came to help her out. In return, Süreyya did the same when she called on her for help with domestic tasks. In addition, Süreyya made bread out of a 50 kg sack of flour she bought. The home-made bread proved a cheaper alternative, as Süreyya avoided paying the labour costs by exchanging her labour reciprocally with four of her neighbours; Gülistan, Perihan, Nesrin and her sister-in-law. The reciprocal transaction between them was balanced in nature:

Interviewer:  It appears that you had some support from your circle…

Süreyya:      What kind of support is that?

Interviewer:  For instance, the tin sheet of bread.

Süreyya:      Well but I'm doing the same for them. One day, I'll also make [bread] for them in return. Do you think they'd do without expecting a return? It was in the past; it remained in the old days; those people who used to do you a favour without asking for the same in return.

Interviewer:  Why do you think this happened?

Süreyya:      I really don't know. Within the last three or four years, people have become very different, they're such different that… Is it because of poverty, I don't know. We used to visit the folks a lot; we used to have a dialogue; we used to have things we gave and took. We had such a community that I could hardly describe to you. Now, not even a single mortal of Allah visits each other.

Interviewer:  Why?

Süreyya:      Is it because people [in] poverty; or because there's crisis? [S] he says, I don't know what; she perhaps says 'if I drink a glass of tea at her place, she'll come to drink at my place; so I'd better sit and drink it at my own place'. I guess that's what it's about. Everybody is in agitation of their own survival.

Süreyya was resentful that her social contacts no longer helped each other without expecting a balanced return, but this appears to be due to erosion in the benefit delivery capacity of the Cansevers' social contacts. In the face of economic crisis, their contacts of fragile economic capacity seemed to have become more concerned with their own immediate needs.

The scope of the Cansevers' semi-commodified practices was very restricted in other areas of expenditure, such as home-maintenance, household items, transportation and clothing. In the field of housing, some labour costs could be avoided because the landlord himself replaced the broken door lock, sealed the windows, painted the doors and windows but charged his tenants for the material used in the process. Regarding household items, the door mat that Süreyya hand knitted was the only example of semi-commodified consumption. With regard to transportation, Nazlı's student status made her eligible for a 33 per cent concession on the municipal bus and underground services. Finally as for clothing, Süreyya stopped knitting cardigans and jumpers for her children, as they no longer liked to wear hand knitted clothes. Moreover, it was cheaper to buy clothes in the Ulus market.

The Cansevers' achievements in the semi-commodified sphere of consumption remained very limited. They had some success in the area of food through the use of household and social contact labour resources free of charge. Two main reasons can be postulated for their limited success. First of all, they lacked access to beneficial entitlements such as those allowing access to state-subsidised medicine. Secondly, there were limits to their self-provisioning activities. In expenditure areas such as clothing, self-provisioning was dying out because it ceased to offer a cheaper alternative to its market equivalents. For the Cansevers, the decline of some self-provisioning activities did not necessarily mean that they were successfully replaced with market activities. Furthermore, self-provisioning was inapplicable to some areas of expenditures such as utilities to which the Cansevers allocated a significant portion of their budget. For these reasons, their semi-commodified practices enabled the removal of little income pressure, and left a significant portion of their basic needs to be met through the market.

*Commodified Consumption*

The Cansevers were involved in a series of commodified practices, including using cheaper and flexible purchasing methods, as well as cutting down on the amount, or going completely without certain items. These practices and their effects on the household's deprivation level will be described below.

Süreyya used some methods for purchasing certain goods and services cheaply. She bought food items in bulk. However, use of this method was confined only to a few staples such as two sacks of potatoes and onions and a sack of rice due to lack of ready cash. Süreyya thus began to buy such staples from the local bazaar on a kilo basis, which still worked out cheaper. Süreyya also used the local bazaar for the weekly fruit and vegetable shopping. No matter how regular her bazaar visits were, she could hardly fill her shopping basket, as in April her weekly bazaar allowance hardly exceeded 5 million TL. Sometimes, as when purchasing tomatoes for puree, Süreyya did her bazaar shopping in the evening when the bazaar vendors lowered their prices even further to get rid of unsold low quality produce.

She used similar methods in the areas of education, household items, utilities and clothing. Regarding education, Süreyya went to a place called Hacı Bayram where books and note-pads were cheaper. Umut bought his uniform cheaply from the market in Ulus where the products were generally of low quality. As for household items, the family purchased most items also from the Ulus market in cash. As for utilities, Süreyya bargained with the wood distributor-on-wheels, by means of which she managed to get 10 million TL reductions for 500 kilos of wood. Finally, Süreyya purchased cheap clothing from markets, such as the Russian, Samanpazarı and Ulus Bazaars. Usually, Süreyya bought clothing in summer when her bootee sales were higher; yet this summer, Süreyya was able to afford none. There were a significant number of areas to which the Cansevers had no cheaper access, such as health, housing, home-maintenance, most utilities and transportation. For instance, despite their acquaintance with the landlord, the rent of their *gecekondu* was not any cheaper than that of an average *gecekondu* in the area.

The Cansevers made a few flexible purchasing arrangements. Süreyya had a credit account with some food distributors-on-wheels such as the milkman. Fifteen years ago, they purchased a TV in instalments from a shop owned by their *hemşehri*. The previous winter, they purchased 500 kilos of coal in the same fashion to top up the coal aid. There is not enough evidence to ascertain whether their flexible arrangements worked out cheaper, but neither cheaper nor flexible purchasing arrangements prevented the family from cutting down or doing without certain goods and services, which can indisputably be regarded as necessary.

With regard to food, the family members had at least two meals per day. However, the regularity of their meals tells us little about the content of their diet. The lunch box that Süreyya prepared for Nazlı for instance contained a potato chip sandwich. Their diet was thus rich in carbohydrates and their protein intake from meat products was very limited. Their monthly meat consumption in April barely exceeded a kilo of chicken, six times less than the amount recommended by dieticians for a four member household. The Cansevers had been unable to afford even a kilo of meat for the last two months before October. There must be many more food items which the Cansevers had to cut down or do without; the children for instance had to go without soft drink beverages despite watching adverts on TV, which created the desire for such products.

Health was another targeted area of expenditure. In case of illness, the Cansever family members had to go without the hospital treatment and medicine. Süreyya was very proud of her children's healthy upbringing, and hoped that *Allah* would protect them from any serious illnesses. Unfortunately, before April, Nazlı had an ear infection so Süreyya took her to the local medical centre, but then could not afford the prescribed medicine. None of their social contacts could help either:

| | |
|---|---|
| Interviewer: | What do you do when one of your family members are ill? |
| Süreyya: | I take them to the medical centre. Sometime ago, my daughter's ear ached so I took her there. He [the doctor] said 'have you got social insurance'; I said no. He said 'have you got any relatives [with social insurance]; I can prescribe on theirs'. I said, I have relatives but this cannot happen. He said 'what kind of relative are they'; I said 'my siblings do no favours to me, would I ever ask for medicine from my relatives?' The doctor laughed. The doctor prescribed the low price medicine; he told 'go to this pharmacy and tell them about me [tell that I sent you]. I walked in the pharmacy; the medicine amounted to 17 million [TL]. I asked 'how much is the full price?' He [the pharmacist] said 24 million [TL]. I couldn't afford it. |
| Interviewer: | Anyone who provide you with medical help at all? |

Süreyya:        No. If we buy pain killer, we buy it from the local shop [cheap].
                I brought up my kids in a healthy way. For the first time, at the
                age of 13, I took her to the doctor as her ear ached, I said [to
                the doctor]. This year their classroom was very cold; it was not
                heated properly; that's why it happened.

Nazlı was attending a school in the area, which was probably highly under-resourced as most residents in the area were poor and hence unable to pay the 'contributory fees'. Also in the area of education, the Cansevers had to cut down on and go without certain items. The children's pocket money was a 'good' target for such practices. Nazlı was given no pocket money at all. The school was nearby so Nazlı needed no money for her bus fare; Süreyya prepared her a lunch box. Umut's pocket money was by no means regular. His bus fares were paid, but he was hardly given money towards his lunch, instead he had some lunch at his father's bakery. Moreover, Umut had to go without any private coaching for the university exams, which cost around one billion TL.

As for household items, the Cansevers had a fridge, hob, stereo, TV, vacuum cleaner, and washing machine. The furniture included two beds, two carpets, two sofas one of which was also used as a bed, wardrobe and wooden table. The Cansevers were unable to replace their old household items although the time seems to have arrived. The mean age for their furniture was around nine, and ten years for electrical appliances. These were by no means viewed as assets to be sold in the future. Süreyya was right: their household items could not possibly fetch a good price if they put them on the market. However, it seems that even if the items had been newer, the family would most probably have not sold them as they symbolised the unity and self-sufficiency of the family.

Similar practices were undertaken also in the area of utilities. The Cansevers individually subscribed to telephone but shared the electricity and water bills with the landlord. To save on the utility bill, Süreyya used the rinsing water from the washing machine to water the plants in the garden, wash the toilet and bathroom etc. The family used the water boiler only at bath times. For washing up, Süreyya heated the water on a stove kept in the front-room. Süreyya was also very careful with their coal consumption. Despite the harsh weather conditions of the previous year, Süreyya managed to save six sacks of coal (approx 30 kg) and some wood that she purchased last year. She achieved this by waiting in the cold or by using the small gas stove until her daughter came back from school. In the area of transportation, Süreyya minimised shopping led travel costs by doing her shopping in the local bazaar and from the distributors-on-wheels. The area of clothing suffered more from such consumption practices as Süreyya was unable to purchase any clothing for any family member after April.

In brief, the Cansevers' commodified practices were hardly successful, firstly because the cheap goods and services they purchased were often of low quality and secondly because the cheap and flexible purchasing methods the Cansevers used did little to remove income pressure. This in turn made it unavoidable to cut down or go without certain goods and services, which were indisputably part of their basic needs. The overall effects of their consumption practices were also limited in terms of bridging the gap between their tight income and consumption needs. The family thus had no choice but to borrow. In April, their consumption-related debts amounted to:

$200      to Nezahat, a neighbour [husband, a civil servant]
50 m. TL   to Remzi, a *hemşehri* neighbour [a regular worker]

Their dollar debts enabled them to pay for four months' rent. By October, Süreyya managed to pay $180 of it back by using the *gün* lump-sum. The debt in Turkish lira remained unpaid. No consumption-related debts were created after April as the family had no capacity to pay any of them back. They thus had to cut down or go without basic consumption items, which might also shed light on the mystery of how Süreyya saved for the monthly *gün* payments. Thus, the Cansevers' consumption practices proved unsuccessful in counteracting income shortfalls. The limited and inconsistent access to beneficial entitlements and social capital resources seems responsible for their failure.

## Conclusion

The Cansevers entered the month of April as highly deprived and became even more deprived over the next six months. The main reasons for this are summarised below in relation to four main areas of behaviour. Starting with income generation, the Cansevers deployed all three labour resources in two distinct cash-generating activities. They hence had a fairly diversified income and a low dependency ratio, neither of which however brought significant success. This has partly to do with market pressures which affected the Cansevers in different ways given the self-employed status of the working members. Wider conditions of economic crisis and seasonal market fluctuations prevented them from accumulating adequate economic capital to stabilise the family business and hence to have it registered with the tax system, which would help initiate or reactive the social insurance membership of the workers in the family.

Supply side influences, such as cultural and social capital, were also of little help in reducing their deprivation. Despite having relatively greater stock of formal cultural capital, the market appeared not to offer family members jobs with more favourable working conditions. Their social capital resources were in fact of some use in finding business loans but borrowing was highly disadvantageous given the high rates of real return from gold and foreign currency. Similarly, they were helpful in term of finding jobs and clients, but had a limited capacity to shift the family labour resources to the upper echelons of the market. In the face of economic crisis, it appears that support from their social contacts have gradually declined not only because the benefit delivery capacity of these contacts have become (further) restricted but also because the Cansevers lost their capacity to reciprocate.

As for income allocation, the typical 'female whole-wage' system was used for income management, but rather unusually household finances were controlled by the female spouse. In allocating the total income, the family members acted in a highly collective manner; 'all of them made sacrifices for 'the common good'' and thereby managed to avoid 'secondary poverty' to a great extent.

With regard to investment, the asset portfolio of the Cansevers was composed of rural land and bakery equipment, neither of which had a significant capacity to a) generate income, b) promote further asset accumulation or c) to provide any other forms of future security.

Finally, the Cansevers undertook various consumption activities extending from the commodified to non-commodified spheres. The extent of their involvement in non-commodified consumption was very limited. Of particular importance, they lacked access to both rent-free accommodation and state healthcare. The type of semi-commodified practices undertaken by the family was similar the other two households. Although the adoption of cheaper and/or flexible purchasing methods and the use of free labour and skills of the household members and social contacts within these practices brought some success, the Cansevers still had to cut back on or go without basic goods and services or had to borrow money for consumption purposes. Thus, their overall consumption practices were of little help in reducing income pressure.

Like the Ayhans and the Hikmets, the Cansevers were a highly enterprising family, making skilful use of their resources and acting collectively to avoid 'secondary poverty'. However, this did not help prevent their 'fall' since they were neither able to take any part in the processes of *gecekondu* acquisition nor to avoid seasonal and informal conditions within the labour market. They were therefore denied the opportunity to enjoy higher and more stable earnings, rights to social insurance, rent-free accommodation and potential returns from *gecekondu* redevelopment.

# Chapter 11
# Conclusion

This book has sought to understand how households respond to poverty and explain why some households are more successful than others in reducing their deprivation. These questions were explored based on the data drawn from a longitudinal study of low-income households living in a *gecekondu* settlement of Ankara in April and October 2002. The book consisted of two major parts. The first provided a critical overview of the relevant literature and outlined the approach taken here to understand poverty and behavioural responses households devise to counter it. The second part depicted the research base for the book and presented results from the analysis of the entire sample and three individual cases.

The concluding chapter evaluates the contributions of the book to theory, research and policy making. It starts by outlining the strengths and weakness of the theoretical model advanced here. This is followed by a summary of the key research findings and a discussion of their significance for current debates about poverty and coping and implications for policy. The chapter concludes with a presentation of the research limitations and an agenda for future studies.

## A Review of the Theoretical Background

The main theoretical drive of this book was to provide a sound basis for understanding poverty and socio-economic behaviour of poor households, based on a critical examination of the relevant literatures. To begin with, existing approaches to poverty were reviewed to address major debates about the definition and measurement of the concept. One such debate concerns whether poverty is a relative or an absolute concept. Here, the absolutist viewpoint was favoured, in line with scholars who argue for the universality of human needs and emphasise the need to maintain the conceptual distinction between poverty and inequality. Furthermore, a middle ground was taken between the two poles of the debates about objective vs. subjective poverty. It was considered necessary to combine the expert view with the bearers' perceptions and/or feelings of poverty in order to obtain a fuller understanding of this phenomenon.

An innovative method of measurement was then proposed to integrate 'objective' and subjective dimensions of poverty. Poverty was understood here from a deprivation perspective, i.e. based on the absence of living standards that are deemed necessary to lead a decent life. The new method incorporated three 'objective' dimensions of deprivation (i.e. monetary, consumption and work-related). The justification for this was that reliance on any one of these dimensions would have resulted in a very narrow understanding of deprivation. All three were included to capture the fact that each represents a different aspect of deprivation and that a household's position on one of these dimensions would not determine their position on others. For example, a household's low income might be associated with more or less work-related deprivation, depending on their job situation and the benefits it gave rise to. Furthermore, each dimension was weighted according to the subjective views of respondents regarding which items are more critical to deprivation. A unique application of factor analysis was used to select the final measures and determine their respective weights.

The proposed method was considered more advantageous than the previous works on deprivation index development. The key advantages are that it a) provides a broader representation of poverty, b) reconciles direct and indirect (i.e. income-based) methods of measurement which tend to be used in isolation, c) moves away from the majoritarian thinking that dominates researchers' evaluations of subjective views about poverty towards a perspective that is more inclusive, d) helps determine a core of deprivation measures in a way that is less dependent on arbitrary decisions, and hence e) retains a capacity to distinguish between choice and constraints more reliably than earlier methods that promote separate exploration of wants and affordability.

In addition to a review of the poverty literature, current approaches to the socio-economic behaviour of poor households were critically examined to assess the workability of a model built upon the idea that households devise strategies to survive, cope with poverty or make a livelihood. This led to the rejection of the widely used concepts of household survival, coping and livelihood strategy in favour of the broader term household responses to poverty. Further reviews were focused on two major frameworks used previously to explain household survival (livelihood) strategies, which draw on Polanyi's three modes of integration and the resource-based approach to livelihoods. This study was built upon the latter perspective due to its advantage of allowing a focus on resource constraints on household responses and their outcomes for poverty.

An alternative model was then proposed to extend the earlier variants of the resource-based framework. The new model draws on a division of household responses to poverty into four key types, i.e. income generation, income allocation, consumption and investment, and identifies three sets of influences on household responses and their outcomes for poverty: a) wider structure (including economic processes, state policies and cultural context), b) household characteristics (i.e. size, structure and life-cycle stage) and c) household resource portfolio (containing time, labour power, bodily resources, social, economic and cultural forms of capital, institutional entitlements and public resources).

I believe this model makes significant advances on earlier variants of the resource-based approach. Major lines of improvement are four-fold. First of all, through a focus on four key types of responses, it establishes the missing behavioural link between resources and poverty, which thereby allows us to systematically explore the composition of resources used in a particular response and their outcomes for poverty. Secondly, while some of the earlier variants, in principle, acknowledge the poverty effects of wider structural forces, the model not only takes account of these forces and explores them empirically, but also recognises the dual nature of the household as an object of decisions about e.g. relocation and restructuring and as a separate factor with possible effects on resources, responses and hence poverty. Thirdly, it specifies the possible effects of wider structure and household characteristics based on a new distinction between the *availability* and *benefit delivery capacity* of resources.

Last but not least, the overall reconstruction of the household resource portfolio is, in many ways, an improvement on the models used previously. The portfolio was reconstructed to clarify the conceptual boundaries of each resource component alongside the term resource, and unify the key resources addressed elsewhere in a fragmented fashion. As a result, the model a) circumvents the problem with indiscriminate application of the terms such as 'resource' and 'social capital' inherent within most poverty and livelihood research; b) avoids the use of vague resource categories such as 'claims and access' (Swift 1989), 'household relations' (Moser 1996), c) draws a clear distinction between household resources and factors that affect their availability or capacity to deliver benefits (e.g. cultural context, religion), d) provides mutually exclusive and jointly exhaustive resource categories; and e) directs attention to key resources that were given little emphasis within the existing literature. Of particular importance is the category of institutional entitlements which enables us to explore the effects of state policies on household responses and their outcomes for poverty. Others include bodily resources separated from labour resources to capture responses that do not require the use of labour power (e.g. organ sale), and the category of economic capital to allow a focus on both financial and non-financial assets owned by low-income households. Overall, the result is a theoretically more sophisticated portfolio of resources with greater conceptual clarity and empirical applicability.

The proposed model is however not without its limitations. First of all, like all models, it relies on concepts (e.g. wider structure, household responses and resources) which are ways of dividing reality, and as such can be challenged as being less useful than others. Second, any concept can be further subdivided. For instance, researchers whose primary focus on macro effects on household responses to poverty would need to further differentiate the notion of wider structure. Third, causal paths shown in this model are the ones which I believe most likely to exist, but this does not exhaust the range of possibilities. Despite these drawbacks, the substantive advantages of this model remain relevant to studies aimed at exploring household responses to poverty in an urban environment.

## An Overview of the Main Research Findings

This section presents the key findings obtained from the analysis of the entire sample and three case studies. Above all, the findings have shown that households' experience of deprivation was associated more with 'primary' than 'secondary' poverty'. This means that poverty was less likely to be caused by decisions and practices concerning income allocation, as when men control the money and spend it on themselves rather than on family. Contrary to the dominant view, which associates male management and/or control of household finances with increased deprivation, no significant difference was observed between male or female managed and controlled systems. This was attributed to the general concern by both spouses for the 'collective good' in their decisions about income allocation. Women were found to create secret kitties, but their kitty keeping was seen more as an attempt to gain greater financial agency than to reduce male-induced deprivation, In keeping with the previous research on female personal spending, it was shown that women generally use their kitty money to meet the needs of the overall household and the children, and this hence tends not to increase deprivation. It can therefore be suggested that households achieved considerable success by their income allocation practices. Other sources of success (or failure) are discussed below in relation to the behavioural areas of income generation, investment and consumption.

The type of resources deployed in income generation activities were found to include both labour and non-labour resources (e.g. economic capital and institutional entitlements), but as expected, a greater use of labour resources was in evidence. It was shown that neither income diversification nor dependency (one/several earners) levels explain differences in household deprivation. This was because high levels of participation in informal and seasonal labour market activities led both to increased deprivation by restricting access to state healthcare and pensions, which were employment-based. It was also demonstrated that the size of cultural capital accumulated by households has little bearing upon deprivation, given the general tendency for members to be educated below the level required for participation in economically more secure parts of the labour market. Likewise, the volume of social capital was found to make no significant difference. This was attributed to a number of factors which restrict the flow of support between social contacts. These include: a) economic decline which further reduces the parties' financial capacity to provide support and the 'creditworthiness' of poor households in the eyes of others, b) the presence of rivalries within one's social circle, and c) the pride taken in the male role as the main provider and/or in the self-sufficiency of the family unit. In fact, the research revealed extensive use of social capital in job seeking. However, neither engagement in power-based relationships with urban patrons nor deployment of weak ties or transient contacts was found to yield better jobs for the majority of those who were dependent on them.

The likely effects of religion on the resources used in income generation were left deliberately unexplored due to the way the sample was stratified. All the *Alevi*s were selected from the Northern part of the settlement whose inhabitants had no entitlements to *gecekondu* redevelopment. This would have biased the comparisons between deprivation and religious affiliation against the *Alevi* households. Instead, the relationship between religion and women's work history was explored to verify assumptions about the *Alevi*s being less segregated along gender lines. It was found that *Alevi* women were more likely to work outside home than their *Sünni* counterparts. However, there was an observed tendency for *Alevi* households to view women's work outside home as a last resort, which may suggest that patriarchal pressures were strong in both religious groups.

Turning to discuss the sources of success by investment practices, households were found to acquire assets through the deployment of resources such as economic capital (e.g. income and assets), social capital and institutional entitlements. However, the findings demonstrated that the majority of assets obtained in this way had a limited capacity to generate income, promote further asset acquisition and/or to ensure future security. Exceptions to these include *gecekondu* housing and land, and lump-sums acquired through retirement. This explains why success in reducing deprivation was dependent more on the ownership of entitlements to social insurance and *gecekondu* redevelopment. Furthermore, social capital was shown to play a particular role in the organisation of rotating savings and credit associations whereby households obtain the discipline to save. However, its contributions to acquisition of beneficial assets proved very limited.

Finally, household success by consumption practices was shown to depend on the type rather than the number or range of resources deployed in these activities. In particular, households with access to resources such as public land and social security entitlements were found to be better off since these resource types enabled access to rent-free accommodation and heavily subsidised medicine.

The conclusions drawn above are also supported by the analysis of change, performed to understand whether households were experiencing short or long spells of poverty. The analysis demonstrated that nearly half of the households had been able to reduce their overall deprivation levels. This was attributed to the April-October period being the peak time for seasonal work. However, the majority of those which experienced improvement remained below the poverty threshold because other structural factors, e.g. the general conditions of economic crisis and informality in the labour market, continued to restrict the benefit delivery capacity of resources available to them. Moreover, the minority who managed to rise above the threshold are most likely to have experienced short-lived success due to the subsequent winter decline in labour market opportunities.

Overall, the research findings confirm the general argument of this book by demonstrating that household (relative) success has little to do with the deployment of more or more varied resources. It rather depends on the capacity of resources to deliver benefits, which tends to be restricted by structural forces such as wider conditions of economic decline, informal, seasonal and casual conditions of work, and state housing and social security policies. Table 11.1 outlines the main research findings for reasons of comparison with the relationships hypothesised earlier (see Chapter 3).

**Table 11.1    Summary of main research findings**

| Hypothesis | Findings from the sample and case analyses |
|---|---|
| A | Higher levels of income diversification did not significantly reduce deprivation |
| B | Labour resources comprised the main source of income generation |
| C | *Alevi* women had a greater tendency to work outside home |
| D | Lower dependency ratio did not significantly reduce deprivation |
| E | Greater formal sector participation led to reduced deprivation |
| F | Economic capital investment in income generation was either low or non-existent |
| G | Higher levels of formal cultural capital accumulation did not significantly reduce deprivation |
| H | Social capital was extensively used in job search |
| I | Greater volume of social capital did not significantly reduce deprivation |
| J | The use of clientelist ties in job search made little difference to deprivation |
| K | The use of weak ties (transient contacts) did not significantly reduce deprivation |
| L | Household asset portfolios generally had a limited capacity to generate income |
| M | Great majority did not use *gecekondu* housing as a source of income generation |
| N | Institutional entitlements had a limited capacity to generate income |
| O | Social capital had a limited capacity as a direct source of income |
| P | Female-managed systems comprised the most common ways of managing income |
| Q | Financial management and control systems were not significantly associated with household deprivation, which seems due to general concern by both spouses for the 'collective good' |
| R | Secret kitty keeping was more common among women in households where finances were predominantly managed or controlled by men |
| S | Secret kitties did not increase deprivation |

| Hypothesis | Findings from the sample and case analyses |
|---|---|
| T | Neither greater involvement in non-commodified consumption practices nor use of more varied resources in these practices reduced deprivation |
| U | Households were not only unable to benefit from financial conditions which were highly favourable for investors but were also adversely affected by them given their tendency to accumulate debts in the form of foreign currency and gold |
| V | Rosca participation did not yield assets with high benefit delivery capacity |
| W | Social capital had a limited capacity to provide access to beneficial assets |
| X | Access to labour and land-based entitlements had a significant capacity to provide access to beneficial assets. More importantly than the year of migration to the city, entitlements to *gecekondu* redevelopment made a significant difference to household deprivation. |
| Y | Overall, deployment of a greater range of resources did not reduce deprivation |
| Z | The majority of households were unable to move out of poverty and the success of those who could tended to be short-lived mainly due to the seasonality factor |

## Policy Implications

This section discusses research contributions to the development of an effective poverty reduction strategy – an urgent matter for countries like Turkey where the state response was piecemeal. For some time, the Turkish government has given a central role to means-tested social safety nets. Since 2003, activation policies have also been made a priority area for both employment and poverty reduction (İŞ-KUR 2007, MLSS 2007, SPO 2006). Micro-credit programmes which have proliferated in recent years were considered as another component of this policy mixture (Buğra and Yakut-Çakar 2010). In what follows, I shall seek to demonstrate why high levels of poverty in the country cannot be tackled effectively from such a policy perspective, and set out a direction for a comprehensive and well-integrated poverty reduction strategy. I believe this research makes a significant contribution towards the development of such a strategy given its wider implications for policy in the areas of employment, labour market, social security, education and housing. These are outlined below in turn.

Within the Turkish context, the conditions that an individual is exposed to within the labour market have significant implications for poverty, since labour market participation not only comprises an important source of income but also a gateway to the state welfare services and benefits. This is why a strong association was found between poverty and informal sector participation. The low wages/ earnings and violations of employee rights observed within this sector were also shown to permeate the tax-regulated parts of the labour market.

Major policy issues emerging from these findings are three-fold. One of them relates to the informalisation of the labour force, and can, to some extent, be counteracted through further regulation of the labour market and proper enforcement via the courts. The recent social security reform policy introduces a new regulation whereby employers are obliged to make wage payments via the banking system. I believe this measure is unlikely to make a significant difference as it neither encourages those businesses that do not appear in the official records to register with the system nor deter the already registered ones from manipulating their employee records. For more effective results, heavier sanctions should be exercised upon employers who do not abide by the minimum wage regulations and who doctor the social security records of their employees. Labour market regulations can be complemented by an incentive mechanism whereby businesses are encouraged to register with the system and/or keep proper records. Small scale businesses can for instance be incentivised through tax discounts and/or subsidies, a possible win-win solution in that it compensates for the loss of employer earnings arising from increased regulation, as well as protecting the social security rights of the employees.

A second issue concerns the low level of hourly wages and earnings observed within both formal and informal ends of the labour market. One way forward is to increase the minimum wage level and replace the monthly minima with an hourly rate. The latter may help reduce incidences where employees are made to work long hours for very little return. Also policy measures need to be taken to support self-employed enterprisers with limited economic capital. One such measure involves the provision of subsidies, which is likely to work more effectively than lending money through micro-credit programmes given the observed difficulties poor households experience in dealing with debt repayments. Furthermore, self-employed people with similar trades can be organised around co-operatives to enhance their access to the commodity markets.

A third issue relates to the conditions for access to the social security system. In recent years, the close connection between employment and access to state health services and pensions has been weakened by allowing optional contributions. However, this by no means makes the social security system more pro-poor because the essence of the old system, which is insurance-based, remains unchanged. As shown in this study, the means-tested solutions offered to provide health coverage for those without social insurance fall short of the demand. Likewise, the majority of the unemployed are unable to receive cash support due to sizeable contributions required for access to the existing benefit scheme. The current social assistance system also far from provides a sustained and sizeable cash support for the needy groups within the working or non-working population. Consequently, the country needs a pro-poor and egalitarian social security system whereby every

Turkish citizen is granted universal access to state health services, pensions and unemployment benefits regardless of his/her employment status and contribution history. The development of such a system entails long-term planning. In the short run, policy measures should be taken to relax the conditions for access to health services and unemployment insurance.

Further findings from this research are relevant to both education and employment policy. Of critical importance is the evidence that indicates a weak association between cultural capital and household deprivation. The limited effects of cultural capital can be explained by the low level of formal education observed across the working household members. The fact that most of them were primary or secondary school graduates may be suggestive of a need to move beyond compulsory education to improve one's job chances. However, given the high rates of unemployment among university graduates, further cultural capital accumulation may well have a small effect on reducing poverty unless decent employment opportunities are created. Yet two policy developments over the last decade attest to the fact that job creation has not been given the attention that it does require. One involves the adoption of an aggressive privatisation policy, resulting in a loss of secure jobs in state enterprises. The other concerns the implementation of IMF-led policies without interruption between the years 1998 and 2008 to obtain fiscal discipline and increase currency reserves. These policies designed to encourage the inflow of financial capital were shown to have led the economy into a state of 'jobless growth' (BSB 2007).[1] This makes it imperative to designate job creation as a priority area for poverty reduction. Along similar lines with scholars who emphasise the need for productive employment (see e.g. Şenses 2008), this study promotes policies that give a central role to the generation of secure jobs with decent working conditions.

Going back to the educational needs of the labour force, one recent state response was to adopt activation policies whereby the third sector was encouraged to provide short-term training opportunities for the unemployed. In fact, very little remains known about the impact of these policies on the lives of recipients and non-recipients, but according to one study, their role in reducing unemployment remains limited (Çapar 2007). Likewise, I consider them to be an unlikely route out of poverty primarily because the activation policies construe the problem as one of a mismatch between jobs and people, and ignore poverty caused by job unavailability, and as shown in this study, unfavourable labour market conditions. An upward movement towards economically more secure parts of the labour market is unlikely to be achieved through short-term skills training provided by voluntary organisations. I suspect training recipients from poor backgrounds will at best be churned at the bottom of the labour market.

---

1   For macro-economic policy models designed to counteract jobless growth and produce fiscal policy alternatives see BSB (2006), Telli et al. (2006), Voyvoda and Yeldan (2005).

Therefore, I believe the state should assume greater responsibility for the creation of a well-educated labour force. A stronger public education system is needed to achieve this task as well as to give children from poor backgrounds an equal chance of access to educational opportunities. Public education at all levels is supposedly free, but families are still expected to pay entry/tuition fees and make further contributions to other school expenses (e.g. water bill) in addition to their children's own educational needs. When these expenses are coupled with the loss of earnings due to the withdrawal of children from the labour market, education becomes unaffordable for households on low income. Sustained and sizeable cash support may thus need to be granted to poor families to help them keep their children in education. However, this alone does not suffice to eliminate inequalities caused by the public vs. private division, which has become a more prominent feature of the Turkish education system in recent years. A reassessment of this division is imperative, especially in terms of improving access to tertiary education. In Turkey, access to state universities is through a national exam for which private coaching is virtually a requirement. High costs involved in taking private courses, coupled with low educational standards particularly in public schools located in low-income settlements, reduce the chances of children from poor backgrounds to succeed in this exam. Clearly, these growing inequalities cannot be counteracted with a public education system that is acutely under-resourced.[2] Thus, the level of funds channelled to the system needs to be substantially increased to improve the educational standards across the country, starting from public schools situated within disadvantaged areas.

Finally, the research implications for housing policy are as follows. The *gecekondu* policies designed in the early 1980s with a clientelist intention to win over votes and suppress social unrest were shown to play a crucial role in determining household success. Especially through the enactment of the Redevelopment Law which authorised the pre-1985 built *gecekondu*s and enabled some owners of these *gecekondu*s to benefit from land speculation, new divisions were created within the *gecekondu* population, which tend to be less emphasised than the divide between the *gecekondu* and non-*gecekondu* population. It was shown here that the redevelopment process leads to increased housing insecurity for illegal occupiers and makes displacement an imminent risk for those dwellers with limited or no access to authorised *gecekondu* land. Hence, a concerted policy approach is needed to deal with the housing needs of this particular risk group.

Moreover, since the enactment of the Redevelopment Law, the possibility of a localised or nationwide amnesty has continued to be used to raise expectations of *gecekondu* dwellers for clientelist purposes. As long as this expectation is kept alive, one force in the creation of informal housing and hence in the perpetuation

---

2   As a matter of interest, the percentage of the national budget allocated to public education fell from 19.25 per cent in 1992 to 9.64 per cent in 2002 (TURKSTAT 2003c). Moreover, the GDP share of the public spending on education was only 3.51 per cent in 2002, which further declined to 3.37 per cent in 2008 (SPO 2010).

of wider urban inequalities will remain. Therefore, alternatives to *gecekondu* amnesty and redevelopment should be considered, such as a) the renovation of the existing *gecekondu* stock (see e.g. YEŞKEP 1996) and b) the development of new social housing. The latter entails re-prioritising the target population for social housing in such a way as to meet the housing needs of the low income groups rather than of civil servants as at present.

Overall, it is clear from this study that poverty can neither be tackled from a perspective centred on means-tested safety nets nor by expecting the social capital to support those who fall through the net. This book rather calls for an employment-centred approach to poverty reduction which promotes job creation and decent working conditions, complemented by a strong state which ensures universal access to key welfare services and benefits. This requires moving away from macro-economic policies which prioritise fiscal discipline over the well-being of the disadvantaged groups in the society.

**Research Limitations**

This section discusses research limitations and their repercussions for the reliability of the data generated as well as the generalisability and validity of the conclusions drawn from it. To begin with, the research was carried out within a single country context where the economy was highly depressed, the degree of informalisation in the labour market was high and access to social welfare provisions were dependent heavily on employment status. The findings may therefore be relevant only to those contexts with similar socio-economic characteristics. Moreover, the data was drawn from a small subset of *gecekondu* households living within a single settlement. However, I believe the generalisability of the findings was enhanced through careful selection of the sample and the setting to reflect the typical characteristics of the wider *gecekondu* population concentrated in large cities. This population usually includes early rural-to-urban migrants who had moved to cities through chain migration and four-member families on low-income who are *Alevi* or *Sünni* by background. Naturally, there is variation in terms of rural origin but the typicality of Ankara *gecekondu*s was captured through the choice of a settlement populated with migrants from rural parts of Central Anatolia. The study also represented the bottom 15 per cent of the lowest income group within the Ankara population. However, one cannot assume that the results apply to households in other economic and social situations (e.g. single or extended households, households at the stage of dispersion or those above the chosen income threshold).

Another limitation stems from the choice of sampling technique. The stratified random sampling method used here to reduce selection bias and to improve representativeness of the sample obstructed the achievement of the target of 20 households, as interviews had to be requested from strangers. The application of multiple eligibility criteria also played a role in this. Of those households who met the criteria, the rate of refusal was approximately 30 per cent. This is unlikely to have introduced significant bias given the selection of households with certain characteristics, and the use of effective methods to persuade those who initially showed less willingness to take part.

A further drawback results from the application of quantitative data analysis techniques to a small sample. The analyses combined qualitative and quantitative approaches; the former was used to describe household responses to poverty and provide insight into the dynamic processes shaping these responses and their outcomes, whereas the latter was employed to shed light on reasons as to why some households were more successful than others in reducing their deprivation. However, the application of statistical techniques to a small sample (n = 17) may raise questions as to the validity of the research findings. Nevertheless, I sought to restore some validity through a) using 'strong', 'moderate' and 'weak' degrees of association rather than precise values, b) relying more on descriptive and bi-variate statistical tests which are relatively safer to apply on a small sample, and c) collecting rich and reliable data. Given the constraints upon the resources available to this study, conducting a large-scale survey would have resulted in a superficial data set. The use of a small sample along with longitudinal design and separate spousal interviews contributed greatly to the acquisition of detailed and high quality data. In particular, the choice of research design helped with rapport-building, which proved a gradual process, and separate interviews allowed cross-checks between spouses' accounts of sensitive topics such as household finances.

Here, a comment is also necessary about casual inference. By definition, correlation does not establish causation. Any causal inferences based on correlations thus involve our understanding of the social processes likely to be involved. Earlier in this book, some causal interpretations were made of the observed correlations, based on theories and research in the literature and my own qualitative data. The possibility that the causal relationships are reciprocal or complex (e.g. including unknown third or fourth factors) remains ever-present and we have noted certain cases where this seemed to be likely (e.g. the relationship between income allocation and deprivation). However, this is not only a limitation of this research but of all empirical studies except for those which adopt very complex mathematical modelling to capture causal complexity.

Finally, three drawbacks can be identified with the use of a composite index in measuring deprivation. First, theoretically a composite index runs the risk of containing more than one indicator measuring the same aspect of deprivation, and hence biasing the scores. Second, the selection of deprivation measures to be included within the index often remains an arbitrary decision. In this research, both these problems were minimised through the application of factor analysis to the data on subjective perceptions of respondents with a view to determining the final list of measures and their respective weights. However, a certain degree of arbitrariness was inevitable since both the initial list of deprivation measures and the factor loadings used for finalising these measures were selected by the researcher. Third, the index was designed to measure overall aspects of household deprivation and therefore remains rather insensitive to intra-household differences in deprivation experienced by individual members.

## An Agenda for Future Research

There are limits to the number of questions any piece of research can feasibly explore. This book therefore leaves many questions for future studies. To start with, certain sources of effect are reduced or removed from the research through the selection of households with the same size, structure and stage in the life-cycle that fell below an income threshold. Thus, it remains for other studies to explore households in other economic or social situations. Researchers may also consider applying the model proposed by this book to other socio-economic contexts or replicating the research on a larger sample.

Another line of inquiry concerns the poverty implications of planned actions. This study has challenged the idea of the poor as 'chronic non-planners' (Aksham 1974 cited in Anderson et al. 1994), by documenting households' involvement in planning e.g. within areas of work and investment (see Anderson et al 1994 and Eroğlu 2010a for similar findings). There is, however, need for further research to explore whether households which plan their actions are significantly better off than those who do not or who cannot.

Issues surrounding income allocation also provoke interesting questions for future examination, such as what dimensions of deprivation would best capture differences between household members? How can objective and subjective views be combined to measure intra-household levels of deprivation? How far can the differences in members' deprivation be attributed the overt and covert mechanisms of income allocation? One may also want to focus on the extent of and reasons for secret kitty keeping of men – an area which has not been explored beyond allusions to a couple of cases where men have concealed separate accounts (Tichenor 1999).

An additional area of interest concerns the relationship between social capital and poverty. This book has focused on certain aspects of social capital such as volume and contact status in order to shed some light upon the factors likely to affect the benefit delivery capacity of this resource and hence household success. One tentative conclusion drawn from this inquiry needs further verification, i.e. the idea that the position of the contact status within the wider (urban) opportunity structure is more critical to household success than his/her occupational characteristics. This throws up further questions about the significance of contact status for poverty, such as whether households with more links to well-positioned people fare better than those with fewer or no such links. If so, who among the poor tend to have access to these beneficial links? To what extent their superior links are clientelist in character? What benefits are accrued on these relationships and at what cost? Alternatively, one may want to take on board a question left unanswered by this research due to lack of sample variation, i.e. whether those who are able to mobilise their social capital resources in job finding are significantly better off than those who cannot. Moreover, this study presents an opportunity to further evaluate the poverty outcomes of the state housing policies. The fact that the research was conducted in a *gecekondu* area planned for gradual redevelopment on a plot-by-plot basis makes it possible to conduct a follow up of the sample to compare the periods before and after transformation. Of particular interest are questions about whether the legal occupiers' expectations about urban rent were actually met, and how successful the illegal occupiers were in coping with the risk of evacuation.

Finally, through an empirical analysis of the wider structural forces such as labour market processes and state housing and social security policies and their role in shaping household resources and behaviour, this book contributes to an area that is little explored within the existing literature. It is therefore of great importance that future research from the livelihood (coping or survival) perspective gives due weight to understanding macro-level constraints, as the chance that households will permanently move out of poverty depends more on changes operating at this level.

# Appendix A
# Measuring Poverty: Designing an Index which Combines 'Objective' and Subjective Dimensions of Deprivation

The appendix outlines the steps taken to develop the Factor Weighted Index of Deprivation (FWID), and explains how weighted aggregate deprivation and change scores were obtained. The aim in building this index is not only to improve on the methods used previously to measure deprivation, but also to create an instrument that provides a broader representation of poverty than the past instruments applied within studies on Turkey. [1]

### Developing the FWID: Towards an Alternative Methodology

The overall process of index development, including the selection of the deprivation measures, took place in three stages. The first stage referred to the period prior to the April interviews, the second to the period between April and October, and the third to the period following the October interviews. In the first stage, I identified

---

1 Studies that have sought to measure the extent of poverty in the country prior to the field research can be subsumed under five groups. The first group takes a capability approach to poverty measurement and calculates the HDI and HPI indices for urban and rural areas (Akder 1999, 2001). The second group determine poverty rates based on a) minimum calorie intake or food expenditure (Bağdadıoğlu 1987-2002, Bulutay 1998, Dağdemir 1999, Dumanlı 1996, Erdoğan 1997, 1998, World Bank 2000), b) basic food and non-food needs (Bağdadıoğlu 1987-2002, Dağdemir 1999, Erdoğan 1997, 1998, World Bank 2000), and c) one-dollar-a-day (World Bank 2000). The third group of studies approaches poverty from an inequality perspective, using diverse thresholds: a) 50% of the median income (Bulutay 1998, Celasun 1989, Derviş and Robinson 1973, Gürsel et al. 2000, Uygur and Kasnakoğlu 1998, World Bank 2000), b) lowest income level for the 40% of the population (Dansuk 1997), c) 50% of the median disposable income (Pamuk 2000), d) regional average consumption expenditure (Dansuk 1997), and e) 50% of the median consumption expenditure (Bulutay 1998). Finally, Gitmez and Morçöl (1995) take a quality of life approach to determining the typology of urban poor, which combines 'objective' and subjective aspects of poverty (e.g. income, assets, housing problems, happiness and life satisfaction). Consequently, a substantial part of the existing literature uses income and/or expenditure as a proxy, which is widely acknowledged to provide only a partial picture of poverty (Alcock 1993, Callan et al. 1993, Rakodi 2002, Şenses 2001, Wratten 1995).

three 'objective' dimensions of deprivation, i.e. monetary, consumption and work-related and broad areas/measures of deprivation from each dimension to be explored during field research. The fundamental decision to incorporate three 'objective' dimensions within a composite index was based on the assumption that a household's position in one of these dimensions would not determine their position on others. Income was considered in conjunction with assets in order to capture likely differences in household capacity to translate income into such resources (e.g. due to patterns of intra-household income allocation), as well as to take account of assets obtained without deploying an income (e.g. through social support). This rationale also applies to the inclusion of commodified and non-commodified elements of consumption separately from income. Also the relationship between income and working conditions was considered in the same fashion since the level of income alone says nothing for instance about excessive work hours or health and safety risks undertaken in generating an income.

On the other hand, the decision regarding the identification of the broad areas of deprivation was made by operationalising ideas already present in the literature regarding the significance of work and welfare-related (or non-commodified) indicators for poverty (e.g. Gutkind 1986, Şenses 2001), and by choosing from earlier poverty studies certain indicators and adapting them to the Turkish case (e.g. Baharoğlu and Kessides 2001, Callan et al. 1993, Gitmez and Morçöl 1995, Gordon et al. 2000, Mack and Lansley 1985, Moser 1996a, Townsend 1979, 1993). As a result, the initial list took the following shape:

*Monetary*
    Income
    Financial assets (debts, savings)
    Non-financial assets

*Consumption*
    Food (e.g. no. of meals, meat consumption)
    Education
    Health (access to and quality of medical services)
    Housing (room, heating, insulation, tenure security, environmental safety)
    Household items (furniture and electrical appliances)
    Urban services (water, electricity, telephone)
    Clothing
    Recreation

*Work*
    Health and safety risks
    Social insurance coverage
    Work hours.

In the second stage, the above items were subjected to further revision in the light of personal impressions obtained through semi-structured interviews and participant observation. As a result, broadly defined areas of deprivation were refined. Some measures were omitted because they either required excessively detailed data (i.e. clothing and recreation) or failed to capture the true extent of deprivation (i.e. number of daily meals per member). Finally, three new measures were added to the list: a) each member's access to subsidized medicine (in order to represent differences in welfare entitlements to medical treatment), b) household winter food stock (in order to reflect habitual ways of coping with lack of income and/or seasonal changes in income), and finally, c) pension prospects (in order to take account of past premium contributions as well as current social insurance status). The last measure focuses on the male partner as neither the female partner nor children had a sufficient employment history on which to base my predictions. Consequently, the revised list contained the 29 'objective' measures presented below:

*Monetary*
1. Real disposable monthly household income
2. Real total household savings
3. Real total household debts
4. Housing security
5. Urban plot ownership
6. Second urban house ownership
7. Rural land ownership
8. Car ownership
9. Work related assets, equipment and supplies

*Consumption*
10. Monthly meat consumption
11. Winter food stock
12. Number of children in compulsory or higher education
13. Quality of education being received by the children
14. Number of household members with access to free/discounted medicine
15. Quality of medical service being received by all members
16. Optimum housing size
17. Private room availability
18. Fuel type and quantity
19. Hot water use
20. Insulation of the heated room
21. Environmental hygiene and safety
22. Individual subscription to utilities
23. Number of furniture items
24. Number of electrical appliances
25. Age and purchase type (i.e. first or second hand) of furniture and appliances

*Work*

    26. Household occupational risk grade
    27. Household social insurance ratio
    28. Household income to work hour ratio
    29. Pension prospects.

Based on this list, a short questionnaire was constructed to explore *the extent to which* respondents perceived the listed items as critical to deprivation. This subjective deprivation questionnaire enquires about partners' perceptions of all listed items from a total of 24 questions; for instance, asking how necessary it is to be able to save for rainy days, or to support children who wish to stay on in further education. These questions were administered during the October interviews with both partners of 17 households, except two males, yielding a total of 32 cases. Their responses were recorded on a Likert scale of five divisions in which number one indicated the item to be seen as 'very unnecessary' whereas five indicated 'very necessary'.

In the last stage, the data obtained from the subjective deprivation questionnaire was used to a) finalize the list of measures, and b) determine the weights for each selected measure. In so doing, two sets of statistics were referred to: The first involved the mean and standard deviation. Items with means equal to or lower than three and standard deviations above one were excluded from the study. This meant that only those items whose significance for deprivation was largely agreed upon were retained within the index. Two items, i.e. car and rural land ownership were omitted due to the lack of such agreement.

The second set included the statistics obtained from factor analysis, which is a technique of identifying underlying dimensions of variation on which the observed variables are loading by means of various extraction and rotation methods (Tabachnick and Fidell 2001). In this study, the SSPSS data reduction facility was used to conduct trials on 24 items, combining different extraction and rotation techniques with a number of factors ranging from three to five. The decision regarding the number of factors depends more on the researcher's judgment than any robust criteria. Nevertheless, Eigenvalues representing variance or the scree test of Eigenvalues plotted against factors can aid this decision. The latter was used in this study to determine the number of factors trialled. After several trials, a three factor solution obtained through combining principal components analysis with varimax rotation technique (orthogonal) was extracted. In fact, this particular solution did not prove significantly different from those produced by other combinations. Nevertheless, I decided to interpret this solution as the techniques involved were better suited to my research purposes. My ultimate aim in conducting factor analysis was to explore how variables were correlated with each other, and how they can be summarized to avoid any risk of repetition. Principal components extraction technique is deemed more suitable for this purpose than testing a hypothesis about underlying processes (Tabachnick and Fidell 2001). Additionally, varimax rotation technique, which maximizes variance of factor loadings, was preferred to increase the sensitivity of the weights to the perceptions of the minority.

As for the selection of variables to be interpreted by each factor, or to be retained within the index, this decision was based on the factor loading scores of the individual variables on it. Factor loading scores indicate the weights used in determining the unique contribution of each factor to the variance in a variable. In solutions using orthogonal rotation, they also refer to the correlations between variables and factors (Tabachnick and Fidell 2001). As a principle, statisticians recommend interpreting only those variables with a score of 0.32 and above. In this study, the cut-off point was set at 0.30, as a result of which the items relating to schooling expenses and environmental hygiene/safety were eliminated. In fact, the omitted items related to a similar feature of deprivation to that sought by measures of housing security and the capacity to send children to higher education. Thus, by eliminating them, the risk of biasing the results through repetitive measurement was reduced. Factor loading scores were also used to determine the weights corresponding to each selected measure, in other words, the relative importance respondents attached to each perceived item of necessity. The extracted factors and variables contributing to each factor are presented in Table A.1 in association with the size of the loading scores.

**Table A.1**   **Order (by size of loadings) in which variables contribute to factors**

| Factor | I. *Quality* | II. *Basic needs* | III. *Financial stability* |
|---|---|---|---|
| Variables | Age of household items (.733) | Urban utilities (.722) | No debts (.749) |
| | Separate study-bedroom (.727) | Health (.679) | Savings (.722) |
| | Health & safety at work (.666) | Home repairs (.666) | Meat consumption (.717) |
| | Furniture (.636) | Sufficient income (.627) | Social ins., pension (.385) |
| | First hand clothes (.587) | Housing security (.568) | Winter food stock (.369) |
| | Electrical appliances (.455) | Urban house/plot (.518) | |
| | Work hours (.407) | Higher education (.392) | |
| | Heating & hot water (.299) | | |
| Variance | 14.61% | 14.36% | 11.11% |
| Means | 4.34 | 4.73 | 4.57 |

Extraction Method: Principal Component Analysis

Rotation Method: Varimax

The labels in italics refer to my own interpretation of each factor with regard to how respondents might perceive each dimension of deprivation. Although my aim in conducting factor analysis was not to test whether my conception of deprivation matched their perceptions, it is interesting to observe that they depart significantly from my understanding of deprivation as having monetary, consumption and work-related dimensions. The respondents seem more inclined to conceive of deprivation in terms of the lack of basic needs, financial stability and quality of life. The significance of each factor is established by looking at the percentage of variation explained by it. As can be seen from Table A.1, the three factors proved almost equally significant in terms of the amount of variance they explained. However, the distribution of their total means seems to indicate a slight order to the way in which each dimension was valued; the basic needs come first, financial stability second, and the quality of life last. This may suggest that respondents were rather rational in their judgments as to how these dimensions/necessities should be prioritised.

Before concluding the discussion of the factor analysis outcomes, a few points need to be made in order to address the question of reliability when this technique is applied to a very small sample. In fact, there exists no precise way to check the reliability of a factor solution. However, the results presented above can be claimed to be reliable on two grounds. Firstly, the factor solutions obtained from numerous trials proved rather stable across different extraction and rotation methods. Secondly, the variables meaningfully loaded on to each extracted factor. At first sight, the relationship between the factor of financial stability and the variables of meat consumption and winter food stock might appear meaningless. However, I consider them to be meaningfully associated because, as my personal observations suggested, neither item was perceived by respondents merely as elements of basic consumption. For them, meat consumption, which was more likely to happen when guests were around, was more symbolic of an economically established family, and food stock preparations meant a safety net against the winter decline in the level of earnings and increase in the food prices.

By the end of the factor analysis, the number of measures retained within the index was reduced to 25. Ideally, I would have liked to explore the nature of deprivation being indicated by all of these measures. However, further measures had to be eliminated prior to coding in order to give each household an equal chance of scoring the maximum. Thus, despite their significance in explaining deprivation, the measures concerning work-related assets, equipments and supplies as well as quality of children's education had to be excluded. As a result, 23 measures were contained within the index. The composition of the retained measures is presented in Table A.2 together with their respective weights.

**Table A.2    Final list of deprivation measures and their corresponding weights**

| Areas of deprivation | Deprivation measure(s) | Weights |
|---|---|---|
| *Monetary* | | |
| Financial deprivation | 1. Real disposable monthly household income i.e. income – [rent + fixed travel expenses] | 0.68 |
| | 2. Real total household savings | 0.72 |
| | 3. Real total household debts | 0.75 |
| Asset deprivation | 4. Housing security (risk of eviction) | 0.57 |
| | 5. Urban plot ownership (inc. the one occupied) in $m^2$ | 0.52 |
| | 6. Second urban house ownership | 0.52 |
| *Consumption* | | |
| Household items | 7. Total no. of pieces of furniture | 0.64 |
| | 8. Total no of electrical appliances | 0.46 |
| | 9. Total no of old/second hand pieces of furniture | 0.72 |
| | 10. Total no of old/second hand appliances | 0.72 |
| Housing | 11. Optimum housing size in $m^2$ | 0.52 |
| | 12. Bedroom availability | 0.73 |
| | 13. Aggregate heating & insulation score $(a + b + c)/3$ a. Fuel type & quantity b. Hot water use c. Insulation of ceiling in the heated room | 0.30 |
| Urban services | 14. Individual subscription to urban utilities (water,electricity, phone) | 0.72 |
| Health | 15. Number of household members with free / discounted access to prescribed medicine | 0.68 |
| | 16. The quality of medical service received by each household member | 0.68 |
| Education | 17. Number of children in compulsory or higher education | 0.39 |
| Food | 18. Monthly meat consumption of any sort in kg | 0.72 |
| | 19. Winter food stock | 0.37 |
| *Work* | | |
| Work hours | 20. Mean household income/work hours ratio (i.e. monthly weighted average ratio of the real income/work hours per working household member) | 0.41 |
| Social security | 21. Household social insurance ratio (i.e. ratio of insured members to total workers) | 0.39 |
| Pension prospects | 22. Male partner's likelihood of drawing full pension | 0.39 |
| Job health & safety | 23. Mean household occupational risk grades (i.e. average risk of having an accident at work per working member) | 0.67 |

## Coding Procedure: Calculating the Aggregate Scores

Table A.2 does not demonstrate the codes for each measure. Details regarding the coding procedure can be made available for viewing on request (see also Eroğlu 2004). However, in brief, the underlying principle was to code each selected measure in such a way as to allow a maximum score of three, which indicated being better off. The nature of deprivation being sought by a particular measure did not always allow for neat categories of three. In such cases, the scores were divided by three to give the same effect. In determining the codes for interval data, cut-off points for three equal groups were obtained through the SPSS descriptive/frequency facility.

The scores for each measure were multiplied by their respective weights (i.e. factor loading scores) and then added up to obtain the weighted aggregate deprivation scores. The same procedure was applied to both April and October data; the only difference being the use of separate sets of cut-off points for grouping April and October interval data. However, a slight modification of this procedure was required for the calculation of the weighted aggregate change scores. Interval data for April and October were merged to generate another set of cut-off points, followed by the regrouping of these data sets. The above procedure was then repeated to determine the weighted aggregates for April and October. Finally, the latter was subtracted from the former to obtain the change scores. The application of April cut-offs to October data was avoided because this would have biased change scores against those who in April scored the maximum on any of the measures containing interval data. This merging of interval data might have had a small effect on the level of accuracy achieved in the amount of change observed, but was needed to reduce bias.

## Conclusion

The appendix explained the stages involved in the development of the FWID. In particular, it has demonstrated how a unique application of factor analysis was used to combine expert opinion with the subjective perceptions of poor respondents in tackling questions of which standards of living should be included in the measurement of deprivation, and how their relative value should be estimated. The outcome is a robust and theoretically sophisticated instrument in that it a) measures a wide range of actual deprivations; b) combines direct and indirect (i.e. income-based) measures of poverty; c) reduces bias due to arbitrary, normative and pragmatic decisions involved in various stages of measure selection, d) contains a core of measures deemed critical to deprivation, and e) includes views of every respondent in determining the weights for each measure. Despite its origin in a small scale study of Turkish households and potential challenges this may lead to, the substantive and methodological advantages of this index are relevant to studies aimed at measuring deprivation, poverty, capability, well-being or social exclusion on any scale in both developing and developed parts of the world.

# Appendix B
# Social Security Reform: Potential Outcomes for Poor Households

The Social Security and General Health Insurance Law No. 5510 enacted in 2008 has brought changes to the conditions of access to state pensions and healthcare. This appendix briefly examines the potential implications of these policy changes for the studied households.

**Access to Pensions**

Starting with the retirement requirements, the new law redefines the minimum age and contribution size for post-2000 entries. The age thresholds are currently set at 58 for women and 60 for men, and from 2036 onwards will both be raised to 65 in stages. The minimum days of contribution are kept at their previous levels for ES and BAĞ-KUR members (i.e. 9000 days), and will be increased incrementally from 7000 to 9000 days for SSK members by 2027. The vested rights of pre-2000 entries are however protected.

Since the male spouses in the sample belonged to the second group of entries, the above changes would not affect their pension prospects. Hence the possibility of drawing a full pension would remain high for 35 percent (6 out of 17) of male spouses provided they stayed in the same job. The risk of redundancy has however increased especially for the private sector employees comprising 50 per cent (3 out of 6) of male spouses from this group, in the face of a subsequent economic crisis which led to a contraction in the economy by 7.8 per cent between October 2008 and September 2009 (Boratav 2010). As a matter of fact, the urban unemployment rates, according to the conservative official figures, rose from 11.6 per cent in 2001 to 15.6 per cent in 2009 (TURKSTAT 2003c, 2010b).

The remaining 65 per cent (11 out of 17) of male spouses, all but one of whom was employed in the private sector without social insurance, are unlikely to have improved on their low to medium prospects for three reasons. First of all, the economic crisis in 2008 is likely to have further reduced their chances of activating their social insurance through regular work. Second, they are likely to have remained subject to violations of social security rights despite the preventative measures proposed by the new law, according to which: a) banks and public bodies will be responsible for informing the Social Security Institution as to whether the users of their services have social security registration; b) wages will be paid through banks; and c) those working less than 30 days will be allowed to make optional contributions. Of these measures, the second might help reduce the incidence of employers making illegal cuts from the net minimum wage, but none of them goes far enough to discourage employers from doctoring the records of employees to pay premiums at the lowest possible rate or from keeping them completely off the books. Finally, the optional scheme continues to be off limits for low-income groups unable to obtain social insurance through work given the new regulations which make it compulsory to make joint payments for health and pension premiums. At the time of research, 90 per cent of male spouses working without social insurance were unable to afford the latter alone. Hence it is highly unlikely that they will have the financial ability to meet the increased payment requirements for the new scheme. For these reasons, the new law can be claimed to have brought no improvement to the pension prospects of male spouses in the sample.

**Access to Healthcare**

Law no. 5510 launched in 2008 an umbrella scheme called General Health Insurance (GSS), unifying the existing social insurance schemes differentiated along employment status, namely ES, SSK and BAĞ-KUR. Access to state healthcare was previously dependent upon labour-based contributions to these three schemes. The minimum premium size, as well as the type of hospitals active and retired members were allowed to use, varied according to the scheme type. ES members consisting of civil servants were entitled to state and university hospitals from the beginning of their employment whereas SSK members embracing the remaining employees had to contribute a minimum of 90 days for themselves and 120 for their dependants. The minimum days of contribution were 240 days for those BAĞ-KUR members who are the self-employed. By the new law, individuals are allowed to make premium payments optionally or through work, and in the latter alternative, employee and employer share the cost of premium payments. There are also plans to provide state help for those unable to make the premium payments. Those with a minimum of 30 days' worth of premium contributions within the year prior to their application to a health provider and without outstanding premiums exceeding 60 days are now allowed access to all public, university and private hospitals contracted by the state.

The GSS futures of the respondent households are discussed below, starting with those composed of active or retired members of the past schemes and their dependants. Active ES and SSK members comprised 26 per cent (9 out of 35) of the working population in the sample and there was only one male spouse who retired from the SSK. Within the group of active and retired members, only the male spouses had dependants (two or more), corresponding to 35 per cent (6 out of 17) of the sample. Active and retired members continue to receive health coverage under the new system but there have been some changes to the status of their dependants. While the non-working wives and children aged between 18 and 25 in education are allowed to remain as their dependants, unmarried and non-working female children above the age of 18 are now denied this status but their vested rights are protected until they get married or resume work. Furthermore, children below the age of 18 cease to count as dependants since the state now provides insurance for them independently of their parents' social insurance status.

Thus, in 35 per cent (6 out of 17) of households, female spouses are likely to have GSS coverage through their husbands – this seems to be the most likely option for them since their prospect for obtaining insurance through work remains rather low. The GSS status of their children is however less straightforward. At the time of research, 17 per cent (2 out of 12) of these children lacked access to state healthcare despite being in full-time employment. If the GSS scheme had been in place in 2002, the figure would have stayed the same, as they were males above the age of 18. However, by 2010, the number of male children who will have passed the age threshold for state coverage will have reached eight, which means that the percentage of children without coverage may increase to 58 per cent (7 out of 12) given their restricted chance of attending higher education or obtaining work-based insurance. It will be shown later that their likelihood of obtaining optional or state coverage also remains rather limited.

Concerning the effects of changes to the premium requirements, as long as the their job status stays the same, active and retired members within the sample would remain unaffected by the newly set conditions, which are generally considered a move forward in terms of eliminating inequalities in access to healthcare resulting from the application of different minima across schemes (e.g. it may allow quicker access to healthcare by SSK and BAĞ-KUR members). However, this claim is based on the optimistic assumption that all individuals will have sustained GSS coverage. However, we have seen already that the children of low-income active or retired members above 18 could well be faced with exclusion. The same future may be awaiting those without social insurance, which comprised 74 per cent (26 out of 35) of the working population in the sample. Of these, 69 per cent (18 out of 26) represented private sector employees and 27 per cent (7 out of 26) constituted the self-employed, who have either never been registered with BAĞ-KUR or been registered but unable to keep up with the premium payments. Given the persistence of adverse labour market conditions, the numbers with work-based insurance are unlikely to have increased, meaning that changes to the premium requirements would make no difference to 65 per cent (11 out of 17) of households unless they are able to obtain optional or state coverage, which, as will be shown later, remains rather unlikely.

Likewise, the extension to the scope of medical services to which the insured are allowed access is unlikely to produce the desired effect of eliminating inequalities arising from the differences in the nature and quality of healthcare provided across hospitals. This is so not only because a portion of the population will remain uninsured but also because of the newly introduced charges for outpatients that are likely to create new inequalities among the insured, including active and retired members of the past schemes. According to the new regulations, outpatients are now expected to pay a doctor/dentist fee per consultation in addition to increased prescription charges, which now consist of a fixed handling fee and a variable amount corresponding to 10 to 20 per cent of the medicine or medical apparatus such as orthesis and prothesis. The patients using primary health services (e.g. GP surgeries) are made liable for prescription charges only while the users of public, university and private hospitals have to pay both consultation and prescription charges. Moreover, the new law gives hospitals the right to apply variable rates; for example, public hospitals can now charge up to 30 per cent higher than the base amount set by the government and the figure goes up to 70 per cent for private hospitals.

In the face of an increased cost of healthcare, the insured members of low-income households are likely to turn to cheaper health providers with the following possible consequences which are rather inter-related. They are likely to find it increasingly difficult to use healthcare providers beyond the first stage. Active and retired members of the past schemes on low-income may thus have to downgrade. Even if they manage to pass the first stage, the likelihood of access to private hospitals would remain close to zero.

All of the above predictions concerning active and retired members across the sample are based on the assumption that there were no job losses, which however remains a real possibility especially for private sector employees and the self-employed with little economic capital to cushion their fragile businesses at a time of economic crisis. In the likely event of redundancy or bankruptcy, only 20 per cent (7 out of 35) of the working population and their dependants within 18 per cent (3 out of 17) of the sample households would have GSS coverage through unemployment insurance for six, eight or ten months, depending on the size of past premium contributions. The numbers eligible for this scheme are unlikely to have improved since the fieldwork, as no revisions have been made to loosen the strict access criteria. Those ineligible for unemployment insurance are provided GSS coverage for 90 days on the condition that they made 90 days of contribution within the year prior to redundancy. Those who fail to meet this requirement are covered for 10 days only. The new system thus provides short but improved access for the active ES members were previously entitled to no healthcare after redundancy. However, it abolishes the right of all SSK members who became unemployed to use the state healthcare services for a period of six months and makes it conditional upon the past premium contributions; thereby penalising not only those made to work without social insurance, but also the active members who fail to meet the strict eligibility criteria for unemployment insurance. So what happens to those ineligible for unemployment insurance or those still unemployed at the end of the claim period? They will be subjected to the same conditions as those working without social insurance. Let us now explore the GSS futures of this particular group.

Households where the male spouse worked without social insurance represented 65 per cent (11 out of 17) of the sample. Of these, 27 per cent (3 out 17) were entitled to a green card which at the time of research allowed access to hospital treatment only. Since the field research, the green card scheme has been subject to revisions. According to the most recent changes, beneficiaries are reimbursed for the consultation and prescription charges from a social assistance fund. The green card scheme is planned to be abolished on the 1st of October 2010, and those on low incomes will be means-tested to determine their eligibility for state-paid GSS premiums. The plan is to continue applying the revised green card selection criterion (see law no. 5222 enacted in 2004) to identify the recipients of state-paid premiums. However, this time gross rather than net minimum wage will be taken as the basis. Those ineligible for state help will on the other hand be expected to pay a monthly premium at a rate adjusted to their household income. According to this, individuals whose per capita household income: a) falls below one third of the gross minimum wage will have their premiums paid by the state; b) remains between one third of the gross minimum wage and the gross minimum wage will pay 12 per cent of the former; c) remains between the gross minimum wage and double the amount will pay 12 per cent of the former, and finally, d) is more than double the gross minimum wage will pay 12 percent of this amount as a monthly premium.

The following hypothetical picture emerges from the application of the above criteria to the sample households, based on the gross minimum wage in place at the time of fieldwork which amounted to 220,000,750 TL. Only 27 per cent (3 out of 11) of households where the male spouse worked without social insurance would be eligible for state-paid premiums. The GSS premiums for a minority of households might be paid by the state but as mentioned earlier, the story does not end with premium contributions; outpatients are now expected to pay new charges to gain access to healthcare. Therefore, those eligible for state paid-premiums may find themselves in a similar situation as the low-income active and retired members of the past schemes, i.e. faced with exclusion from healthcare providers beyond the first stage. Even if those eligible for state help are, like the existing green card holders, reimbursed for the consultation and prescription charges, their exclusion remains a real possibility due to a lack of ready cash.

On the other hand, 73 per cent (8 out of 11) of households where the male spouse worked without social insurance, which comprise 47 per cent (8 out of 17) of the overall sample, would be considered ineligible and hence be expected to pay a monthly premium at a rate defined in category (b) for each member above the age of 18 who are unable to obtain insurance through work. Let us now estimate the number of members within these households who are likely to pay a premium. At the time of research, 55 per cent (12 out of 22) of their children lacked health coverage. If the GSS system had been in place then, the figure would have declined to 18 per cent (4 out of 22) as those below the age of 18 would have been covered by the state. This would have reduced the number of household members requiring premium contributions to two for most households, i.e. male and female spouse, as the latter is most likely to stay outside employment. However, by 2010, the percentage of uninsured children is likely to have reached 55 per cent as more of them will have passed the age threshold with little prospect for obtaining insurance through regular work. Assuming that they will be unmarried and continue to live with their parents, these households would thus be expected to pay a monthly premium for three to four members, which in the 2002 figures would amount to 26.4 and 35.2 million TL respectively.

Likewise, 35 per cent (6 out of 17) of households where the male spouse was an active or retired member of a past scheme would have to make a contribution for one or both children at the same rate, which comes to 8.8 or 17.6 million TL per month. The rates may seem reasonable to some, but when they are considered in conjunction with the newly introduced charges, it becomes rather unlikely that either group of households will be able to ensure sustained GSS coverage for members without work-based insurance. This is also supported by the fact that the majority of men eligible for the optional pension scheme were unable to afford the premium payments. Thus, it remains highly probable that 47 per cent of households (8 out of 17) and 58 per cent (19 out of 34) of children within the sample can face complete exclusion from the new system.

Overall, despite being called 'General Health Insurance', the new scheme is far from offering sustained coverage for all, and continues to punish the poorer segments of the population for having to settle for work without social insurance.

# Bibliography

Abrams, F. 2002a. The breadline: a month on the minimum wage. *The Guardian G2*, 28 January, 1–5.

Abrams, F. 2002b. Can you survive on the minimum wage in London? *The Guardian G2*, 29 January, 2.

Agarwal, B. 1992. Gender relations and food security: coping with seasonality, drought and famine in South Asia, in *Unequal Burden: Economic Crisis, Persistent Poverty and Women's Work*, edited by L. Beneria and S. Feldman. London: Westview Press.

Akder, H. 1999. *Türkiye'de Kırsal Yoksulluğun Boyutları* (The Dimensions of Rural Poverty in Turkey). Ankara: The World Bank.

Akder, H. 2001. *Human Development Report: Turkey 2001*. Ankara: UNDP.

Akşam 2000. Gecekonducuların öfkesi (The rage of squatters). *Akşam*, 26 September.

Akyüz, Y. and Boratav, K. 2003. The making of the Turkish financial crisis. *World Development*, 3(9), 1549–66.

Alkire, S. 2002. *Valuing Freedoms: Sen's Capability Approach and Poverty Reduction*. Oxford: Oxford University Press.

Alkire, S. 2007. Measuring freedoms alongside wellbeing, in *Wellbeing in Developing Countries: from Theory to Research*, edited by I. Gough and J.A. McGregor. Cambridge: Cambridge University Press.

Almedon, A.M. 1995. A note on ROSCAs among Ethiopian in Addis Ababa and Eritrean women in Oxford, in *Money-Go-Rounds: The Importance of Rotating Savings and Credit Associations for Women*, edited by S. Ardener and S. Burman. Oxford/Washington D.C.: BERG.

Alpar, İ. and Yener, S. 1991. *Gecekondu Araştırması* (A *Gecekondu* Study). Ankara: Devlet Planlama Teşkilatı Sosyal Planlama Başkanlığı (State Planning Organisation Social Planning Department).

Amis, P. 1995. Making sense of poverty. *Environment and Urbanization*, 7(1), 145–57.

Anderson, M. 1971. *Family Structure in Nineteenth Century Lancashire*. Cambridge: Cambridge University Press.

Anderson, M., Bechhofer, F. and Kendrick, S. 1994. Individual and household strategies, in *The Social and Political Economy of the Household*, edited by M. Anderson et al. Oxford: Oxford University Press.

Andreotti, A. 2006. Coping strategies in a wealthy city of Northern Italy. *International Journal of Urban and Regional Research*, 30(2), 328–45.

Ardener, S. 1964. The comparative study of rotating credit associations. *The Journal of the Royal Anthropological Institute of Great Britain and Ireland*, 94(2), 201–29.

Ardener, S. 1995. Women making money go round: ROSCAs revisited, in *Money-Go-Rounds: The Importance of Rotating Savings and Credit Associations for Women*, edited by S. Ardener and S. Burman. Oxford/Washington D.C.: BERG.

Ayata, A. 1997. The emergence of identity politics in Turkey. *New Perspectives on Turkey*, 17 (Fall), 59–73.

Ayers, P. and Lambertz, J. 1986. Marriage relations, money and domestic violence in working-class Liverpool 1919–1939, in *Labour and Love: Women's Experience of Home and Family, 1850–1940*, edited by J. Lewis. Oxford: Basil Blackwell.

Bağdadıoğlu, E. 2002a. *TÜRK-İŞ Haber Bülteni, 26 Mart 2002* (TÜRK-İŞ Bulletin, 26 March 2002). Ankara: TÜRK-İŞ (The Confederation of Turkish Workers Trade Unions).

Bağdadıoğlu, E. 2002b. *TÜRK-İŞ Haber Bülteni, 27 Nisan 2002* (TÜRK-İŞ Bulletin, 27 April 2002). Ankara: TÜRK-İŞ.

Bağdadıoğlu, E. 2002c. *TÜRK-İŞ Haber Bülteni, 26 Kasım 2002* (TÜRK-İŞ Bulletin, 26 November 2002). Ankara: TÜRK-İŞ.

Baharoğlu, D. and Kessides, C. 2001. *Urban Poverty*. Unpublished Working Paper. Washington D.C.: The World Bank.

Baker, J. 1995. Survival and accumulation strategies at the rural-urban interface in the North-West Tanzania. *Environment and Urbanization*, 7(1), 117–32.

Banck, G.A. 1986. Poverty politics and the shaping of urban space: a Brazilian example. *International Journal of Urban and Regional Research*, 10(4), 522–39.

Bartolome, L.J. 1984. Forced resettlement and the survival systems of the urban poor. *Ethnology*, 23(3), 177–92.

Başaran, F. 1982. Attitude changes related to sex roles in the family, in *Family in Turkish Society*, edited by T. Erder. Ankara: Türk Sosyal Bilimler Derneği (Turkish Social Science Association).

Başlevent, C. and Dayıoğlu, M. 2005. The effect of squatter housing in income distribution in Turkey. *Urban Studies*, 42(1), 31–45.

Beall, J. and Kanji, N. 1999. *Households, Livelihoods and Urban Poverty*. Urban Governance, Partnership and Poverty Theme Paper no.3. London School of Economics: Department of Social Policy and Administration.

Beall, J., Crankshaw, O. and Parnell, S. 2000. The causes of unemployment in post-apartheid Johannesburg and the livelihood strategies of the poor. *Tridschrift voor Economische en Sociale Geografie* (Journal of Economic and Social Geography), 91(4), 379–96.

Bebbington, A. 1999. Capitals and capabilities: a framework for analysing peasant viability, rural livelihoods and poverty. *World Development*, 27(2), 2021–44.

Bebbington, A., Hinojosa-Valencia, L., and Rojas Lizarazú, R. E. 2007. Livelihoods and resources in accessing the Andes: *desencuentros* in theory and practice, in *Wellbeing in Developing Countries: from Theory to Research*, edited by I. Gough and J.A. McGregor. Cambridge: Cambridge University Press.

Beck, T. 1989. Survival strategies and power amongst the poorest in a West Bengal Village. *IDS Bulletin*, 20(2), 23–32.

Bellér-Hann, I. 1996. Informal associations among women in North-East Turkey, in *Turkish Families in Transition*, edited by G. Rasuly-Paleczek. Frankfurt: Peter Lang.

Beneria, L. 1992. The Mexican debt crisis: restructuring the economy and the household, in *Unequal Burden: Economic Crisis, Persistent Poverty and Women's Work*, edited by L. Beneria and S. Feldman. London: Westview Press.

Beneria, L. and Feldman S. (eds.) 1992. *Unequal Burden: Economic Crisis, Persistent Poverty and Women's Work*. London: Westview Press.

Beneria, L. and Roldan, M. 1987. *The Crossroads of Class and Gender*. Chicago: The University of Chicago Press.

Berthoud, R. 1976. *The Disadvantages of Inequality: A Study of Social Deprivation*. London: Macdonald and Jane's.

Bird, K. and Shepherd, A. 2003. Livelihoods and chronic poverty in semi-arid Zimbabwe. *World Development,* 31(3), 591–610.

Björnberg, U. and Kollind, A.K. 2005. *Individualism and Families*. London: Routledge.

Blau, P. 1964. *Exchange and Power in Social Life*. Chichester: John Wiley and Sons.

Blau, P. 1968. Interaction: social exchange, in *International Encyclopædia of the Social Sciences*, edited by D.L. Sills. New York: Macmillan and The Free Press.

Blumberg, R.L. 1991. Income under female versus male control: hypotheses from a theory of gender stratification and data from the third world, in *Gender, Family and Economy: The Triple Overlap*, edited by R. L. Blumberg. London: Sage.

Boissevain, J. 1974. *Friends of Friends*. London: Blackwell.

Bolak, H. 1997. Marital power dynamics: women providers and working class households in Istanbul, in *Cities in the Developing World*, edited by J. Gugler. New York: Oxford University Press.

Booth, C. 1891. *Life and Labour of the People of London: Volume I*. London: Macmillan.

Bora, A. 2002. Olmayanın nesini idare edeceksin? (What can you manage about the non-existent?), in *Yoksulluk Halleri: Türkiye'de Kentsel Yoksulluğun Toplumsal Görünümleri*, (States of Poverty: Social Manifestations of Urban Poverty in Turkey), edited by N. Erdoğan. İstanbul: De:ki.

Boratav, K. 1988. *Türkiye İktisat Tarihi 1908–1985* (Turkish Economic History 1908–1985). İstanbul: Gerçek.

Boratav, K. 1994. *İstanbul ve Anadolu'dan Sınıf Profilleri* (Class Profiles from Istanbul and Anatolia). İstanbul: Tarih ve Toplum Vakfı (History and Society Association).

Boratav, K. 2010. 2009'da milli gelir (National income in 2009). [Online: Sol]. Available at: http://haber.sol.org.tr/yazarlar/korkut-boratav/2009da-milli-gelir-26321 [accessed: 8 April 2010].

Boratav, K., Yeldan, A.E. and Köse A.H. 2000. *Globalization, Distribution and Social Policy: Turkey 1980–1998*. CEPA Working Paper Series I no.20. New York: New School University Centre for Economic Policy Analysis.

Bourdieu, P. 1977a. *Outline of a Theory of Practice*. Nice, R. trans. Cambridge: Cambridge University Press.

Bourdieu, P. 1977b. Marriage strategies as strategies of social reproduction, in *Family and Society: Selections from the Annales: Economes, Societes and Civilisations*, edited by E. Forster and P. M. Ranum. Baltimore: The John Hopkins University Press.

Bourdieu, P. 1986. *Handbook of Theory and Research for the Sociology of Education*. New York: Green Wood Press.

Boxman, E.A.W., De Graaf, P.M. and Flap, H. D. 1991. The impact of social and human capital on the income attainment of Dutch managers. *Social Networks*, 13(1), 51–73.

Bruce, J. 1989. Home divided. *World Development*, 17(7), 979–91.

Buğra, A. 1998. The immoral economy of housing in Turkey. *International Journal of Urban and Regional Research*, 22(2), 303–17.

Buğra, A. and Keyder, Ç. 2003. *New Poverty and New Welfare Regime of Turkey*. Ankara: UNDP.

Buğra, A. and Keyder, Ç. 2006. The Turkish welfare regime in transformation. *Journal of European Social Policy*, 16(3), 211–28.

Buğra, A. and Yakut-Cakar, B. 2010. Structural change, the social policy environment and female employment in Turkey. *Development and Change*, 41(3), 517–38.

Bulutay, T. 1998. *Employment and Training Project Labour Market Information: Informal Sector II*. Ankara: Devlet İstatistik Enstitüsü (State Institute of Statistics).

Burgoyne, C.B. 1990. Money in marriage: how patterns of allocation both reflect and conceal power. *Sociological Review*, 38(4), 634–65.

Burgoyne, C.B. and Lewis, A. 1994. Distributive justice in marriage: equality or equity. *Journal of Community and Applied Social Psychology*, 4(2), 101–14.

Burgwal, G. 1995. *Struggle of the Poor: Neighborhood Organization and Clientelist Practice in a Quito Squatter Settlement*. Amsterdam: CEDLA.

Burman, S. and Lembete, L. 1995. Building new realities: African women and ROSCAs in urban South Africa, in *Money-Go-Rounds: The Importance of Rotating Savings and Credit Associations for Women*, edited by S. Ardener and S. Burman. Oxford/Washington D.C.: BERG.

Burt, R.S. 2001. Structural holes versus network closure as social capital, in *Social Capital: Theory and Research*, edited by N. Lin et al. New York: Aldine de Gruyter.

BSB 2006. *Bağımsız Sosyal Bilimciler 2006 Yılı Raporu: IMF Gözetiminde On Uzun Yıl 1998–2008 – Farklı Hükümetler, Tek Siyaset.* (Independent Social Scientists Annual Report 2006: Long Ten Years under the Scrutiny of the IMF 1998–2008 – Different Governments, Single Politics). [Online: Bağımsız Sosyal Bilimciler (Independent Social Scientists)]. Available at: http://www. bagimsizsosyalbilimciler.org/Yazilar_BSB/BSB2006_Final.pdf. [accessed: October 2007].

BSB 2007. *Bağımsız Sosyal Bilimciler 2007 Yılı Raporu: 2007 İlkyazında Türkiye ve Dünya Ekonomisine Bakış* (Independent Social Scientists Annual Report 2007: A Glance at the Turkish and World Economy in Spring 2007). [Online: Bağımsız Sosyal Bilimciler (Independent Social Scientists)]. Available at: http://www.bagimsizsosyalbilimciler.org/Yazilar_BSB/BSB2007_Final.pdf. [accessed: September 2010].

Calhoun, C. 1993. Habitus, field and capital: the question of historical specifity, in *Bourdieu: Critical Perspectives,* edited by C. Calhoun. Cambridge: Polity Press.

Callan, T., Nolan, B., and Whelan, C.T. 1993. Resources, deprivation and the measurement of poverty. *Journal of Social Policy*, 22(2), 141–72.

Carney, D., Drinkwater, M., Rusinow, T., Neefjes, K., Wanmali, S. and Singh, N. 1999. *Livelihood Approaches Compared.* London: Department for International Development.

Carter, M.R. and May, J. 1999. Poverty, livelihood and class in rural South Africa. *World Development*, 27(1), 1–20.

Celasun, M. 1989. Income distribution and employment aspects of Turkey's 1980 adjustment. *ODTÜ Gelişme Dergisi* (METU Studies in Development), 16 (3–4), 1–31.

Certeau, M. de 1984. *The Practice of Everyday Life.* Translated by S. Rendall. Berkeley, Los Angeles and London: University of California Press.

Chamber of City Planners 2003. Imar Affı Raporu (Development Amnesty Report). [Online: Şehir Plancıları Odası Chamber of City Planners]. Available at: http://www.spo.org.tr/imar afii[sic]tmmob.shtml [accessed September 2003].

Chambers, R. and Conway, G.R. 1991. *Sustainable Livelihoods: Practical Concepts for the 21st Century*. IDS Discussion Paper 296. Sussex: Sussex University, Institute of Development Studies.

Chambers, R. 1995. Poverty and livelihoods: whose reality counts? *Environment and Urbanization*, 7(1), 173–204.

Chambers, R. 1997. Editorial: responsible wellbeing – a personal agenda for development. *World Development*, 25(11), 1743–54.

Chant, S. 1985. Single-parent families: choice or constraint? The formation of female-headed households in Mexican shanty towns. *Development and Change*, 16(4), 635–56.

Chant, S. 1991. *Women and Survival in Mexican Cities: Perspectives on Gender, Labour Market and Low Income Households*. Manchester: Manchester University Press.

Chant, S. 1994. Women and poverty in urban Latin America: Mexican and Costa Rican experiences, in *Poverty in the 1990s: the Responses of Women*, edited by F. Meer. Paris: UNESCO and International Social Science Council.

Chant, S. 1996. Kadın, konut ve varolma stratejileri: kalkınmakta olan ülkelerde dikkate alınması gereken konular (Woman, housing and survival strategies: issues to be considered in developing countries), in *Diğerlerinin Konut Sorunları* (Housing Problems of Others), edited by E. M. Komut. Ankara: Mimarlar Odası (The Chamber of Architects).

Chubb, J. 1982. *Patronage, Power and Poverty in Southern Italy*. Cambridge: Cambridge University Press.

Clark, D.A. 2006. *The Capability Approach: Its Development, Critiques and Recent Advances*. GPRG-WPS-032. Oxford and Manchester: Centre of the Study of African Economies and Institute for Development Policy and Management.

Clarke, S. 1999. *New Forms of Employment and Household Survival Strategies in Russia*. Coventry and Moscow: ISITO/CCLS.

Cleaver, F. 2005. The inequality of social capital and the reproduction of chronic poverty. *World Development*, 33(6), 893–906.

Coleman, J.S. 1988. Social capital in the creation of human capital. *American Journal of Sociology*, 94(Suppl. S), 95–120.

Coleman, J.S. 1990. *Foundations of Social Theory*. Cambridge: Belknap Press of Harvard University Press.

Colin, W.L., McGregor, J.A.and Saltmarshe, D.K. 2000. Surviving and thriving: differentiation in a peri-urban community in Northern Albania. *World Development*, 28(8), 1499–514.

Corbet, J. 1988. Famine and household coping strategies. *World Development*, 16(9), 1099–112.

Cornelius, W. A. 1975. *Politics and the Migrant Poor in Mexico City*. California: Stanford University Press.

Cornell, L.L. 1987. Where can family strategies exist? *Historical Methods*, 20(3), 120–23.

Cornia, G., Jolly, R., and Stewart, F. 1987. *Adjustment with a Human Face Volume 1*. Oxford: Oxford University Press.

Crow, G. 1989. The use of concept of strategy in recent sociological literature. *Sociology*, 23(1), 1–24.

Cumhuriyet 1994. Mamak çöplüğünde heran felaket yaşanabilir (A disaster can be experienced any moment in Mamak dump). *Cumhuriyet*, 17 March.

Cuong, N.V. 2008. Is a governmental micro-credit program for the poor really pro-poor? Evidence from Vietnam. *Developing Economies*, 46(2), 151–87.

Çapar, S. 2007. *İstihdamın Artırılmasında Aktif İşgücü Politikalarının Rolü* (The Role of Active Labour Market Policies in Increasing Employment). Planning Expertise Thesis. Ankara: Devlet Planlama Teşkilatı (State Planning Organisation).

Çınar, M.E. 1994. Unskilled urban migrant women and disguised employment: home-working women in Istanbul, Turkey. *World Development*, 22 (3), 369–80.

Dağdemir, Ö. 1999. Türkiye Ekonomisi'nde yoksulluk sorunu ve yoksulluk analizi, 1987–1994 (Poverty Problem in Turkish Economy and Poverty Analysis 1987–1994). *Hacettepe Üniversitesi İktisadi ve İdari Bilimler Fakültesi Dergisi* (Journal of Hacettepe University Economic and Public Administration Faculty), 7(1).

Daines, V. and Seddon, D. 1991. *Survival Struggles: Protest and Resistance: Women's Responses to 'Austerity' and 'Structural Adjustment'*. Norwich: University of East Anglia, School of Development Studies.

Dansuk, E. 1997. *Türkiye'de Yoksulluğun Ölçülmesi ve Sosyo-Ekonomik Yapılarla İlişkisi* (Measuremet of Poverty in Turkey and Its Relationship with Socio-Economic Structures). Specialisation Thesis no. 2472. Ankara: Devlet Planlama Teşkilatı (State Planning Organisation).

Davies, S. 1993. Are coping strategies a cop out? *IDS Bulletin*, 24(4), 60–72.

Dean, H. 2003. *Discursive Repertoires and the Negotiation of Well-being: Reflections on the Resource Profiles, Human Needs and Quality of Life Frameworks*. Unpublished Working Paper Presented to the Inaugural Workshop of the ESRC Research Group on Well-Being in Developing Countries (WeD). Bath: University of Bath.

Demir, E. 1991. *The Impact of the Economic Policies on the Survival Strategies of the Urban Poor*. Unpublished Master Thesis. Ankara: Middle East Technical University.

Demir, E. 2002. Yeni kentli ailelerde geçimlik üretim ve yoksulluk (Subsistence production and poverty in new urban families), in *Yoksulluk, Şiddet ve İnsan Hakları* (Poverty, Violence and Human Rights), edited by Y. Özdek. Ankara: Türkiye ve Orta Doğu Amme İdaresi Enstitüsü (Turkey and Middle East Public Administration Institute).

Dercon, S. and Krishnan, P. 1996. Income portfolios in rural Ethiopia and Tanzania: choices and constraints. *Journal of Development Studies*, 32(6), 850–75.

Dercon, S. 2000. *Income Risk, Coping Strategies and Safety Nets*. Background Paper for World Development Report 2000/2001. Oxford University: Centre for the Study of African Economies.

Dercon, S. 2002. Income risk, coping strategies and safety nets. *World Bank Research Observer*, 17(2), 141–66.

Derviş, K. and Robinson, S. 1980. The structure of income inequality in Turkey 1950–1973, in *The Political Economy of Income Distribution in Turkey*, edited by E. Özbudun and A. Ulusan. London: Holmes and Meier Publishers.

Devereux, S. 1993. Goats before ploughs: dilemmas of household response sequencing during food shortages. *IDS Bulletin*, 24(4), 52–9.

*Dirty Pretty Things*, (dir. Stephan Frears, 2002).

Doğan, L. 1993. Türkiye Nüfusu'nun özellikleri (The characteristics of the Turkish population), in *Türkiye'de Nüfus Konuları, Politika Öncelikleri* (Population

Issues and Policy Priorities for Turkey), edited by A. Toros Ankara: Hacettepe Üniversitesi Nüfus Etüdleri Enstitüsü (Hacettepe University Population Studies Institute).

Doyal, L and Gough, I. 1991. *A Theory of Human Need.* London: Macmillan.

Duben, A. 1982. The significance of family and kinship in Turkey, in *Sex Roles, Family and Community in Turkey,* edited by Ç. Kağıtçıbaşı. Bloomington: Indiana University Press.

Dubetsky, A. 1976. Kinship, primordial ties, and factory organisation in Turkey: an anthropological view. *International Journal of Middle East* Studies, 7(3), 433–51.

Dumanlı, R. 1996. *Türkiye'de Yoksulluk ve Boyutları* (Poverty and Its Dimensions in Turkey). Specialisation Thesis no. 2449. Ankara: Devlet Planlama Teşkilatı (State Planning Organisation).

Dündar, Ö. 2001. Models of urban transformation: informal housing in Ankara. *Cities,* 18(6), 391–401.

Dwyer, D. and Bruce, J. (eds.) 1988. *Home Divided: Women and Income in the Third World.* California: Stansford University Press.

Eames, E. and Goode, J.G. 1973. *Urban Poverty in a Cross-Cultural Context.* New York: Free Press.

Ecevit, Y. 1995. Kentsel üretim sürecinde kadın emeğinin konumu ve değişen biçimleri (The position and changing forms of female labour in urban production process), in *Kadın Bakış Açısından Kadınlar* (Women from Woman's Perspective), edited by S. Tekeli. İstanbul: İletişim.

Ecevit, Y. 1998. Küreselleşme, yapısal uyum ve kadın emeğinin kullanımında değişmeler (Globalisation, structural adjustment and changes in the use of female labour), in *Kadın Emeği ve İstihdamında Değişimler: Türkiye Örneği* (Changes Female Labour and its Employment: Turkish Case), edited by F. Özbay. İstanbul: Human Resources Development Foundation.

Edin, K. and Lein, L. 1997. Work, welfare and single mothers' economic survival strategies. *American Sociological Review,* 62 (2), 253–66.

Eisenstadt, S.N. and Roniger, L. 1984. *Patrons, Clients and Friends: Interpersonal relations and Structure of Trust in Society.* Cambridge: Cambridge University Press.

Eke, F. 1982. Absorption of low income groups in Ankara. *Progress in Planning,* 19(1), 1–88.

Elizabeth, V. 2001. Managing money, managing coupledom: a critical examination of cohabitants' money management strategies. *Sociological Review,* 49 (3), 389–411.

Ellis, F. 1998. Household strategies and rural livelihood diversification. *Journal of Development Studies,* 35(1), 1–38.

Ellis, F. 2000a. *Rural Livelihoods and Diversity in Developing Countries.* Oxford: Oxford University Press.

Ellis, F. 2000b. The determinants of rural livelihood diversification in developing countries. *Journal of Agricultural Economics,* 51(2), 289–302.

Elson, D. 1992. From survival strategies to transformation strategies: women's needs and structural adjustment, in *Unequal Burden: Economic Crisis, Persistent Poverty and Women's Work*, edited by L. Beneria and S. Feldman. London: Westview Press.

Erder, S. 1994. Yeni kentliler ve kentin yeni yoksulları (New urbanites and the new urban poor). *Toplum–Bilim* (Society-Science), Fall, 106–19.

Erder, S. 1996. *İstanbul'a Bir Kent Kondu: Ümraniye* (A City is Squatted on Istanbul: Ümraniye). İstanbul: İletişim.

Erder, S. 1997. *Kentsel Gerilim* (Urban Tension). Ankara: Um:ag.

Erdoğan, G. 1997. *Poverty and Poverty Line in Turkey*. Conference paper presented in a session of the International Statistical Institute 18–26 August. İstanbul.

Erdoğan, G. 1998. *Poverty in Turkey: Its Dimension and Profile*. Ankara: Devlet İstatistik Enstitüsü (State Institute of Statistics).

Erdoğan, N. (ed.) 2002. *Yoksulluk Halleri: Türkiye'de Kentsel Yoksulluğun Toplumsal Görünümleri* (Conditions of Poverty: Social Manifestations of Urban Poverty in Turkey). İstanbul: De:ki.

Erickson, B.H. 2001. Good networks and good jobs: the value of social capital to employers and employees, in *Social Capital: Theory and Research*, edited by N. Lin et al. New York: Aldine de Gruyter.

Erman, T. 1997. The meaning of city living for rural migrant women and their role in migration: the case of Turkey. *Women's Studies International Forum*, 20(2), 263–73.

Erman, T. 1998. The impact of migration on Turkish rural women. *Gender and Society*, 12(2), 146–67.

Erman, T. 2001. Rural migrants and patriarchy in Turkish cities. *International Journal of Urban and Regional Research*, 25(1), 118–33.

Erman, T., Kalaycıoğlu, S. and Rittersberger-Tılıç, H. 2002. Money earning activities and empowerment experiences of rural migrant women in the city: the case of Turkey. *Women's Studies International Forum*, 25 (4), 395–410.

Erman, T. and Türkyılmaz, S. 2008. Neighbourhood effects and women's agency regarding poverty and patriarchy within a Turkish slum. *Environment and Planning*, 40(7), 1760–76.

Eroğlu, Ş. 2000. *The Role of Reciprocity Networks and Patron-Client Relationships in the Survival of the Urban Poor: A Review of Concepts and Research Findings*. Unpublished MA Thesis. Canterbury: University of Kent.

Eroğlu, Ş. 2004. *What Difference Do Resources Make? A Longitudinal Study of Household Responses to Poverty in a Gecekondu Settlement in Ankara, Turkey*. PhD thesis. Canterbury: University of Kent.

Eroğlu, Ş. 2007. Developing an index of deprivation which integrates objective and subjective dimensions: Extending the work of Townsend, Mack and Lansley and Halleröd. *Social Indicators Research*, 80(3), 493–510.

Eroğlu, Ş. 2009. Patterns of income allocation among poor *gecekondu* households in Turkey: overt mechanisms and women's secret kitties. *The Sociological Review*, 57(1), 58–80.

Eroğlu, Ş. 2010a. Informal finance and the urban poor: an investigation of rotating savings and credit associations in Turkey. *Journal of Social Policy*, 39(3), 461–81.

Eroğlu, Ş. 2010b. The irrelevance of social capital in explaining deprivation: a case study of Turkish *gecekondu* households. *Tijdschrift voor Economische en Sociale Geografie* (Journal of Economic and Social Geography), 101(1), 37–54.

Espinoza, V. 1999. Social networks among the urban poor: inequality and integration in a Latin American City, in *Networks in the Global Village*, edited by B. Wellman. London: Westview Press.

Evrensel 2000a. Gökçek'e ev' protestosu ('Home' protest against Gökçek). *Evrensel*, 23 September.

Evrensel 2000b. Belediye önünde oturma eylemi (Sit-down protest in front of municipality). *Evrensel*, 26 September.

Fapohunda, E.R. 1988. The non-pooling household: a challenge to theory, in *Home Divided: Women and Income in the Third World*, edited by D. Dwyer and J. Bruce. Stanford: Stanford University Press.

Ferman, L.A. and Brendt, L. 1981. The irregular economy, in *Can I have It in Cash?* edited by S. Henry. London: Astragel Books.

Fernandez-Kelly, M. P. 1982. *For We Are Sold, I and My People: Women and Industry in Mexico's Frontier*. New York: SUNY Press.

Field, J. 2003. *Social Capital*. London: Routledge.

Finch, J. and Mason, J. 1992. *Negotiating Family Responsibilities*. London: Tavistock.

Fine, B. and Green, F. 2000. Economics, social capital and colonization of the social sciences, in *Social Capital: Critical Perspectives*, edited by S. Baron et al. Oxford: Oxford University Press.

Fine, B. 2001. *Social Capital versus Social Theory: Political Economy and Social Science at the Turn of the Millennium*. London: Routledge.

Flap, H. and Boxman, E. 2001. Getting started: the influence of social capital on the start of occupational career, in *Social Capital: Theory and Research*, edited by N. Lin et al. New York: Aldine de Gruyter.

Folbre, N. 1986a. Cleaning house: new perspectives on households and economic development. *Journal of Development Economics*, 20(1), 5–40.

Folbre, N. 1986b. Hearts and spades: paradigms of household economics. *World Development*, 14(2), 245–55.

Folbre, N. 1987. Family strategy, feminist strategy. *Historical Methods*, 20(3), 113–25.

Folbre, N. 1988. The black four of hearts: towards a new paradigm of household economics, in *Home Divided: Women and Income in the Third World*, edited by D. Dwyer and J. Bruce. Stanford: Stanford University Press.

Fontaine, L. and Schlumbohm, J. 2000. Household strategies for survival: an introduction. *International Review of Social History*, 45(8), 1–17.

Forrest, R. and Kearns, A. 2001. Social cohesion, social capital and the neighbourhood. *Urban Studies,* 38(12), 2125–43.

Foster, G.M. 1963. Dyadic contract in Tzintzuntzan, II: patron-client relationships. *American Anthropologist*, 65(6), 1280–94.

Frayne, B. 2004. Migration and urban survival strategies in Windhoek, Namibia. *Geoforum*, 35(4), 489–505.

Friedman, K. 1984. Households as income-pooling units, in *Households and the World Economy*, edited by J. Smith, I. Wallerstein and H.D. Evers. London: Sage.

Fukuyama, F. 1995. *Trust: The Social Virtues and the Creation of Prosperity*. New York: Free Press.

George, V. 1988. *Wealth, Poverty and Starvation: An International Perspective*. England: Weatsheaf Books, New York: St. Martin's Press.

Gershuny, G. 1983. *Social Innovation and Division of Labour*. Oxford: Oxford University Press.

Gitmez, A. and Morçöl, G. 1995. A typology of the urban poor in Turkey. *Journal of Urban Affairs*, 17(4), 413–22.

Gonzales de la Rocha, M. 1988. Economic crisis, domestic reorganisation and women's work in Guadalajara, Mexico. *Bulletin of Latin American Research*, 5(2), 207–23.

Gonzales de la Rocha, M. 1994. *Resources of Poverty: Women and Survival in a Mexican City*. London: Blackwell.

Gonzales de la Rocha, M. 2001a. *From the Resources of Poverty to the Poverty of Resources? The Erosion of a Survival Model.* Working Paper no.01–09a. Princeton: Princeton University, Centre for Migration and Development.

Gonzales de la Rocha, M. 2001b. Private adjustments: household responses to erosion of work, in *Negotiating Poverty: New Directions, Renewed Debate*, edited by N. Middleton et al. London: Pluto Press.

Gonzales de la Rocha, M. 2007. The construction of the myth of survival. *Development and Change*, 38(1), 45–66.

Goode J., Callender, C. and Lister, R. 1998. *Purse or Wallet? Gender Inequalities and Income Distribution within Families on Benefits*. London: Policy Studies Institute.

Gordon, D. 2000. The scientific measurement of poverty: recent theoretical advances, in *Researching Poverty*, edited by J. Bradshaw and R. Sainsbury. Aldershot: Ashgate.

Gordon, D., Adelman, L., Ashworth, K., Bradshaw, J., Levitas, R., Middleton, S., Pantazis, C., Patsios, D., Payne, S., Townsend, P. and Willias J. 2000. *Poverty and Exclusion in Britain*. York: Joseph Rowntree Foundation.

Gough, I., McGregor, J.A. and Camfield, L. 2007. Theorising wellbeing in international development, in *Wellbeing in Developing Countries: from Theory to Research*, edited by I. Gough and J.A. McGregor. Cambridge: Cambridge University Press.

Gökçe, B., Acar, F., Ayata, A., Kasapoğlu, A., Özer, I. and Uygun H. 1993. *Gecekondularda Ailelerarası Geleneksel Dayanışmanın Çağdaş Organizasyonlara Dönüşümü* (Transformation of Traditional Inter-family Solidarity into Modern Organisations in *Gecekondu* Areas). Ankara: T.C. Başbakanlık Kadın ve Sosyal Hizmetler Müsteşarlığı Yayınları (T.R. Presidency Woman and Social Services Undersecretariat Press).

Graham, H. 1984. *Women, Health and Family*. Brighton: Wheatsheaf.

Granovetter, M.S. 1973. The strength of weak ties. *American Journal of Sociology*, 78(6), 1360–80.

Granovetter, M.S. 1982. The strength of weak ties: a network theory revisited, in *Social Structures and Network Analysis*, edited by P.V. Marsden and Lin. London: Sage.

Grieco, M. 1987. *Keeping It in the Family*. London: Tavistock.

Grootaert, C., Kanbur, R. and Oh, G.1995. *The Dynamics of Poverty: Why Some People Escape from Poverty and Others Don't*. Policy Research Working Paper 1499. Washington D.C.: The World Bank.

Grootaert, C. 1998. *Social Capital, Household Welfare and Poverty in Indonesia*. Local Level Institutions Study Working Paper 6. Washington D.C.: The World Bank.

Grootaert, C. and Narayan, D. 2001. *Local Institutions, Poverty and Household Welfare in Bolivia*. Washington D.C.: The World Bank.

Grootaert, C., Oh, G.T. and Swamy, A. 2002. Social capital, household welfare and poverty in Burkino Faso. *Journal of African Economies*, 11(1), 4–38.

Grown, C.A. and Sebstad, J. 1989. Introduction: toward a wider perspective on women's employment. *World Development*, 17(7), 937–52.

Gutkind, E. 1986. *Patterns of Economic Behaviour among the American Poor*. New York: St. Martin's Press.

Günçiner, E. 1993. Gaz tahliyesi tehlikeli (Gas release is dangerous). *Aydınlık*, 09 July.

Güneş 2000. Kadınların isyanı (Women's rebellion). *Güneş*, 26 September.

Güneş-Ayata, A. 1991. Gecekondularda kimlik sorunu, dayanışma örüntüleri ve hemşehrilik (The identity issues, solidarity patterns and *hemşehrilik* in *gecekondu* areas). *Toplum-Bilim (Society-Science)*, 1990–1991, 89–101.

Güneş-Ayata, A. 1994. Roots and trends of clientelism in *Democracy, Clientelism and Civil Society in Turkey,* edited by L. Roniger and A. Güneş-Ayata. London: L. Rienner Publishers.

Güneş-Ayata, A. 1996. Solidarity in urban Turkish family, in *Turkish Families in Transition*, edited by Rasuly-Paleczek. Frankfurt: Peter Lang.

Güneş-Ayata, A. and Ayata, S. 2003. The benefit dependent and the regular income earning poor: the analysis of the interview data, in *Turkey: Poverty and Coping After Crises, Volume II Background Papers*. Washington D.C.: The World Bank.

Gürsel, S., Levent, H., Selim, R., and Sarıca, O. 2000. *Gelir Dağılımı ve Türkiye'de Yoksulluk* (Income Distribution and Poverty in Turkey). Report no. TÜSİAD-T/2000-12/295. İstanbul: Türk Sanayici ve İş Adamları Derneği (Turkish Industrialists and Businessmen Association).

Güvenç, M. 2001. Ankara'da statü-köken farklılaşması: 1990 sayım örneklemleri üzerinde 'blok model' çözümlemeleri (Status-ethnicity segregation in Ankara: 'block-model' solutions based on 1990 census samples), in *Tarih içinde Ankara* (Ankara within History), edited by Y. Yavuz. Ankara: Orta Doğu Teknik Üniversitesi (Middle East Technical University).

Haan, L. de and Zoomers, A. 2005. Exploring the frontiers of livelihood research. *Development and Change*, 36(1), 27–47.

Hacettepe University 1994. *Tuzluçayır Eski Deponi Alanı Rehabilitasyon Projesi: Ön Araştırmalar* (Tuzluçayır Former Dump Area Rehabilitatin Project: Preliminary Investigations). Ankara: Hacettepe Üniversitesi Çevre Uygulama ve Araştırma Merkezi (Hacettepe University Environmental Implementation and Research Centre).

Hackenberg, R., Murphy, A.D. and Selby, H.A. 1984. The urban household in dependent development, in *Households: Comparative and Historical Studies of the Domestic Group*, edited by R. M. Netting et al. Los Angeles: University of California Press.

Hagenaars, A. and De Vos, K. 1987. The definition and measurement of poverty. *Journal of Human Resources*, 23(2), 211–21.

Halleröd, B., Bradshaw, J. and Holmes, H. 1997. Adapting the consensual definition of poverty, in *Breadline Britain in the 1990s,* edited by D. Gordon and C. Pantazis. Aldershot: Ashgate.

Halleröd, B. 1994. *A New Approach to the Direct Consensual Measurement of Poverty*. Social Policy Research Centre Discussion Paper No. 50. Sydney: University of New South Wales.

Halleröd, B. 1995. The truly poor: direct and indirect consensual measurement of poverty in Sweden. *Journal of European Social Policy*, 5(2), 111–29.

Halpern, D. 2005. *Social Capital*. Cambridge: Polity Press.

Hammersley, M. and Atkinson, P. 1983. *Ethnography: Principles in Practice*. London: Tavistock.

Hannerz, U. 1974. Ethnicity and opportunity in urban America, in *Urban Ethnicity*, edited by A. Cohen. London: Tavistock.

Harari, D. and Garcia-Bouza, J. 1982. *Social Conflict and Development: Basic Needs and Survival Strategies in Four National Settings*. Paris: OECD Development Centre Studies.

Hareven, T. 1982. *Family Time and Industrial Time*. Cambridge: Cambridge University Press.

Harris, O. 1981. Households as natural units, in *Of Marriage and the Market*, edited by K. Young et al. London: CSE Books.

Hart, G. 1986. *Power, Labor and Livelihood: Process of Change in Rural Java.* Berkeley: University of California Press.

Heper, M. 1982. The plight of urban migrants: dynamics of service procurement in a squatter area, in *Sex Roles, Family and Community in Turkey*, edited by Ç. Kağıtçıbaşı. Bloomington: Indiana University Press.

Heper, M. 1983. *Türkiye'de Kent Göçmenleri ve Bürokratik Örgütler* (The Urban Migrants and Bureucratic Organisations in Turkey). İstanbul:Üç-Dal Neşriyat.

Hertz, R. 1992. Money and Authority in Dual-Earner Marriage, in *Dual-Earner Families: International Perspectives*, edited by S. Lewis et al. London: Sage.

Heyer, J. 1989. Landless agricultural labourers' asset strategies. *IDS Bulletin*, 20(2), 33–40.

Hogan, M.J., Solheim, C., Wolfgram S., Nkosi, B. and Rodrigues, N. 2004. The working poor: from the economic margins to asset building. *Family Relations*, 53(2), 229–36.

Hoodfar, H. 1988a. *Survival strategies in the low-income neighbourhoods of Cairo Egypt*. Unpublished PhD thesis. Canterbury: University of Kent.

Hoodfar, H. 1988b. Household budgeting and financial management in a lower-income Cairo neighbourhood, in *Home Divided: Women and Income in the Third World*, edited by D. Dwyer and J. Bruce. California: Stanford University Press.

Hoodfar, H. 1996. Survival strategies and political economy of low income households in Cairo, in *Development, Change and Gender in Cairo: A View from the Household*, edited by D. Singerman. Bloomington and Indianapolis: Indiana University Press.

Hospes, O. 1995. Women's differential use of ROSCAs in Indonesia, in *Money-Go-Rounds: The Importance of Rotating Savings and Credit Associations for Women*, edited by S. Ardener and S. Burman. Oxford/Washington D.C.: BERG.

Hussein, K. and Nelson, J. 1998. *Sustainable Livelihoods and Livelihood Diversification*. IDS Working Paper 69. Sussex: Sussex University, Institute of Development Studies.

ILO 1976. *Employment Growth and Basic Needs: A One-World Problem*. Geneva: International Labour Organization.

Inglehart, R. 1997. *Modernization and Postmodernization: Cultural, Economic and Political Change in 41 Societies*. Princeton: Princeton University Press.

Işık, O. and Pınarcıoğlu, M. 2001. *Nöbetleşe Yoksulluk* (Taking Turns in Poverty). İstanbul: İletişim.

Itzigson, J. 1995. Migrant remittances, labour markets and household strategies: a comparative analysis of low-income household strategies in the Caribbean Basin. *Social Forces*, 72(2), 633–35.

İsvan, N.A. 1991. Productive and reproductive decisions in Turkey: the role of domestic bargaining. *Journal of Marriage and the Family*, 53(4), 1058–70.

İŞ-KUR 2007. *EU-Turkey Joint Assessment Paper for Employment Priorities* (final draft). Ankara: General Directorate of Turkish Employment Organisation.

Jacobs, J. 1961. *The Life and Death of Great American Cities*. New York: Random House.

Jiggins, J. 1989. How poor women earn their income in Sub-Saharan Africa and what works against them. *World Development*, 17(7), 953–63.

Kalaycıoğlu, S. and Rittersberger-Tılıç, H. 2000. Intergenerational solidarity networks of instrumental and cultural transfers within migrant families in Turkey. *Ageing and Society*, 20(5), 523–42.

Kalaycıoğlu, S. and Rittersberger-Tılıç, H. 2001. *Evlerimizdeki Gündelikçi Kadınlar* (Daily Cleaners in Our Houses). İstanbul: Su Yayınları.

Kalaycıoğlu, S. and Rittersberger-Tılıç, H. 2002. Yapısal uyum programlarıyla ortaya çıkan yoksullukla başetme stratejileri (Strategies for combating poverty resulting from structural adjustment programs), in *Kentleşme, Göç ve Yoksulluk: Türk Sosyal Bilimler Derneği 7. Ulusal Sosyal Bilimler Kongresi Bildirileri* (Urbanisation, Migration and Poverty: Proceedings of the 7th National Social Sciences Congress of the Turkish Social Science Association), edited by A.A. Dikmen. Ankara: İmaj.

Kandiyoti, D. 1982. Urban change and women's roles in Turkey: an overview and evaluation, in *Sex Roles, Family and Community in Turkey*, edited by Ç. Kağıtçıbaşı. Bloomington: Indiana University Press.

Kandiyoti, D. 1988. Bargaining with patriarchy. *Gender and Society*, 2(3), 274–90.

Kanji, N. 1994. Structural adjustment in Zimbabwe: the way forward for low-income urban women, in *Poverty in the 1990s: The Responses of Women*, edited by F. Meer. Paris: UNSECO and International Social Science Council.

Karpat, K.H. 1976. *The Gecekondu: Rural Migration and Urbanisation*. Cambridge: Cambridge University Press.

Kartal, K. 1982. Kentleşme sürecinde toplumsal değişme odağı olarak Ankara (Ankara as a focus of social change in the process of urbanisation), in *Kentsel Bütünleşme* (Urban Integration), edited by T. Erder. Ankara: Türk Sosyal Bilimler Derneği (Turkish Social Science Association).

Kazepov, Y. 2005. Cities of Europe: changing contexts, local arrangements and the challenge to social cohesion. in *Cities of Europe: Changing Contexts, Local Arrangements and the Challenge to Social Cohesion*, edited by Y. Kazepov. Oxford: Blackwell Publishing.

Kempson, E. 1996. *Life on a Low Income*. York: Joseph Rowntree Foundation Publications.

Kempson, E., Bryson, A. and Rowlingson, K. 1995. *Hard Times? How Poor Families Makes Ends Meet*. London: Policy Studies Institute.

Kentkur 2002. *Ege Kentsel Dönüşüm Projesi: Revizyon Uygulama Plan Raporu* (Ege Urban Transformation Project: Revision Implementation Plan Report). Ankara: Kentkur.

Khatib-Chahidi, J. 1995. Gold coins and coffee roscas: coping with inflation the Turkish way in Northern Cyprus, in *Money-Go-Rounds: The Importance of Rotating Savings and Credit Associations for Women*, edited by S. Ardener and S. Burman. Oxford/Washington D.C.: BERG.

Kıray, M. 1982. Changing patterns of patronage: a study in structural change, in *Sex Roles, Family and Community in Turkey*, edited by Ç. Kağıtçıbaşı. Bloomington: Indiana University Press.

Kimuyu, P. K. 1999. Rotating credit and saving associations in rural East Africa. *World Development*, 27(7), 1299–308.

Kirkby, J. and Moyo, S. 2001. Environmental security, livelihoods and entitlements, in *Negotiating Poverty: New Directions, Renewed Debate*, edited by N. Middleton et al. London: Pluto Press.

Kongar, E. 1972. *İzmir'de Kentsel Aile Yapısı: Akrabalarla ve Bürokratik Örgütlerle İlişkiler ve Zaman İçinde Bazı Değişme Eğilimleri* (Urban Family Structure in Izmir: Relations with Kin and Bureaucratic Organisations and Some Change Trends over Time). Ankara: Ayyıldız Matbaası.

Krishna, A. 2004. Escaping poverty and becoming poor: who gains, who loses and why? *World Development*, 32(1), 121–36.

Krishna, A., Kristjanson P., Kuan J., Quilca M.R. and Sanchez-Urello A. 2006. Fixing the hole in the bucket: household poverty dynamics in the Peruvian Andes. *Development and Change*, 37(5), 997–1021.

Kurtz, D.V. 1973. The rotating credit association: an adaptation to poverty. *Human Organization*, 32(1), 49–58.

Kuyaş, N. F. 1982. The effects of female labour on power relations in the urban Turkish family, in *Sex Roles, Family and Community in Turkey*, edited by Ç. Kağıtçıbaşı. Bloomington: Indiana University Press.

Land, H. 1969. *Large Families in London*. London: Bell and Sons.

Lande, C.H. 1977. Introduction: the dyadic basis of clientelism, in *Friends, Followers and Factions*, edited by S.W. Schmidt et al. California: University of California Press.

Latapi, E. and Gonzales de la Rocha, M. 1995. Crisis, restructuring and urban poverty in Mexico. *Environment and Urbanization*, 7(1), 57–75.

Leach, M., Mearns, R. and Scoones, I. 1999. Environmental entitlements: dynamics and institutions in community-based resource management. *World Development*, 27(2), 225–47.

Leithman, J. and Baharoğlu, D. 1998. Using informal rules! Using institutional economics to understand service provision in turkey's spontaneous settlements. *Journal of Development Studies*, 34(5), 98–122.

Leonard M. 1992. Ourselves alone: household work strategies in a deprived community. *Irish Journal of Sociology*, 2, 70–84.

Leonard, M. 1998. *Invisible Work, Invisible Workers*. London: Macmillan.

Levenson A.R. and Besley, T. 1996. The anatomy of an informal financial market: rosca participation in Taiwan. *Journal of Development Economics*, 51(1), 45–68.

Levi-Strauss, C. 1969. *Elementary Structures of Kinship*, edited by R. Needham, translated by J.H. Bell and J.R. von Sturmer. London: Eyre and Spottiswoode.

Liebow, E. 1967. *Tally's Corner*. Boston and Toronto: Little Brown.

Lin, N. 1982. Social resources and instrumental action, in *Social Structures and Network Analysis*, edited by P.V. Marsden and N. Lin. London: Sage.

Lin, N. 1999. Social networks and status attainment. *Annual Review of Sociology*, 25 (1), 365–85.

Lin, N. 2001. Building a network theory of social capital, in *Social Capital: Theory and Research*, edited by N. Lin et al. New York: Aldine de Gruyter.

Lin, N., Fu, Y.C. and Hsung, R.M. 2001. The position generator: measurement techniques for investigating social capital, in *Social Capital: Theory and Research*, edited by N. Lin et al. New York: Aldine de Gruyter.

Logan, K. 1981. Getting by with less: economic strategies of lower income households in Guadalajara. *Urban Anthropology*, 10(3), 231–46.

Lokshin, M. and Harris, K.M. 2000. Single mothers in Russia: household strategies for coping with poverty. *World Development*, 28(12), 2183–98.

Lokshin, M. M., and Yemtsov, R. 2001. *Housing Strategies for Coping with Poverty and Social Exclusion in Post-Crisis Russia*. Policy Research Working Paper no. 2556. Washington D.C.: The World Bank.

Lomnitz, L.A. 1971. Reciprocity of favours in the urban middle class of Chile, in *Studies in Economic Anthropology*, edited by G. Dalton. Washington: American Anthropological Association.

Lomnitz, L.A. 1977. *Networks and Marginality: Life in a Mexican Shantytown*. New York: Academic Press.

Lomnitz, L.A. 1988. Informal exchange systems in formal systems: a theoretical model. *American Anthropologist*, 90(1), 42–55.

Lopez-Gonzaga, V. 1996. Rafina and Tia Lilia: sagas of poverty, hardship and survival. *Southeast Asian Journal of Social Science*, 24(1), 112–19.

Mack, J. and Lansley, S. 1985. *Poor Britain*. London: George Allen and Unwin.

Magnarella, P. 1970. Sociological review: from villagers to townsman in Turkey. *The Middle East Journal*, 24 (Spring), 229–40.

Maluccio, J., Lawrence H., and May, J. 2000. Social capital and income generation in South Africa, 1993–98. *Journal of Development Studies*, 36(5), 56–81.

Marsden, P. and Hulbert, J.S. 1988. Social resources and mobility outcomes. *Social Forces,* 66(4), 1038–59.

Martin G.M. and Beittel, M. 1987. The hidden abode of reproduction: conceptualising households in South Africa. *Development and Change*, 18(2), 215–34.

Massiah, J. 1989. Women's lives and livelihoods: a view from the Commonwealth Caribbean. *World Development*, 17(7), 956–77.

Mayoux, L. and Anand, S. 1995. Gender inequality, roscas and sectoral employment strategies: questions from the south indian silk industry, in *Money-Go-Rounds: The Importance of Rotating Savings and Credit Associations for Women*, edited by S. Ardener and S. Burman. Oxford/Washington D.C.: BERG

McCrone, D. 1994. Getting by and making out in Kirkcaldy, in *The Social and Political Economy of the Household,* edited by M. Anderson et al. Oxford: Oxford University Press.

McGregor A.J and Kebede, B. 2002. *Resource Profiles and the Social Construction of Wellbeing.* A paper presented to the Inaugural Workshop of the ESRC Research Group on Wellbeing in Developing Countries. Bath: University of Bath.

Meer, F. 1994. Women and poverty in the 1990s: the responses of women in South Africa, in *Poverty in the 1990s: the Responses of Urban Women,* edited by F. Meer. Paris: UNESCO and International Social Science Council.

Meert, H., Mistiaen, P. and Kesteloot, C. 1997. The geography of survival: household strategies in urban settings. *Tridschrift voor Economische en Sociale Geografie* (Journal of Economic and Social Geography), 88(2), 169–81.

Meert, H. 2000. Rural community life and the importance of reciprocal survival strategies. *Sociologia Ruralis,* 40(3), 319–38.

Meikle, S. 2002. Urban context and poor people, in *Urban Livelihoods: A People Centred Approach to Reducing Poverty,* edited by C. Rakodi and T. Lloyd-Jones. London and Sterling VA: Earthscan.

Mencher, J. P. 1988. Women's work and poverty: women's contribution to household maintenance in South India, in *Home Divided: Women and Income in the Third World,* edited by D. Dwyer and J. Bruce. California: Stanford University Press.

METU 2003. Interim report: assessment of social solidarity fund beneficiaries, in *Turkey: Poverty and Coping after Crises. Volume II Background Papers.* Washingthon D.C.: The World Bank.

Mingione, E. 1983. Informalisation, restructuring and the survival strategies of the working class. *International Journal of Urban and Regional Research,* 7(3), 311–33.

Mingione, E. 1985. Social reproduction of the surplus labour force: the case of Southern Italy, in *Beyond Employment: Household, Gender and Subsistence,* edited by N. Redclift and E. Mingione. Oxford: Basil Blackwell.

Mingione, E. 1987. Urban survival strategies, family structure and informal practices, in *The Capitalist City: Global Restructuring and Community Politics,* edited by M.P. Smith and J.R. Feagin. Oxford: Basil Blackwell.

Mingione, E. 1991. *Fragmented Societies.* Goodrick, P. trans. Oxford: Basil Blackwell.

Ministry of Health 2001. *Yeşil Kart Uygulaması Hakkında Genelge no. 1519* (Circular regarding the Implementation of Green Card no. 1519). [Online: Sağlık Bakanlığı (Ministry of Health)]. Available at: http://www.saglik.gov.tr/ sb/codes/mevzuat [accessed: December 2002).

Mitchell, J.C. 1969. The concept and use of social networks, in *Social Networks in Urban Situations,* edited by J.C. Mitchell. Manchester: University of Manchester Press.

MLSS 2003. *İşçi Sayısı ve Sendikalaşma Oranları* (Number of Workers and Unionisation Statistics). [Online: Çalışma ve Sosyal Güvenlik Bakanlığı (Ministry of Labour and Social Security)]. Available at http://www.calisma. gov.tr [accessed: September 2003].

MLSS 2007. *EU-Turkey Joint Inclusion Memorandum*. Ankara: Ministry of Labour and Social Security.

MMA 2002. *1999 Yerel Seçim Sonuçları* (1999 Local Election Results). [Online: Ankara Büyükşehir Belediyesi (Metropolitan Municipality of Ankara)]. Available at: http://www.ankara-bel.gov.tr/secim.htm [accessed February 2002].

MMDPB (Metropolitan Master Development Planning Bureau) (Ankara Metropolitan Nazım İmar Planlama Bürosu) 2000. *Ankara 2025 Metropolitan Nazım İmar Plan Raporu* (Ankara 2025 Metropolitan Master Development Plan Report). Ankara: Ankara Büyükşehir Belediyesi, Kentsel Planlama ve İmar Müdürlüğü (Greater Municipality of Ankara, Directorate of Urban Planning and Development).

Morgan, D.H.J. 1989. Strategies and sociologists: a comment on Crow. *Sociology,* 23(1), 25–9.

Morris, L. 1990. *The Workings of the Household*. Cambridge: Polity Press.

Moser, C.O.N. 1996a. *Household Responses to Poverty and Vulnerability, Volume I: Confronting Crisis in Cisne Dos, Guayaquil, Ecuador*. Washington D.C.: The World Bank.

Moser, C.O.N. 1996b. *Household Responses to Poverty and Vulnerability, Volume II: Confronting Crisis in Angyafold, Budapest, Hungary*. Washington D.C.: The World Bank.

Moser, C.O.N. 1996c. *Household Responses to Poverty and Vulnerability, Volume III: Confronting Crisis in Commonwealth, Metromanila, The Philippines*. Washington D.C.: The World Bank.

Moser, C.O.N. 1998. The asset vulnerability framework: reassessing urban poverty reduction strategies. *World Development*, 26(1), 1–19.

Muica, N., Turnock, D. and Urucu, V. 2000. Coping strategies in rural areas of the Buzau Sub-Carpathians. *GeoJournal*, 50(2/3), 157–72.

Narayan, D. 1997. *Voices of the Poor: Poverty and Social Capital in Tanzania*. Environmentally and Socially Sustainable Development Studies and Monographs Series 20. Washington D.C.: The World Bank.

Narayan, D. 1999. Bonds and Bridges: Social Capital and Poverty. Mimeo. Washington D.C.: The World Bank.

Narayan, D. and Pritchett, L. 1999. Cents and sociability: household income and social capital in rural Tanzania. *Economic Development and Cultural Change*, 47(4), 871–97.

Nelson, J. 1979. *Access to Power: Politics and the Urban Poor in Developing Nations*. Princeton: Princeton University Press.

Nelson, N. 1995. The Kiambu groups: a succesful women's rosca in Mathare Valley, Nairobi (1971 to 1990). *Money-Go-Rounds: The Importance of Rotating Savings and Credit Associations for Women*, edited by S. Ardener and Burman. Oxford/Washington D.C.: BERG *In*:

Norris, W.P. 1984. Patron-client relationships in the urban social structure: A Brazilian case study. *Human Organisation*, 43(1), 16–26.

Norris, W.P. 1988. Household survival in the face of poverty in Salvador, Brazil: towards an integrated model of household activities. *Urban Anthropology*, 17(4), 299–321.

Nussbaum, M. 2000. *Women and Human Development. The Capabilities Approach.* Cambridge: Cambridge University Press.

Nyman, C. 1999. Gender equality in 'the most equal country in the world'? Money and marriage in Sweden. *Sociological Review*, 47(4), 766–93.

Oakley, R. 1979. Family, kinship and patronage, in *Minority Families in Britain*, edited by S. Khan. London: Macmillan.

OECD 2010. *Social Expenditure Database* [Online: Organisation for Economic Co-operation and Development]. Available at http://stats.oecd.org/Index. aspx?datasetcode=SOCX_AGG. [accessed September 2010].

Oktik, N. ed. 2008. *Türkiye'de Yoksulluk Çalışmaları* (Poverty Studies in Turkey). İzmir: Yakın Kitabevi.

Öncü, A. 1988. The politics of urban land market in Turkey: 1950–1980. *International Journal of Urban and Regional Research*, 12(1), 38–64.

Öğretmen, İ. 1957. *Ankara'da 158 Gecekondu Hakkında Monografi* (A Monograph about 158 *Gecekondu*s in Ankara). Ankara: Ankara Üniversitesi Siyasal Bilgiler Fakültesi Yayınları (Ankara University Political Science Department Press).

Özbay, F. 1995. Kadınların eviçi ve evdışı uğraşlarındaki değişme (Changes in the women's tasks at home and outside home), in *Kadın Bakış Açısından Kadınlar* (Women from Woman's Perspective), edited by Ş. Tekeli. İstanbul: İletişim.

Özbudun, E. 1981. Turkey: the politics of political clientelism, in *Political Clientelism, Patronage and Development,* edited by S.N. Eisenstadt and R. Lemarchand. London: Sage.

Özdek, Y. ed. 2002. *Yoksulluk, Şiddet ve İnsan Hakları* (Poverty, Violence and Human Rights). Ankara: Türkiye ve Orta doğu Amme İdaresi Enstitüsü (Turkey and Middle East Public Administration Institute).

Pahl, J. 1980. Patterns of money management within marriage. *Journal of Social Policy*, 9(3), 313–35.

Pahl, J. 1983. The allocation of money and the structuring of inequality within marriage. *Sociological Review*, 31(2), 237–62.

Pahl, J. 1989. *Money and Marriage*. London: Macmillan.

Pahl, J. 1990. Household spending, personal spending and the control of money in marriage. *Sociology*, 24(1): 119–38.

Pahl, R.E. 1984. *Division of Labour*. Oxford: Basil Blackwell.

Pahl, R.E. 1985. The restructuring of capital, the local political economy and household work strategies, in *Social Relations and Spatial Structures*, edited by D. Gregory and J. Urry. London: Macmillan.

Pahl. R.E. 1988. Some remarks on informal work, social polarization and the social structure. *International Journal of Urban and Regional Research*, 4(1), 247–67.

Pahl, R.E 1989. From informal economy to the forms of work, in *Industrial Societies: Crisis and Division in Western Capitalism and State Socialism*, edited by R. Scase. London: Unwin and Hyman.

Pahl, R.E. and Wallace, C. 1985. Household work strategies in economic recession, in *Beyond Employment: Household, Gender and Subsistence*, edited by E. Mingione and R. Nanneke. London: Blackwell.

Pak, O. 1996. Resourcefulness without resources: the life history of a landless Minangkabau village woman. *Southeast Asian Journal of Social Science*, 24(1), 97–111.

Pamuk, M. 2000. Kırsal yerlerde yoksulluk (Poverty in rural areas), in *İşgücü Piyasası Analizleri 1999-I* (Labour Market Analyses 1999-I). Ankara: Devlet İstatistik Enstitüsü (State Institute of Statistics).

Papanek, H. 1979. Family status production work: the work and non-work of women. *Signs*, 4(4), 775–81.

Papanek, H. and Schwede, L. 1988. Women are good with money: earning and managing in an Indonesian city, in *Home Divided: Women and Income in the Third World*, edited by D. Dwyer and J. Bruce. California: Stanford University Press.

Patterson, S.A. 1994. Women's survival strategies in urban areas: Caricom and Guyana, in *Poverty in the 1990s: The Responses of Women*, edited by F. Meer. Paris: UNSECO and International Social Science Council.

Peattie, L.R. 1968. *A View from the Barrio*. Michigan: Ann Arbor.

Perez-Aleman, P. 1992. Economic crisis and women in Nicaragua, in *Unequal Burden: Economic Crisis, Persistent Poverty and Women's Work*, edited by L. Beneria and S. Feldman. London: Westview Press.

Pınarcıoğlu, M. and Işık, O. 2001. 1980 sonrası dönemde kent yoksulları arasında güce dayalı ağ ilişkileri (Power-based network relationships among the urban poor in post-1980s). *Toplum-Bilim* (Society-Science), 89, 31–61

Piachaud, D. 1981. Peter Townsend and the Holy Grail. *New Statesman*, 57(982), 419–21.

Piachaud, D. 1987. Problems in the definition and measurement of poverty. *Journal of Social Policy*, 16(2), 147–64.

Piachaud, D. 2002. *Capital and the Determinants of Poverty and Social Exclusion*. CASE Paper 60. London: London School of Economics, Centre for Analysis of Social Exclusion.

Pickvance, C.G. and Pickvance K. 1994. Towards a strategic approach to housing behaviour. *Sociology*, 28(3), 657–77.

Pizzorno, A. 2001. *Why Pay for Petrol? Notes for a Theory of Social Capital*. Paper presented at EURESCO Conference. Exeter: University of Exeter.

Polanyi, K. 1977. Forms of integration and supporting structures, in *The Livelihood of Man*, edited by H.W. Pearson. London: Academic Press.

Portes, A. 1995. Economic sociology and the sociology of migration: a conceptual overview, in *Essays on Networks, Ethnicity and Entrepreneurship*, edited by A. Portes. New York: Russell Sage Foundation.

Portes, A. 1998. Social capital: its origins and applications in modern sociology. *Annual Review of Sociology.* 24(1), 1–24.

Portes, A. and Castells, M. 1989. World underneath: the origins, dynamics and effects of the informal economy. *Informal Economy*, edited by L.A. Benton et al. Baltimore and London: The John Hopkins University Press.

Portes, A. and Landolt, P. 1996. The downside of social capital. *American Prospect*, no.26, 18–21, 94.

Portes, A and Sensenbrenner, J. 1993. Embeddedness and immigration: notes on the social determinants of the economic action. *American Journal of Sociology*, 98(6), 1320-50.

Pryer, J.A. 2003. *Poverty and Vulnerability in Dhaka Slums: The Urban Livelihood Study*. Hampshire: Ashgate.

Putnam, R.D. 1993. *Making Democracy Work: Civic Traditions in Modern Italy.* Princeton N.J.: Princeton University Press.

Putnam, R.D. 2000. *Bowling Alone: The Collapse and Revival of American Community*. New York: Simon and Schuster.

Rake, K. and Jayatilaka, G. 2002. *Home Truths: An Analysis of Financial Decision Making Within the Home*. London: Fawcett Society.

Rakodi, C. 1991. Women's work or household strategies? *Environment and Urbanization*, 3(2), 39–45.

Rakodi, C. 1999. A capital assets frameworks for analysing household livelihood strategies: implications for policy. *Development Policy Review*, 17(3), 315–42.

Rakodi, C. 2002. A livelihoods approach: conceptual issues and definitions, in *Urban Livelihoods: A People Centred Approach to Reducing Poverty*, edited by C. Rakodi and T. Lloyd-Jones. London and Sterling VA: Earthscan.

Reardon, T., Delgado, C. and Matlon, P. 1992. Determinants and effects of income diversification amongst households in Burkino Faso. *Journal of Development Studies*, 28(2), 264–96.

Roberts, B. 1970. Urban poverty and political behaviour in Guatemala. *Human Organization*, 29(1), 20–28.

Roberts, B. 1973. *Organising Strangers*. Austin: University of Texas Press.

Roberts, B. 1989. Employment structure, life cycle and life chances: formal and informal sectors in Guadalajara, in *Informal Economy: Studies in Advanced and Less Developed Countries*, edited by A. Portes et al. Baltimore: John Hopkins University Press.

Roberts, B. 1991. Household coping strategies and urban poverty in a comparative perspective, in *Urban Life in* Transition, edited by C.G. Pickvance and M. Gottdiener. London: Sage.

Roberts, B. 1994. Informal economy and family strategies. *International Journal of Urban and Regional Research*, 18(1), 6–23.

Roberts, B. 1995. *The Making of Citizens*. London: Arnold.

Roberts, P. 1991. Anthropological perspectives on the household. *IDS Bulletin*, 22(1), 60–64.

Rodriguez, l. 1994. Housing and household survival strategies in urban areas, in *Poverty in the 1990s: The Responses of Women,* edited by F. Meer. Paris: UNSECO & International Social Science Council.

Roldan, M. 1988. Renegotiating the marital cntract: intra-household patterns of money allocation and women's subordination among domestic outworkers in Mexico City, in *Home Divided: Women and Income in the Third World,* edited by D. Dwyer and J. Bruce. California: Stanford University Press.

Rose, R. 1994. *Getting By Without Government; Everyday Life in a Stressful Society.* University of Strathclyde Studies in Public Policy no.227. Glasgow: University of Strathclyde.

Rose, R. 1998. *Getting Things Done in an Anti-Modern Society: Social Capital Networks in Russia.* Studies in Public Policy no.304. Glasgow: University of Strathclyde.

Rose, R. 1999. What does social capital add to individual welfare: an empirical analysis of Russia. Paper presented at Social Capital and Poverty Reduction Conference 22–24 June 1999. Washington D.C.: The World Bank.

Rowntree, B. S. 1910. *Poverty: A Study of Town Life.* London: Macmillan.

Roy, K. M., Tubbs, C. Y. and Burton, L. M. 2004. Don't have no time: daily rhythms and the organization of time for low-income families. *Family Relations,* 53(2), 229–36.

Rubin, L. B. 1976. *Worlds of Pain: Life in the Working Class Family.* New York: Basic Books.

Saaw, E. and Akpınar, E. 2007. Assessing poverty and related factors in Turkey. *Croatian Medical Journal,* 48(5), 628–35.

Sabah 1994. *Mamak çöplüğü için dehşet veren rapor* (Horrifying report for Mamak Dump). *Sabah,* 22 February.

Sabah 2000a. Ege Mahallesi direniyor (Ege Mahallesi is resisting). *Sabah,* 22 September.

Sabah 2000b. Gökçek: 'yeni ihale açarım' (Gökçek: 'I would assign a new bid'). *Sabah,* 25 September.

Safa, H.I. and Antrobus, P. 1992. Women and the economic crisis in the Carribean, in *Unequal Burden: Economic Crisis, Persistent Poverty and Women's Work,* edited by L. Beneria and S. Feldman. London: Westview Press.

Safilios-Rothschild, C. 1984. The role of the family in development, in *Women in the Third World Development,* edited by S.E. Charlton, London: Westview.

Sahlins, M. 1974. *Stone Age Economics.* London: Tavistock.

Saltmarshe, D. 2002. The resource profile approach: a Kosovo case study. *Public Administration and Development,* 22(2), 179–90.

Sandbrook, R. 1982. *The Politics of Basic Needs.* London: Heinemann.

Sayarı, S. 1977. Political patronage in Turkey. *Patrons and Clients in Mediterranean Societies,* edited by E. Gellner and J. Waterbury eds. London: Ducksworth.

Schindler, K. 2010. Credit for what? Informal credit as a coping strategy of market women in Northern Ghana. *Journal of Development Studies,* 46(2), 234–53.

Schmink, M. 1984. Household economic strategies: review and research agenda. *Latin American Research Review*, 19(3), 87–101.

Schuller, T., Baron, S.and Field, J. 2000. Social capital: a review and critique, in *Social Capital: Critical Perspectives*, edited by S. Baron et al. Oxford: Oxford University Press.

Scoones, I. 1998. *Sustainable Rural Livelihoods: A Framework For Analysis*. IDS Working Paper 72. Sussex: University of Sussex, Institute of Development Studies.

Scott, J. 1977. Patronage or exploitation? in *Patrons and Clients in Mediterranean Societies*, edited by E. Gellner and J. Waterbury. London: Ducksworth.

Selby, H.A., Murphy, A.D. and Lorenzen, S.A. 1990. *The Mexican Urban Household: Organizing for Self-Defense* [sic]. Austin: University of Texas Press.

Sen, A. K. 1982. *Poverty and Famines: An Essay on Entitlement and Deprivation*. Oxford: Clarendon Press.

Sen, A.K. 1983. Poor, relatively speaking. *Oxford Economic Papers*, 35(2), 153–69.

Sen, A. K. 1987. *The Standard of Living*. Cambridge: Cambridge University Press.

Sen, A.K. 1990. Gender and cooperative conflicts, in *Persistent Inequalities: Women and World Development*, edited by I. Tinker. Oxford: Oxford University Press.

Sen, A.K. 1993. Capabilities and well-being, in *Quality of Life*, edited by M. Nussbaum and A.K. Sen. Oxford: Oxford University Press.

Sen, A.K. 1999. *Commodities and Capabilities*. New Delhi: Oxford University Press.

Shankland, D. 1996. Changing gender relations among Alevi and Sunni in Turkey. *Turkish Families in Transition*, edited by G. Rasuly-Paleczek. Frankfurt: Peter Lang.

Sharma, U. 1986. *Women's Work, Class and the Urban Household: A Study of Shimla, North India*. London: Tavistock.

Smith, D. and Macnicol, J. 2001. Social insecurity and the informal economy: survival strategies on a London estate, in *Risk and Citizenship: Key Issues in Welfare*, edited by R. Edwards and J. Glover. London: Routledge.

Social Security Institution (Sosyal Sigortalar Kurumu) 1981. *İş Kazaları ve Meslek Hastalıkları Sigortaları Prim Tarifesi* (The Premium Tariff for Occupational Illness and Accident Insurance). Publication no. 597. Ankara: Sosyal Sigortalar Kurumu Genel Müdürlüğü (General Directorate of Social Security Institution).

Sönmez, M. 2001. *Gelir Uçurumu: Türkiye'de Gelirin Adaletsiz Bölüşümü* (The Income Gap: Unjust Distribution of Income in Turkey). İstanbul: OM.

Sönmez, İ.Ö. 2007. Concentrated urban poverty: the case of İzmir inner area, Turkey. *European Planning Studies*, 15(3), 319–38.

Sönmez, M. 2009. TÜİK'in Son zırvası: en zenginler, ücretliler (The last nonsense from TURKSTAT: the richest, wage earners.). Cumhuriyet

[Online, 29 December] Available at: http://www.cumok.org/tr/index. php?option=com_content&view=article&id=100:tuekin-son-zrvas-en-zenginler-uecretliler&catid=37:guencel-yazlar [accessed: April 2010].

Spicer, E. 1970. Patrons of the poor. *Human Organisation,* 29(1), 12–19.

Spicker, P. 1990. Charles Booth: the examination of poverty. *Social Policy and Administration,* 24(1), 21–38.

Stack, C.B. 1974. *All Our Kin: Strategies for Survival in a Black Community.* New York: Harper and Row.

Stamp, P. 1985. Research note: balance of financial power in marriage: an explanatory study of breadwinning wives. *Sociological Review,* 33(3), 546–57.

SPO 2001. *Gelir Dağılımının İyileştirilmesi ve Yoksullukla Mücadele: Özel İhtisas Komisyon Raporu* (Improvement of Income Distribution and Fight against Poverty: Special Expertise Commision Report) no. 2599-OIK: 610. Ankara: Devlet Planlama Teşkilatı (State Planning Organisation).

SPO 2006. *IX. Kalkınma Planı 2007–2013* (IX. Development Plan 2007–2013). Ankara: Devlet Planlama Teşkilatı (State Planning Organisation).

SPO 2010. Kamu Kesimi Sosyal Harcama İstatistikleri (Public Social Expenditure Statistics). [Online: Devlet Planlama Teşkilatı (State Planning Organisation)]. Available at: www.dpt.gov.tr [accessed: September 2010].

Stauth, G. 1984. Households, modes of living and production systems, in *Households and the World Economy,* edited by J. Smith, I. Wallerstein and H.D. Evers. London: Sage.

Staveren, I. van 2003. Beyond social capital in poverty research. *Journal of Economic Issues,* 37(2), 415–23.

Sterling, L. 1995. Partners: the social organisation of rotating savings and credit societies among exilic Jamaicans. *Sociology,* 29(4), 653–66.

Streeton, P., Burki, S.J., Haq, M., Hicks, N. and Stewart F. 1981. *First Things First: Meeting Basic Needs in Developing Countries.* London: Oxford University Press.

Swift, J. 1989. Why are rural people vulnerable to famine? *IDS Bulletin,* 20(2), 8–15.

Şen, M. 2002. Kökene dayalı dayanışma-yardımlaşma: zor iş… (Ethnic solidarity-support: a difficult task…), in *Yoksulluk Halleri: Türkiye'de Kentsel Yoksulluğun Toplumsal Görünümleri* (States of Poverty: Social Manifestations of Urban Poverty in Turkey), edited by N. Erdoğan. İstanbul: De:ki.

Şenol-Cantek, F. 2001. Fakir/haneler: yoksulluğun 'ev hali' (Poor/homes: the 'home situation' of poverty). *Toplum-Bilim* (Society-Science), 89, 102–31.

Şenses, F. 2001. *Küreselleşmenin Öteki Yüzü: Yoksulluk* (The Other Face of Globalisation: Poverty). İstanbul: İletişim.

Şenses, F. 2008. Missing links in poverty analysis in the age of neoliberal globalization: some lessons from Turkey. *New Perspectives on Turkey,* Spring Issue 38, 61–81.

Şenyapılı, T. 1978. *Bütünleşmemiş Kentli Nüfusun Sorunu* (The Non-Integrated Urban Population Question). Ankara: Orta Doğu Teknik Üniversitesi (Middle East Technical University).

Şenyapılı, T. 1981. *Gecekondu: Çevre İşçilerin Mekanı* (*Gecekondu*: The Space of Peripheral Workers). Ankara: Orta Doğu Teknik Üniversitesi (Middle East Technical University).

Şenyapılı, T. 1998. Cumhuriyet'in 75. yılı, gecekondunun 50. Yılı. (75. anniversary of the Republic, 50. anniversary of the *gecekondu*), in *75. Yılda Değişen Kent ve Mimarlık* (Urban Change and Architecture in the 75th Anniversary of the Turkish Republic), edited by Y. Sey. İstanbul: Türk Tarih Vakfı (Turkish History Foundation).

Taal, H. 1989. How farmers cope with risk and stress in rural Gambia. *IDS Bulletin*, 20(2), 16–22.

Tabachnik, B.G. and Fidell, L.S. 2000. *Using Multivariate Statistics* (Fourth Edition). Boston: Allyn and Bacon.

Tacoli, C. 1995. Gender and international survival strategies. *Third World Planning Review*, 17(2), 199–212.

Tatlıdil, E. 1989. *Kentleşme ve Gecekondu* (Urbanisation and *Gecekondu* Housing). İzmir: Ege Üniversitesi Edebiyat Fakültesi Yayınları (Ege University Literature Department Press).

Tchernina, N.V. and Tchernin, E.A. 2002. Older people in Russia's transitional society: multiple deprivation and coping responses. *Ageing and Society*, 22(5), 543–62.

Telli, Ç., Voyvoda, E. And Yeldan, E. 2006. General equilibrium modelling for socially responsible macroeconomics: seeking for the alternatives to fight jobless growth in Turkey. *METU Studies in Development*, 33(2), 255–93.

Tichenor, V.J. 1999. Status and income as gendered resources. *Journal of Marriage and the Family*, 61(3), 638–50.

Tilly, L.A. 1987. Beyond family strategies, what? *Historical Methods*, 20(3), 123–25.

Tipple, G. and Coulson, J. 2007. Funding the home-based enterprise- finance and credit in development country livelihoods. *International Development Planning Review*, 29(2), 125–59.

TMMOB 1993. *Çöp Deplama Alanları ve Mamak Eski Cöp Depolama Alanı* (Solid Waste Dumps and Former Mamak Solid Waste Dump). Ankara: Türk Mimar ve Mühendis Odaları Birliği (The Union of Turkish Architect and Engineer Chambers).

Townsend, P. 1979. *Poverty in the United Kingdom: A Survey of Household Resources and Standards of Living*. Harmondsworth: Penguin Books.

Townsend, P. 1985. A sociological approach to the measurement of poverty: a rejoinder to Professor Amartya Sen. *Oxford Economic Papers*, 37(4), 659–68.

Townsend, P. 1993. *The International Analysis of Poverty*. Harvester: Wheatsheaf.

Toynbee, P. 2003. *Hard Work: Life in Low-Pay Britain*. London: Bloomsbury.

Treas, J. 1993. Money in the bank: transaction costs and the economic organization of marriage. *American Sociological Review*, 58(5), 723–34.

TTB 1994. Mamak Eski Cöp Depolama Alanı Halk Sağlığı Komisyon Raporu (Public Health Commision Report on Former Mamak Solid Waste Dump). Ankara: Türk Tabipler Birliği (The Union of Turkish Doctors).

TURKSTAT 2002a. Üç Aylık Gayri Safi Milli Hasıla Bülteni, 31 Mart 2002 (Quarterly Gross National Product Bulletin, 31 March 2002). [Online: Türkiye İstatistik Kurumu (Turkish Statistical Institute)]. Available at http:// at www. die.gov.tr/TURKISH/SONIST/GSMH [accessed: September 2003].

TURKSTAT 2002b. Fiyat İstatistikleri ve İndeks Veritabanı (Price Statistics and Indices Database). [Online: Türkiye İstatistik Kurumu (Turkish Statistical Institute)]. Available at: http://www.die.gov.tr [accessed: December 2002].

TURKSTAT 2002c. Seçilmiş Finansal Yatırım Araçlarının Aylık Gerçekleşen Reel Getiri Oranları Haber Bülteni, 9 Mayıs 2002 (The Materialised Monthly Real Revenues from Selected Means of Financial Investment, News Bulletin, 9 May 2002). [Online: Türkiye İstatistik Kurumu (Turkish Statistical Institute)]. Available at: http://www.die.gov.tr/TURKISH/SONIST/YATIRIM> [accessed: March 2003].

TURKSTAT 2002d. Seçilmiş Finansal Yatırım Araçlarının Aylık Gerçekleşen Reel Getiri Oranları Haber Bülteni, 11 Kasım 2002 (The Materialised Monthly Real Revenues from Selected Means of Financial Investment, News Bulletin, 11 November 2002). [Online: Türkiye İstatistik Kurumu (Turkish Statistical Institute)]. Available at: http://www.die.gov.tr/TURKISH/SONIST/YATIRIM [accessed: March 2003].

TURKSTAT 2003a. Hanehalkı İşgücü Veritabanı (Household Labour Force Database). [Online: Türkiye İstatistik Kurumu (Turkish Statistical Institute)]. Available at: http://www.die.gov.tr [accessed: April and September 2003].

TURKSTAT 2003b. 2000 Kentsel Yerler Küçük ve Şirketleşmemiş İşyerleri Anketi Sonuçları (2000 Urban Areas Small-Scale and Non-Corporatist Work Places Survey Results). [Online: Türkiye İstatistik Kurumu (Turkish Statistical Institute)]. Available at: http:// www.die.gov.tr/arsiv.htm [accessed: April 2003].

TURKSTAT 2003c. Nüfus ve Kalkınma Göstergeleri (Population and Development Indicators). [Online: Türkiye İstatistik Kurumu (Turkish Statistical Institute)]. Available at: http://www.nkg.die.gov.tr [accessed: September 2003].

TURKSTAT 2006. 2004 Gelir Dağılımı Haber Bülteni, 27 Şubat 2006 (2004 Income Distribution Bulletin, 27 February 2006). [Online: Türkiye İstatistik Kurumu (Turkish Statistical Institute)]. Available at: http://www.tuik.gov.tr [accessed: June 2010].

TURKSTAT 2009a. 2008 Yoksulluk Çalışması Sonuçları Haber Bülteni, 1 Aralık 2009 (2008 Poverty Study Results Bulletin, 1 December 2009). [Online: Türkiye İstatistik Kurumu (Turkish Statistical Institute)]. Available at: http:// www.tuik.gov.tr [accessed: June 2010].

TURKSTAT 2009b. 2006–2007 Gelir ve Yaşam Koşulları Araştırması Sonuçları Haber Bülteni, 17 Aralık 2009 (2006–2007 Income and Living Conditions Research Results Bulletin, 17 December 2009). [Online: Türkiye İstatistik Kurumu (Turkish Statistical Institute)]. Available at: http://www.tuik.gov.tr [accessed: June 2010].

TURKSTAT 2010a. 2008 Gelir ve Yaşam Koşulları Araştırması Sonuçları Haber Bülteni, 29 Temmuz 2009 (2008 Income and Living Conditions Research Bulletin, 29 July 2009). [Online: Türkiye İstatistik Kurumu (Turkish Statistical Institute)]. Available at: http://www.tuik.gov.tr [accessed: June 2010].

TURKSTAT 2010b. 2009 Hanehalkı İşgücü Araştırması Yıllık Sonuçları Haber Bülteni, 15 Mart 2010 (2009 Household Labour Survey Annual Results Bulletin, 15 March 2010). [Online: Türkiye İstatistik Kurumu (Turkish Statistical Institute)]. Available at: http://www.tuik.gov.tr [accessed: April 2010].

Türkdoğan, O. 1974. *Yoksulluk Kültürü: Gecekonduların Toplumsal Yapısı* (Culture of Poverty: The Social Structure of *Gecekondu*s). Erzurum: Atatürk Üniversitesi (Atatürk University).

Türker-Devecigil, P. 2005. Urban transformation projects as a model to transform *gecekondu* areas in Turkey: the example of Dikmen Valley. *European Journal of Housing Policy*, 5(2), 211–29.

UNDP 1990. *Human Development Report 1990*. Oxford and New York: Oxford University Press.

UNDP 1996. Human *Development Report 1996*. Oxford and New York: Oxford University Press.

UNDP 1999. *Women in Turkey*. [Online: United Nations Development Programme, Turkey]. Available at: http://www.undp.org.tr [accessed: April 2003].

UPL 2000. *Kentsel Yoksulluk ve Kentsel Geçim Stratejileri: Ankara Örneği.* (Urban Poverty and Urban Survival Strategies: Ankara Case). Ankara: Orta Doğu Teknik Üniversitesi (Middle East Technical University).

UPL 2001. *Kente Göç ve Yoksulluk:Diyarbakır Örneği* (Migration to the City and Poverty: Diyarbakır Case). Ankara: Orta Doğu Teknik Üniversitesi (Middle East Technical University).

Uygur, S. and Kasnakoğlu, Z. 1998. *Yoksulluk Sınırının Ölçülmesi: Türkiye 1994* (Estimation of Poverty Line: Turkey 1994). Ankara: Devlet İstatistik Enstitüsü (State Institute of Statistics).

Uzun, N. 2005. Residential transformation of squatter settlements: urban redevelopment projects in Ankara. *Journal of Housing and the Built Environment*, 20, 183–99.

Veit-Wilson, J.H. 1986. Paradigms of poverty: A rehabilitation of B.S. Rowntree. *Journal of Social Policy*, 15(1), 69–99.

Veit-Wilson, J.H. 1987. Consensual approaches to poverty lines and social security. *Journal of Social Policy*, 16(2), 183–211.

Vinay, P. 1985. Family life-cyle and the informal economy in central Italy. *International Journal of Urban and Regional Research*, 9(1), 82–98.

Vogler, C. and Pahl, J. 1993. Social and economic change and organisation of money within marriage'. *Work, Employment and Society*, 7(1), 71–95.

Vogler C. and Pahl, J. 1994. Money, power and inequality within marriage. *Sociological Review*, 42(2), 263–88.

Vogler, C. 1994. Money in the household, in *The Social and Political Economy of the Household*, edited by M. Anderson et al. Oxford: Oxford University Press.

Vogler, C. 2005. Cohabiting couples: rethinking money in the household at the beginning of the twenty first century. *Sociological Review*, 53(1), 1–29.

Vogler, C., Borckman, M. and Wiggings, R.D. 2006. Intimate relationships and changing patterns of money management at the beginning of twenty-first century. *Sociology*, 57(3), 455–82.

Voyvoda, E. and Yeldan, E. 2005. Managing Turkish debt: An OLG investigation of the IMF's fiscal programme model for Turkey. *Journal of Policy Modelling*, 27(6), 743–65.

Wacquant, L.J.D. 1999. Inside the 'zone': the social art of the hustler in the American Ghetto, in *Weight of the World: Social Suffering in Contemporary Society*, edited by P. Bourdieu, translated by P.P. Ferguson. Cambridge: Polity Press.

Walker, C. and Walker, A. 1994. Poverty and the poor, in *Developments in Sociology*, edited by M. Haralambos. Lancashire: Causeway Press.

Walker, M. 1998. Survival strategies in an industrial town in East Ukraine, in *Surviving Post-Socialism: Local Strategies and Regional Responses in Eastern Europe and the Former Soviet Union*, edited by S. Bridger and F. Pine. London: Routledge.

Weingrod, A. 1977. Patrons, patronage and political parties, in *Friends, Followers and Factions*, edited by S.W. Schmidt et al. California: University of California Press.

Wellman, B. and Frank, K. 2001. Network capital in a multi-level world: getting support from personal communities, in *Social Capital: Theory and Research*, edited by N. Lin et al. New York: Aldine de Gruyter.

White, J. 1994. *Money Makes Us Relatives: Women's Labor in Urban Turkey*. Austin: University of Texas Press.

White, S. and Ellison, M. 2007. Wellbeing, livelihoods and resources in social practice, in *Wellbeing in Developing Countries: from Theory to Research*, edited by I. Gough and J.A. McGregor. Cambridge: Cambridge University Press.

Whitehead, A. 1981. I'm hungry, mum': The politics of domestic budgeting, in *Of Marriage and the Market*, edited by K. Young, et al. London: CSE Books.

Wilson, G. 1987. *Money in the Family: Financial Organisation and Women's Responsibility*. Aldershot: Avebury.

Wolf, D.L. 1990. Daughters, decisions and domination: an empirical and conceptual critique of household strategies. *Development and Change*, 21(1), 43–74.

Wolf, E.R. 1966. Kinship, friendship, and patron-client relations in complex societies, in *The Social Anthropology of Complex Societies*, edited by M. Banton. London: Tavistock.

Wong, D. 1984. The limits of using the household as a unit of analysis. *Households and the World Economy*, edited by J. Smith, I. Wallerstein and H.D. Evers. London: Sage.

Woolcock, M. 1998. Social Capital and economic development: toward a theoretical synthesis and policy framework. *Theory and Society*, 27(2), 151–208.

World Bank 1999. *Migrant Women's Participation in the Labour Force in Urban Turkey*. Washington D.C.: The World Bank.

World Bank 2000. *Turkey, Economic Reforms, Living Standards and Social Welfare Study*. Report no. 20029-TU. Washington D.C.: The World Bank.

World Bank 2003. *Turkey: Poverty and Coping after Crises: Volume 1*. Washington D.C.: The World Bank.

World Bank 2005. *Turkey Joint Poverty Assessment Report Volume I: Main Report*. Washington D.C.: Human Development Sector Unit Europe and Central Asia Region and State Institute of Statistics.

Wratten, E. 1995. Conceptualizing urban poverty. *Environment and Urbanization*, 7(1), 11–38.

Yakubovich, V. 1999. *Economic Constraints and Social Opportunities: Participation in Informal Support Networks of Russian Urban Households*. Unpublished Project Paper for Household Survival Strategies, Job Creation and New Forms of Employment in Russia. Coventry and Moscow: CCLS/ISITO.

Yasa, İ. 1966. *Ankara'da Gecekondu Aileleri* (*Gecekondu* Families in Ankara). Ankara: Akın.

Yasa, İ. 1973. Gecekondu ailesi mozayiği (The mosaic of *gecekondu* family). *Amme İdaresi Dergisi* (Public Administration Journal), 6(2), 41–6.

Yeldan, E. 2001. *Küreselleşme Sürecinde Türkiye Ekonomisi* (Turkish Economy in the Process of Globalisation). İstanbul: İletişim.

Yeldan, A.E. 2004. The impact of financial liberalization and the rise of financial rents on income inequality: The case of Turkey, in *Inequality, Growth and Poverty in the Era of Liberalization and Globalization*, edited by G.A. Cornia. Oxford: Oxford University Press.

YEŞKEP 1996. *Yenimahalle, Şentepe Konut Edinme Projesi* (Yenimahalle Şentepe Housing Acquisition Project Report). Ankara: UNDP.

Yönder, A. 1998. Implications of double standards in housing policy: development of informal settlements in Istanbul, Turkey, in *Illegal Cities: Law and Urban Change in Developing Countries*, edited by E. Fernandes and A. Varley. London and New York: Zed Books.

Yörükhan, T. 1968. *Gecekondular ve Gecekondu Bölgelerinin Sosyo-Kültürel Özellikleri* (*Gecekondu*s and Socio-Economic Characteristics of *Gecekondu*

Areas). Ankara: İmar ve İskan Bakanlığı Mesken Genel Müdürlüğü (Ministry of Development and Public Works, General Directorate of Housing).

Zaman 2000. Ege Mahallesi sakinleri eylem yaptı (Ege Mahallesi inhabitants protested). *Zaman*, 23 September.

Zimmerman, F.J. and Carter, M.R. 2003. Asset smoothing, consumption smoothing and the reproduction of inequality under risk and subsistence constraints. *Journal of Development Economics*, 71(2), 233–60.

Zoomers, A. 2006. Pro-indigenous reforms in Bolivia: is there an Andean way to escape poverty? *Development and Change*, 37(5), 1023–46.

# Index